The Case Book for Russian

THE CASE BOOK
FOR RUSSIAN

LAURA A. JANDA
STEVEN J. CLANCY

BLOOMINGTON, INDIANA, 2002

SLAVICA

ISBN: 0-89357-307-8

Printed in the United States of America.

Slavica Publishers
Indiana University
2611 E. 10th St.
Bloomington, IN 47408-2603
USA

[Tel.] 1-812-856-4186
[Toll-free] 1-877-SLAVICA
[Fax] 1-812-856-4187
[Email] slavica@indiana.edu
[www] http://www.slavica.com/

Contents

SUGGESTIONS ON HOW TO USE THIS BOOK

The Case Book for Russian is unusual because it focuses on a single important issue confronting learners of Russian: the use of grammatical cases. Rather than targeting a specific audience (for example, second-year students) and giving a smattering of information on a variety of topics, this book is a thorough, comprehensive analysis of a single, but absolutely essential feature of Russian grammar, empowering learners to achieve complete mastery of case usage. *The Case Book for Russian* departs from standard textbook approaches in other ways as well. It demonstrates that proficiency-based materials can be successfully implemented while actually enhancing rather than compromising the acquisition of grammar. This book and its analysis draw upon a large database of naturally-occurring Russian sentences, presenting the reader with real native Russian rather than stripped-down textbook examples. Just as *The Case Book for Russian* refuses to feed its users unnaturally simplified samples of Russian, it also avoids offering sterile rules. This book focuses instead on explaining coherent groupings of motives that drive case use, on the understanding that Russian uses its six cases to produce a potentially infinite number of sentences, and learners will need to recognize novel as well as commonplace uses. Because *The Case Book for Russian* is so unlike most textbooks, a guide for its use might be of value to readers. The following suggestions for integrating this book into Russian language programs are offered in the confidence that readers will make their own more specific (and possibly more creative!) adjustments.

NO SPECIAL KNOWLEDGE IS ASSUMED FOR TEACHERS OR STUDENTS

Aside from the names of the cases (nominative, instrumental, etc.), there is virtually no linguistic terminology used in *The Case Book for Russian*, and no knowledge of linguistics or semantics is assumed. Users are not expected to master any special formalism or to memorize new terms, and students who have used this book report that it is written in an accessible style. Most instructors with a good working knowledge of Russian will recognize the value of this book and feel comfortable with the explanations it contains.

FOR USE AT A VARIETY OF LEVELS IN A VARIETY OF SETTINGS

The material presented here is most valuable to students who have already been exposed to the Russian case system, and now need to cement what they have learned about the case endings to a thorough understanding of how they are used. This point will be reached by learners at different times, depending upon their strengths and the structure of the program they are in. It is perhaps most likely that *The Case Book for Russian* will be used in second- or third-year Russian courses, although it is certainly not limited to any given time slot or environment. *The Case Book for Russian* is designed to be sufficiently self-explanatory to be used for self-study, while maintaining enough rigor to be useful also in highly structured learning situations such as military and foreign service language instruction. One could alternatively envision integrating this book into a course on the structure of Russian; all of the talented graduate students who worked on this project reported learning facts about Russian case usage that were valuable to their work as teaching assistants in our Russian courses.

FOR USE BY ITSELF OR WITH ANY OTHER TEXTBOOKS OR READINGS

The Case Book for Russian is entirely self-contained and can be used alone or in combination with any other materials. Most college-level Russian courses will develop conversation, reading, writing, and grammar skills simultaneously, and the use of this book can support all of these endeavors, regardless of what other materials and approaches are used. At one extreme, an instructor could simply assign *The Case Book for Russian*, and require students to work through it on their own (a process that can be monitored by collecting periodic homework assignments or asking students to hand in printed logs of their progress from the electronic version of this book). At the other extreme, this book could be the primary focus of a course that could include intensive analysis of case usage in various media (texts, audio, video, etc.). It is more likely, however, that *The Case Book for Russian* will be used in conjunction with other grammar and reading materials, and that part of one class per week will be devoted to discussing this book and applying its explanations to other materials covered in the course (i.e., intensive analysis only of excerpts that students find hard to understand). Since the meaning of every sentence in Russian is partially a function of case usage, virtually any source of Russian language material provides ample opportunities to enlarge upon what students will learn from this book.

CHAPTERS MAY BE USED IN ANY ORDER

Each chapter in *The Case Book for Russian* is a separate, stand-alone module, designed to be used in any order. There is no need to follow the order presented in the book. The table gives four plans for using *The Case Book for Russian*, depending upon whether the goal is to complete it in one semester or over a whole year, and upon whether the user chooses to follow the order of the book (nominative, instrumental, accusative, dative, genitive, locative) or another order (this model presents the cases in an alternative order of nominative, accusative, genitive, dative, instrumental, locative, although absolutely any order can be accommodated). The table presumes standard semesters of 14-15 weeks, but of course this plan can be contracted or expanded to meet the needs of users on trimester or quarter systems or on more extended schedules such as at the Defense Language Institute. *The Case Book for Russian* contains several other features that contribute to its overall flexibility and ease of navigation. The appendix is a comprehensive review of all the case endings for nouns, adjectives, pronouns, and numerals, and all the endings relevant to a given case appear in a table at the beginning of that chapter. The Table of Contents is highly detailed. There are both Russian and English indices, as well as margin notes on every page to enable users to find the exact section of the book they seek. It is hoped that even after users have worked through all the text and exercises, they will continue to find *The Case Book for Russian* a handy reference book, to be consulted for all their case needs.

THE SEMESTER PLAN

The Case Book for Russian in one semester (14 weeks; if you have a 15-week semester, you can add a second week of review with exercises)

	Assuming order in book (NIADGL)	Assuming different order (NAGDIL)
Week 1	Preliminaries; Nominative case and exercises	Preliminaries; Nominative case and exercises
Week 2	Instrumental Prologue Instrumental: a means	Accusative Prologue Accusative: a destination
Week 3	Instrumental: a label Instrumental: an adjunct Instrumental: a landmark	Accusative: a dimension Accusative: an endpoint
Week 4	Instrumental Epilogue Instrumental exercises	Accusative Epilogue Accusative exercises
Week 5	Accusative Prologue Accusative: a destination	Genitive Prologue Genitive: a source Genitive: a goal
Week 6	Accusative: a dimension Accusative: an endpoint	Genitive: a whole Genitive: a reference
Week 7	Accusative Epilogue Accusative exercises	Genitive Epilogue Genitive exercises
Week 8	Dative Prologue Dative: a receiver Dative: an experiencer	Dative Prologue Dative: a receiver Dative: an experiencer
Week 9	Dative: a competitor Dative Epilogue Dative exercises	Dative: a competitor Dative Epilogue Dative exercises
Week 10	Genitive Prologue Genitive: a source Genitive: a goal	Instrumental Prologue Instrumental: a means
Week 11	Genitive: a whole Genitive: a reference	Instrumental: a label Instrumental: an adjunct Instrumental: a landmark
Week 12	Genitive Epilogue Genitive exercises	Instrumental Epilogue Instrumental exercises
Week 13	Locative: a place Locative exercises	Locative: a place Locative exercises
Week 14	Multiple case review and exercises	Multiple case review and exercises

THE YEAR PLAN
The Case Book for Russian in two semesters (14 weeks each)

	Assuming order in book (NIADGL)		Assuming different order (NAGDIL)	
	FALL	SPRING	FALL	SPRING
Week 1	Preliminaries	Dative Prologue Dative: receiver	Preliminaries	Dative Prologue Dative: receiver
Week 2	Nominative:name Nominative:identity Nominative exercises	Dative: experiencer	Nominative:name Nominative:identity Nominative exercises	Dative: experiencer
Week 3	Instrumental Prologue Instrumental:means 1-6	Dative: competitor	Accusative Prologue Accusative:destination 1-5	Dative:competitor
Week 4	Instrumental:means 7-12	Dative Epilogue Dative exercises	Accusative:destination 6-10	Dative Epilogue Dative exercises
Week 5	Instrumental:label Instrumental:adjunct	Genitive Prologue Genitive: source	Accusative: dimension	Instrumental Prologue Instrumental:means 1-6
Week 6	Instrumental:landmark	Genitive:goal	Accusative:endpoint	Instrumental:means 7-12
Week 7	Instrumental Epilogue Instrumental exercises I	Genitive:whole	Accusative Epilogue Accusative exercises I	Instrumental:label Instrumental:adjunct
Week 8	Instrumental exercises II	Genitive:reference	Accusative exercises II	Instrumental:landmark
Week 9	Accusative Prologue Accusative:destination 1-5	Genitive Epilogue Genitive exercises I	Genitive Prologue Genitive: source	Instrumental Epilogue Instrumental exercises I
Week 10	Accusative:destination 6-10	Genitive exercises II	Genitive:goal	Instrumental exercises II
Week 11	Accusative:dimension	Locative Prologue Locative:place	Genitive:whole	Locative Prologue Locative:place
Week 12	Accusative:endpoint	Locative Epilogue Locative exercises	Genitive:reference	Locative Epilogue Locative exercises
Week 13	Accusative Epilogue Accusative exercises I	Multiple case review exercises	Genitive Epilogue Genitive exercises I	Multiple case review exercises
Week 14	Accusative exercises II	Multiple case review exercises	Genitive exercises II	Multiple case review exercises

ACKNOWLEDGMENTS

This book derives from over a decade of work on case semantics, and we are grateful to many people and grant funds that have made it possible for us to complete this work. First there are the people who helped to administer funds for the project: Meredith Clason and Glenda Thompson. There were a number of graduate students who worked on collection of data and discussions of how they would be presented: Mi-hi Lee, George Stackpole, and Maria Stalnaker. Sebastian Kempgen created a beautiful font custom-designed for the project. We are especially thankful to Eleonora Magomedova who helped us edit the Russian examples and lent us her fabulous voice for the audio recordings. A number of colleagues have made comments and suggestions that have enhanced the project, including: Edna Andrews, Larry Feinberg, Ron Feldstein, George Fowler, Robert Greenberg, Tore Nesset, George Rubinstein, Charles Townsend, and Nadia Zilper. In the summer of 1999, we tested an earlier version of these materials with two brave undergraduate volunteers at UNC, who gave us valuable feedback from the perspective of student users, they are: Ramona Carey and Claire Horn. Grants from a number of sources have helped to keep the case book fires burning over the years, including: a Fulbright award to conduct the original research on cases in 1987, an American Council of Learned Societies/Social Science Research Council grant in 1992 and 1994 to work on a book on the role of analogy in Slavic historical linguistics (which gave us a good perspective on certain aspects of the Russian case system that are presented in this book, such as the second genitive and locative, the distribution of genitive plural endings, and the development of animacy), a Chancellor's Instructional Technology grant in 1997-1998 to launch the actual case book project, a University Research Council grant in 1998-1999 to fund further work on audio recordings and digitization of the project, course development money from a Title VI National Resource Center grant to prepare the text for implementation in courses, and funds from a Title VI Language Resource Center grant helped complete the project. An IREX short-term travel grant in 1999 made it possible to compare notes with our Russian colleagues.

Finally, we are grateful to all the students in many language courses who appreciated presentations on case meaning in various Slavic languages and encouraged us to undertake this project. We are also thankful to all of our colleagues who have listened to papers and presentations on the subject of case semantics at conferences for so many years.

Mrs. Glass ... went over to the medicine cabinet. It was stationed above the washbowl, against the wall. She opened its mirror-faced door and surveyed the congested shelves with the eye — or, rather, the masterly squint — of a dedicated medicine-cabinet gardener. Before her, in overly luxuriant rows, was a host, so to speak, of golden pharmaceuticals, plus a few technically less indigenous whatnots. The shelves bore iodine, Mercurochrome, vitamin capsules, dental floss, aspirin, Anacin, Bufferin, Argyrol, Musterole, Ex-Lax, Milk of Magnesia, Sal Hepatica, Aspergum, two Gillette razors, one Schick Injector razor, two tubes of shaving cream, a bent and somewhat torn snapshot of a fat black-and-white cat asleep on a porch railing, three combs, two hairbrushes, a bottle of Wildroot hair ointment, a bottle of Fitch Dandruff Remover, a small, unlabeled box of glycerin suppositories, Vicks Nose Drops, Vicks Vapo Rub, six bars of castile soap, the stubs of three tickets to a 1946 musical comedy ("Call Me Mister"), a tube of depilatory cream, a box of Kleenex, two sea-shells, an assortment of used-looking emery boards, two jars of cleansing cream, three pairs of scissors, a nail file, an unclouded blue marble (known to marble-shooters, at least in the twenties, as a "purey"), a cream for contracting enlarged pores, a pair of tweezers, the strapless chassis of a girl's or woman's gold wristwatch, a box of bicarbonate of soda, a girl's boarding-school class ring with a chipped onyx stone, a bottle of Stopette — and, inconceivably or no, quite a good deal more.

—from *Franny and Zooey*, J. D. Salinger

PRELIMINARIES 1—The mission of this book

Open a Russian-English dictionary and you will find the meanings of every kind of word. Many dictionaries will even list translations for prefixes. But you won't find meanings for cases in your trusty dictionary. If you are lucky, you might have a reference grammar with an entry for each case, but chances are these entries will look rather like the contents of Mrs. Glass' medicine cabinet, and be just as appealing. Take the dative case, for example. Your reference grammar might tell you that the dative is used in the following contexts: for the indirect object; with the prepositions к 'toward' and по 'along'; with certain verbs such as отвечáть 'answer', апплодúровать 'applaud', платúть 'pay', подражáть 'imitate', помогáть 'help', принадлежáть 'belong to', вéрить 'believe', мстить 'avenge', угождáть 'please', завúдовать 'envy'; in impersonal expressions of age and comfort such as *мне* двáдцать лет/хóлодно [me-DAT twenty-NOM years-GEN/cold] '*I* am twenty years old/cold'. There's no obvious pattern in such an explanation, and it doesn't prepare you to predict what other words might be associated with the dative, or to interpret a sentence like Онá наступúла *емý* на портфéль [She-NOM stepped him-DAT on briefcase-ACC] 'She stepped on *his* briefcase'. The incoherent assortments of case usage offered up in this fashion are incomplete and suggest no logical motive. There is also no logical motive for the student to try to learn them, since they don't make sense. The only choice seems to be to memorize lists of case uses, and this proves to be a formidable if not impossible task, since it is exceedingly difficult to assimilate information if it looks to you like just so much nonsense.

Traditional explanations of Russian cases usually look like lists of random items.

The goal of this text and accompanying exercises is to show you that there are patterns to case usage that make sense and can be learned fairly easily. This book can be used by students at any level of study, from beginner through advanced. Ideally a student could read through the basic text in the first year of study and then work through the examples and exercises in the second or third year. The margin notes and extensive indexing make it possible to access and use the text in any order, and for a variety of purposes, from general orientation to troubleshooting specific case meanings.

This text explains the coherent patterns of case meanings and can be used at any level of study.

The meanings of the grammatical cases are probably the biggest obstacle faced by English-speaking students trying to learn Russian. Even advanced learners will often run into sentences they can't interpret. Students often know plenty of vocabulary and how to find unfamiliar words in the dictionary, and maybe they can even figure out what cases all the nouns, pronouns, and adjectives are in, but if they cannot figure out what the cases mean, the meaning of the sentence remains a mystery.

Learning the meanings of Russian cases is an obstacle to students.

The meaning of a sentence is a product of two interdependent forces: the words it contains, and the relationships those words have to each other. In English these relationships are usually expressed by means of word order and prepositions, but in Russian this job is done by case. The words are fairly self-contained and concrete, since they can exist by themselves, outside of any sentence. The relationships that hold between words are relatively abstract and largely dependent upon context. The relationships themselves can be likened to a bare conceptual structure that is fleshed out by the actual words chosen. You can compare this to the concept *sandwich*, which indicates a set of relationships between bread, spreads, and fillings. By itself, *sandwich* is abstract, and if somebody asked you to

Russian cases show the relationship between words in a sentence.

"make a sandwich," you would probably ask for more information. If instead the request sounded something like "give me an open-faced turkey sandwich on rye with lettuce, tomato, and mustard, hold the mayo," you would find that more satisfactory, because you would know both the relationship (sandwich) and the specific items in that relationship (one slice of rye, mustard [not mayonnaise] for spread, filling of turkey, lettuce, and tomato).

Understanding Russian cases is like understanding how a game structures play.

Our culture has some abstract relationships that can't be expressed in a single word, or even in a common expression. Take for example the various types of games that involve two teams of people, each of which tries to control the movement of a round object into a space belonging to another team. Variations in the type of object, parts of body or implements used to move it, playing environments, rules, etc. yield specific games such as basketball, football, soccer, volleyball, field hockey, ice hockey, lacrosse, rugby, water-polo, tennis, and ping-pong. The abstract relationship that holds between all the players, objects, playing environments, and rules is so familiar that it is transparent to us. We don't even think about it, and we apply it effortlessly even when we encounter a new game we haven't seen before. Now, imagine that there are some people who live in a radically different culture, where there are no such sports. If you led them onto a lacrosse field and handed them some sticks and a ball, they would be utterly clueless. Without any extra help, it's extremely unlikely that these people would start playing anything remotely like lacrosse. The sticks might seem handy for gathering apples from some nearby trees, and maybe the ball could serve as the head of a child's doll or ritual effigy. Goodness knows what they would make of the goals.

Nobody ever explained to you the principle relationship behind lacrosse or all the other games that work the same way. They didn't have to. You saw plenty of examples all around you and internalized the principle without even thinking about it. In order to gain the kind of understanding you have for such games, newcomers who have never been exposed to such an idea will need an explanation, not just of the principle itself, but of how it functions in various actual games. The situation of a student learning Russian is very similar to the culture-shock of these outsiders. Until you get acculturated to the games Russians play with their cases, it is impossible for you to interpret and manipulate Russian sentences the way that Russians do. The objective is to make you into effective players of the case game. There are challenges to face, as in any game, but they are part of the sport, and the rewards of really mastering the language far outweigh the difficulties.

Every case has a coherent meaning.

If a Russian asked you to explain the meaning of the English preposition *for*, you might be surprised and frustrated by the difficulty of this task. Even if you couldn't give your Russian friend a satisfactory answer, that wouldn't mean that *for* doesn't mean anything or that there are lots of different *for*s that are not related to each other in any systematic way. Intuitively you sense that *for* does mean something and that all uses of *for* relate to that meaning. The same goes for Russians and cases: they may not be able to tell you why all those different verbs take the dative case, but they have an intuitive sense that the dative case does mean something and the contexts in which the dative appears has to do with that meaning.

PRELIMINARIES 2—How information is presented in this book

The notation and presentation of case in this book.

This book will present to you the basic meaning of each case, and it will also show you all the specific uses and how they relate to the basic meaning. To help you focus on the cases and their meanings, all examples are presented with both a word-by-word gloss and a smooth translation. The cases will be marked with abbreviated tags in the word-by-word gloss: NOM for nominative, INST for instrumental, ACC for accusative, DAT for dative, GEN for genitive, and LOC for locative (also known in some textbooks as "prepositional"). Each case will further be associated with two labels, one of which is a word and the other a diagram. For example, the instrumental will look like this:

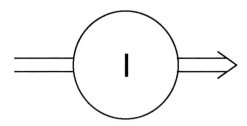

A force (arrow) passes through INSTRUMENTAL: A MEANS (circle labeled I)

Both the word and the diagram are meant to suggest the basic meaning of the case, to give you a handle to grip your memory to. They are not definitions, nor do they imply that Russians have such labels or think in pictograms or anything of that sort. They are merely reference points for the process of working through the meanings. Both the word and the diagram focus only on the meaning of the case itself, which is usually embedded in a sentence that uses several cases. For example, a sentence like the following could be represented by a larger diagram in which INSTRUMENTAL: A MEANS would be only a component:

Режиссёр протёр очки́ *платко́м.*
[Director-NOM wiped glasses-ACC handkerchief-INST.]
The director wiped his glasses *with a handkerchief.*

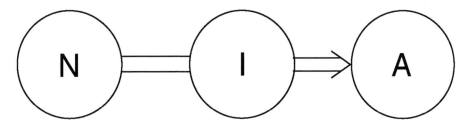

A force from a NOMINATIVE: A NAME (circle labeled N)
passes through an INSTRUMENTAL: A MEANS (circle labeled I) and
arrives at an ACCUSATIVE: A DESTINATION (circle labeled A)

However, such diagrams would quickly become clumsy and distracting. We will focus on only one case at a time instead of diagramming entire sentences this way.

Most cases have submeanings related to the basic meaning:

INSTRUMENTAL: A LABEL

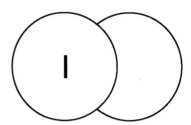

INSTRUMENTAL: A LABEL
(circle labeled I) is juxtaposed
with another item (other circle)

When there are submeanings, they will be arranged in a network to show how they are related like this:

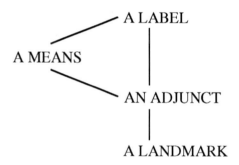

INSTRUMENTAL Network

This book focuses on case meaning, not endings; tables of endings appear in every chapter and in the appendix.

    The object of this text is not to teach you the case endings for nouns, adjectives, pronouns, and numerals. Working through these materials will certainly reinforce your knowledge of what these paradigms look like, but there are many other books and materials for achieving that goal. Drilling the endings would distract you from concentrating on the meanings. However, if you want to review the case endings at any time, there are tables in the appendix giving complete declensions for your reference, and shortened tables specific to each given case are at the beginning of each chapter.

Spatial relations and metaphor motivate case meaning.

    In addition to basic meanings and submeanings, metaphor plays an important role in case meaning. Case meaning takes as its point of departure the relationships that hold between physical objects placed or moving in space. These relationships can be metaphorically transferred to other domains such as time or social interaction, just as we see in English:

> *on* in space: I already have dinner *on* the table.
> *on* in time: I have a doctor's appointment *on* Monday.
> *toward* in space: The troops are advancing *toward* the border.
> *toward* in social interaction: That director is favorably inclined *toward* English actresses.

In these examples, time and social interaction are treated as if they were physical spaces. For the most part, Russians use these metaphors in ways very similar to those familiar from English, though some uses might surprise you. Throughout the text mention is made of meanings that are extended to domains other than space. These metaphorical extensions, in conjunction with items specific to certain contexts, such as negation, numerals, certain verbs and prepositions, are responsible for the more specific meanings that you will find nested under the basic meanings and submeanings.

There are also relations that hold between the cases. It is not essential for you to memorize or appreciate these relations at this point, but since these relations motivate the order in which the cases are presented and to some extent the descriptions they are given, a brief overview is in order. This overview is purely for purposes of general orientation; the statements it makes are abstract and will probably make more sense to you after you have completed all the text and exercises.

The relationships between cases.

	no direction	*direction*	*section*
center	NOMINATIVE: A NAME	ACCUSATIVE: A DESTINATION	GENITIVE: A SOURCE
periphery	INSTRUMENTAL: A MEANS	DATIVE: A RECEIVER	LOCATIVE: A PLACE

The nominative basically names an item, and has no particular designation. The instrumental is relatively peripheral to the nominative, and names an item through which something happens; it is a mere conduit, envelope, or accompaniment for something else. Both the accusative and the dative signal direction; the accusative is the destination for some item or activity, and the dative, relatively more peripheral, is a receiver or experiencer of some item or activity, usually capable of producing some further action in response. The sectioning of a part from its source is expressed by the genitive; more abstractly such sectioning can involve background elements of the setting, expressed by the locative.

The examples in this book are real, not concocted.

You will notice that the examples in both the text and exercises are very different from the examples you have seen in other textbooks. That is because these are not textbook examples; not a single one of them was cooked up for this book. Most of the examples in here have been taken from literature or periodicals printed in the past decade. Trying to learn Russian cases from traditional textbook examples is a little like trying to learn about the water cycle by studying the steam in your bathroom. It leads to the syndrome described at the beginning of this chapter, where you know all the words and endings, but still can't make sense of the sentence. Many people hit this plateau in their third year of study, but if you're a fast learner, you risk getting stuck there even sooner. Rather than being contrived and antiseptic, the examples in this book and exercises will expose you to the cases as they really are, raw and unadulterated. This means that the examples will be somewhat messier than the ones you are used to seeing. But hopefully this guided tour of case realia will help to make your transition from language study to language use a confident, seamless stride rather than a desperate leap into a void.

NOMINATIVE Forms

Feminine declension nouns	hard type: 'room'		soft type: 'week'
	singular	plural	singular	plural
	ко́мната	ко́мнаты	неде́ля	неде́ли

	-ь: 'talent'	
	singular	plural
	спосо́бность	спосо́бности

Masculine declension nouns	hard type: 'courtyard'		soft type: 'nail'
	singular	plural	singular	plural
	дво́р	дворы́	гво́здь	гво́зди

Neuter declension nouns	hard type: 'body'		soft type: 'schedule'
	singular	plural	singular	plural
	те́ло	тела́	расписа́ние	расписа́ния

Adjectives

hard type: 'first'

feminine	masculine	neuter	plural
пе́рвая	пе́рвый	пе́рвое	пе́рвые
	-**о́й** if stressed		

soft type: 'last'

feminine	masculine	neuter	plural
после́дняя	после́дний	после́днее	после́дние

Pronouns

'I'	'we'	'you' informal	'you'
я	мы	ты	вы

'she'	'he'	'it'	'they'
она́	он	оно́	они́

'who'	'what'
кто	что

'this'

feminine	masculine	neuter	plural
э́та	э́тот	э́то	э́ти

'all, every'

feminine	masculine	neuter	plural
вся	весь	всё	все

Possessives

feminine	masculine	neuter	plural
'my'			
моя́	мой	моё	мои́

'our'			
на́ша	на́ш	на́ше	на́ши

Numerals

'one'

feminine	masculine	neuter	plural
одна́	оди́н	одно́	одни́

'two'	'three'	'four'	'five'
дв**е** (fem)	три	четы́ре	пя́ть
дв**а** (masc/neut)			

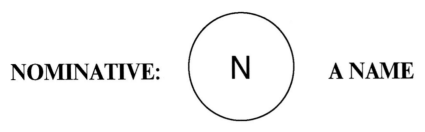

The nominative network:

A NAME ——————— AN IDENTITY

PROLOGUE

As you probably suspect, the nominative case is relatively simple and straightforward. It is the logical starting point both for our survey of the cases and for many sentences. In addition to its basic meaning, NOMINATIVE: A NAME, this case has just one submeaning, NOMINATIVE: AN IDENTITY. Whereas NOMINATIVE: A NAME has a very broad naming function, NOMINATIVE: AN IDENTITY has a more narrow function, targeting a characteristic of something that has already been named. You can think of NOMINATIVE: AN IDENTITY as being a specialized version of NOMINATIVE: A NAME, used when we want to convey more information.

An overview of the nominative case.

NOMINATIVE: A NAME 1—Naming and calling

Because it does not have any other more specific meaning, the nominative is ideal even for use outside of a sentence, such as: pointing to an object and naming it; signs, tags,

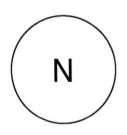

NOMINATIVE: A NAME
(circle labeled N)

labels, titles, and similar naming devices. The fact that dictionaries cite nouns in the nominative case is a symptom of the nominative's function as the primary name for an item or idea; the other case forms are all variations on the nominative, secondary and derived. There are two ways in which Russian uses this naming function just like a sign: either by setting it off with a comma, or by using a comma and *как* 'like'. In both situations the nominative item is set apart from the rest of the sentence; it is merely a parenthetical piece of commentary:

The naming function of NOMINATIVE: A NAME.

Ты не в Мордо́вии, *чу́чело*!
[You-NOM not in Mordovia-LOC, scarecrow-NOM!]
You're not in Mordovia, *you scarecrow*!

Не трожь Росси́ю, *иноро́дец*!
[Not touch Russia-ACC, foreigner-NOM!]
Don't touch Russia, *you foreigner*!

NOMINATIVE: A NAME used to call someone a name or to get their attention.

Только скажу́ — *молоды́е*, не губи́те себя́, не про́буйте.
[Only say — young people-NOM, not destroy self-ACC, not try.]
I have only one thing to say — *young people*, don't destroy yourselves, don't try it.

In the first two examples above, the naming function is being used to call someone a name. As the third example shows (a plea for young people not to use drugs), you can similarly use the nominative case to call out to someone to get their attention. Some languages have a separate vocative case with its own endings where Russian uses NOMINATIVE: A NAME. Russian does have some special vocative case forms with people's names and names of family members. If a name (usually a diminutive form) ends in -а or -я it is not uncommon to hear Russians drop the last vowel when calling to a friend or relative. Thus you might hear *Оль!* as well as *Óля!*, *Алёш!* as well as *Алёша!*, and *мáм!* as well as *мáма!* Here's an example of this truncated use of the NOMINATIVE: A NAME with the name *Дúма*:

Дим, как ты ду́маешь, любо́вь ме́жду му́жем и жено́й мо́жет быть ве́чной?
[Dima-NOM, how you-NOM think, love-NOM between husband-INST and wife-INST can be eternal-INST?]
Dima, what do you think, can the love between a husband and a wife last forever?

There are two special naming forms (historical leftovers from a vocative case long ago lost in Russian) that can be used to appeal for divine assistance: *Бóже!* 'O God!' (from *Бог* 'God') and *Гóсподи* 'O Lord' (from *Госпóдь* 'Lord').

As mentioned above, NOMINATIVE: A NAME can be introduced by the word как 'like'. Here are two examples of the parenthetical use of как with the NOMINATIVE: A NAME:

Оказа́лось, что и танцева́ть не уме́ла и сиде́ла ти́хо, как *мышь*.
[Turned-out, that even dance not knew and sat quietly, like mouse-NOM.]
It turned out that she didn't even know how to dance, and she sat quietly, like *a mouse*.

И я, как *áндерсеновский коро́ль*, из всех сил стара́лся разгляде́ть э́ту о́блачность и прозра́чность, э́ту му́зыку без слов.
[And I-NOM, like Andersen's king-NOM, from all strengths-GEN tried to see-through this cloudiness-ACC and transparency-ACC, this music-ACC without words-GEN.]
And I, like *Andersen's king* (in the tale "The Emporer's New Clothes"), tried with all my strength to see through this cloudiness and transparency, this music without words.

NOMINATIVE: A NAME 2—The subject of a sentence

In the expression of any more complex thought, the nominative names the subject, the active head of most sentences. Because words are marked with cases, there is no need for a nominative subject to be the first item in a sentence, as in English. The thing that identifies the subject is its nominative case, not its position; no matter where it is, it can be identified as nominative and therefore subject. As we will see, the same goes for the other cases as well: since each item in a sentence is flagged with a case ending indicating its role, the order of words doesn't matter as much. The word order we are familiar with from English is probably the most common one used in Russian, but there are many other possibilities, thanks to the fact that speakers of Russian can read the case flags no matter where they are waving. Here are some examples of nominative subjects, both at the beginnings of sentences and elsewhere:

Никако́е друго́е и́мя в ру́сской про́зе после́днего десятиле́тия не звучи́т так гро́мко и вня́тно и, гла́вное, — привлека́тельно.
[No other name-NOM in Russian prose-LOC last decade-GEN not sound as loudly and distinctly and, mainly, — appealingly.]
No other name in Russian prose of the last decade sounds as loud and distinct and, most importantly, — as appealing.

Осо́бенно скорби́т *а́втор* по приснопа́мятным времена́м СССР тридца́тых - пятидеся́тых годо́в.
[Especially laments author-NOM along memorable times-DAT USSR-GEN thirties-GEN - fities years-GEN.]
The author particularly laments the memorable times of the USSR of the 1930's - 1950's.

Чем обернётся для Росси́и *поте́ря* стратеги́ческого се́верного форпо́ста.
[What-INST turn-into for Russia-GEN loss-NOM strategic northern outpost-GEN.]
What *the loss* of a strategic northern outpost will mean for Russia.

Ви́дно, на по́чте что́-то перепу́тали. Нет, на паке́те то́чно зна́чился *мой а́дрес.*
[Clearly, at post-office-LOC something-ACC mixed-up. No, on package-LOC precisely appeared my address-NOM.]
Clearly they had made a mistake at the post office. No, it was precisely *my address* that appeared on the package.

Во мне́, есте́ственно, нака́пливался *проте́ст* проти́в их "пра́вды".
[In me-LOC, naturally, welled-up protest-NOM against their "truth-GEN".]
A feeling of *protest* against their "truth" naturally welled up in me.

Поэ́тому-то и *развито́й социали́зм* ру́хнул не то́лько из-за того́, что его́ возглавля́ли *дря́хлые ста́рцы*, кото́рых приводи́ли на заседа́ние *колле́ги* по́д руку...
[For that reason even mature socialism-NOM collapsed not just because that-GEN, that it-ACC headed decrepit elders-NOM, whom-ACC led at meeting-ACC colleagues-NOM under hand-ACC...]
That's why even *mature socialism* collapsed, not just because it was headed *by decrepit elders* whom *colleagues* led by the hand to the meeting...

NOMINATIVE: A NAME as the subject of быть 'be'.

The first example has the NOMINATIVE: A NAME subject at the beginning, the second example places it after the verb. The third example (the title of a newspaper article) shows the NOMINATIVE: A NAME subject deeply embedded in the sentence, and the same goes for the last three examples. Notice that the last example here has three clauses, all with nominative subjects; the second one is actually active ('decrepit elders headed it'), but we used the passive voice in the smooth translation because English word order is not as flexible as Russian. The active phrase 'decrepit elders headed it' would have put 'decrepit elders' too far away from 'whom'. You will often encounter Russian sentences that cannot be said in the same way in English, and this will be reflected in our translations.

The subject of a sentence need not engage in any real action in order to serve as the source of energy for a verb; it can merely exist. Here is an example of NOMINATIVE: A NAME serving as the subject for the verb быть 'be':

В це́нтре перегово́ров — *вопро́сы* ира́но-росси́йского сотру́дничества.
[In center-LOC negotiations-GEN — questions-NOM Iranian-Russian collaboration-GEN.]
Questions about Iranian-Russian collaboration are at the center of the negotiations.

NOMINATIVE: A NAME as the subject of быть 'be', when used to express 'have'.

This example follows the pattern of "at a location [*center of negotiations*] there is *an item (subject)*[*questions*]". Russian uses a specialized version of this construction to express 'have', employing у 'by' + GEN to describe the location. Thus у меня́ (есть) *кни́га* [by me-GEN (is) book-NOM], literally 'by me there is *a book*', is the most usual way of saying 'I have *a book*'. The following example contains a metaphorical assertion of having familial attachments (roots being ancestors and shoots being offspring), followed by an assertion of existence (expressed by an archaic form of the verb быть 'be'):

У меня́ есть *ко́рни* и есть *ростки́*. Зна́чит, я есмь.
[By me-GEN are roots-NOM and are shoots-NOM. Means, I-NOM am.]
I have *roots* and I have *shoots*. Therefore, *I* exist.

NOMINATIVE: AN IDENTITY 1—The Y in an X = Y sentence

NOMINATIVE: AN IDENTITY with the verb 'be'.

Even when you have already given something a name, you might want to give more information about the item, to tell us that it is big or unusual or whatever. The basis of this submeaning is a simple equation of the type $x = y$, where y is NOMINATIVE: AN IDENTITY. The bond between x and y is typically the verb быть 'be' (which usually has a zero form in the present tense). The other item, x,

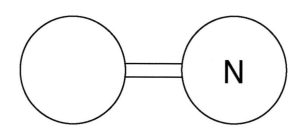

NOMINATIVE:: AN IDENTITY (circle labeled N) is associated with another item (other circle)

is typically NOMINATIVE: A NAME (just like the examples with быть 'be' immediately above). This use of NOMINATIVE: AN IDENTITY is traditionally known as the "predicate nominative".

Найма́н — *интеллектуа́льный ковбо́й.*
[Naiman-NOM — intellectual cowboy-NOM.]
Naiman is *an intellectual cowboy.*

Вообще́, ру́сский Се́вер — ещё *неразга́данная та́йна* Росси́и.
[In-general, Russian North-NOM — still unsolved mystery-NOM Russia-GEN.]
In general, the Russian North is Russia's as yet *unsolved mystery.*

До́лжен призна́ться, что я не совсе́м *журнали́ст.*
[Must admit, that I-NOM not completely journalist-NOM.]
I must admit that I am not exactly *a journalist.*

На́до име́ть в виду́, что она́ *челове́к* глубоко́ *ве́рующий.*
[Necessary have in view-LOC, that she-NOM person-NOM deeply faithful-NOM.]
One has to keep in mind the fact that she is *a person of* profound *faith.*

Since both terms in the equation refer to the same thing, the item marked as NOMINATIVE: AN IDENTITY can be just an adjective, adding extra information, as in:

NOMINATIVE: AN IDENTITY with adjectives.

Коври́гин стра́шно *рани́мый* и боле́зненно *чу́ткий.*
[Kovrigin-NOM terribly woundable-NOM and painfully sensitive-NOM.]
Kovrigin is terribly *easy to wound* and painfully *sensitive.*

NOMINATIVE: AN IDENTITY in sentences with the $x = y$ structure also marks the place where short-form adjectives appear in Russian; indeed when you have only an adjective in this position, it is usually short-form, and short-form adjectives can only appear in the nominative case. Here are some examples:

NOMINATIVE: AN IDENTITY with short-form adjectives.

Побе́да Довла́това *несомне́нна.*
[Victory-NOM Dovlatov-GEN indisputable-NOM.]
Dovlatov's victory is *indisputable.*

Уби́йцы на́шего вождя́ пока́ не *на́йдены.*
[Murderers-NOM our leader-GEN as-yet not found-NOM.]
The people who murdered our leader have not yet been *found.*

Изве́стно, ю́ность *дове́рчива* и *любопы́тна*, а потому́ и *бесстра́шна.*
[Known, youth-NOM trusting-NOM and curious-NOM, and for-that-reason also fearless-NOM.]
It is well known that youth is *trusting* and *curious* and for that reason also *fearless.*

In reality there are two kinds of $x = y$ expressions, the relatively simple identity described here, and a different one that involves labeling x as a member of category y, in which case y is marked as INSTRUMENTAL: A LABEL. Here is one example for comparison:

Contrast between NOMINATIVE: AN IDENTITY and INSTRUMENTAL: A LABEL with the verb 'be'.

Я был одновреме́нно *хи́щником и же́ртвой.*
[I-NOM was simultaneously predator-INST and victim-INST.]
I was simultaneously *a predator* and *a victim*.

The use of INSTRUMENTAL: A LABELwill become clearer in the discussion of the instrumental case in the following chapter. For now it is enough to note that although both the nominative and the instrumental cases can be used to describe an item, NOMINATIVE: AN IDENTITY tends to describe inherent, unchanging properties, whereas INSTRUMENTAL: A LABEL tends to describe temporary, changing properties. Remember that an identity is something that is permanent, whereas a label can be taken off and exchanged.

Word order can be rearranged for this use of the nominative as well, as in this example:

Найвные мы всё же *люди!*
[Naive-NOM we-NOM after all people-NOM]
We are after all *naive people!*

The normal word order, corresponding to the other examples we have seen, would of course be мы всё же *найвные люди,* but the word найвные has been moved to the beginning for emphasis.

NOMINATIVE: AN IDENTITY 2—Fixed X = Y expressions

There are a couple of fixed expressions that use NOMINATIVE: AN IDENTITY. One is the phrase что тако́е + NOM 'what is Y?', which asks the hearer to identify the meaning of a word that the speaker does not know. Here is an example of how this simple question can be embedded in a sentence for rhetorical effect:

Здесь, когда́ стрясло́сь у меня́ большо́е го́ре, я позна́ла и что тако́е *настоя́щие друзья́.*
[Here, when shook-off by me-GEN big grief-NOM, I-NOM found-out also what-NOM such-NOM real friends-NOM.]
Here, when I shook off the burden of grief, I also found out what *true friends* really are.

The use of NOMINATIVE: AN IDENTITY with the preposition за 'behind' to mean 'what kind of Y is that?' is not uncommon in spoken Russian:

Ты мне лу́чше объясни́, что э́то за *люди!*
[You-NOM me-DAT better explain, what-NOM that-NOM for people-NOM!]
Then you explain to me what kind of *people* those are!

Э́то ещё что за *но́вости?*
[That-NOM still what-NOM for news-NOM?]
What kind of *news* is that now?

Что за *оппозицио́нная па́ртия* — бы́ло ещё не совсе́м я́сно.
[What-NOM for opposition party-NOM — was still not entirely clear.]
What kind of *opposition party* — that was still not entirely clear.

NOMINATIVE: AN IDENTITY 3—X = Y reduced to X, Y

The construction associated with NOMINATIVE: AN IDENTITY can appear in an abbreviated form, without any verb to connect the two entities (perhaps not such a big loss, since the most common verb is 'to be', which is usually not expressed in the present tense, as shown in most of the examples in the preceding two sections). In this construction we see a word that refers to a generic category (like 'state' or 'novel') followed by the specific name or title of something in that category (like 'Nevada' or 'The White Guard'), as in these two examples:

> 1992 г. — в шта́те *Нева́да* произведён после́дний я́дерный взрыв.
> [1992 year-NOM — in state-LOC Nevada-NOM produced-NOM last nuclear explosion-NOM.]
> The year 1992 — in the state *of Nevada* the last nuclear explosion is produced.

> Éсли в "Ма́стере и Маргари́те" ирреа́льное и фантасти́ческое определено́ за́мыслом, то от рома́на "*Бе́лая гва́рдия*" никто́ не ожида́л мисти́ческих приключе́ний.
> [If in "Master-LOC and Margarita-LOC" unreal-NOM and fantastic-NOM determined-NOM design-INST, then from novel-GEN "White Guard-NOM" no-one-NOM not expected mystical adventures-GEN.]
> Whereas in *The Master and Margarita* unreal and fantastic elements were determined by design, no one expected mystical adventures from the novel *The White Guard*.

Notice that the word for the generic category can be in any case (in these examples, шта́те 'state' is in the locative, and рома́на 'novel' is in the genitive), but the actual name (commonly known as an appositive) is in the nominative. The second example provides us with an opportunity to compare the effect of this use of the NOMINATIVE: AN IDENTITY with its absence. When the generic category is not stated, the title of the first book mentioned (*The Master and Margarita*) is declined, but when the generic term meaning 'novel' is used, the title (*The White Guard*) appears in the nominative case.

EPILOGUE

To recap: the nominative case can be used to call someone or something by name, to name the subject of a sentence, and also to indicate the identity of an item. The nominative is all about naming, and it should not surprise you that the very term "nominative" is related to our English word *name*. Though not all Russian sentences have nominative subjects, the vast majority do, and your strategy should be to look first for a nominative subject and its

NOMINATIVE: AN IDENTITY can be used to give specific names to examples of categories.

verb; once you find these two items, the rest of the sentence becomes easier to unpack. The remaining chapters of this book will reveal the meanings of the other cases and demonstrate their functions. Russian operates on an austere and powerful little system, using only six cases to describe all the possible relationships that human beings encounter in their lives. As the pieces fall into place, you will gradually become acculturated to the logic of Russian sentences and you will find that each case takes on a life of its own.

INSTRUMENTAL Forms

Feminine declension nouns

hard type: 'room'		soft type: 'week'	
singular	plural	singular	plural
ко́мнатой	ко́мнатами	неде́лей	неде́лями

-ь: 'talent'	
singular	plural
спосо́бностью	спосо́бностями

Masculine declension nouns

hard type: 'courtyard'		soft type: 'nail'	
singular	plural	singular	plural
дворо́м	двора́ми	гвоздём	гвоздя́ми

Neuter declension nouns

hard type: 'body'		soft type: 'schedule'	
singular	plural	singular	plural
те́лом	тела́ми	расписа́нием	расписа́ниями

Adjectives

hard type: 'first'			
feminine	masculine	neuter	plural
пе́рвой	пе́рвым	пе́рвым	пе́рвыми

soft type: 'last'			
feminine	masculine	neuter	plural
после́дней	после́дним	после́дним	после́дними

Pronouns

'I'	'we'	'you' informal	'you'
мной	на́ми	тобо́й	ва́ми

'she'	'he'	'it'	'they'
(н)ей	(н)им	(н)им	(н)и́ми

'who'	'what'	'oneself'	
кем	чем	собо́й	

'this'			
feminine	masculine	neuter	plural
э́той	э́тим	э́тим	э́тими

'all, every'			
feminine	masculine	neuter	plural
всей	всем	всем	все́ми

Possessives

feminine	masculine	neuter	plural
'my'			
мое́й	мои́м	мои́м	мои́ми

'our'			
на́шей	на́шим	на́шим	на́шими

Numerals

'one'			
feminine	masculine	neuter	plural
одно́й	одни́м	одни́м	одни́ми

'two'	'three'	'four'	'five'
двумя́	тремя́	четырьмя́	пятью́

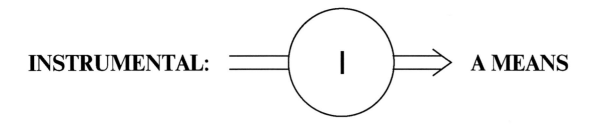

INSTRUMENTAL: ⟶ **A MEANS**

The instrumental network:

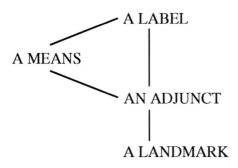

A LABEL

A MEANS

AN ADJUNCT

A LANDMARK

Prologue

The instrumental is one of the most complex Russian cases, but the idea behind it is fairly simple. You can think of it as an accessory for something else. Rather than serving as a source for energy (which is the primary task of NOMINATIVE: A NAME), the instrumental is a peripheral attachment for something else. The peripheral accessory named by the instrumental can be associated either with an activity or with an item. When an item in the instrumental case is associated with an activity, we have INSTRUMENTAL: A MEANS, and the instrumental item is a conduit for the activity. When an item in the instrumental case is attached to another item, it serves as an address for that item; this can be done by tagging it in some way, in which case we have INSTRUMENTAL: A LABEL, by identifying something to which it is joined, in which case we have INSTRUMENTAL: AN ADJUNCT (here we use the Russian preposition c 'with'), or by locating it in reference to a landmark, in which case we have INSTRUMENTAL: A LANDMARK (used with the prepositions над 'above', под 'under', пе́ред 'in front of', за 'behind', and ме́жду 'between').

Your first task when confronted with an item in the instrumental case will be to figure out which part of the network it is using. If any of the prepositions (c, над, под, пе́ред, за, ме́жду) are present, you can put this task behind you, since you will have INSTRUMENTAL: AN ADJUNCT with the preposition c, and INSTRUMENTAL: A LANDMARK with the remaining prepositions. If not, you will need to think about whether the instrumental is being used to augment a description of an activity (INSTRUMENTAL: A MEANS) or a thing (INSTRUMENTAL: A LABEL). The explanations and examples below should help you get used to looking for this difference.

An overview of the instrumental case.

The instrumental case marks an item associated with an activity or another item.

INSTRUMENTAL: A MEANS 1—A map of the mental leaps involved

Though INSTRUMENTAL: A MEANS always designates a conduit for action, there is an intricate web of specific uses, and it is worth mapping them out ahead of time before diving right into them. INSTRUMENTAL: A MEANS can be divided into two smaller groups: one takes the concept of a path as its point of departure (sections 2-9), and the other focuses on the agents of actions (sections 10-11). The following diagram might help you to think about how the ideas in the first group (the path group) are organized:

path >
      facilitator/instrument/means >
           person/object under control >
               person/object possessed >
                   person/object evaluated positively/negatively

A path, because it facilitates movement, can also be conceived of as a facilitator for action, an instrument, or a means (think of our English expression of *a way to do things*, where we also understand means and instruments in terms of a path by using the word *way*). The fact that instruments are objects under our control motivates the use of the instrumental with verbs expressing domination, facilitating a mental leap from instrument to person or object under control. Since having control is a special kind of having, some verbs of possession also have instrumental objects, and this brings us to person or object possessed. Finally, an item under control can be variously evaluated and as a result we use the instrumental with certain verbs meaning 'enjoy' and 'despise'. The next eight sections will take you through all these mental leaps, with enough examples and explanations to ensure a safe landing for every jump.

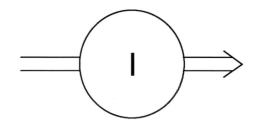

A force (arrow) passes through
INSTRUMENTAL: A MEANS
(circle labeled I)

INSTRUMENTAL: A MEANS 2—Paths through space

When an instrumental item is associated with a verb, its purpose is to tell us something about the means by which the verbal activity takes place. It can be thought of as a channel for realizing the activity of the verb. The instrumental item thus serves as a conduit for the flow of energy named by the verb. This can involve simply passing through a space or following a path, as in:

Мы свернули к набережной и прошли *дощатым трапом* над колеблющейся водой.
[We-NOM turned toward embankment-DAT and walked planked ladder-INST above quavering water-INST.]
We turned toward the embankment and walked *along the planked ladder* above the quavering water.

Он ре́зко сверну́л в сто́рону и пошёл *суходо́лом* на́искось.
[He-NOM sharply turned to side-ACC and went riverbed-INST diagonally.]
He turned sharply to the side and walked diagonally *across the riverbed.*

Пе́гий пёс, бегу́щий *кра́ем* мо́ря
[Skewbald dog-NOM, running-NOM edge-INST sea-GEN]
A skewbald dog, running *along the edge* of the sea

In the above examples, the planked ladder, the riverbed, and the edge of the sea are all paths for movement.

A path can of course be conceived of abstractly, giving us examples like this one:

Мы все обожа́ем Довла́това за то, как он жил, но мы-то пойдём *други́м путём.*
[We all-NOM adore Dovlatov-ACC for that-ACC, how he-NOM lived, but we-NOM will-go another way-INST.]
We all adore Dovlatov for how he lived, but we will go *another way.*

INSTRUMENTAL: A MEANS as an abstract path.

In both English and Russian we think of life as a journey along a path; this makes it possible for us to talk of *the path of life* and *life's obstacles.* Because life is a path, a Russian can substitute *life* for *path* to get:

Я жил *той* же *жи́знью,* что и все, и волнова́ло меня́ то же, что и всех.
[I-NOM lived same life-INST, that and everyone-NOM, and upset me-ACC that-NOM, that and everyone-ACC.]
I lived *the same life* as everyone and got upset by the same things as everyone.

In this example, life is the path along which living is realized. Living goes down the path of life.

If the verb describes a state rather than a movement, the space marked in the instrumental is a container for the state. You can think of this as a stationary path. The connection of paths of movement with stationary routes is one that is very well motivated, since repeated motion along a given route carves stationary paths through meadows and forests, and nowadays we often ensure the stability of these stationary paths with layers of asphalt. Here is an example of a stationary path along another kind of terrain, namely a woman's face:

INSTRUMENTAL: A MEANS as a stationary path, the container of a state of being.

Она́ была́ бледна́ *лицо́м.*
[She-NOM was pale-NOM face-INST.]
She was pale *in the face.*

Paleness extends along the face just as movement extends along a path. A common example of this meaning is found in the idiom вверх *нога́ми* [up legs-INST] 'upside-down'; the legs are the place where "up" is happening. The same principle is at work, albeit more abstractly, with the instrumental item naming a domain that can be measured, in the following example:

INSTRUMENTAL: A
MEANS as a path
through time.

Оди́н из слоно́в — трёхле́тний Раджа́ *ве́сом* в 850 килогра́ммов — воспо́льзовался прогу́лкой, чтобы загляну́ть в посу́дную ла́вку.
[One-NOM of elephants-GEN — three-year-old Rajah-NOM weight-INST in 850-ACC kilograms-GEN — took-advantage outing-INST, to peek to china shop-ACC.]
One of the elephants — three-year-old Rajah, *weighing* 850 kilograms — took advantage of the outing to take a peek into a china shop.

Thus, in the case of Rajah the elephant, the parameter of weight is the instrumental container for a measurement of 850 kilograms.

INSTRUMENTAL: A MEANS 3—Paths through time

As we saw in Preliminaries, time can often behave in a way similar to space, or at least we think of it as behaving similarly and talk about it as if it did. Stretches of time can also serve as paths for activity. Duration is essential, since a point that is instantaneous does not have enough dimension to be conceived of as a path. You are probably already familiar with the use of the instrumental case with the names of seasons of the year and parts of the day; here is a list of them:

seasons of the year		parts of the day	
весно́й	*in the spring*	*у́тром*	*in the morning*
ле́том	*in the summer*	*днём*	*in the afternoon*
о́сенью	*in the fall*	*ве́чером*	*in the evening*
зимо́й	*in the winter*	*но́чью*	*at night*

The use of INSTRUMENTAL: A MEANS with these words is so well entrenched in Russian that dictionaries commonly list them as adverbs. These words can, however, be modified, as in:

Ны́нешней зимо́й ко всем бе́дам Владивосто́ка доба́вится ещё и отсу́тствие воды́.
[Current winter-INST to all misfortunes-DAT Vladivostok-GEN is-added still and absence-NOM water-GEN.]
This winter, in addition to all of Vladivostok's misfortunes, there is also a water shortage.

А́вгустовской но́чью мы ме́дленно шли по тротуа́ру, и́зредка обме́ниваясь слова́ми.
[August night-INST we-NOM slowly walked along sidewalk-DAT, rarely exchanging words-INST.]
In that August night we walked slowly down the sidewalk, rarely exchanging words.

And other words for durations of time can also be used:

Вели́ким посто́м меня́ заста́вили гове́ть.
[Great Lent-INST me-ACC forced fast.]
During Great Lent they forced me to fast.

Па́мятным пари́жским ма́ем шестьдеся́т восьмо́го, когда́ в Лати́нском кварта́ле возводи́лись баррика́ды бунту́ющих студе́нтов, аристократи́ческий шестна́дцатый кварта́л наслажда́лся поко́ем и тишино́й.
[Memorable Paris May-INST sixty eighth-GEN, when in Latin quarter-LOC were-raised barricades-NOM rioting students-GEN, aristocratic sixteenth quarter-NOM enjoyed peace-INST and quiet-INST.]
During that memorable May in Paris in 1968, when the rioting students' barricades were going up in the Latin quarter, the aristocratic sixteenth quarter was enjoying peace and quiet.

The previous four examples prove that the use of SMALL CAPS INSTRUMENTAL: A MEANS for durations of time is a productive phenomenon in Russian.

INSTRUMENTAL: A MEANS 4—Expanses of time and space

Expanses of both time and space can appear in the plural, creating either continuous (as in *века́ми, часа́ми* below) or discontinuous (as in *ноча́ми, места́ми*) locations for objects and events. This use of the instrumental builds on the notion of a stationary path through space or time (the latter interpreted as duration, as we saw in section 3), but multiplies these stationary paths. If the paths connect neatly end-to-end, we simply have a very long stretch of time, as in the first two examples below. If the paths do not connect, then the activity is distributed along a patchwork of stationary paths, as in the second two examples.

Plural paths— INSTRUMENTAL: A MEANS in places and at times.

Э́то — традицио́нное приве́тствие, знако́мое челове́честву *века́ми*.
[It-NOM — traditional greeting-NOM, known-NOM humankind-DAT centuries-INST.]
It is a traditional greeting, known to humankind *for centuries*.

Неизме́нно вы́пивший, он *часа́ми* броди́л по коридо́ру.
[Invariably drunk-NOM, he-NOM hours-INST wandered along corridor-DAT.]
Invariably drunk, he wandered *for hours* along the corridor.

Она́ поджида́ла му́жа *ноча́ми*.
[She-NOM waited-up husband-ACC nights-INST.]
She waited up for her husband *during the nights*.

В лесу́ *места́ми* ещё лежа́л снег.
[In forest-LOC places-INST still lay snow.]
In the forest there was still snow lying *in places*.

Instrumental: a means 5—Path > facilitator/instrument

INSTRUMENTAL: A
MEANS as a
facilitator,
instrument, or
means.

Let's go back again to that idea of a path. In an abstract sense, a path is something that facilitates movement; the existence of a way to go makes it possible for you to go. We can get more mileage out of the concept of facilitation by doing some substitutions. Instead of looking only at movement, we can expand our view to include any activity named by a verb. And instead of looking only at paths as facilitators, we can look at anything that makes activity possible. By taking the original concept of *path for movement* and extending it to *facilitator for activity* we open up a wide horizon of ideas. All other uses of INSTRUMENTAL: A MEANS take advantage of this horizon, empowering the instrumental case to signify a wide variety of instruments and agents of actions.

INSTRUMENTAL: A
MEANS with
physical
instruments.

We will start with instruments facilitating action. Examples of concrete physical instruments are fairly common:

Пóмню егó молодóго, огрóмного, в мя́той сéрой шинéли, перепоя́санной *ремнём* с мéдной бля́хой.
[Remember him young, huge-ACC, in wrinkled grey overcoat-LOC, girded-LOC belt-INST with brass buckle-INST.]
I remember him young, huge, in a wrinkled grey overcoat, girded *with a belt* with a brass buckle.

И как раз в э́тот момéнт с лéстницы стáли нáшу кóмнату открывáть *ключóм*.
[And like once in that moment-ACC from stairway-GEN began our room-ACC open key-INST.]
And right at that moment they started to open our room from the stairway *with a key*.

Смéх углубля́ет дыхáние, обогащáет *кислорóдом* кровь и вентили́рует лёгкие.
[Laughter-NOM deepens breathing-ACC, enriches oxygen-INST blood-ACC and ventilates lungs-ACC.]
Laughter deepens the breathing, enriches the blood *with oxygen*, and ventilates the lungs.

INSTRUMENTAL: A
MEANS with
metaphorical
instruments.

These next three examples are fairly typical metaphorical extensions of the idea of a physical instrument:

Я мог летéть домóй *ближáйшим рéйсом*.
[I-NOM could fly home next flight-INST.]
I could fly home *on the next flight*.

Онá грози́ла емý *развóдом*.
[She-NOM threatened him-DAT divorce-INST.]
She threatened him *with divorce*.

Побе́ды Суво́рова и пораже́ния Куропа́ткина определя́лись не то́лько *их лйчными талáнтами*, но и *истори́ческим контéкстом* их войн и похо́дов.
[Victories-NOM Suvorov-GEN and defeats-NOM Kuropatkin-GEN were-determined not only their personal talents-INST, but also historical context-INST their wars-GEN and campaigns-GEN.]
Suvorov's victories and Kuropatkin's defeats were determined not only *by their personal talents*, but also *by the historical context* of their wars and campaigns.

The next flight is a way to realize a trip home, a divorce is wielded as a threat, and talents and context serve to determine military successes and failures. In the next example the speaker declares that he was ready to pay any price as an instrument to dispel his depressing thoughts:

Любо́й ценóй я захотéл избáвиться от э́тих тя́жких мы́слей.
[Any price-INST I-NOM wanted get-rid from these grave thoughts-GEN.]
I wanted to get rid of these grave thoughts *at any price*.

Now let's try something a bit more challenging:

По́мню блистáющий, осо́бенно *людьмй*, ресторáн Кры́ша.
[Remember shining-ACC, especially people-INST, restaurant-ACC Krysha.]
I remember the Krysha restaurant, shining especially *by means of the people* there.

The restaurant shines in the memory of the speaker, and the reason it shines is because it was filled with brilliant people. The people caused the brilliance that made the restaurant shine. Or to follow the logic of the example, the restaurant shone *by means of the people*. This use of the instrumental is very much parallel to English *with* in phrases like the air was buzzing *with bees*, the yard was crawling *with ants*, the sky was glittering *with stars*. Here's a more typical Russian example:

По́сле пое́здки к мáтери и до вечéрней рабóты в ресторáне онá успéла убрáть в квартйре, и тепéрь кýхня сия́ла *чистотóй*.
[After trip-GEN to mother-DAT and before evening work-GEN in restaurant-LOC she-NOM managed clean-up in apartment-LOC, and now kitchen-NOM shone cleanliness-INST.]
After visiting her mother and before her evening shift in the restaurant she managed to clean up the apartment, and now the kitchen shone *with cleanliness*.

You'll also need some imagination to tackle an example like:

Я тут *проéздом*.
[I-NOM here trip-INST.]
I'm here *on a trip* / I'm *just stopping through* here.

The journey has facilitated the fact that the speaker is here; it has brought about his presence. The verbal activity in this example is "being", and it is still valid even when the present tense forms of the verb быть are omitted.

The instrument used can be very close to home, including a part of one's own person:

> Бу́дучи америка́нцем, он *всей душо́й* мечта́л разбогате́ть.
> [Being American-INST, he-NOM all soul-INST dreamed get-rich.]
> Being an American, he dreamed of getting rich *with all his soul*.

In this case the soul serves to facilitate dreams of riches.

INSTRUMENTAL: A MEANS 6—Actions facilitated by instruments

INSTRUMENTAL: A
MEANS can
express the item
necessary for an
action.

Expressions using INSTRUMENTAL: A MEANS of the type 'produce an action by means of X' are quite common. Here is an example:

> Вон! — кри́кнула фрау неожи́данно *зво́нким го́лосом*.
> [Out! — shouted frau-NOM unexpectedly sonorous voice-INST.]
> Out! — shouted the frau unexpectedly *in a sonorous voice*.

Often the instrumental item represents something necessary to the performance of the action. The following combinations are standard fare:

Expressions of moving an item associated with INSTRUMENTAL: A MEANS

броса́ться *ка́мнями*	'throw *stones*'	пожа́ть *плеча́ми*	'shrug *one's shoulders*'
дви́гать/дви́нуть *руко́й/ного́й*	'move *one's hand/foot*'	пока́зывать/показа́ть *па́льцем*	'point *one's finger*'
		покры́ть стол *ска́тертью*	'cover a table *with a tablecloth*'
крути́ть/закрути́ть *рулём*	'turn *a steering wheel*'		
маха́ть/замаха́ть *руко́й*	'wave *one's hand*'	хло́пнуть *две́рью*	'slam *a door*'

These collocations, many of which involve body parts, function to some extent as fixed phrases in Russian. Here are a few of them presented in context:

> Они́ ма́шут *рука́ми*: да ла́дно тебе́!
> [They-NOM wave hands-INST: well all-right you-DAT!]
> They wave *their hands*: that's enough!

> Он стоя́л как парали́тик, не мог дви́нуть ни *руко́й* ни *ного́й*.
> [He-NOM stood like paralytic-NOM, not was-able move neither arm-INST neither leg-INST.]
> He stood like a paralytic, unable to move either *an arm* or *a leg*.

Она́ показа́ла *па́льцем* на взлётную площа́дку, от кото́рой, крутя́ *пропе́ллером*, отделя́лся вертолёт.
[She-NOM showed finger-INST on take-off pad-ACC, from which-GEN, spinning propeller-INST, separated helicopter-NOM.]
She pointed *her finger* at the helipad, from which the helicopter, spinning *its propeller*, was taking off.

The last example above contains two instances of this type of instrumental, one a fixed collocation (показа́ла *па́льцем* 'pointed *her finger*'), and one a relatively novel use (крутя́ *пропе́ллером* 'spinning *its propeller*'). Whether in a fixed collocation or in a more novel use of INSTRUMENTAL: A MEANS to identify an item necessary to an action, the instrumental marks the object through which the action is realized. Slamming takes place *by means of a door*, turning is actualized *on the steering wheel*, waving is done *with the hand*, etc. Here are a few more examples to demonstrate the versatility of this meaning of the instrumental case:

Они́ иногда́ выхо́дят во двор и садя́тся на ла́вочку подыша́ть *све́жим во́здухом*.
[They-NOM sometimes go-out in yard-ACC and sit on bench-ACC breathe fresh air-INST.]
They sometimes go out in the yard and sit on the bench to breathe *the fresh air*.

Де́вочка бе́гала в коро́тенькой ю́бочке, трясла́ *смешны́ми коси́чками*, кача́ла ку́клу.
[Girl-NOM ran in short skirt-LOC, shook cute braids-INST, rocked doll-ACC.]
The girl ran in a short little skirt, shook *her cute little braids*, and rocked her doll.

Она́ сжима́ет *зуба́ми* сигаре́ту, щёлкает *зажига́лкой* и затя́гивается.
[She-NOM presses teeth-INST cigarette-ACC, flicks lighter-INST and takes-drag.]
She grips the cigarette *with her teeth*, flicks *the lighter*, and takes a drag.

In this next example, the nose indicates a direction for action in such a vivid way that no verb (hold, point, move?) is needed:

Сле́дующие пять дней дя́дя Ко́ля лежи́т безмо́лвный, *но́сом* в потоло́к.
[Following five-ACC days-GEN uncle Kolya-NOM lies silent-NOM, nose-INST in ceiling-ACC.]
For the next five days uncle Kolya lies silently, *with his nose pointing* toward the ceiling.

When Russians play chess, they of course move by means of the playing pieces, so it is normal to use an expression like идти́ *ферзём* [walk queen-INST] 'move *the queen*'. Here is an example of this type of INSTRUMENTAL: A MEANS in sentences describing a woman applying cosmetics:

Она́ провела́ *ро́зовой ки́сточкой* о́коло глаз.
[She-NOM drew pink brush-INST around eyes-GEN.]
She drew *a pink brush* around her eyes.

An item can also use its own self as an instrument to realize an action:

Э́то представля́ет *собо́й* исключе́ние.
[That-NOM represents self-INST exception-ACC.]
That *in itself* represents an exception.

INSTRUMENTAL: A MEANS 7—Questions, adverbs, groups

Often an activity is not facilitated by an instrument, but it is brought about more abstractly by some means. Here's a simple, very common example; you can think of it as meaning '*By what means* can I help you?' There is no actual instrument involved, but there is something that should serve as a catalyst for action:

Чем я могу́ вам помо́чь?
[What-INST I-NOM can you-DAT help?]
How can I help you?

Adverbs
expressing
INSTRUMENTAL: A
MEANS.

Note that in this and many of the examples of INSTRUMENTAL: A MEANS, it is possible to apply the question *How?* Similar to the adverbs of time and кругом listed above, the use of the instrumental to describe how an action is performed has become so conventional that for some words the instrumental case form is considered an adverb of manner; here are some examples:

укра́дкой	*stealthily*
бего́м	*at a run*
ша́гом	*at a walk*
пешко́м	*on foot*
ползко́м	*at a crawl*
верхо́м	*on horseback*
ра́зом	*at once*
тайко́м	*secretly*
круго́м	*around*

In this example, the adverb *бего́м 'at a run'* depicts motion so vividly that the speaker doesn't even bother using a verb to describe her movements:

Бего́м до ко́мнаты, хвата́ю су́мку и *бего́м* же до раздева́лки.
[Run-INST to room-GEN, grab purse-ACC and run-INST also to cloak-room-GEN.]
I run to the room, grab my purse, and *run* again to the cloak-room.

It is worth noting that this meaning of manner also motivates the use of *чем* [what-INST] 'how, by what means; than' and *тем* [that-INST] 'by that means' with adverbs and comparative forms, as we see in the following common phrases:

INSTRUMENTAL: A MEANS with comparatives.

Лу́чше по́здно, *чем* никогда́.
[Better late, what-INST never.]
Better late *than* never.

Чем бо́льше, *тем* лу́чше.
[What-INST more/bigger, that-INST better.]
The more/bigger, the better.

One way of describing *how* something is done is by measuring the quantities involved; a number or unit of measurement gives us this use of the instrumental, which is similar to the English use of *by* with numerals:

INSTRUMENTAL: A MEANS with quantities.

Уже́ не *деся́тками*, как пре́жде, *со́тнями* за незако́нный перехо́д грани́цы заде́рживают наруши́телей пограни́чники.
[Already not tens-INST, like before, hundreds-INST for illegal crossing-ACC border-GEN detain violators-ACC border-guards-NOM.]
Border guards are not detaining violators for illegal border crossing *by the tens* any more like they used to, but *by the hundreds*.

This use of the instrumental is common in the metaphorical domain of mathematics, where one multiplies one number *by* another, as in (note unusual stress):

Ше́стью пять — три́дцать.
[Six-INST five-NOM — thirty-NOM.]
Six times five is thirty.

The same quantification of participants in an action can be expressed with words naming groups marked by INSTRUMENTAL: A MEANS. A common phrase based on this idea is де́лать что́-то *всей семьёй* [do something-ACC all family-INST] 'do something *all together, as a family*'. Here's an example to demonstrate this usage:

Он не переноси́л е́здить в ли́фте *компа́нией*, остава́ться в за́мкнутом простра́нстве с незнако́мым челове́ком.
[He-NOM not endure ride in elevator-LOC group-INST, stay in closed space-LOC with unfamiliar person-INST.]
He couldn't stand riding in an elevator *with other people (as part of a group)*, staying in a closed space with an unfamiliar person.

INSTRUMENTAL: A MEANS 8—Person or object under control

Textbooks often give lists of verbs that govern the instrumental case, like кома́ндовать 'command' and руководи́ть 'lead, direct'. Now it should be easy for you to see why verbs with these meanings have instrumental objects. Just as the chess pieces are instruments of players, so too can human beings serve as pawns to their leaders. Indeed government and leadership cannot happen without there being someone to govern. The underlings are the conduit for domination, which is realized through them. The very fact that we can use the words *pawns, conduit, through* in the sentences above should prove to you that the concept is not impossibly foreign. Russian has taken this fairly natural concept of power requiring a relationship to the powerless and made it a convention. This covers verbs with meanings such as 'manipulate' as well. Here are more words you should expect to see with INSTRUMENTAL: A MEANS:

Expressions of governance and leadership associated with INSTRUMENTAL: A MEANS

'lead'
верхово́дить

'manage'
заве́довать
заве́дование 'managing, management'
заве́дующий 'manager'

'abuse'
злоупотребля́ть/злоупотреби́ть
злоупотребле́ние 'abuse'

'command'
кома́ндовать
кома́ндование 'commanding'

'conduct (a musical group)'
дирижи́ровать
дирижи́рование 'conducting'

'use'
по́льзоваться/воспо́льзоваться
по́льзование 'use'

'govern'
пра́вить
правле́ние 'governing, government'

'lead'
предводи́тельствовать
предводи́тельствование 'leading'

'manage'
распоряжа́ться/распоряди́ться
распоряже́ние 'managing, management'

'lead, direct'
руководи́ть
руково́дство 'leadership, guidance'

'govern, administer, manage'
управля́ть
управле́ние 'governing, government'

The concept of governing and having control works for both people and things. Here are a couple of sentences so that you can see these words in action:

Á рмии быва́ют ра́зные; всё зави́сит от того́, кто *и́ми* кома́ндует.
[Armies-NOM are various-NOM; everything-NOM depends from that-GEN, who-NOM them-INST commands.]
There are different kinds of armies; everything depends on who commands *them.*

Ва́ше фина́нсовое положе́ние упро́чится, е́сли нау́читесь лу́чше управля́ть *ва́шим бюдже́том.*
[Your financial situation-NOM becomes-stronger, if learn better manage your budget-INST.]
Your financial situation will become stronger if you learn how to manage *your budget* better.

Instrumental: a means 9—Person or object possessed

If items governed are the instruments of their governors, then it does not take a large mental leap to view them as possessions. The connection between "having" and "having control over" is a natural one. And indeed, there are a number of Russian words that express possession and require the use of the instrumental case for the object possessed. Here are some examples:

INSTRUMENTAL: A MEANS with words meaning possession.

Expressions of possession associated with INSTRUMENTAL: A MEANS

'possess' владе́ть владе́ние 'possession'	'possess' облада́ть облада́ние 'possession'	'have at one's disposal' располага́ть
'have control of' воро́чать воро́чание 'controlling'	'take possession of' овладева́ть/овладе́ть овладева́ние 'taking possession of'	

Of course not all words meaning 'possess' have instrumental objects. The verb име́ть 'have' uses the accusative, and the most normal way to say 'have' in Russian is by using the y + GEN есть + NOM construction, which literally means 'by someone there is'. However, all of the words that use the instrumental imply a possession that involves more than just "having"; they actually equate "having" with "having control over". Here are some examples so that you can see how these words are used in the context of sentences:

Мы не располага́ем *таки́ми сре́дствами.*
[We-NOM not have-at-disposal such means-INST.]
We don't have *the means* at our disposal. / We don't have *that kind of money.*

О́н облада́л *краси́вым ни́зким барито́ном* удиви́тельного те́мбра.
[He-NOM possessed a beautiful deep baritone-INST surprising timbre-GEN.]
He possessed *a beautiful deep baritone* of surprising timbre.

И вот *Мару́сей* овладе́ло чу́вство трево́ги.
[And then Marusya-INST took-possession feeling-NOM alarm-GEN.]
And then a feeling of alarm took possession of *Marusya.*

Sharing is a special kind of possession, and certainly involves power and control. The Russian word дели́ться/подели́ться 'share' also uses the instrumental case, as we see in this example:

Все мы по о́череди дели́лись *но́вой информа́цией.*
[All we-NOM along line-DAT shared new information-INST.]
We all in turn shared *new information.*

There are a few other words involving the manipulation of possessions which you should expect to see with the instrumental, among them:

Expressions of exchange associated with INSTRUMENTAL: A MEANS

'trade'
торговать
торговец 'merchant, trader'
торговля 'trade, commerce'

'sacrifice, give up'
жёртвовать/пожёртвовать
жёртвование/пожёртвование
'sacrificing/sacrifice'

'waive, forgo'
поступаться/поступиться

'supply, provide'
снабжать/снабдить
снабжёние 'supply, supplying'

'exchange'
меняться

Filling and occupying are also a kind of manipulation, and can involve the body and the mind as well:

Expressions of filling and occupying associated with INSTRUMENTAL: A MEANS

'be/get sick with'
болеть/заболеть
болен 'sick'

'be occupied with, study'
заниматься
занятие 'occupation, studies'

'be filled with'
исполняться/исполниться
полон 'full of'

'get filled up with'
наполняться/наполниться

'suffer from'
страдать

INSTRUMENTAL: A MEANS 10—Positive/negative evaluation

INSTRUMENTAL: A
MEANS with
words meaning
positive and
negative
evaluation.

We will need to make one more mental leap in order to finish out our tour of the *conduit* meaning of INSTRUMENTAL: A MEANS, and we can rely on what we know about English to help us once again. Remember that in English we can use the word *enjoy* as a synonym for *have (at one's disposal)*. So we can say things like *Judy Garland enjoyed tremendous popularity* or *I hope to enjoy good health for many years to come* or *Bill Gates enjoys both fame and fortune*. In a certain sense, one has to have something in order to appreciate it. However, this evaluation can be both positive or negative, and Russian takes advantage of both of these options. Here are some words that use the instrumental in this meaning:

Expressions of enjoyment and strong emotion associated with INSTRUMENTAL: A MEANS

'be indignant at'
возмущаться/возмутиться
возмущён 'indignant at'
возмущёние 'indignation at'

'be delighted with'
восторгаться

'be carried away by, admire'
восхищаться/восхититься
восхищёние 'delight, admiration'

'abhor, disdain'
гнушаться/погнушаться

'be proud of'
гордиться
горд 'proud of'

Expressions of enjoyment and strong emotion associated with INSTRUMENTAL: A MEANS

'be satisfied with'
дово́льствоваться/
удово́льствоваться
дово́лен 'satisfied with'
дово́льство 'satisfaction with'

'value'
дорожи́ть

'be interested'
интересова́ться

'enjoy'
наслажда́ться
наслажде́ние 'enjoyment'

'be fascinated by'
пленя́ться

'despise'
пренебрега́ть

'be mad about, get carried away with'
увлека́ться/увле́чься
увлече́ние 'passion for, enthusiasm for'

'boast of'
хвали́ться/похвали́ться

These examples will give you an idea of how these words are used:

Жи́знью свое́й я в о́бщем-то дово́лен.
[Life own-INST I-NOM in general-LOC satisfied-NOM.]
In general I am satisfied *with my life.*

Пи́шущие не о́чень дорожа́т *свое́й рабо́той.*
[Writing-NOM not very value own work-INST.]
People who write do not really value *their work.*

Он увлёкся *выра́щиванием* грибо́в.
[He-NOM became-mad-about cultivating-INST mushrooms-GEN.]
He became mad about *cultivating* mushrooms.

INSTRUMENTAL: A MEANS 11—The passive agent

The examples we have seen of the *conduit* meaning of INSTRUMENTAL: A MEANS are based on this model: a nominative subject + an active verb form + an instrumental *conduit* + whatever else is in the sentence. The crucial item here is the active verb; this doesn't necessarily mean that any real activity is going on, it just means that the verb is not passive. You can think of active as being the default mode for most verbs, where the nominative subject serves as the energy source for the verb. When you have a passive verb, the nominative subject is not the energy source for the verb. Active is about doing something. Passive is about something being done, by someone or something else, the *passive agent.* Given what we already know about the instrumental case, it is no surprise that Russians use it to mark the passive agent, since it is the someone or something by means of which the verbal action takes place. The construction that we are going to be looking at now contains the following elements: a nominative subject + a passive verb form + an instrumental *passive agent* + whatever else is in the sentence.

INSTRUMENTAL: A MEANS can mark a passive agent.

-ся/-сь sometimes indicates passive, passive participles always indicate passive.

Comparison of passive and active.

Russian has two ways to express passive verbal action: either by adding -ся/-сь to the verb or by using passive participles (past passive participles are the most common and are formed from verbs by adding -н or -т and act like adjectives; here are some examples: сде́ланный 'done', ку́пленный 'bought', откры́тый 'opened'). Unfortunately -ся/-сь is not a reliable indicator of passive verb forms, but it can alert you to the possibility that you might be looking at a passive verb. When you have a past passive participle, on the other hand, you can be certain that you have a passive verb form. In general, -ся/-сь will be used with imperfective verbs, whereas the past passive participle will be used with perfective verbs.

Sometimes there is an obvious correspondence between the active and passive voices. For example, we can talk about students reading books in a variety of ways: Студе́нты чита́ют э́ти кни́ги [Students-NOM read these books-ACC] 'Students read these books', or Э́ти кни́ги чита́ются *студе́нтами* [These books-NOM are-read students-INST] 'These books are read *by students*', or Э́ти кни́ги бы́ли прочи́таны *студе́нтами* [These books-NOM were read students-INST] 'These books were read *by students*', or even Э́ти кни́ги, чита́емые *студе́нтами* [These books-NOM, read students-INST] 'These books, read *by students*'. In examples like this it is clear that the instrumental passive agent plays the same role as the nominative subject in the corresponding active sentence. This correspondence will not always be so clear, but it is the conceptual motive for the use of the instrumental with passive verb forms. Here are some typical examples employing passive verb forms:

И да́льше всё э́то воспринима́лось *на́ми* лишь издева́тельски.
[And further all this-NOM was-perceived us-INST only scoffingly.]
And what's more, all this was perceived *by us* only scoffingly.

Э́ти деклара́ции не подтвержда́лись *каки́ми-либо фа́ктами*.
[These declarations-NOM not were-confirmed any facts-INST.]
These declarations were not confirmed *by any facts whatsoever*.

А телеви́зор у нас есть — ста́рый <<КВН-49>>, бро́шенный *тётей Со́ней*.
[But television-NOM by us-GEN is — old KVN-49-NOM, thrown-NOM aunt Sonya-INST.]
But we do have a television — an old KVN-49 thrown out *by aunt Sonya*.

Впервы́е "озо́новая дыра́" над Анта́рктикой была́ обнару́жена *специали́стами* в 1981 году́.
[First "ozone hole"-NOM above Antarctica-INST was discovered-NOM specialists-INST in 1981 year-LOC.]
The "ozone hole" above Antarctica was first discovered *by specialists* in 1981.

Ру́бенс рисова́л безу́мных своего́ вре́мени, Мунк сам бы́л одержи́м *маниака́льной депре́ссией*.
[Rubens-NOM drew madmen-ACC own time-GEN, Munch himself-NOM was afflicted-NOM manic depression-INST.]
Rubens drew the madmen of his time, and Munch was himself afflicted *by manic depression*.

There are a few ways in which the *conduit* and *passive agent* type of instrumental overlap. On the one hand, it is fairly common for adjectives to be used to express being in a certain state, and this is something that they share with past passive participles (which are, after all, adjectives derived from verbs) and many -ся/-сь verbs. Take an example like:

Пётр симпати́чен *свое́й и́скренностью.*
[Pyotr-NOM likeable-NOM own sincerity-INST.]
Pyotr is likeable *for his sincerity.*

Is Pyotr using his sincerity as a tool to make himself likeable, or is sincerity the agent in bringing about his state of likeableness? It probably doesn't matter. On the other hand, sometimes even when you have a passive verb form, an instrumental item can identify either an instrument or an agent, and sometimes you can't tell for sure.

На скамье́ сиди́т же́нщина, оку́танная *чёрной ша́лью.*
[On bench-LOC sits woman-NOM, wrapped-NOM black shawl-INST.]
On the bench sits a woman wrapped in *a black shawl.*

Here the shawl is almost certainly not the agent, but an instrument, the *conduit* for an act of wrapping carried out by the woman herself or someone else. But what about this example:

Они́ объединены́ *о́бщим го́рем.*
[They-NOM united-NOM shared grief-INST.]
They are united *by shared grief.*

Have they (or someone else) performed the uniting by using shared grief (as a *conduit*), or is shared grief the *agent* that has united them? Once again, it doesn't really matter. One of the beauties of language is that there is room for ambiguity and overlap.

INSTRUMENTAL: A MEANS 12—An agent with no subject

You may have noticed that Russian can form sentences without subjects. With the *raw force* use of INSTRUMENTAL: A MEANS, you get sentences based on the model of "something happened *by means of X*", where X is the instrumental item, but there is no agent in sight. The effect is rather similar to the *conduit* reading of the example with *shared grief* just above, but *raw force* uses active instead of passive verb forms, and the verb forms are neuter singular, the "default mode" for verbs that have no subject. *Raw force* is typically used to express the production of smells, movements of air, and other agentless (and frequently disastrous) acts of God. The most common verb to use the instrumental this way is па́хнуть 'smell', as in:

Па́хло *горя́чим хле́бом* из то́стера.
[Smelled hot bread-INST from toaster-GEN.]
There was a smell *of hot bread* from the toaster.

Ambiguity between conduit and passive agent uses of INSTRUMENTAL: A MEANS.

INSTRUMENTAL: A MEANS can express raw force in an event with no agent.

Smells and drafts as raw forces expressed by INSTRUMENTAL: A MEANS.

The verbs нести́ and отдава́ть can both mean 'reek, stink' and work the same way; so one could say от неё несёт/отдаёт *во́дкой* [from her-GEN reeks/stinks vodka-INST] 'she reeks/ stinks *of vodka*'. This construction also works for drafts of air, as in: от реки́ потяну́ло *прохла́дой* [from river-GEN wafted chill-INST] '*a chill* came off the river' and can be used metaphorically as in the common expression ве́ет *весно́й* [blows spring-INST] '*spring* is in the air'.

Perhaps the most peculiar use of the *raw force* meaning is the one that expresses the "acts of God" referred to above. These subjectless sentences can have an accusative object, and are usually translated into English with passive forms. Here are some examples:

> Ма́льчика задави́ло *электри́чкой.*
> [Boy-ACC ran-over commuter-train-INST.]
> The boy was run over *by a commuter train.*

> Хоти́те знать, что чу́вствует челове́к, когда́ его́ пережига́ет *шарово́й мо́лнией?*
> [Want know, what-ACC feels person-NOM, when him-ACC burns ball lightning-INST?]
> Do you want to know what a person feels when he is burned *by ball lightning?*

> Ло́дку переверну́ло *волно́й.*
> [Boat-ACC overturned wave-INST.]
> The boat was overturned *by a wave.*

Acts of God as raw forces expressed by INSTRUMENTAL: A MEANS.

INSTRUMENTAL: A LABEL 1—Being, becoming, seeming

INSTRUMENTAL: A MEANS is devoted to empowering Russians to express how an item can cause or facilitate the action of a verb. The remaining uses of the instrumental, IN-STRUMENTAL: A LABEL, INSTRUMENTAL: AN ADJUNCT, and INSTRUMENTAL: A LANDMARK, relate the instrumental item not to a verb, but to another item. The type of relationship, however, remains the same. The instrumental is something peripheral in relation to something else: an accessory, a companion, or a backgrounded landmark.

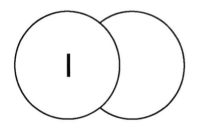

INSTRUMENTAL:: A LABEL (circle labeled I)
is juxtaposed with another item (other circle)

Although a label can be permanent, it doesn't have to be, and is often associated with a certain period of time for which it is valid. A label tells you how to categorize something, what set of things it belongs to. Very often INSTRUMENTAL: A LABEL is used with verbs meaning 'be' or 'become' to describe labels with a varying degree of impermanence:

> Не сомнева́юсь в том, что тот рома́н был *паро́дией.*
> [Not doubt in that-LOC, that that novel-NOM was parody-INST.]
> I do not doubt that that novel was *a parody.*

Relation of INSTRUMENTAL: A MEANS to the other uses of the instrumental.

INSTRUMENTAL: A LABEL with non-permanent labels.

Бу́дучи *революционе́ром*, он мечта́л доби́ться справедли́вости.
[Being revolutionary-INST, he-NOM dreamed achieve justice-GEN.]
Being a *revolutionary*, he dreamed of achieving justice.

Беда́ в том, что хоро́ший писа́тель, реши́в стать *вели́ким*, перестаёт быть *хоро́шим*.
[Trouble-NOM in that-LOC, that good writer-NOM, having-decided become great-INST, stops be good-INST.]
The trouble is that a good writer, once he has decided to become *great*, stops being *good*.

Он стал *фана́тиком* пунктуа́ции.
[He-NOM became fanatic-INST punctuation-GEN.]
He became a punctuation *fanatic*.

Note that even *oneself* can behave like a label. In English we can say things like *Just be yourself* or *He's not acting like himself this morning*, and Russians also use this concept of a self that can be viewed from various perspectives:

Не мо́жет челове́к одновреме́нно быть *собо́й* и находи́ться ря́дом.
[Not can person-NOM simultaneously be self-INST and be-located beside.]
A person cannot simultaneously be *himself* and be outside of himself.

We also have the sense that when something is true to its label (rather than using it as a disguise), then it is a genuine article. The Russian saying дру́жба *дру́жбой*, а слу́жба *слу́жбой* [friendship-NOM friendship-INST, but service-NOM service-INST] 'friendship is *friendship*, but work is *work*' captures the idea that friendship is all about friendship, just as work is all about work; the two items are pure and cannot be mixed together. Perhaps the closest English equivalent would be *Let's not mix business with pleasure*.

There are many words that serve more or less as synonyms of 'be' and 'become' and share this construction of NOMINATIVE: A NAME + verb + INSTRUMENTAL: A LABEL, and all roughly mean 'X is a Y', where X is a specific item, and Y is the category used to label it. Here are some of these words:

INSTRUMENTAL: A LABEL with words meaning 'be', 'become'.

Expressions of being and becoming associated with INSTRUMENTAL:: A LABEL

'behave oneself as' вести́ себя́	'appear, be mentioned as' зна́читься	'turn into' обора́чиваться/оберну́ться
'look like' вы́глядеть	'seem, appear' каза́ться/показа́ться	'turn out to be' ока́зываться/оказа́ться
'grow up to be' вы́расти	'be named' называ́ться/назва́ться	'stay, remain, continue to be' остава́ться/оста́ться

Expressions of being and becoming associated with INSTRUMENTAL:: A LABEL (continued)		

'die (as)'
погибнуть

'proclaim, report oneself (as)'
сказа́ться

'get a job (as)'
устра́иваться/устро́иться

'pretend to be'
представля́ться/предста́виться

'serve (as)'
служи́ть

'be listed (as)'
чи́слиться

'pretend to be'
притворя́ться/притвори́ться

'be known (as), pass for'
слыть/прослы́ть

'feel (like)'
чу́вствовать/почу́вствовать себя́

'work (as)'
рабо́тать

'be'
состоя́ть

'be'
явля́ться

'be born (as)'
роди́ться

'be considered'
счита́ться

Here are a few examples of these verbs being used to apply the INSTRUMENTAL: A LABEL:

За су́тки состоя́ние больно́го незначи́тельно меня́ется то в лу́чшую, то в ху́дшую сто́рону, но о́бщая карти́на остаётся неизме́нно *тяжёлой*.
[Beyond day-ACC condition-NOM patient-GEN imperceptibly changes that in better-ACC, that in worse side-ACC, but general picture-NOM remains invariably serious-INST.]
In the course of a day the patient's condition changes imperceptibly alternately for the better and for the worse, but the general picture remains invariably *serious*.

Почему́ я с таки́м вот лицо́м не родила́сь *мужчи́ной*?
[Why I-NOM with such-INST here face-INST not born man-INST?]
With a face like this, why wasn't I born *a man*?

Ба́йрон поги́б сравни́тельно молоды́м челове́ком.
[Byron-NOM died relatively young person-INST.]
Byron died *a* relatively *young man*.

INSTRUMENTAL: A LABEL used to mean 'is like.'

When a label is applied metaphorically, INSTRUMENTAL: A LABEL has the power to invoke a comparison, stating that 'X is like a Y', in cases where we know that X cannot literally be a Y. The next two examples were inspired by a visit to the zoo, where the author found that the animals reminded him of various people:

Тигр был *приукра́шенной ко́пией* Ста́лина.
[Tiger-NOM was made-over copy-INST Stalin-GEN.]
The tiger was *a made-over copy* of Stalin.

Орангута́нг вы́глядел *старе́ющим актёром*, за плеча́ми у кото́рого бу́рная жизнь.
[Orangutang-NOM looked-like aging actor-INST, behind shoulders-INST by whom-GEN stormy life-NOM.]
The orangutang looked like *an aging actor* with a stormy life behind him.

INSTRUMENTAL: A LABEL can be applied even when there is no triggering word. Note its use in the following two examples, where it has a meaning similar to English 'like' or 'as':

Вокру́г него́ *зы́бким голубы́м тума́ном* плывёт дым.
[Around him-GEN quivering blue cloud-INST floats smoke-NOM.]
Smoke floats around him *in the form of a quivering blue cloud*.

Односельча́не нашли́ его́ *мёртвым*.
[Fellow-villagers-NOM found him-ACC dead-INST.]
His fellow villagers found him *dead*.

Consistent with the construction in the last example above, it is common for verbs with meanings like 'consider', 'choose', 'make' to apply the INSTRUMENTAL: A LABEL to the items marked as their accusative direct objects. Here are a few examples to show you how this works:

INSTRUMENTAL: A LABEL with words meaning 'apply a label'.

Мо́жет быть он возьмёт тебя́ на рабо́ту *корре́ктором*.
[May be he-NOM will-take you-ACC on work-ACC proof-reader-INST.]
Maybe he will give you a job as *a proof-reader*.

Телеви́дение де́лает мир *пло́ским* и *примити́вным*.
[Television-NOM makes world-ACC flat-INST and primitive-INST.]
Television makes the world *flat* and *primitive*.

Врач назва́л *чу́дом* то, что семидесятишестиле́тний челове́к, перенёсший 40-мину́тную клини́ческую смерть, живёт уже́ две неде́ли.
[Doctor-NOM named miracle-INST that-ACC, that seventy-six-year-old man-NOM, experienced-NOM 40-minute clinical death-ACC, lives already two weeks-ACC.]
The doctor called it *a miracle* that a seventy-six-year-old man who had been clinically dead for 40 minutes, has survived for two weeks thus far.

Слу́чай э́тот специали́сты до сих пор счита́ют *небыва́лым*.
[Case this-ACC specialists-NOM to this time-GENT consider unprecedented-INST.]
Specialists consider this case *to be unprecedented*.

Among the words that use this structure of [NOMINATIVE: A NAME + verb + ACCUSATIVE: A DIRECTION + INSTRUMENTAL: A LABEL], you will find the following:

Words meaning 'apply a label to an item' associated with INSTRUMENTAL:: A LABEL

'imagine (as)'
вообража́ть/вообрази́ть

'elect (as)'
избира́ть/избра́ть

'declare, announce'
объявля́ть/объяви́ть

'select (as)'
выбира́ть/вы́брать

'depict, portray, represent (as)'
изобража́ть/изобрази́ть

'recognize (as)'
признава́ть/призна́ть

'make'
де́лать/сде́лать

'appoint, nominate (as)'
назнача́ть/назна́чить

'consider'
счита́ть

'find (as)'
застава́ть/заста́ть

'name'
называ́ть/назва́ть

INSTRUMENTAL: AN ADJUNCT 1 — Companions

INSTRUMENTAL: AN ADJUNCT with с 'with'.

It is no accident that the two relationships expressed in English by the word *with* can both be translated using the instrumental case in Russian. Ива́н ре́зал хлеб *ножо́м* [Ivan-NOM cut bread-ACC knife-INST] 'Ivan cut bread *with a knife*' is of course an example of INSTRUMENTAL: A MEANS, whereas Сестра́ говори́ла с *Ива́ном* [Sister-NOM talked with Ivan-INST] 'Sister was talking with *Ivan*' is an example of INSTRUMENTAL: AN ADJUNCT. Russian is more fastidious than English, reserving the use of the preposition с 'with' only for INSTRUMENTAL: AN ADJUNCT to introduce an accomplice, companion, or other peripheral adjunct to an item of more central importance.

с + INSTRUMENTAL: AN ADJUNCT with companions.

Just about any activity that a person engages in can become a joint project when there is someone else to share it with, as we see in these examples:

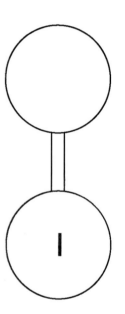

INSTRUMENTAL:: AN ADJUNCT (circle labeled I) is an adjunct of another item (other circle)

Она́ предпочита́ла ти́хую жизнь с *му́жем* и *двумя́ детьми́*.
[She-NOM preferred quiet life-ACC with husband-INST and two children-INST.]
She preferred a quiet life with *her husband* and *two children*.

Подчёркивается, что существу́ют возмо́жности для многосторо́ннего сотру́дничества с *Москво́й* и для разви́тия торго́вых конта́ктов.
[Emphasizes, that exist opportunities-NOM for multi-lateral collaboration-GEN with Moscow-INST and for development-GEN commercial contacts-GEN.]
It should be emphasized that there exist opportunities for multi-lateral collaboration with *Moscow* and for the development of commercial contacts.

с + INSTRUMENTAL: AN ADJUNCT with interpersonal relationships.

Many activities that are part of interpersonal relationships require a partner to engage *with*. All of the words below can use с 'with' to name such a partner:

Expressions of engagement associated with INSTRUMENTAL:: AN ADJUNCT

'converse'
бесе́довать с
бесе́да с 'conversation'

'struggle, fight'
боро́ться с
борьба́ с 'struggle, fight'

'see (each other)'
ви́деться с

'wage war'
воева́ть с
война́ с 'war'

'romp, play'
вози́ться/повози́ться с
возня́ с 'romp(ing), play(ing)'

'meet'
встреча́ться/встре́титься с
встре́ча с 'meeting'

'share'
дели́ться с

'come to an agreement, make an arrangement'
догова́риваться/договори́ться с
догово́р с 'agreement, arrangement'

'fight'
дра́ться/подра́ться с
дра́ка с 'fight'

'become acquainted'
знако́миться/познако́миться с
знако́м с 'acquainted'
(short forms only)
знако́мство с 'acquaintance'

'associate, be friendly'
обща́ться с
обще́ние с 'associating, association'

'correspond (exchange letters)'
перепи́сываться с
перепи́ска с 'correspondence (exchange of letters)'

'say farewell'
проща́ться/прости́ться с
проще́ние с 'saying farewell'

'converse'
разгова́ривать с
разгово́р с 'conversation'

'settle accounts'
рассчи́тываться/рассчита́ться с

'communicate, get in contact, be associated'
свя́зываться/связа́ться с
связь с 'association, contact'

'agree'
соглаша́ться/согласи́ться с
согла́сие с 'agreement'

'compete'
соревнова́ться с
соревнова́ние с 'competition'

'argue'
ссо́риться/поссо́риться с
ссо́ра с 'argument'

'collide with, run into, encounter'
ста́лкиваться/столкну́ться с
столкнове́ние с 'collision'

The following examples illustrate the use of INSTRUMENTAL: AN ADJUNCT with these words:

Я люблю́ ве́чер пя́тницы: мо́жно посиде́ть подо́льше за столо́м, повози́ться с *ребя́тами*, уложи́ть их на полчаса́ по́зже.
[I-NOM love evening-ACC Friday-GEN: possible sit longer behind table-INST, play with kids-INST, put-to-bed them-ACC on half-hour-ACC later.]
I love Friday evening: I can sit a while longer at the table, play with *the kids*, and put them to bed a half hour later.

По ро́ду свое́й рабо́ты я каждодне́вно ста́лкиваюсь с *людьми́, пострада́вшими* от уку́сов живо́тных.
[Along nature-DAT own work-GEN I-NOM daily encounter with people-INST, suffered-INST from bites-GEN animals-GEN.]
Due to the nature of my work I daily encounter *people who have suffered* animal bites.

Когда́ Наполео́н просну́лся и реши́л продолжа́ть бой, то уви́дел, что воева́ть не с *кем.*
[When Napoleon-NOM woke-up and decided continue battle-ACC, then saw, that wage-war not with who-INST.]
When Napoleon woke up and decided to continue the battle, then he saw that there was *no one* to wage war with.

INSTRUMENTAL: AN ADJUNCT 2 — Idioms and other uses

Russian uses the idiom мы с + INST (literally 'we with *so-and-so*') to express '*so-and-so* and I'. This seems to involve a politeness strategy similar to that imposed in English, where we consider it improper to say *I and Anna*, but are supposed to say *Anna and I* instead. In Russian, instead of inverting to be polite, you include the partner by saying 'we' in place of 'I': мы с *А́нной* [we-NOM with Anna-INST] '*Anna* and I'. Here is an example of the мы с + INST idiom where мы appears in the dative case as нам:

Одна́жды Му́ся загляну́ла к нам с *жено́й.*
[Once Musya-NOM glanced-in to us-DAT with wife-INST.]
Once Musya stopped by to see *my wife* and me.

One idiomatic use of с + INSTRUMENTAL: AN ADJUNCT has an exact parallel in English:

Что с *тобо́й?*
[What-NOM with you-INST?]
What's with *you?*

The phrase поздравля́ю вас/тебя́ с + INSTRUMENTAL: AN ADJUNCT, literally 'I congratulate you with', motivates another idiomatic construction used for greetings on the occasion of holidays and events. The first part of the phrase is rarely heard, leaving just the preposition с + INST. Here is a table of common greetings:

С *днём* а́нгела!	Happy Name's *Day!*
С *днём* рожде́ния!	Happy Birth*day!*
С *лёгким па́ром!*	Have *a nice bath!*
С *но́вым го́дом!*	*Happy New Year!*
С *пра́здником!*	*Happy Holiday!*
С *причаще́нием!*	Congratulations on *receiving Holy Communion!*
С *Рождество́м!*	*Merry Christmas!*

As the idioms with holidays above show, the use of the preposition с 'with' is not limited to human companions; it can be used with objects, abstractions, and attributes, much as *with* is used in English. Here are some examples:

Она́ что-то проде́лала с *волоса́ми*.
[She-NOM something-ACC with hair-INST.]
She did something with *her hair*.

с + INSTRUMEN-
TAL: AN ADJUNCT
with objects.

Одна́жды он возвраща́лся из овощно́го магази́на со *свёклой* в аво́ське —
кру́пной и *кру́глой*, как футбо́льный мяч.
[Once he-NOM returned from grocery store-GEN with beet-INST in shopping-bag-
LOC — big-INST and round-INST, like soccer ball-NOM.]
Once he came back from the grocery store with *a beet* in his shopping bag — *big*
and *round* like a soccer ball.

Но в ней всё э́то каки́м-то о́бразом совмеща́лось — наи́вность с *цини́змом*,
ум с *глу́постью* и че́стность с *тяготе́нием* к вранью́.
[But in her-LOC all this-NOM some manner-INST was-combined — naivete-NOM
with cynicism-INST, intelligence-NOM with stupidity-INST and honesty-NOM with
tendency-INST to lying-DAT.]
But somehow all these things were combined in her — naivete with *cynicism*, intel-
ligence with *stupidity*, and honesty with *a tendency* to lie.

с + INSTRUMEN-
TAL: AN ADJUNCT
with abstrac-
tions.

Приро́да с и́стинно *послевое́нной ще́дростью* разгуля́лась.
[Nature-NOM with truly post-war generosity-INST blossomed-forth.]
Nature was blossoming forth with true *post-war generosity*.

Рабо́тала то́лько одна́ ка́сса, и вдоль магази́на текла́ о́чередь, как река́ с
изги́бами и *излу́чинами* и *ответвлёнными ручейка́ми*.
[Worked only one cash-register-NOM, and along store-GEN flowed line-NOM, like
river-NOM with twists-INST and turns-INST and branched streams-INST.]
Only one cash register was open, and a line flowed around the store, like a river with
twists and *turns* and *little branching streams*.

с + INSTRUMEN-
TAL: AN ADJUNCT
with attributes.

INSTRUMENTAL: A LANDMARK 1—пе́ред 'in front of, before'

Five Russian prepositions are used with the INSTRUMENTAL: A LANDMARK to describe the
peripheral location of one item in alignment with another item or items. Two of these prepositions view this alignment in a horizontal plane: пе́ред 'in front of' and за 'behind'. Two
more are exactly parallel to these, but view the alignment in a vertical plane: над 'above'
and под 'below'. The fifth preposition, ме́жду 'between, among' uses two or more items to
establish the alignment independent of any geographic orientation.

Overview of
INSTRUMENTAL: A
LANDMARK.

In terms of physical location, пе́ред 'in front of' + INSTRUMENTAL: A LANDMARK identifies
an item that serves as a peripheral landmark for another item. In this example, the administration building serves as a peripheral landmark for the square where students' passions are
seething:

пе́ред +
INSTRUMENTAL: A
LANDMARK 'in
front of, before'
in the domain of
space.

перед +
INSTRUMENTAL: A
LANDMARK 'in
front of, before'
in the domain of
time.

Два дня на площади перед *зданием* администрации города кипели страсти — демонстрировали студенты.
[Two days-ACC on square-LOC in-front-of building-INST administration-GEN city-GEN seethed passions-NOM — demonstrated students-NOM.]
For two days passions seethed on the square in front of *the* municipal administration *building* — the students were demonstrating.

In the domain of time, перед means 'before, until such time as', and can be used directly with the landmark time in the instrumental, or with the fixed phrase перед тем, как [before that-INST, how] 'before', as illustrated in these two examples, where the meeting and the loss of contact serve as temporal landmarks for the announcement of health and for wandering in the Alaskan hinterland:

INSTRUMENTAL:: A LANDMARK (circle or circles labeled I) is in a proximate relationship to another item (small circle)

"Никаких остатков болезни нет", отметил вчера президент перед *встречей* с премьер-министром.
["No remains-GEN illness-GEN no", remarked yesterday president-NOM before meeting-INST with prime-minister-INST.]
"I show no signs of illness," remarked the president yesterday before *his meeting* with the prime minister.

Норвежский путешественник два месяца провёл в центральных районах Аляски, перед *тем*, как связь с ним неожиданно прервалась.
[Norwegian traveler-NOM two months-ACC spent in central regions-LOC Alaska-GEN, before that-INST, how contact-NOM with him-INST unexpectedly was-broken-off.]
The Norwegian traveler spent two months in the central regions of Alaska before contact with him was suddenly broken off.

перед +
INSTRUMENTAL: A
LANDMARK in the
domain of
morality and
justice.

Перед is frequently deployed in the domain of morality and justice, where it designates a position in terms of merits and obligations. The first example below describes a moral achievement, the following ones refer to legal and financial obligations, respectively.

В сообщении пресс-службы президента говорится, что господин Куликов "удостоен высокой награды за заслуги перед *государством*".
[In report-LOC press-service-GEN president-GEN says, that Mr. Kulikov-NOM "awarded-NOM high award-GEN for services-ACC before state-INST."]
In the president's press report it says that Mr. Kulikov "has received an exalted award for his service to *the state*."

Олимпи́йский чемпио́н в гре́бле на кано́э слова́к Ми́хал Ма́ртикан в ско́ром вре́мени предста́нет пе́ред *судо́м*.
[Olympic champion-NOM in rowing-LOC on canoe-LOC Slovak Michal Martikan-NOM in soon time-LOC appear before court-INST.]
Olympic canoeing champion Slovak Michal Martikan will soon appear in *court*.

Премье́р-мини́стр отме́тил, что в настоя́щее вре́мя фи́рма "Татне́фть" не име́ет долго́в пе́ред *федера́льным бюджѐтом*.
[Prime-minister-NOM noted, that in present time-ACC company "Tatneft"-NOM no have debts-GEN before federal budget-INST.]
The prime-minister noted that at the present time the "Tatneft" company is not indebted to *the federal budget*.

Here is an example of a self-imposed obligation:

Вы́ставка Слова́цкой респу́блики ста́вит пе́ред *собо́й* цель ознако́мить росси́йских предпринима́телей с э́кспортными возмо́жностями Слова́кии.
[Exhibition-NOM Slovak Republic-GEN places before self-INST goal-ACC acquaint Russian entrepreneurs-ACC with export opportunities-INST Slovakia-GEN.]
The Slovak Republic's exhibit is setting *itself* the goal of acquainting Russian entrepreneurs with Slovakia's export opportunities.

INSTRUMENTAL: A LANDMARK 2—за 'beyond, behind'

За + INSTRUMENTAL: A LANDMARK indicates a spatial alignment that is the opposite of пе́ред. The landmark is an item that is between us and another item which is 'behind' or 'beyond' it. Here are a couple of examples of за used to locate items in space.

На́шему сосе́ду пообеща́ли за кварти́ру всего́ лишь де́вять миллио́нов рубле́й, зато́ взаме́н предложи́ли жить в своё удово́льствие на да́че за *го́родом*.
[Our neighbor-DAT promised for apartment-ACC all-GEN only nine-ACC millions-GEN rubles-GEN, but in-exchange offered live in own pleasure-ACC at dacha-LOC beyond city-INST.]
They promised our neighbor only nine million rubles for his apartment, but in return they offered him a life of pleasure in a dacha outside of *town*.

За *воро́тами* же́нщину вы́толкнули из маши́ны и скры́лись.
[Beyond gate-INST woman-ACC pushed-out from car-GEN and hid.]
On the other side of *the gate* they pushed the woman out of the car and hid.

The notion that за identifies a barrier between us and another item is capitalized on in the Russian translation of 'You can't see the forest for *the trees*', За *дере́вьями* не вида́ть ле́са [Beyond trees-INST not see forest-GEN].

There are two spatial uses of за that are especially worth noting. One is за *рулём* [behind wheel-INST] 'behind *the (steering) wheel*', and the other is за *столóм* [behind table-INST] 'at *the table (while eating a meal).*'

Чу́вствовалось, что за *рулём* сиде́л суперме́н, владе́ющий маши́ной, как ковбóй мустáнгом.
[Felt, that behind wheel-INST sat superman-NOM, commanding-NOM car-INST, like cowboy-NOM mustang-INST.]
One got the feeling that there was a superman sitting behind *the wheel* who was controlling the car like a cowboy controls a mustang.

За *столóм* сиди́м дóлго, еди́м не спешá.
[Behind table-INST sit long, eat not hurrying.]
We sit for a long time at *the table*, eating without hurrying.

The за *столóм* construction above motivates за *обéдом* [behind lunch-INST] 'during *lunch*', where the spatial location is juxtaposed with a given time.

за + INSTRUMEN-
TAL: A LANDMARK
'following after'.

Just as we use 'behind' with the word 'follow', so do Russians associate за + INSTRUMENTAL: A LANDMARK with following. The following examples demonstrate this use in physical movement through space, in sequential action along the dimension of time, and in the metaphorical domain of verification:

Собáки бегу́т за *звéрем.*
[Dogs-NOM run following beast-INST.]
The dogs are running after *the beast.*

Он ку́рит сигарéту за *сигарéтой.*
[He-NOM smokes cigarette-ACC following cigarette-INST.]
He smokes one cigarette after *another.*

Абонемéнтную плáту за пóльзование телефóном внóсят не позднéе деся́того числá мéсяца, слéдующего за *мéсяцем* предоставлéния услу́ги.
[Subscription fee-ACC for use-ACC telephone-INST enter not later tenth number-GEN month-GEN, following-GEN behind month-INST rendering-GEN service-GEN.]
They enter the subscription fee for telephone use no later than the tenth of the month following *the month* in which the service was rendered.

С 1 января́ во всём региóне ввóдится жёсткий контрóль за *кáчеством* алкогóльной проду́кции, её *произвóдством, хранéнием,* и *реализáцией.*
[From first-GEN January-GEN in all region-LOC is-introduced strict control-NOM following quality-INST alcohol production-GEN, its manufacture-INST, storage-INST, and sale-INST.]
Throughout the region beginning January 1, strict control is being introduced on *the quality* of alcohol production, its *manufacture, storage,* and *sale.*

In English 'following' is synonymous with 'going after' something, and we can 'go after' something in order to get it; in Russian за + INSTRUMENTAL: A LANDMARK can likewise be used to mean 'fetch':

за + INSTRUMEN-TAL: A LANDMARK 'fetch'.

> Реши́ли сде́лать имени́нику прия́тный сюрпри́з и пое́хали за *де́вочками и дополни́тельной вы́пивкой.*
> [Decided make birthday-boy-DAT pleasant surprise-ACC and rode fetch girls-INST and supplementary drink-INST.]
> They decided to give the birthday boy a nice surprise and went to get *some girls* and *something more to drink.*

> Я зайду́ за *тобо́й* в шко́лу.
> [I-NOM go-by fetch you-INST in school-ACC.]
> I'll come to pick *you* up at school.

INSTRUMENTAL: A LANDMARK 3—над 'above'

In the vertical plane, над locates an item 'above' another item. The use of this preposition in the doman of space is just what we would expect:

над + INSTRU-MENTAL: A LANDMARK 'above'.

> Озо́новая дыра́ над *Анта́рктикой* дости́гла реко́рдных разме́ров.
> [Ozone hole-NOM above Antarctica-INST reached record proportions-GEN.]
> The ozone hole above *Antarctica* has reached record proportions.

> В не́бе над *Лос-А́нджелесом* едва́ не столкну́лись два самолёта.
> [In sky-LOC above Los-Angeles-INST barely not collided two airplanes-NOM.]
> Two airplanes almost collided in the sky above *Los Angeles.*

> Про семью́ Га́нди говоря́т, что над *ней* гори́т несчастли́вая звезда́.
> [About family-ACC Gandhi say, that above it-INST burns unlucky star-NOM.]
> They say about the Gandhi family that an unlucky star burns above *it.*

As with English 'above', над identifies a vantage point that has certain implications. It is a location from which one can make observations:

> Корреспонде́нт попроси́л профе́ссора Левинсо́на подели́ться свои́ми наблюде́ниями над *поведе́нием* городско́го населе́ния в ра́зные го́ды, эпо́хи и режи́мы.
> [Correspondent-NOM asked professor Levinson-ACC share own observations-INST above behavior-INST city population-GEN in various years-ACC, epochs-ACC and regimes-ACC.]
> The correspondent asked Professor Levinson to share his observations of *the behavior* of the city's population in various years, epochs, and regimes.

над + INSTRU-
MENTAL: A
LANDMARK can
express derision.

In English we can 'look down at someone' from a higher vantage point of superiority; Russian uses this idea to motivate the expression смея́ться над + INSTRUMENTAL: A LANDMARK 'laugh at', as illustrated in this example:

Снача́ла над *ним* смея́лись, пото́м ста́ли отмеча́ть успе́хи в иску́сстве, а в конце́ концо́в позво́лили откры́ть "Дом худо́жников".
[At-first above him-INST laughed, then started notice successes-ACC in art-LOC, and in end-LOC ends-GEN allowed open "House-ACC artists-GEN".]
At first they laughed at *him*, but then they started to notice his successes in art, and finally they allowed him to open a "House of Artists."

над + INSTRU-
MENTAL: A
LANDMARK can
express work
'on' and control
'over'.

A position 'above' an item facilitates manipulation and control. Notice the parallels to vertical relationships in English translations of рабо́тать над 'work on' and контро́ль над 'control over' in these examples:

Президе́нт акти́вно рабо́тает над *формирова́нием* структу́ры прави́тельства.
[President-NOM actively works above formation-INST structure-GEN government-GEN.]
The president is actively working on *the formation* of the structure of the government.

В апре́ле в Москве́ состои́тся Междунаро́дная конфере́нция по сотру́дничеству с Росси́ей в о́бласти контро́ля над *нарко́тиками*.
[In April-LOC in Moscow-LOC takes-place International conference-NOM along collaboration-DAT with Russia-INST in area-LOC control-GEN above narcotics-INST.]
In April in Moscow there is an International Conference on Collaboration with Russia in the area of *narcotics* control.

Control over an item can likewise be wielded by legal or governmental authority, as in the following two examples:

Вчера́ в Де́ли начался́ суд над *бы́вшим премьер-мини́стром* И́ндии.
[Yesterday in Delhi-LOC began legal-proceedings-NOM above former prime-minister-INST India-GEN.]
Legal proceedings against *the former prime minister* of India began in Delhi yesterday.

Бальмо́нт це́лое десятиле́тие безразде́льно цари́л над *ру́сской поэ́зией*.
[Balmont-NOM whole decade-ACC indivisibly was-tsar above Russian poetry-INST.]
For a whole decade, Balmont reigned over *Russian poetry* unchallenged.

INSTRUMENTAL: A LANDMARK 4—под 'under'

Opposing над in the vertical plane is под 'under'. Once again we will look first at examples of how this preposition indicates physical locations:

под + INSTRU-
MENTAL: A
LANDMARK
'under'.

> Тигр поги́б под *колёсами* лесово́за.
> [Tiger-NOM died under wheels-INST lumber-truck-GEN.]
> The tiger died under *the wheels* of the lumber truck.

> По не́которым све́дениям, под *обло́мками* зда́ний всё ещё нахо́дятся о́коло двадцати́ семе́й.
> [Along certain reports-DAT, under wreckage-INST buildings-GEN all still are-located about twenty families-GEN.]
> According to certain reports, there are still about twenty families under *the wreckage* of the buildings.

Because cities were traditionally built on hills and locations outside them were at lower elevations, the preposition под with the name of a city indicates a position outside or on the outskirts of town:

> Четы́ре челове́ка поги́бли в результа́те авиакатастро́фы, произше́дшей вчера́ под *Ту́лой*.
> [Four people-NOM died in result-LOC aviation-catastrophe-GEN took-place-GEN yesterday under Tula-INST.]
> Four people died as a result of the aviation catastrophe which took place outside of *Tula* yesterday.

Just as над gave us the perspective of control 'over', под can conversely describe being 'under' control:

под + INSTRU-
MENTAL: A
LANDMARK can
express
subordination,
protection, and
both covert and
overt identities.

> Солда́ты под *кома́ндованием* полко́вника овладе́ли после́дним уголко́м респу́блики Абха́зии, находи́вшимся под *контро́лем* грузи́нских формирова́ний.
> [Soldiers-NOM under command-INST lieutenant-GEN took-possession last corner-INST republic-GEN Abkhazia-GEN located-INST under control-INST Georgian units-GEN.]
> Soldiers under *the command* of the lieutenant took possession of the last corner of the Republic of Abhxazia that was under *the control* of Georgian military units.

> В настоя́щее вре́мя банки́р остаётся под *дома́шним аре́стом*.
> [In present time-ACC banker-NOM remains under house arrest-INST.]
> At the present time the banker remains under *house arrest*.

Being 'under' an item can have its benefits, since this location implies a relationship of protection, as in these examples:

Отны́не музе́й бу́дет находи́ться под *покрови́тельством* президе́нта.
[From-henceforth museum-NOM will be-located under protection-INST president-GEN.]
From henceforth the museum will be under *the protection* of the president.

Вы́ставка прохо́дит под *патрона́жем* пе́рвого вице-премье́ра Бори́са Немцо́ва.
[Exhibit-NOM takes-place under patronage-INST first vice-premier Boris Nemtsov-GEN.]
The exhibit is taking place under *the patronage* of the first vice-premier Boris Nemtsov.

One can also go 'under' cover by taking on a disguise:

Грузи́нская сторона́ ссыла́ется на возмо́жность передвиже́ния под *ви́дом* военнослу́жащих не́ких банди́тских гру́пп.
[Georgian side-NOM cites on possibility-ACC travel-GEN under guise-INST servicemen-GEN certain bandit groups-GEN.]
The Georgian side cites the possibility that some groups of bandits are traveling under *the guise* of military servicemen.

More innocently под can indicate the name given to buildings, organizations, and events, as in this example:

Вчера́ в Берли́не откры́лся фестива́ль под *назва́нием* "Волше́бный лес".
[Yesterday in Berlin-LOC opened festival-NOM under title-INST "Magical forest"-NOM.]
A festival *entitled* "Magical Forest" opened yesterday in Berlin.

INSTRUMENTAL: A LANDMARK 5—ме́жду 'between, among'

ме́жду +
INSTRUMENTAL: A
LANDMARK
'between'.

The preposition ме́жду 'between, among' is used in spatial and metaphorical domains in ways very similar to its English counterparts. Here are a few examples:

По федера́льным авиацио́нным пра́вилам, расстоя́ние ме́жду *лета́тельными объе́ктами* должно́ составля́ть не ме́нее 6,5 км.
[Along federal aviation rules-DAT, distance-NOM between flying objects-INST must be not less 6.5 km-GEN.]
According to federal aviation rules, the distance between *flying objects* must not be less than 6.5 km.

Э́кспортно-и́мпортный банк Япо́нии вы́делил 200 миллио́нов до́лларов для созда́ния микроволно́вой телефо́нной свя́зи ме́жду *Москво́й* и *Хаба́ровском*.
[Export-import bank-NOM Japan-GEN allocated 200-ACC million-GEN dollars-

GEN for creation-GEN microwave telephone link-GEN between Moscow-INST and Khabarovsk-INST.]

The export-import bank of Japan allocated 200 million dollars to create a microwave telephone link between *Moscow* and *Khabarovsk*.

Герма́нский бундеста́г ратифици́ровал вчера́ соглаше́ние о партнёрстве и сотру́дничестве ме́жду *Европе́йским сою́зом* и *Росси́ей*.

[German Bundestag-NOM ratified yesterday agreement-ACC about partnership-LOC and collaboration-LOC between European Union-INST and Russia-INST.]

Yesterday the German Bundestag ratified an agreement on partnership and collaboration between *the European Union* and *Russia*.

This last example demonstrates both an idiomatic usage, ме́жду *тем* [between that-INST] 'meanwhile', and the 'among' meaning that is present when the preposition refers to more than two items:

Ме́жду *тем*, распределе́ние обя́занностей ме́жду *замести́телями* руководи́теля аппара́та прави́тельства ещё не заверши́лось.

[Between that-INST, assignment-NOM responsibilities-GEN among deputies-INST leader-GEN apparatus-GEN government-GEN still not completed.]

Meanwhile the assignment of responsibilities among *the deputy leaders* of the organs of government has not yet been completed.

EPILOGUE

The meaning of the word *instrumental* is transparent to us, and it's a good name for this case because Russians use it not only for instruments, but for a variety of items that are instrumental to whatever a sentence describes: a path for motion, a way to do something, a time to do it, the agent or cause of an event, the category something falls in, a companion or opponent, a landmark for locating something. As promised in the Preliminaries, we have seen that time is understood as a kind of metaphorical space, and so are many other abstract domains. We will explore similar extensions of our experience from physical space to other realms in all the remaining chapters. This survey of the instrumental case has also given us a peek into the conceptual world of Russian. It is a world where life is a journey, where power is wielded by manipulating those who are subject to it, where possession is a special type of control, where enjoyment and disdain are special types of possession, where disaster can have a means without having a cause, where obligations are something people stand in front of, where power is up and submission is down. Most of these ideas are familiar from the conceptual structure of English; even the ideas that strike us as foreign make sense in the overall structure of the instrumental case, because even though the instrumental is quite complex, all the parts fit together to make a coherent whole. Understanding the whole helps you orient to the individual meanings of the instrumental because you have a structure to relate those meanings to. Even if you don't memorize all the meanings right off, you will now have a "feel" for the instrumental, and you'll be surprised how well your new-found intuitions will serve you.

ACCUSATIVE Forms

Feminine declension nouns	hard type: 'room'		soft type: 'week'	
	singular	plural	singular	plural
	ко́мнату	ко́мнаты	неде́лю	неде́ли
		= GEN if animate		= GEN if animate
	-ь: 'talent'			
	singular	plural		
	спосо́бность	спосо́бности		

Masculine declension nouns	hard type: 'courtyard'			soft type: 'nail'
	singular	plural	singular	plural
	двор	дворы́	гвоздь	гво́зди
	= GEN if animate	= GEN if animate	= GEN if animate	= GEN if animate

Neuter declension nouns	hard type: 'body'		soft type: 'schedule'	
	singular	plural	singular	plural
	те́ло	тела́	расписа́ние	расписа́ния

Adjectives

hard type: 'first'			
feminine	masculine	neuter	plural
пе́рвую	пе́рвый	пе́рвое	пе́рвые
	= GEN if animate		= GEN if animate

soft type: 'last'			
feminine	masculine	neuter	plural
после́днюю	после́дний	после́днее	после́дние
	= GEN if animate		= GEN if animate

Pronouns

'I'	'we'	'you' informal	'you'
меня́	нас	тебя́	вас
'she'	'he'	'it'	'they'
(н)её	(н)его́	(н)его́	(н)их
'who'	'what'	'oneself'	
кого́	что	себя́	

'this'			
feminine	masculine	neuter	plural
э́ту	э́тот	э́то	э́ти
	э́того if animate		э́тих if animate

'all, every'			
feminine	masculine	neuter	plural
всю	весь	всё	все
	всего́ if animate		всех if animate

Possessives

feminine	masculine	neuter	plural
'my'			
мою́	мой	моё	мои́
	моего́ if animate		мои́х if animate
'our'			
на́шу	наш	на́ше	на́ши
	на́шего if animate		на́ших if animate

Numerals

'one'			
feminine	masculine	neuter	plural
одну́	оди́н	одно́	одни́
	одного́ if animate		одни́х if animate

'two'	'three'	'four'	'five'
две/два	три	четы́ре	пять
двух if animate	трёх if animate	четырёх if animate	

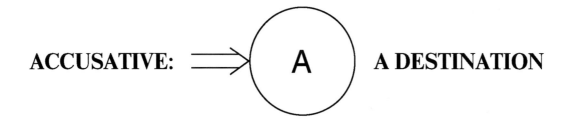

ACCUSATIVE: **A DESTINATION**

The accusative network:

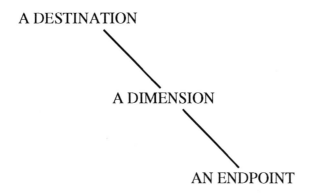

A DESTINATION

A DIMENSION

AN ENDPOINT

Prologue

An overview of the accusative case.

An apt subtitle for this chapter would be "Toward, down, and at the bottom of a slippery slope." The accusative case can do all three things: it can take you to a place (toward a slippery slope = ACCUSATIVE: A DESTINATION), it can take you along a place (down a slippery slope = ACCUSATIVE: A DIMENSION), and it can take you to the end of a place (to the bottom of a slippery slope = ACCUSATIVE: AN ENDPOINT). Just as running up to, sliding down, and getting to the bottom of a slippery slope can be all folded into one continuous action, the three meanings of the accusative are really all parts of a continuum without precise boundaries between them. And the accusative is itself a slippery slope.

Above all else, the accusative describes a destination, and this is equally true for all of its meanings. The relations between the three meanings of the accusative are noticeably different from those that we see in the other cases with multiple meanings (the nominative, instrumental, dative, and genitive). Rather than being relatively discrete and independent (but related), the meanings of the accusative are like the nesting parts of a матрёшка doll. The basic meaning of ACCUSATIVE: A DESTINATION is the biggest, least specific meaning; it does not analyze its object in any way[2]. An item marked by ACCUSATIVE: A DESTINATION is just a destination, its structure is of no particular interest. ACCUSATIVE: A DIMENSION, however, focuses on a destination extended through time, space, or some other dimension. ACCUSATIVE: AN ENDPOINT takes this concept even further, focusing specifically on the endpoint of a destination extended through some dimension; you might think of it as a destination (endpoint) within a destination. Overall, you can visualize the accusative meanings as a megaphone or a telescope, with ACCUSATIVE: A DESTINATION at the wide end, ACCUSATIVE: AN ENDPOINT at the narrow end, and ACCUSATIVE: A DIMENSION in between. The accusative operates on

The meanings of the accusative case are increasingly specific, identifying first a destination in general, then extension along a dimension, and then an endpoint.

The distribution of prepositions among the meanings of the accusative case.

a scale from general to specific, and the boundaries between submeanings are rather diffuse.

Another hallmark of the accusative case is the way it deploys prepositions. With all other cases, each preposition is associated with only one submeaning. Not so the accusative. It is not uncommon for prepositions to use two or even all three meanings of the accusative. This table will give you some idea of how versatile prepositions are in the accusative case, and the individual uses of each will be discussed below.

Distribution of prepositions among the meanings of the accusative case

ACCUSATIVE: A DESTINATION	ACCUSATIVE:: A DIMENSION	ACCUSATIVE:: AN ENDPOINT
в 'to, in, into; on, at; for'	в 'in, during; like'	в 'in, at; at the end of'
на 'to, on, onto; on, at; for'	на 'for, lasting; to'	
за 'behind; for'	за 'during'	за 'away; by the end of'
о 'against'	о 'with'	
по 'up to; after, to get'	по 'through; each'	
под 'under, toward; for use as'	под 'like; to the tune of'	
про 'for'	про 'about'	
	с 'approximately'	
	сквозь 'through'	
	чéрез 'through'	чéрез 'across, after; in, at the end of'

We often spend so much time learning the prepositions in Russian that we neglect the fact that it also has postpositions. Just as a preposition is a word that comes before other words, a postposition is a word that comes after other words. All the postpositions associated with the accusative case are used to express time with ACCUSATIVE: AN ENDPOINT, and appear in the last section of this chapter.

ACCUSATIVE: A DESTINATION 1—в 'in, into'

ACCUSATIVE: A DESTINATION with space, time, action, and purpose.

ACCUSATIVE: A DESTINATION operates in four domains: space, time, action, and purpose. In the spatial domain ACCUSATIVE: A DESTINATION is a destination of physical motion; in terms of time it is a temporal destination, a time when something happens; in the domain of action it is the destination of a verbal activity — what we usually call the direct object; and in the domain of purpose its meaning is roughly equivalent to the English word *for*.

ACCUSATIVE: A DESTINATION in the domain of space is explored in sections 1-6.

в + ACCUSATIVE: A DESTINATION in the domain of space means 'in, into'.

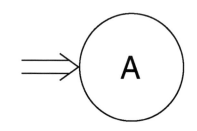

A force (arrow) arrives at an ACCUSATIVE: A DESTINATION (circle labeled A)

In the domain of space, ACCUSATIVE: A DESTINATION always requires a preposition to tell us what sort of trajectory is envisioned. The prepositions that can appear here are: в 'to, into', на 'to, onto', за 'to the far/back side of', о 'against', по 'up to; after, to get', под 'to the underside of, approaching', and про 'for'. We will look at each preposition, including its metaphorical uses, in turn.

Physical movement through space in the direction of or entering something is the most basic use of в expressing ACCUSATIVE: A DESTINATION.

Лишь 7 проце́нтов люде́й вы́разили жела́ние вы́ехать в *други́е места́.*
[Only 7-NOM percent-GEN people-GEN expressed desire-ACC move to other places-ACC.]
Only 7 percent of the people expressed a desire to move to *other places.*

Э́та де́вушка ра́ньше учи́лась в их кла́ссе, а пото́м перешла́ в *другу́ю шко́лу.*
[That girl-NOM earlier studied in their class-LOC, but later transferred to another school-ACC.]
That girl used to study in their class, but later she transferred to *another school.*

Ма́ма попа́ла в *сумасше́дший до́м.*
[Mama-NOM wound-up in lunatic asylum-ACC.]
Mama wound up in *a lunatic asylum.*

The last example shows that Russian will often express the idea of moving toward a destination even when the equivalent English doesn't. Here's another typical example:

Я разде́лась и легла́ в *посте́ль.*
[I-NOM got-undressed and lay-down in bed-ACC.]
I got undressed and lay down in *bed.*

в + ACCUSATIVE: A DESTINATION with motion in Russian, conceived of as location in English.

Many kinds of motion, large and small, may be conceived of as showing direction. Here are some examples that you might not expect to use the accusative, given the way we think of them in English. Still, they do show directed motion, and thus the logic of using ACCUSATIVE: A DESTINATION is justified.

уда́р в *грудь*, стуча́ть в *дверь*
[blow-NOM to chest-ACC, knock to door-ACC]
a blow to *the chest*, to knock on *a door*

Я как сумасше́дший захло́пал в *ладо́ши.*
[I-NOM like crazy-person-NOM began-clapping to palms-ACC.]
I started clapping *my hands* like a crazy person.

Of course, in addition to moving oneself, one can also move other objects to accusative destinations, as in the following example:

Ван Гог отре́зал себе́ у́хо и отда́л в *борде́ль.*
[Van Gogh-NOM cut-off self-DAT ear-ACC and sent to brothel-ACC.]
Van Gogh cut off his ear and sent it to *the brothel.*

ACCUSATIVE: A DESTINATION is also used when the motion is more imaginary than actual, as in the following to examples:

в + ACCUSATIVE: A DESTINATION with metaphorical motion.

В Япо́нии всё ча́ще звучи́т ло́зунг: Отбро́сим Евро́пу, вернёмся в *Азию*.
[In Japan-LOC all more-frequently sounds slogan-NOM: Cast-away Europe-ACC, return to Asia-ACC.]
In Japan one more and more frequently hears the slogan: Let's cast off Europe and return to *Asia*.

Э́то должно́ снять основно́е препя́тствие на пути́ за́падных инвести́ций в *на́шу эконо́мику*.
[This-NOM should remove primary barrier-ACC on path-LOC western investments-GEN to our economy-ACC.]
This should remove the primary barrier on the path leading western investments into *our economy*.

Vision is conceived of as moving along a path from the eyes to what they perceive. We therefore look at something using ACCUSATIVE: A DESTINATION.

Он ей посмотре́л в *глаза́*.
[He-NOM her-DAT looked into eyes-ACC.]
He looked into her *eyes*.

Just as light travels, so do sound and telephone signals, motivating the use of the accusative with verbs like звони́ть 'call':

Он звони́л в *разли́чные организа́ции*.
[He-NOM called to various organizations-ACC.]
He called *various organizations*.

Idiomatic uses of
B + ACCUSATIVE:
A DESTINATION.

There are also some idiomatic uses of ACCUSATIVE: A DESTINATION; here are some common examples:

Э́то в *пе́рвую о́чередь* пробле́ма президе́нта.
[This-NOM in first line-ACC problem-NOM president-GEN.]
In *the first place* this is the president's problem.

Э́то мо́жет уси́лить кри́тику в *а́дрес* президе́нта.
[This-NOM can intensify criticism-ACC in address-ACC president-GEN.]
This can intensify the criticism *directed toward* the president.

Два го́да наза́д я посети́л э́тот го́род и буква́льно влюби́лся в *него́*.
[Two years-ACC ago I-NOM visited that city-ACC and literally fell-in-love to it-ACC.]
Two years ago I visited that city and literally fell in love with *it*.

B + ACCUSATIVE:
A DESTINATION
expresses
changes of state.

Sometimes movement can also cause a change in the object itself, as in hair, which via movement goes from a free state to one in which it forms a braid:

У Пе́ти бы́ли дли́нные бе́лые во́лосы, кото́рые он заплета́л сза́ди в *ко́су*.
[By Petya-GEN were long white hairs-NOM, which-ACC he-NOM wove in-back to braid-ACC.]
Petya had long white hair which he wove into *a braid* in back.

This sort of movement as a transformation inspires a metaphorical usage of ACCUSATIVE: A DESTINATION in which objects move from one state of existence to another, as in the following three examples:

Иногда́ любо́вь перехо́дит в *не́нависть*.
[Sometimes love-NOM passes to hatred-ACC.]
Sometimes love turns into *hatred*.

Реда́ктор переименова́л своё изда́тельство в *"Неви́димую кни́гу"*.
[Editor-NOM renamed his publishing-house-ACC to "Invisible book"-ACC.]
The editor renamed his publishing house *"The Invisible Book."*

С по́мощью световы́х эффе́ктов зда́ние МГУ преврати́лось в *ба́шню* Кремля́.
[With help-INST light effects-GEN building-NOM MGU-GEN turned to tower-ACC Kremlin-GEN.]
With the help of light effects the MGU building turned into *a tower* of the Kremlin.

In the abstract domain of mathematics, a "destination" is a factor involved in multiplication, motivating this common use of в + ACCUSATIVE: A DESTINATION:

В + ACCUSATIVE: A DESTINATION expresses multiplication.

За после́дние пять лет престу́пность увели́чилась почти́ в *четы́ре ра́за*.
[In past five-ACC years-GEN crime-rate-NOM increased nearly in four times-ACC.]
In the past five years the crime rate has nearly *quadrupled*.

There is one use of the preposition в with ACCUSATIVE: A DESTINATION that refers exclusively to people who are taking on an identity or joining a group. The most common example is идти́/е́хать в *го́сти* [go to guests-ACC] 'go on *a visit*' (where the subject takes on the identity of a guest); but you will encounter other examples like вы́двинуться в *руководи́тели* [be-promoted to managers-ACC] 'be promoted to *manager*', and игра́ть в *ко́шки-мы́шки* [play to cats-mice-ACC] 'play *cat-and-mouse*'. What is very strange about this use of the accusative is that even though the items marked with the accusative tend to be plural and animate, there is no use of the genitive-accusative. That is because this use of ACCUSATIVE: A DESTINATION is a historical throw-back — it dates from a time before the genitive-accusative spread to the plural, back when all plural accusatives looked like the inanimate accusatives of today. So that is why you see го́сти instead of госте́й, руководи́тели instead of руководи́телей, and ко́шки-мы́шки instead of ко́шек-мы́шек. Here is a contextualized example:

В + ACCUSATIVE: A DESTINATION expresses joining a group — note that animates are not marked with the genitive-accusative form.

Ло́ра поступи́ла в *учени́цы* к маникю́рше.
[Lora-NOM entered to apprentices-ACC to manicurist-DAT.]
Lora joined (became one of) the manicurist's *apprentices*.

ACCUSATIVE: A DESTINATION 2—на 'to, on, onto'

на + ACCUSATIVE:
A DESTINATION in
the domain of
space means 'to,
on, onto'.

The behavior of на is very similar to that of в. The only difference is that в can imply entering the accusative object, whereas на treats it like a two-dimensional surface. See the chapter on the locative case for a list of common "на words", including ones we wouldn't think of as surfaces in English. Like в, на is often used to describe the destination to which objects move or are moved:

> Ма́ленькая змея́ влеза́ла на *горя́чий ка́мень* и поднима́ла го́лову.
> [Small snake-NOM crawled-up on hot stone-ACC and lifted head-ACC.]
> The small snake crawled up on *the hot stone* and lifted its head.

> Я причёсываюсь, положи́в шпи́льки на *умыва́льник* под зе́ркалом.
> [I-NOM brush-hair, having-laid hairpins-ACC on sink-ACC under mirror-INST.]
> I brush my hair, having laid the hairpins on *the sink* under the mirror.

> Он усе́лся на *со́бственные очки́*.
> [He-NOM sat-down on own glasses-ACC.]
> He sat down on *his own glasses*.

на + ACCUSATIVE:
A DESTINATION
with metaphori-
cal motion.

Sometimes the motion involved is more imaginary than real:

> Сли́шком ра́но отправля́ет он Росси́ю на *дно морско́е*!
> [Too early sends he-NOM Russia-ACC to bottom sea-ACC!]
> It's too early for him to be sending Russia to *the bottom of the sea*!

As we saw above, vision is understood as directed motion, motivating the use of на with things that can be looked upon or at:

> Я смотрю́ на *её ли́чико, гла́денькое* и *ова́льное*, как яи́чко.
> [I-NOM look on her face-ACC, smooth and oval-ACC, like an egg-NOM.]
> I look at *her face, smooth* and *oval* like an egg.

The fact that there is a direction indicated, even if there is no actual motion, is often sufficient to trigger the ACCUSATIVE: A DESTINATION meaning:

> Президе́нт прово́дит поли́тику, напра́вленную на *поддержа́ние* те́сных свя́зей с Кита́ем.
> [President-NOM conduct policy-ACC, directed-ACC on support-ACC close ties-GEN with China-INST.]
> The president is setting policy aimed at *supporting* close ties with China.

Idiomatic uses of
на + ACCUSATIVE:
A DESTINATION.

This idea of energy rather than actual objects moving toward a destination inspires further uses of на, which function to some degree as fixed phrases. Here are a few typical examples:

Го́рький никогда́ не претендова́л на *роль* "верхо́вного судьи́" литерату́ры.
[Gorky-NOM never not aspired/claimed on role-ACC "supreme judge"-GEN literature-GEN.]
Gorky never claimed *to be* the "supreme judge" of literature.

Вероя́тно, вели́кие лю́ди име́ют пра́во на *осо́бые пристра́стия* и *предпочте́ния*.
[Probably great people-NOM have right-ACC on peculiar passions-ACC and preferences-ACC.]
Great people probably have a right to *their peculiar passions* and *preferences*.

В отве́т на *предложе́ние* Го́рького прие́хать Цвета́ева написа́ла ему́ второ́е письмо́.
[In answer-ACC on suggestion-ACC Gorky-GEN come Tsvetaeva-NOM wrote him-DAT second letter-ACC.]
In answer to Gorky's *suggestion* to come, Tsvetaeva wrote him a second letter.

ACCUSATIVE: A DESTINATION 3—за 'beyond, behind'

The preposition за takes an object beyond or behind its destination; this is clearly expressed in concrete examples:

за + ACCUSATIVE: A DESTINATION in the domain of space means 'behind, to the far/back side of'.

Вечере́ло и со́лнце зака́тывалось за *горизо́нт*.
[Night-fell and sun-NOM rolled-away behind horizon-ACC.]
Night was falling and the sun was rolling away behind *the horizon*.

Лётчик схвати́л его́, завёл ему́ ру́ку за́ *спину*, повали́л на зе́млю, а сам сел све́рху.
[Pilot-NOM grabbed him-ACC, put him-DAT arm-ACC behind back-ACC, threw-down on ground-ACC, and self-NOM sat on-top.]
The pilot grabbed him, put his arm behind *his back*, threw him to the ground and sat on top of him.

Sitting down is of course also a movement toward a destination, and there are important idioms associated with this idea, such as: сесть за *стол* [sit-down behind table-ACC] 'sit down at *the table*' and сесть за *руль* [sit-down behind steering-wheel-ACC] 'take *the wheel*'. The first one seems odd because in English we talk about being *at*, not *behind*, tables. The insistence on mentioning sitting when assuming control of a car will likewise strike us as odd, though the logic behind it is clear. Less clear is the idiomatic use of за to express marriage for women; a man "marries on" a woman at the altar (using the construction жени́ться на — see the chapter on the locative case), but a woman "goes behind" her man (since this book is about grammar, let's leave the explanation to the cultural historians):

Idiomatic uses of за + ACCUSATIVE: A DESTINATION.

Тётя Йра вы́шла за́муж за *америка́нца*.
[Aunt Ira-NOM went-out married behind American-ACC.]
Aunt Ira got married to *an American*.

Another common idiomatic use is за *грани́цу* [behind border-ACC] '*abroad*', as in this example:

Ещё когда́ я в пе́рвый раз пое́хала со свои́ми фи́льмами за *грани́цу*, была́ поражена́ неадеква́тностью восприя́тия зарубе́жной аудито́рией.
[Still when I-NOM in first time-ACC rode with own films-INST behind border-ACC, was shocked-NOM inadequacy-INST perception-GEN foreign audience-INST.]
Even the first time I went *abroad* with my films, I was shocked at the inadequate reception of foreign audiences.

за + ACCUSATIVE: A DESTINATION expresses grabbing or holding.

When one object goes behind another it can get caught there or use that position to restrain the other object (remember the pilot in the example above). You will often see за plus ACCUSATIVE: A DESTINATION used to mean grabbing or holding. Common examples involve hands, as in взя́ться за́ *руку* [take behind hand-ACC] 'join *hands*' and вести́ за́ *руку* [lead behind hand-ACC] 'lead by *the hand*', but grabbing and holding can be invoked in a variety of situations, as illustrated in the following two examples:

Он подошёл к маши́не, взял за *за́дний ба́мпер*, оторва́л за́дние колёса от земли́, пото́м поста́вил и ушёл.
[He-NOM approached to car-DAT, took behind back bumper-ACC, tore-away back wheels-ACC from ground-GEN, then placed and left.]
He walked up to the car, took it by *the back bumper*, tore the back wheels off the ground, then put it down and walked away.

Полице́йские кре́пко держа́ли его́ за *пле́чи*.
[Policemen-NOM firmly held him-ACC behind shoulders-ACC.]
The policemen held him firmly by *the shoulders*.

за + ACCUSATIVE: A DESTINATION expresses replacing or exchanging.

Placing one thing behind another can also be the first step in replacing or exchanging items; the most common transaction of this kind is the receipt of goods or services in exchange for money (here the use of за is very similar to its use meaning 'for' in the domain of purpose):

Англича́не приобрели́ до́чку за *ми́зерную пла́ту* у 17-ле́тней цыга́нки.
[English-people-NOM obtained daughter-ACC for wretched sum-ACC by 17-year-old gypsy-GEN.]
The English [couple] obtained a daughter from a 17-year-old gypsy girl for *a wretched sum*.

за + ACCUSATIVE: A DESTINATION means 'more than'.

Finally, in the metaphorical space of numbers, за can name a number that is exceeded, as in: набрало́сь за *со́тню* жела́ющих [gathered beyond hundred-ACC interested-parties-GEN] 'more than *a hundred* interested parties gathered'.

ACCUSATIVE: A DESTINATION 4—o 'against'

The preposition o, like на, treats the accusative object as a surface, but it requires that contact be made and that there be some kind of force or pressure, usually involving leaning on or striking the object.

> Брала́ их за дли́нный ро́зовый хвост и с разма́ху би́ла голово́й о *цеме́нтный
> пол*.
> [Took them-ACC beyond long pink tail-ACC and from sweep-GEN beat head-INST
> against cement floor-ACC.]
> She took them by their long pink tail and with all her might beat their head against
> *the cement floor*.

> Электромеха́ник рассказа́л, что о́коло четырёх часо́в утра́ послы́шались
> си́льные уда́ры о *ко́рпус* корабля́.
> [Electromechanic-NOM said, that around four hours-GEN morning-GEN were-heard
> strong blows-NOM against hull-ACC ship-GEN.]
> The electromechanic said that heavy blows against *the hull* of the ship were heard at
> about four in the morning.

O + ACCUSATIVE: A DESTINATION also provides the structure for the idiom бок о *бок* [side-NOM against side-ACC] 'side by *side*'.

ACCUSATIVE: A DESTINATION 5—по 'up to'

Most frequently по with the accusative means 'up to' a certain point. Some activity is progressing through some space, and the accusative item is its destination, the place where it stops.

> Бы́ло очеви́дно, что его́ дед привы́к стоя́ть по *коле́но* в наво́зе и шурова́ть
> лопа́той.
> [Was obvious, that his grandfather-NOM accustomed stand up-to knee-ACC in
> manure-LOC and stoke shovel-INST.]
> It was obvious that his grandfather was used to standing up to *his knees* in manure
> and heaving a shovel.

The next two examples demonstrate metaphorical extensions: the arranging of meetings is an activity which has six as its stopping point/destination, and writing is an activity which has eighty pages as its destination (note that this meaning overlaps with the use of по + ACCUSATIVE: A DIMENSION meaning 'each').

> Дире́ктору назнача́ли ежедне́вно по *шесть* деловы́х свида́ний.
> [Director-DAT arranged daily up-to six-ACC business meetings-GEN.]
> They were arranging up to *six* business meetings a day for the director.

Этот журналист писа́л по *во́семьдесят* страни́ц в день.
[That journalist-NOM wrote up-to eighty-ACC pages-GEN in day-ACC.]
That journalist wrote up to *eighty* pages a day.

The use of по to mean 'after, to get' is fairly infrequent, and sounds archaic to most Russians. It can also be paraphrased as 'to fetch', as in идти́ по *я́годы* [to-go after/to get/to fetch strawberries-ACC] 'to go get *strawberries*'.

ACCUSATIVE: A DESTINATION 6—под 'under'

The preposition под expresses a destination 'under' an item. Here's a concrete illustration of how it is used:

На таёжной тра́ссе поги́б тигр, попа́вший под *колёса* проезжа́вшего лесово́за.
[On taiga route-LOC died tiger-NOM, fallen-NOM under wheels-ACC passed logging-truck-GEN.]
A tiger that fell under *the wheels* of a passing logging truck died on the taiga road.

More frequently под is used to describe the creation of metaphorical relationships, often involving power, as in this newspaper headline:

Ру́сские пограни́чники в Гру́зии взя́ты под *наблюде́ние*
[Russian border-guards-NOM in Georgia-LOC taken-NOM under observation-ACC]
Russian border guards are put under *observation* in Georgia

This last example is of 'under'-handed financing, involving the attraction of investments with a promise of state-owned stocks:

Прави́тельство гото́во рассмотре́ть вопро́с привлече́ния инвести́ций под *гара́нтию* а́кций Сберега́тельного ба́нка, принадлежа́щих госуда́рству.
[Government-NOM prepared-NOM examine question-ACC attraction-GEN investments-GEN under guarantee-ACC shares-GEN Savings bank-GEN, belonging-GEN state-DAT.]
The government is prepared to examine the question of how investments were solicited by means of *a guarantee* of Savings Bank shares that belong to the state.

Similar to под *гара́нтию* is the common phrase под *зало́г* [under pledge-ACC] 'on *the security* of'.

ACCUSATIVE: A DESTINATION 7—Destinations in time

If a destination in space is the point where something goes, then a destination in time is the point when something happens.

Both в and на are deployed for this meaning, which is very common, especially for days and times of day:

в and на +
ACCUSATIVE: A
DESTINATION in
the domain
of time
means 'on, at'.

Курс до́ллара в *пя́тницу* не́сколько сни́зился.
[Exchange-rate-NOM dollar-GEN to Friday-ACC somewhat declined.]
The exchange rate for the dollar declined somewhat on *Friday*.

В *семь* часо́в ве́чера она́ стоя́ла во́зле его́ до́ма в чём-то мо́дном, я́рком и кова́рном.
[To seven-ACC hours-GEN evening-GEN she-NOM stood next-to his house-GEN in something fashionable, bright and insidious-LOC.]
At *seven* o'clock in the evening she was standing next to his house in something fashionable, bright, and insidious.

На *сле́дующий день* по́сле подписа́ния контра́кта начала́сь отпра́вка гру́зов.
[On next day-ACC after signing-GEN contract-GEN began shipment-NOM freight-GEN.]
Shipment of freight began *the day* after the contract was signed.

Both в and на are used with *раз* [time-ACC] in time expressions such as: в *пе́рвый раз* 'the first time', в *после́дний раз* 'the last time', на *э́тот раз* 'this/that time'. Here's an example:

Предвы́борный штаб постара́ется опротестова́ть результа́ты вы́боров, тем бо́лее что на *э́тот раз* бы́ло зафикси́ровано нема́ло наруше́ний.
[Election staff-NOM tries protest results-ACC elections-GEN, that-INST more that on this time-ACC was recorded-NOM not-few violations-GEN.]
The election staff will try to protest the election results, especially since *this time* quite a number of violations were recorded.

The preposition по preserves its meaning of 'up to' in the domain of time, as these examples demonstrate:

по + ACCUSATIVE:
A DESTINATION in
the domain
of time means
'up to'.

Ты́сячи люде́й поколе́ния на́ших роди́телей по *пятьдеся́т* лет жи́ли вме́сте, но при э́том нере́дко бы́ли абсолю́тно чужи́ми друг дру́гу людьми́.
[Thousands-NOM people-GEN generation-GEN our parents-GEN up-to fifty-ACC years-GEN lived together, but at this-LOC not-infrequently were aboslutely alien-INST friend-NOM friend-DAT people-INST.]
Thousands of people of our parents' generation lived together for up to *fifty* years, but still were not infrequently absolutely estranged from each other.

С середи́ны января́ по *коне́ц* февраля́ вооружёнными отря́дами ислами́стов уничто́жено свы́ше 600 ми́рных гра́ждан, включа́я старико́в и дете́й.
[From middle-GEN January-GEN up-to end-ACC February-GEN armed divisions-INST Islamists-GEN destroyed-NOM more 600 peaceful citizens-GEN, including old-people-GEN and children-GEN.]
From the middle of January through *the end* of February more than 600 peaceful citizens, including children and the elderly, were killed by armed divisions of Islamists.

под + ACCUSA-
TIVE: A DESTINA-
TION in the
domain of time
means 'toward'.

Parallel to its spatial uses, под can indicate a time approaching another set time (note how we also express directed motion in English by using *toward* in this way):

Возвраща́ясь под *у́тро*, она́ говори́ла себе́: ла́дно, обойдётся. Что́-нибудь приду́маю в такси́.
[Returning under morning-ACC, she-NOM said self-DAT: okay, work-out. Something-ACC think-up in taxi-LOC.]
Returning toward *morning*, she said to herself: okay, things will work out. I'll think something up in the taxi.

ACCUSATIVE: A DESTINATION 8—The direct object

ACCUSATIVE: A
DESTINATION in
the domain of
action expresses
the direct object.

Thus far we have traveled through the domains of space and time in search of destinations. What happens if we enter the domain of action? Where will we find the destination of the activity expressed by the verb in a sentence? The answer is something traditionally called the direct object. Here is the logic that ties it to the ACCUSATIVE: A DESTINATION. Imagine any sentence with both an agent (something that does something) and a patient (something that has something done to it). The patient is the direct object, and it is in the accusative case because the action moves along a path from the agent to the patient. For example, let's take *I* for the agent, *pushed* for the action, and *button* for the patient. Result: *I pushed the button*, where *the button* is the direct object of the verb. Of course in Russian it will appear in the accusative case, and here is what it looks like:

Я нажа́л *большу́ю кру́глую кно́пку* ли́фта.
[I-NOM pressed big round button-ACC elevator-GEN.]
I pressed the elevator's *big round button*.

This formula will work for just about any verb (except the ones that govern the instrumental, dative, or genitive for some special reason explained in those chapters), even verbs that don't involve any real "action".

Вертолёт пошёл вве́рх, увлека́я за собо́й *Бо́нда*.
[Helicopter-NOM went up, dragging behind self-INST Bond-ACC.]
The helicopter went up, dragging *Bond* behind it.

Ка́ждый трудя́щийся соде́ржит *трои́х*.
[Each worker-NOM supports three-ACC.]
Each worker supports *three people*.

Но́вый докуме́нт предполага́ет *откры́тие* национа́льных и междунаро́дных ры́нков.
[New document-NOM proposes opening-ACC national and international markets-GEN.]
The new document proposes *the opening* of national and international markets.

Четы́ре спо́рных о́строва име́ют *ва́жное значе́ние* для безопа́сности Росси́и.
[Four disputed islands-NOM have important meaning-ACC for security-GEN Russia-GEN.]
The four disputed islands are *important* for Russia's security.

Я вёл *двойну́ю жизнь.*
[I-NOM led double life-ACC.]
I led *a double life.*

Thanks to the fact that the direct object is marked with the accusative case (and thus distinct from the nominative agent/subject), the subject, verb, and direct object can be presented in just about any order. Here are a few examples of word orders that won't usually work in English (at least not with active verbs):

ACCUSATIVE: A DESTINATION as the direct object doesn't always come after the verb.

Вита́лика люби́ли о́ба роди́теля, две ба́бушки, праба́бушка, и два де́душки.
[Vitalik-ACC loved both parents-NOM, two grandmothers-NOM, great-grand-mother-NOM, and two grandfathers-NOM.]
Vitalik was loved by both parents, two grandmothers, a great-grandmother, and two grandfathers.

Свою́ двухко́мнатную кварти́ру она́ сдала́ внаём.
[Own two-room apartment-ACC she-NOM let-out to-rent.]
She rented out *her two-room apartment.*

Зави́стники счита́ют, что *же́нщин* привлека́ют в богача́х их де́ньги.
[Envious-people-NOM think, that women-ACC attract in rich-men-LOC their money-NOM.]
Envious people think that what attracts *women* about rich men is their money.

It is possible to have an accusative direct object even when we tamper a bit with the rest of the sentence structure. For example, sometimes the subject might appear in the dative case (for more about such datives, see the following chapter):

ACCUSATIVE: A DESTINATION as the direct object can appear without a nominative subject.

Кабине́ту мини́стров пору́чено разрабо́тать *те́хнико-экономи́ческое обоснова́ние* прое́кта.
[Cabinet-DAT ministers-GEN charged work-out technical-economic basis-ACC project-GEN.]
The cabinet of ministers has been charged with working out *the technical and economic basis* of the project.

Often in Russian we simply use a plural verb with no subject to express a generic "they". Here the subject is implied even though we can't see it, and the direct object stays in the accusative case, just as we would expect it to:

> Печа́льно, но *тех*, кто сча́стлив в бра́ке, по́лностью игнори́руют.
> [Sadly, but those-ACC, who-NOM happy-NOM in marriage-LOC, completely ignore.]
> It's unfortunate, but *people* who are happy in marriage are utterly ignored.

> Вот уж пои́стине ре́жут *ку́рицу, несу́щую золоты́е я́йца*!
> [Well already indeed slaughter hen-ACC, laying-ACC golden eggs-ACC!]
> Well now they really are killing *the goose that lays the golden eggs*!

The first of these two sentences is based on the structure игнори́руют *тех* '[they] ignore *those [people]*'; these two words are inverted and the clause about who is happy in marriage is inserted to explain what *тех* refers to. The second sentence contains two examples of ACCUSATIVE: A DESTINATION in the domain of action: one is *the hen* (with no subject), and the other is *the golden eggs* (with the hen as the subject).

ACCUSATIVE: A DESTINATION 9—Objects without subjects

ACCUSATIVE: A DESTINATION as the direct object can appear without any subject at all.

It is possible to have sentences without even an implied subject, in which case the verb shows "default" agreement of neuter singular. This is required for certain verbs (usually involving feeling sick), and some examples (like the one with the barn below) are clearly parallel with the "raw force" type of INSTRUMENTAL: A MEANS (minus the instrumental itself; note that the accusative items in the "raw force" instrumental examples are all direct objects, too). The verbs most frequenty encountered in this construction are зноби́ть 'have the chills', рвать 'vomit', тошни́ть 'feel nauseated', and трясти́ 'shake, have the shivers'. The following examples demonstrate how these verbs are used in context:

> И когда́ зазвене́л звоно́к на обе́д и все роди́тели столпи́лись у ле́стницы, он по́нял, что э́то зна́чит, и *его́* ста́ло рвать бутербро́дом.
> [And when rang bell-NOM on lunch-ACC and all parents-NOM crowded by staircase-GEN, he-NOM understood, what-ACC this-NOM means, and him-ACC began vomit sandwich-INST.]
> And when the lunch bell rang and all the parents crowded around the staircase, he understood what it meant and *he* began to throw up his sandwich.

> *Вас* не тошни́т от того́, что Чечня́ счита́ется террито́рией Росси́и, а там регуля́рно похища́ют и убива́ют люде́й?
> [You-ACC not feel-nauseated from that-GEN, that Chechnya-NOM is-considered territory-INST Russia-GEN, but there regularly capture and kill people-ACC?]
> It doesn't make *you* sick that Chechnya is considered a Russian territory, but people are being captured and killed there?

Пассажи́ров трясёт ме́ньше, чем в други́х маши́нах.
[Passengers-ACC shakes less, than in other vehicles-LOC.]
Passengers get shaken less than in other vehicles.

As the last example with the shaken passengers above suggests, it is also possible just to name the patient of some (usually damaging) action, and leave the agent anonymous, as in this statement of arson:

Сара́й зажгло́.
[Barn-ACC set-on-fire.]
The barn was set on fire.

Another variant is to leave the verb in the infinitive form, again without a subject, as in:

Курс интенси́вной терапи́и решено́ продо́лжить.
[Course-ACC intensive therapy-GEN decided continue.]
It was decided to continue *the course* of intensive therapy.

Finally, one can even dispense with the verb entirely, provided it can be retrieved from context, as in this expression which you might hear when someone offers their hand to help you up a steep path (where на is an interjection, not a preposition):

На *ру́ку*!
[Here hand-ACC!]
Here, take *my hand*!

ACCUSATIVE: A DESTINATION 10—Destinations of purpose

Now we move to a more nebulous realm, that of the wishes, wants, and hopes that make up the human will. Moving the will in a certain direction means using it as a cause to produce a desired effect. Here we see ACCUSATIVE: A DESTINATION fleshed out as an object toward which an agent is directing its will, its sense of purpose. Usually this takes the form of somebody doing something for *something or somebody* (and perhaps for *a reason*). This kind of 'for' is most commonly expressed by the preposition на, though в, за, and less frequently под and про are deployed for this purpose.

In this first example, the purpose of Moscow's taking action is the defense of one of its citizens; Moscow is obliged to do something for him:

Росси́йский граждани́н преступле́ния не соверши́л, и Москва́ обя́зана вы́ступить в *его́ защи́ту*.
[Russian citizen-NOM crime-GEN not committed, and Moscow-NOM obliged-NOM act for his defense-ACC.]
The Russian citizen has not committed any crime, and Moscow is obliged to act in *his defense*.

ACCUSATIVE: A DESTINATION in the domain of purpose.

в + ACCUSATIVE: A DESTINATION in the domain of purpose means 'for'.

на + ACCUSATIVE: A DESTINATION in the domain of purpose means 'for'.

The next two examples illustrate the use of на in this domain. In the first one the purpose of action is destruction. The second example is actually two examples in one, containing a budget designated for *the following year*, as well as money allocated for *the purposes of public well-being*.

> Нéкоторые маньяки не перенóсят чужóго совершéнства и дéйствуют на *егó истреблéние.*
> [Certain maniacs-NOM not endure strange perfection-GEN and act for its destruction-ACC.]
> Certain maniacs cannot endure others' perfection and work to *destroy it*.

> В бюджéте на *бу́дущий год* предусмóтрено увеличéние расхóдов на *социáльные нýжды, здравоохранéние и образовáние.*
> [In budget-LOC for future year-ACC envisaged increase-NOM expenses-GEN for social needs-ACC, public health-ACC and education-ACC.]
> An increase in the expenses for *social needs*, *public health*, and *education* is envisaged in *next year's* budget.

A common use of на expresses the purposeful act of answering a question. There is a construction in which both на and в act in this domain, namely в *отвéт* на + ACC [in answer-ACC to + ACC] 'in *answer* to', and we also commonly see just на + ACC following the verb отвечáть/отвéтить, as in this example:

> Не могý отвéтить на *егó вопрóс.*
> [Not can answer on his question-ACC.]
> I cannot answer *his question*.

On occasion you may see examples with на that involve a transaction similar to that described under за below:

> На *срéдства* япóнского правѝтельства бýдет пострóено нóвое здáние шкóлы бѝзнеса.
> [For funds-ACC Japanese government-GEN will-be built-NOM new building-NOM school-GEN business-GEN.]
> A new building for the business school will be built with *funds* from the Japanese government.

за + ACCUSATIVE: A DESTINATION in the domain of purpose means 'for'.

The use of за can mean 'for' in the sense of 'in support of'; in asking for a vote one might say кто за, а кто прóтив? [who-NOM for and who-NOM against?] 'who's in favor and who's opposed?', where за implies *наш план, нáшего президéнта* [our plan-ACC, president-ACC] '*our plan, our president*', etc. One can also express other emotional or moral relationships in this way, as in feeling shame for, on account of something or someone:

> Мне сты́дно за *россѝйское орýжие*!
> [Me-DAT shameful for Russian weaponry-ACC!]
> I'm ashamed of *Russian weaponry*!

Very frequently, however, за inspires the concept of exchange, getting this for *that*, fighting for *something*, being punished for *something*, or paying for *something*. We have already seen за play this role in expressing transactions when we looked at the spatial destinations above.

> Ка́жется маловероя́тным, что́бы тако́й челове́к плани́ровал боро́ться за *президе́нтское кре́сло*.
> [Seems unlikely-INST, that such person-NOM planned fight for president's seat-ACC.]
> It seems unlikely that such a person would plan to fight for *the president's seat*.

> Бу́дут ли у нас когда́-нибудь нака́зывать за *враче́бные преступле́ния и оши́бки*?
> [Will whether by us-GEN someday punish for medical crimes-ACC and errors-ACC?]
> Will people someday be punished in our country for *medical crimes* and *errors*?

> Журнали́сты заплати́ли штраф за *незако́нное пребыва́ние* в пограни́чной полосе́.
> [Journalists-NOM paid fine-ACC for illegal stay-ACC in border zone-LOC.]
> The journalists paid a fine for *staying illegally* in the border zone.

When the preposition под is used in the domain of purpose, it means 'for use as', and involves designing or redesigning something to serve a given function, as in this example:

> Одна́ко по́сле револю́ции це́рковь переде́лали под *кремато́рий*.
> [However after revolution-GEN church-ACC remade under crematorium-ACC.]
> However after the revolution they remodeled the church to serve as *a crematorium*.

ПОД + ACCUSATIVE: A DESTINATION in the domain of purpose means 'for use as'.

The use of the preposition про is also relatively restricted in the domain of purpose. It is part of the fixed phrase сохрани́ть про *чёрный день* [save for black day-ACC] 'save for *a rainy day*' and often occurs in the negative with the pronoun нас 'us', as in this example:

> Э́ти ла́комства — не про *нас*.
> [These delicacies-NOM — not for us-ACC.]
> These delicacies aren't for *us*.

ПРО + ACCUSATIVE: A DESTINATION in the domain of purpose means 'for'.

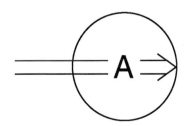

A force (arrow) moves through
an ACCUSATIVE:: A DIMENSION
(circle labeled A)

ACCUSATIVE: A DIMENSION 1—
Distance and duration

The hallmark of the ACCUSATIVE: A DIMENSION is that the action of the verb extends over some dimension. The domains invoked by ACCUSATIVE: A DIMENSION can be grouped as follows: distance and duration, size and capacity, comparison, and perfomance of activities. Each grouping will be examined in turn below.

ACCUSATIVE: A DIMENSION is invoked in the domains of distance and duration, size and capacity, comparison, and performance of activities.

ACCUSATIVE: A
DIMENSION in the
domain of
distance and
duration.

There's a Russian proverb that nicely illustrates the distance and duration uses of AC-CUSATIVE: A DIMENSION:

Жизнь прожи́ть не *по́ле* перейти́.
[Life-ACC live-through not field-ACC walk-across.]
Living through *life* isn't like walking across *a field/Life*'s no bed of roses.

Here life is understood as a stretch of time with a beginning and an end (and punctuated by trials and tribulations), and living is an activity that stretches all along this time period. The field is a bounded space, and walking extends along the distance from one edge of it to the other. Both the life and the field provide dimensions that guide activities.

Although examples of distance are by no means rare, you will encounter many more examples of duration, which can be expressed both without prepositions and with them: в, за, на, and по.

The following four sentences illustrate duration without prepositions. The first two contain obvious cues, such as the idiomatic expression провести́ *вре́мя* 'spend *time*' and the verb дли́ться 'last'. The other two show that duration can be expressed for any activity (walking) or state (being).

Мы с ним обяза́тельно ещё раз схо́дим в рестора́н и опя́ть прекра́сно проведём *вре́мя* вдвоём.
[We-NOM with him-INST surely still one-time-ACC go to restaurant-ACC and again splendidly conduct time-ACC together.]
Surely he and I will go once more to a restaurant and again have a splendid *time* together.

Наркома́ния почти́ неизлечи́ма, и е́сли реми́ссия дли́тся *два-три го́да*, то э́то уже́ хоро́ший результа́т.
[Drug-addiction-NOM almost incurable-NOM and if remission-NOM lasts two-three years-ACC, then that-NOM already good result-NOM.]
Drug addiction is almost incurable, and if a remission lasts *two or three years*, then that's a pretty good result.

Америка́нец купи́л э́ти сапоги́ в спорти́вном магази́не и ходи́л в них по гора́м лет *пять* и́ли *шесть*.
[American-NOM bought these boots-ACC in sport store-LOC and walked in them-LOC along mountains-DAT years-GEN five-ACC or six-ACC.]
An American bought these boots in a sporting goods store and walked around the mountains in them for about *five* or *six* years.

Пять десятиле́тий Япо́ния была́ ве́рным после́дователем США.
[Five-ACC decades-GEN Japan-NOM was loyal follower-INST USA-GEN.]
For five decades Japan was the USA's loyal follower.

Sometimes the duration is made up of small discontinuous pieces of time, usually indicated by the use of words like ка́ждый 'every' and раз 'time', as in говори́ть *сто* раз [say hundred-ACC times-GEN] 'say *a hundred* times', and as in this example:

> Éсли ты лю́бишь меня́, тогда́ заче́м мы *ка́ждый день* расстаёмся?
> [If you-NOM love me-ACC, then why we-NOM every day-ACC break-up?]
> If you love me, then why do we break up *every day*?

With the preposition в, duration is usually expressed in terms of вре́мя/времена́ 'time(s)' or го́ды 'years', as in the following two examples:

> Сати́ра во *все времена́* испы́тывала недоброжела́тельство власте́й и во *все времена́* пита́лась горя́чей подде́ржкой пу́блики.
> [Satire-NOM in all times-ACC experienced disfavor-ACC authorities-GEN and in all times-ACC been-nourished ardent support-INST public-GEN.]
> Satire has at *all times* experienced the disfavor of the authorities and at *all times* been nourished by the ardent support of the public.

> В *те го́ды* всем не хвата́ло нали́чных де́нег.
> [In those years-ACC all-DAT not sufficed available money-GEN.]
> In *those years* everyone had a shortage of available money.

Probably the most common use of в + ACCUSATIVE: A DIMENSION in the domain of time is with the word раз 'time' to express frequency, as in раз в *неде́лю* [time-ACC in week-ACC] 'once *a week*', три ра́за в *ме́сяц* [three times-ACC in month-ACC] 'three times *a month*'.

Like в, на can also identify a duration, specifically one during which something is done, or how long the results should last, usually translatable into English as 'for' or 'lasting'. Thus in Russian you can come on a visit на *одну́ неде́лю* [for one week-ACC] 'for *one week*', and one can also engage in an activity for a specified period of time, as in this example:

> Врачи́ наста́ивают на скоре́йшем ухо́де в о́тпуск не ме́нее чем на *три́дцать* дней.
> [Doctors-NOM insist on fastest departure-LOC in vacation-ACC not less than lasting thirty days-ACC.]
> The doctors insist that he immediately take a vacation lasting at least *thirty* days.

The preposition за can mean 'during, in the course of', as we see in these two examples:

> За *э́тот ме́сяц* никого́ в на́шем до́ме не хорони́ли.
> [During that month-ACC no one-ACC in our house-LOC not buried.]
> During *that month* no one in our house was buried.

в + ACCUSATIVE: A DIMENSION in the domain of duration means 'in, during'.

на + ACCUSATIVE: A DIMENSION in the domain of duration means 'for, lasting'.

за + ACCUSATIVE: A DIMENSION in the domain of duration means 'during'.

За *су́тки* состоя́ние больно́го незначи́тельно меня́ется то в лу́чшую, то в ху́дшую сто́рону.
[During twenty-four-hours-ACC condition-NOM patient-GEN imperceptibly changes now to better-ACC, now to worse side-ACC.]
In the course of *twenty-four hours* the patient's condition changes imperceptibly, getting better and worse by turns.

The meaning of по in this context is usually best translated as 'through':

С января́ по *май* вы бу́дете в олимпи́йской фо́рме.
[From January-GEN through May-ACC you-NOM will-be in olympic form-LOC.]
From January through *May* you will be in olympic form.

ACCUSATIVE: A DIMENSION 2—Size and capacity

In the domain of size and capacity, some feature of an object is measured against a standardized scale (often units of weight and measure) or against another object or objects. You will usually have a preposition here (в is most frequent, на and по are possible, and о is rather rare), followed by the ACCUSATIVE: A DIMENSION marking the scale, units, or object along which size or capacity are measured.

Here are typical examples expressing weight and size:

Оди́н из слоно́в — трёхле́тний Раджа́ ве́сом в *850* килогра́ммов — воспо́льзовался прогу́лкой, чтобы загляну́ть в посу́дную ла́вку.
[One-NOM of elephants-GEN — three-year-old Rajah-NOM weight-INST in 850-ACC kilograms-GEN — took-advantage outing-INST, to take-peek to china shop-ACC.]
One of the elephants — three-year-old Rajah, weighing *850* kilograms — took advantage of the outing to take a peek into a china shop.

Сра́зу броса́ется в глаза́ ваго́нчик в *два этажа́*, сде́ланный в А́нглии незадо́лго до пе́рвой мирово́й войны́.
[Immediately throws in eyes-ACC wagon-NOM in two stories-ACC, made-NOM in England-LOC not-long before first world war-GEN.]
Suddenly there appears a *two-story* wagon, made in England not long before the first World War.

The preposition в can also be used to tell us the amount by which things differ:

Ста́рый ку́рс от но́вого отлича́ется ро́вно в *ты́сячу* раз.
[Old rate-NOM from new-GEN differs exactly in thousand-ACC times-GEN.]
The old rate is exactly *a thousand* times more than the new one.

In this domain, на can tell us how big an item is in phrases like: теа́тр на *пятьсо́т* мест [theater-NOM on five-hundred-ACC places-GEN] 'a *five-hundred*-seat theater', облига́ция на *сто* рубле́й [obligation-NOM on hundred-ACC rubles-GEN] 'a *one-hundred*-ruble obligation', ко́мната на *двои́х* [room-NOM on two-ACC] 'a room for *two*'.

Like в, на can measure the amount by which it differs from some other object. Here you will usually see a comparative adjective (like бо́льше 'bigger', ме́ньше 'smaller', коро́че 'shorter') or a verb indicating exceeding or failing to reach some mark, plus the preposition на:

> В понеде́льник курс до́ллара зафикси́рован на у́ровне 2017 рубле́й, что на *пять* рубле́й вы́ше предыду́щего показа́теля.
> [To Monday-ACC exchange-rate-NOM dollar-GEN fixed-NOM on level-LOC 2017 rubles-GEN, what-NOM to five-ACC rubles higher previous indicator-GEN.]
> On Monday the exchange rate for the dollar is fixed at the level of 2017 rubles, which is *five* rubles higher than the previous indicator.

> Я опозда́ла на *пятна́дцать* мину́т.
> [I-NOM got-late on fifteen-ACC minutes-GEN.]
> I was *fifteen* minutes late.

In this domain the preposition по refers to a distribution such that each of a series of items is assigned the same amount. In the following example the value of two rubles is assigned to each kilo of mimosa:

> В Со́чи мимо́зу мо́жно прода́ть по *два рубля́* за оди́н килогра́мм.
> [In Sochi-LOC mimosa-ACC possible sell along two rubles-ACC for one kilogram-ACC.]
> In Sochi you can sell mimosa for *two rubles* a kilo.

The use of the preposition о in the domain of size and capacity is rare and archaic, but here are two phrases to give you an idea of what it looks like: избу́шка об *одно́ око́нце* [hut-NOM with one window-ACC] 'a hut with just *one little window*', крыльцо́ о *три ступе́ньки* [porch-NOM with three steps-ACC] 'a porch with just *three little steps*'.

A very common use of ACCUSATIVE: A DIMENSION deals with financial rather than physical dimensions, here the cost of an item is presented in the accusative with no preposition. This meaning of the accusative is most frequently associated with the verb сто́ить 'cost', although, as this example illustrates, other verbs can occasionally serve this purpose:

> Обы́чно перевы́пуск ка́рточки сто́ит *пятьдеся́т* до́лларов, се́рвисная пла́та составля́ет *сто пятьдеся́т* до́лларов.
> [Usually reissue-NOM card-GEN costs fifty-ACC dollars, service fee-NOM comes-to hundred fifty-ACC dollars-GEN.]
> Usually the reissue of a card costs *fifty* dollars, and the service fee comes to *one hundred and fifty* dollars.

Margin notes:

на + ACCUSATIVE: A DIMENSION in the domain of size and capacity expresses a number of units.

по + ACCUSATIVE: A DIMENSION in the domain of size and capacity expresses an amount per item.

о + ACCUSATIVE: A DIMENSION in the domain of size and capacity means 'with'.

ACCUSATIVE: A DIMENSION in the domain of size and capacity expresses cost.

Accusative: a dimension 3—Comparison

ACCUSATIVE: A
DIMENSION in the
domain of
comparison
always requires a
preposition.

в + ACCUSATIVE: A
DIMENSION in the
domain of
comparison
indicates a
characteristic.

похо́ж на +
ACCUSATIVE: A
DIMENSION in the
domain of
comparison
means 'resem-
bling'.

The measurement of one thing against another in and of itself implies a comparison of the thing measured with some standard. It is perhaps no surprise that comparison is an important component of the ACCUSATIVE: A DIMENSION, and that comparison can be made in many different ways.

The use of в in the domain of comparison is rather marginal, but one does come across examples such as бума́га в *кле́точку* [paper-NOM like square-ACC] '*graph* paper' and ю́бка в *поло́ску* [skirt-NOM in stripe-ACC] 'a striped skirt.

In comparing objects according to their various characteristics to determine whether they are similar to each other, the accusative object is used as a standard, along which another object is measured in a metaphorical sense. The most common example of this use of ACCUSATIVE: A DIMENSION is the phrase похо́ж на 'looks like, resembling':

> Хоти́те знать, на *кого́* вы похо́жи? На *разби́тую* параличо́м *гори́ллу*, кото́рую де́ржат в зоопа́рке из жа́лости.
> [Want know, to whom-ACC you-NOM resemble? To stricken-ACC paralysis-INST gorilla-ACC, which-ACC keep in zoo-LOC from pity-GEN.]
> Do you want to know *what* you look like? Like *a paralyzed gorilla* that they keep in a zoo out of pity.

под + ACCUSA-
TIVE: A DIMENSION
in the domain of
comparison
means 'like'.

With the preposition под, comparison has the connotation of imitation, as in this bit of conversation from a beauty parlor, where a woman is being offered a haircut 'like *a boy's*':

> Согла́сно ва́шему лицу́, предлага́ю под *ма́льчика* — не возража́ете?
> [In-harmony your face-DAT, suggest under boy-ACC — not object?]
> To suit your face, I suggest giving you *a boy's* haircut — is that okay with you?

с + ACCUSATIVE: A
DIMENSION in the
domain of
comparison
means 'approxi-
mately'.

A specialized type of comparison is approximation, and this use has its own preposition: с 'about the size/length of, approximately'. This is the only meaning that с ever has when it is used with the accusative case. An easy way to recognize this use is to remember the Russian rhyme for 'Tom Thumb', which is Ма́льчик с *па́льчик*, literally [Boy-NOM approximately finger-ACC] 'A boy about the size of *your finger*'. Here are some contextualized examples:

> Наш попуга́й был ро́стом с *ку́рицу*.
> [Our parrot-NOM was size-INST approximately chicken-ACC.]
> Our parrot was about the size of *a chicken*.

> Он с *мину́ту* подержа́л жену́ в объя́тиях.
> [He-NOM approximately minute-ACC held wife-ACC in embraces-LOC.]
> He held his wife in his arms for about *a minute*.

ACCUSATIVE: A DIMENSION 4—Activities in various domains

Measurement and comparison are not the only activities that can extend along the dimensions of an object marked as ACCUSATIVE: A DIMENSION. Almost any kind of activity can behave this way, being guided or limited by the features or dimensions of the accusative object. The concept of activity extending along some defining space is abstract and metaphorical; considering some concrete examples will help you to see how this works.

A very common use of this meaning is in the phrase играть в [play to] which is used when we talk about playing games and sports. The name of the game or sport follows in the accusative. Let's think for a minute about the relationship between a game or sport and playing. Playing in itself is a relatively loosely defined activity. A game or sport, however, brings all kinds of concrete parameters with it: rules, implements used, techniques, etc. In this sense the game or sport lends specific dimensions to the playing activity (otherwise left undefined).

> На но́вом стадио́не мо́жно игра́ть в *ре́гби, бейсбо́л, софтбо́л...*
> [At new stadium-LOC possible play in rugby-ACC, baseball-ACC, softball-ACC...]
> At the new stadium one can play *rugby, baseball, softball...*

The distinction we make in English between 'believe' (say, 'a story') and 'believe in' (say, 'God') has an exact parallel in Russian. Whereas ве́рить is usually followed by a DATIVE: A COMPETITOR (parallel to 'believe'), when speaking of strong convictions Russians use ве́рить/ве́ра в + accusative: a dimension, as in ве́рить/ве́ра в *Бо́га* [believe/belief in God-ACC] 'believe/belief in *God*'.

Here's another example using в, where the activity is crying, defined by the dimension of one voice (unison).

> Но пла́кать в *оди́н го́лос* с ним не хо́чется.
> [But cry to one voice-ACC with him-INST not want-self.]
> But one doesn't feel like crying in *unison* with him.

The extension of an activity along a dimension can be variously expressed by all of the following prepositions: на, под, про, сквозь, and че́рез. На is usually the place where something is or happens. In this example being beautiful is something that extends along the face, but being fat extends along the figure:

> Она́ была́ краси́вая на *лицо́*, но то́лстая на *фигу́ру*.
> [She-NOM was beautiful-NOM to face-ACC, but fat-NOM to figure-ACC.]
> She had a beautiful *face*, but a fat *figure*.

A more abstract, but very common example is the phrase на *мой (твой, её, его́...) взгляд* [to my (your, her, his...) view-ACC] 'in *my (your, her, his...) view/opinion*'. The proposition (whatever it is that the person believes) extends along that person's view; in other words, it is true for the domain of that person's opinion. In the following example, the belief that taking such steps will be beneficial is true for the domain of the ambassador's opinion:

На *взгляд* посла́, таки́е шаги́ создаю́т благоприя́тную атмосфе́ру для реше́ния территориа́льной пробле́мы.
[To view-ACC ambassador-GEN, such steps-NOM create favorable atmosphere-ACC for solution-GEN territorial problem-GEN.]
In the ambassador's *opinion* , such steps create a favorable atmosphere for solving the territorial problem.

под + ACCUSA-
TIVE: A DIMENSION
in the domains
of various
activities means
'to the tune of'.

The preposition под indicates an activity that accompanies another one, most commonly involving music, as in танцева́ть под *му́зыку* [dance under music-ACC] 'dance to *the music*', петь под *гита́ру* [sing under guitar-ACC] 'sing along with *the guitar*'. This idea of musical accompaniment can be extended to other activities involving rhythmic sounds, as in this example:

Под *свире́пую воркотню́* гардеро́бщика оставля́ю свои́ су́мки на полу́, поднима́юсь наве́рх и сра́зу сажу́сь в кре́сло.
[Under fierce growling-ACC coat-check-man-GEN leave own bags-ACC on floor-LOC, raise up and immediately sit in chair-ACC.]
To the tune of the coat-check man's *fierce growls*   I leave my bags on the floor, go upstairs, and sit right down in a chair.

про + ACCUSA-
TIVE: A DIMENSION
in the domains
of various
activities means
'about'.

The preposition про designates dimensions for activities like thinking, talking, and writing. The domain of these cognitive and communicative activities is their topic, literally the thing that you think, talk, or write *about* .

Мы всё зна́ем друг про *дру́га*.
[We-NOM all-ACC know other-NOM for other-ACC.]
We know everything about *each other* .

Я забы́л про *царе́вну-лягу́шку*.
[I-NOM forgot for queen-frog-ACC.]
I forgot about the *frog-queen* .

сквозь +
ACCUSATIVE: A
DIMENSION in the
domains of
various activities
means 'through'.

Сквозь refers to something that has dimensions, 'through' which something else (usually light or sound or the perception of something seen or heard) passes, often with some difficulty or alteration, as we see in these two examples:

Заразительная поэ́тика вели́кой кни́ги заставля́ет смотре́ть сквозь *её о́птику* на мно́гие обы́денные ве́щи.
[Infectious poetics-NOM great book-GEN force look through its lens-ACC on many ordinary things-ACC.]
This great book's captivating poetry forces us to look at a multitude of everyday things through *its lens* .

Я ещё слы́шу сквозь *сон*, как ложи́тся Ди́ма, но не могу́ откры́ть глаза́.
[I-NOM still hear through sleep-ACC, how goes-to-bed Dima-NOM, but not can open eyes-ACC.]
Through *the veil of sleep* , I can still hear Dima going to bed, but I can't open my eyes.

We should also note the common Russian expression смех сквозь слёзы [laughter-NOM through tears-ACC] 'laughter through *tears*', a metaphorical extension of the use of сквозь to the domain of the emotions, where one can bring forth a smile despite the trials and tribulations of life.

Че́рез likewise identifies a dimension through which something passes. The first example describes a money-laundering scheme where funds are being cycled through a firm in order to make it look like they have a legitimate origin. The firm provides the dimensions for this cycling activity:

че́рез + ACCUSATIVE: A DIMENSION in the domains of various activities means 'through'.

Они́ прокру́чивали че́рез *фи́рму* со́тни ты́сяч до́лларов.
[They-NOM cycled through firm-ACC hundreds-ACC thousands dollars-GEN.]
They cycled hundreds of thousands of dollars through *the firm* .

People can also serve this purpose when they act as go-betweens. Here Russian journalists provide a medium for the act of conveying:

Лишь немно́гим бойца́м удаётся переда́ть че́рез случа́йно *встре́ченных российских журнали́стов* запи́ску для ро́дственников.
[Only few soldiers-DAT manage convey through by-chance met Russian journalists-ACC note-ACC for relatives-GEN.]
Only a few soldiers manage to convey a note for their relatives via *Russian journalists that they meet* by chance.

ACCUSATIVE: AN ENDPOINT 1—Space as opposed to time

ACCUSATIVE: AN ENDPOINT is very similar to the ACCUSATIVE: A DIMENSION, except that it focuses just on one part of the accusative object, namely the one furthest away. The accusative object is thus reduced to its logical endpoint. ACCUSATIVE: AN ENDPOINT functions in only two domains, that of space and time; however, space and time actually function rather differently from each other. Imagine yourself standing on a certain spot at a certain time. Space stretches out from your spot in all directions equally. Since all directions are equal, they are all the same in some sense. In other words, if some object is one meter away from you, that fact is essentially the same regardless of the direction in which the object lies: it will always be *one meter* away

ACCUSATIVE: AN ENDPOINT is invoked in the domains of space and time.

An interval of space indicates a distance away.

A force (arrow) arrives at the
ACCUSATIVE:: AN ENDPOINT
(circle labeled A) of a domain

from you. Time is different. It stretches away from you in exactly two directions, and those directions are distinct from each other. One goes forward, into the future. And one goes backward, into the past. If an event is an hour away from you, it does matter which direction it lies in. The event will either happen *in an hour* or it will have happened *an hour ago*. We don't have any one way to say (in normal English) that an event is an hour away without indicating that it is future or past. The same goes for Russian. In terms of space, the ACCUSATIVE: AN ENDPOINT locates something as being a certain distance away (at the end of that distance), whereas in terms of time this meaning locates things as happening later, at the end of a certain period, or has having happened before, at or prior to the beginning of a certain period. In this way Russian shows a parallelism between the two concepts that we would express in English as I'll see him in *a week* and I saw him *a week* ago. In either case you have to reach one week away from where you are now to get to the point where the action is; you are always looking at something that happens at the far end of a week.

In the domain of space, there are three prepositions that identify endpoints: в, за, and чёрез. В is relatively infrequently used to locate items at a given distance, but here is one example:

В *один скачо́к* он очути́лся у двери.
[In one leap-ACC he-NOM found-self by door-GEN.]
In *one leap* he was at the door.

When за 'away' is used in the domain of space, it usually occurs in conjunction with от 'from' or до 'to' (which also means 'from' in this context), as in this example:

За *не́сколько* киломе́тров до го́рода авто́бус сорва́лся с обры́ва в ре́ку.
[Beyond several-ACC kilometers-GEN to city-GEN bus-NOM fell from precipice-GEN in river-ACC.]
Several kilometers before reaching the city the bus fell off the precipice into the river.

In its most simple manifestation, чёрез 'across' locates something at the opposite edge of an item as in клуб — чёрез *доро́гу* [club-NOM — across street-ACC] 'the club is across *the street*'. Usually, however, чёрез refers to something that is repeated in a series, such that you wind up skipping over every other object, as in the common teacher's instruction писа́ть чёрез *стро́чку* [write away line-ACC] 'skip *lines*/write *double-spaced*', which could be literally interpreted as 'go *one line* away and then write, and then repeat that pattern'. Here's an example to show how this works in context:

И чёрез *ка́ждую фра́зу* сло́вно подчёркивали: У Росси́и в ко́смосе всё хорошо́.
[And across every phrase-ACC as-if emphasized: By Russia-GEN in space-LOC all-NOM good.]
And it was as if *every other sentence* they were emphasizing: Everything is okay with the Russian space program.

Sidebar notes (left margin):

An interval of time indicates a point in the future or past.

ACCUSATIVE: AN ENDPOINT in the domain of space.

в + ACCUSATIVE: AN ENDPOINT in the domain of space means 'in'.

за + ACCUSATIVE: AN ENDPOINT in the domain of space means 'away'.

чёрез + ACCUSATIVE: AN ENDPOINT in the domain of space means 'across, after'.

ACCUSATIVE: AN ENDPOINT 2—Time as opposed to space

As we saw above, time differs in important ways from space. There are furthermore some special peculiarities about the way Russian uses ACCUSATIVE: AN ENDPOINT in time expressions. In addition to the usual use of prepositions (в, за, чёрез) followed by the accusative case, you will also see the accusative case preceding words indicating direction of time (these words act as postpositions triggering the accusative). This table gives an overview of the uses, using *одну неделю* [one week-ACC] '*one week*' as our unit of time:

ACCUSATIVE: AN ENDPOINT in the domain of time.

Time expressions associated with ACCUSATIVE:: AN ENDPOINT

time running forward: in, after, later

в *одну неделю*	[to one week-ACC]	in/ by *the end of a week*
за *одну неделю*	[to one week-ACC]	in/ by *the end of a week*
чёрез (*одну*) неделю	[across (one) week-ACC]	after *a week, a week* later; every *other week*
одну неделю погодя	[one week-ACC later]	*one week* later
одну неделю после того	[one week-ACC after that-GEN]	*one week* after that
одну неделю спустя	[one week-ACC later]	*one week* later

time running backward: ago, before

одну неделю до того/перед тем	[one week-ACC until that-GEN/before that-INST]	*one week* before that
за *одну неделю* до того/перед тем	[to one week-ACC until that-GEN/before that-INST]	*one week* before that
одну неделю назад	[one week-ACC ago]	*one week* ago

The preposition в is often used in reference to the ages of people to say 'at *the age of* X this person did Y'; literally it means 'at *the end of so many years* this person did Y':

в, за, and чёрез + ACCUSATIVE: AN ENDPOINT in the domain of time running forward means 'in, at, by the end of'.

> Наш дирижёр родился в семье музыкантов и уже в *пять* лет научился играть на фортепиано.
> [Our conductor-NOM was-born in family-LOC musicians-GEN and already to five-ACC years-GEN learned play on piano-LOC.]
> Our conductor was born in a family of musicians and already at the age of *five* he learned to play the piano.

The meaning of the preposition за is very similar here. You will notice that when за is used with an accusative time expression, if the sentence refers to a completed action (usually with a perfective verb), you get focus on the endpoint, whereas if a process or state is involved, then you have a duration (ACCUSATIVE: A DIMENSION). Here is an example of за expressing ACCUSATIVE: AN ENDPOINT:

> За *месяц* Дима превратился в обыкновенного человека.
> [To month-ACC Dima-NOM transformed to ordinary person-ACC.]
> By the end of *a month* Dima had become an ordinary person.

Че́рез typically indicates a time period that elapses before something else happens:

> Он поста́вил им ультима́тум: сда́ться че́рез *неде́лю*.
> [He-NOM set them-DAT ultimatum-ACC: give-up across week-ACC.]
> He set an ultimatum for them: give up by the end of *a week*.

> Буква́льно че́рез *час* к ней прие́дет расстре́льная брига́да.
> [Literally across hour-ACC to her-DAT arrives firing squad-NOM.]
> Literally in *one hour* a firing squad will arrive at her place.

When the context calls for periodic repetition (often by means of ка́ждый 'every'), then you get the temporal equivalent of what we saw with че́рез and intervals of space: things that happen at regular intervals of time:

> Че́рез *ка́ждую неде́лю* — медици́нский осмо́тр.
> [Across every week-ACC — medical examination-NOM.]
> There's a medical examination *every other week*.

ACCUSATIVE: AN ENDPOINT + спустя́ in the domain of time running forward means 'later'.

The postposition спустя́ 'later' (which can also be used as a preposition) gives Russian yet another way to say 'later' (just as we can also say *thereafter* and *after that*); here's an example:

> *Четы́ре го́да* спустя́, в 1904 году́ на и́грах в Сент-Лу́исе, же́нщины ста́ли ме́риться си́лами в стрельбе́ из лу́ка.
> [Four years-ACC later, in 1904 year-LOC at games-LOC in Saint Louis-LOC, women-NOM started compare strengths-INST in shooting-LOC from bow-GEN.]
> *Four years* later, in 1904 at the games in Saint Louis, women started to compare their abilities in archery.

ACCUSATIVE: AN ENDPOINT + наза́д/тому́ наза́д in the domain of time running backward means 'ago'.

The postposition наза́д is probably the most common Russian equivalent for 'ago'. Here are a couple of examples to show how it works:

> *Ме́сяц* наза́д я забы́ла у него́ очки́ от со́лнца.
> [Month-ACC ago I-NOM forgot by him-GEN glasses-ACC from sun-GEN.]
> *A month* ago I forgot my sunglasses at his place.

> *Неде́лю* наза́д я слы́шала по ра́дио переда́чу о сча́стье.
> [Week-ACC ago I-NOM heard along radio-DAT program-ACC about happiness-LOC.]
> *A week* ago I heard a program on the radio about happiness.

By the way, наза́д has a variant, тому́ наза́д, which also means 'ago' and is also preceded by ACCUSATIVE: AN ENDPOINT.

EPILOGUE

The word *accusative* is not very helpful in summing up this case, although you can think of the parallel between the force of an accusation being released upon the accused and the force of a verb being released upon an object. Accusation is indeed one kind of directed activity, and the accusative case is all about directed activity, particularly motion. Directed motion occupies a prominent place in the linguistic imagination of Russians, and they make a much crisper distinction between motion and location than we do in English. It doesn't matter how short the trip is: even the travel of our backside to a seat or the travel of hairpins to the place we lay them on the sink is described as a movement with a destination. Just looking at something constitutes a visual voyage. Once again our understanding of time is patterned after how we perceive space, motivating the conclusion that if a journey has a spatial destination, then an event has a temporal destination as well. Time is clearly conceived of in Russian as a unidimensional line stretching away from us in two directions. Change to a new state is comprehended as movement to a new location. Going to a destination behind an item can be interpreted as catching hold, replacing, or exceeding that item. Feeling nauseated or shaken up are not activities people engage in; these are things that just happen to us without any apparent agent. The dative case will continue this theme of forces directed at targets, albeit in a less immediate way.

DATIVE Forms

Feminine declension nouns				
hard type: 'room'		soft type: 'week'		
singular	plural	singular	plural	
ко́мнате	ко́мнатам	неде́ле	неде́лям	

-ь: 'talent'	
singular	plural
спосо́бности	спосо́бностям

Masculine declension nouns

hard type: 'courtyard'		soft type: 'nail'	
singular	plural	singular	plural
двору́	двора́м	гвоздю́	гвоздя́м

Neuter declension nouns

hard type: 'body'		soft type: 'schedule'	
singular	plural	singular	plural
те́лу	тела́м	расписа́нию	расписа́ниям

Adjectives

hard type: 'first'			
feminine	masculine	neuter	plural
пе́рвой	пе́рвому	пе́рвому	пе́рвым

soft type: 'last'			
feminine	masculine	neuter	plural
после́дней	после́днему	после́днему	после́дним

Pronouns

'I'	'we'	'you' informal	'you'
мне	нам	тебе́	вам

'she'	'he'	'it'	'they'
(н)ей	(н)ему́	(н)ему́	(н)им

'who'	'what'	'oneself'	
кому́	чему́	себе́	

'this'			
feminine	masculine	neuter	plural
э́той	э́тому	э́тому	э́тим

'all, every'			
feminine	masculine	neuter	plural
всей	всему́	всему́	всем

Possessives

feminine	masculine	neuter	plural
'my'			
мое́й	моему́	моему́	мои́м

'our'			
на́шей	на́шему	на́шему	на́шим

Numerals

'one'			
feminine	masculine	neuter	plural
одно́й	одному́	одному́	одни́м

'two'	'three'	'four'	'five'
двум	трём	четырём	пяти́

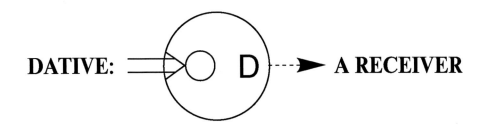

The dative network:

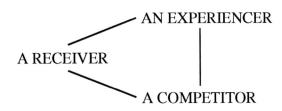

Prologue

Imagine for a moment that you are playing Mad Libs, and you are asked to supply some words, so you suggest *flowerpot*, *mud puddle*, and *refrigerator*. Then the leader of the game reads the story: "Philanthropists are people who like to help flowerpots. Some of them are very gullible and will believe every mud puddle they meet. These do-gooders will even give a refrigerator their last dime." Although they are all grammatically correct, these sentences are not representative of the ordinary repertoire of English. The fun of this game in fact consists in creating nonsensical sentences such as these. The three Mad Libs sentences created here are strange because there is a clash between the expectations of constructions containing *help*, *believe*, and *give* and words like *flowerpot*, *mud puddle*, and *refrigerator* which fail to meet these expectations. All three constructions presume that the object is most likely to be a human being. Help is meaningless to a flowerpot because it cannot appreciate the benefit it receives. A mud puddle doesn't have a story to tell and cannot inspire belief. A refrigerator cannot do anything with money, so there is no point in giving it any. The reason that inanimate objects don't work in these contexts is that they are incapable of serving as the subjects of further action. If you were to play this round of Mad Libs in Russian, you would put all three words in the dative case because the verbs помогáть 'help', вéрить 'believe', and дать 'give' would require you to do so, but they still wouldn't make any more sense in Russian than in English. The dative case shows that all three contexts have something in common, and as we saw above, they all share the expectation that the dative item is capable of being a subject. This doesn't mean that all dative items are going to be human or even animate, but it does mean that when you are dealing with a dative item, it is likely to be able to react or at least to exert forces of its own.

There are three meanings to the dative, all of which involve the dative's capacity to interact with its surroundings. The first two meanings are relatively passive, involving receiving objects (DATIVE: A RECEIVER) and absorbing experiences (DATIVE: AN EXPERIENCER), whereas the third one is relatively active, involving exerting equal or superior strength in relation to something else (DATIVE: A COMPETITOR).

A dative item is one that can react or exert forces of its own.

An overview of the dative case.

DATIVE: A RECEIVER 1—The indirect object

DATIVE: A RECIEVER involves the transfer of an object from one thing or person to another, as in *Sally gave the book to John*. The thing or person on the receiving end (John) is marked with the dative. You might recognize this as the indirect object (the direct object, of course, is the book, marked in the accusative). As we will see, the tricky thing about Russian is that you can sometimes have an indirect object (DATIVE: A RECEIVER) without an obvious direct object (ACCUSATIVE: A DESTINATION). But let's start with some straightforward examples.

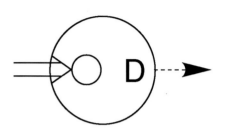

A force (arrow) brings an item (small circle) to a DATIVE: A RECEIVER (circle labeled D), which has the potential to exert a force (dotted arrow)

Giving is a universal experience of human interaction, and it serves as the logical starting point for the meanings of the dative. Russian has two verbs for 'give': давáть/дать (which can have many prefixes) and дарúть/подарúть, and the following examples illustrate their use with the dative:

> Дориáн обхóдит свойх учеников, раздаёт *им* нóты.
> [Dorian-NOM walk-around own pupils-ACC, gives-out them-DAT music-ACC.]
> Dorian makes the rounds of his pupils, handing out music *to them*.

> Идéя былá моя́, я самá подарúла её *своему́ начáльнику*.
> [Idea-NOM was mine-NOM, I myself-NOM gave it-ACC own boss-DAT.]
> The idea was mine, I gave it *to my boss* myself.

You can see that these sentences have parallel structures, as indicated in this table:

subject	verb	*indirect object*	direct object
Dorian	hands out	*to pupils*	music
I	gave	*to my boss*	the idea

You can also see that both the pupils and the boss are much more than passive destinations for the music and the idea. In both instances we presume that they are going to do something with what they have received: the pupils are probably going to play the music on their instruments, and the boss is probably going to implement the idea. Even if they fail to do anything, the fact that they could do something is crucial here.

Giving need not involve tangible objects. In English we can offer more abstract, metaphorical "gifts", such as chances and opportunities, and the same goes for Russian:

> *Ему́* дáли шанс вы́платить долгú по кредúтам.
> [Him-DAT gave chance-ACC pay-off debts-ACC along credits-DAT.]
> They gave *him* the chance to pay off his debts on credit.

Смея́сь, мы широко́ открыва́ем рот, напряга́я все мы́шцы лица́, и даём возмо́жность по́лностью рассла́биться *други́м мы́шцам.*

[Laughing, we-NOM widely open mouth-ACC, tensing all muscles-ACC face-GEN, and give opportunity-ACC completely relax other muscles-DAT.]

When we laugh, we open wide our mouth, tensing all the muscles in our face, and we give *our other muscles* an opportunity to completely relax.

Acts of transferring objects from one party to another are fairly widespread; in English, for example we can *send*, *offer*, *supply*, and *deliver* things to other people. We can even extend this idea of making something available to someone to words like *buy* (She bought *me* a ticket) and *show* (He showed *me* his report card). These words aren't really synonyms of *give*, but they share the same basic conceptual structure, and it is no surprise that in Russian words like these will also have dative indirect objects, as we see in the following table and examples:

> Words meaning 'transfer' or 'make available' trigger DATIVE: A RECEIVER.

Expressions of giving associated with DATIVE: A RECEIVER

'return'
возвраща́ть/возврати́ть/верну́ть

'deliver, entrust'
вруча́ть/вручи́ть
вруче́ние 'delivery'

'give out, issue'
выдава́ть/вы́дать
вы́дача 'issue'

'give'
дава́ть/дать

'give as a gift'
дари́ть/подари́ть
даре́ние 'giving'
пода́рок 'gift'

'bequeath'
завеща́ть

'render'
ока́зывать/оказа́ть

'leave (for)'
оставля́ть/оста́вить

'send, dispatch'
отправля́ть/отпра́вить

'pass, convey'
передава́ть/переда́ть
переда́ча 'passing; broadcast'

'show'
пока́зывать/показа́ть
показа́ние 'testimony, evidence'

'buy'
покупа́ть/купи́ть

'entrust'
поруча́ть/поручи́ть

'dedicate'
посвяща́ть/посвяти́ть
посвяще́ние, 'dedication'

'supply'
поставля́ть/поста́вить
поста́вка 'supply, delivery'

'send'
посыла́ть/посла́ть
посы́лка 'sending; parcel'

'offer'
предлага́ть/предложи́ть
предложе́ние 'offer'

'grant'
предоставля́ть/предоста́вить
предоставле́ние 'grant(ing)'

'bring'
приноси́ть/принести́
приноше́ние 'bringing'

'sell'
продава́ть/прода́ть
прода́жа 'sale'

'hand out, distribute'
раздава́ть/разда́ть
разда́ча 'distribution'

'hand over, surrender'
сдава́ть/сдать
сда́ча 'handing over, surrender'

DATIVE: A
RECEIVER in the
context of
transfer.

Па́ртия монархи́стов напра́вила письмо́ *англи́йскому при́нцу Эдва́рду* с про́сьбой стать эсто́нским королём.
[Party-NOM monarchists-GEN sent letter-ACC English prince Edward-DAT with request-INST become Estonian King-INST.]
The monarchist party sent a letter *to the English Prince Edward* with a request that he become King of Estonia.

Кита́й поставля́л *Ира́ну* компоне́нты, кото́рые мо́гут быть испо́льзованы для созда́ния я́дерного ору́жия.
[China-NOM supplied Iran-DAT components-ACC, which-NOM can be used-NOM for creation-GEN nuclear weapons-GEN.]
China supplied components *to Iran* that can be used to create nuclear weapons.

DATIVE: A
RECEIVER in the
context of
metaphorical
transfer.

Transfer of objects with a variety of verbs also lends itself to abstract, metaphorical usage. Granting status and selling your soul involve a transfer that is more fictive than actual, but still the connection with giving is clear:

Он та́кже предложи́л предоста́вить *восточноевропе́йским стра́нам* ста́тус наблюда́телей при Западноевропе́йском сою́зе.
[He-NOM also suggested grant East-European countries-DAT status-ACC observers-GEN at West-European union-LOC.]
He also suggested granting *the East European countries* the status of observers in the West European union.

Все ду́шу *дья́волу* продаю́т, а я подари́л беспла́тно.
[Everyone-NOM soul-ACC devil-DAT sell, but I-NOM gave for-free.]
Everyone sells their soul *to the devil*, but I gave mine for free.

DATIVE: A
RECEIVER in the
context of
creation.

Another way to give someone something is by creating the gift for the person. If I say *I'll bake you a cake for your birthday*, I'm promising to bring the cake into existence so that you will receive it; in Russian you would be the DATIVE: A RECEIVER. All kinds of words involving making things can be recruited for this purpose, such as building, cooking, sewing, etc. Here's an example:

Себе́ она́ ничего́ не постро́ила.
[Self-DAT she-NOM nothing-GEN not built.]
She didn't build anything *for herself.*

DATIVE: A
RECEIVER in the
absence 'give'.

The force of the dative case is so strong that the role of DATIVE: A RECEIVER comes through loud and clear even when there is no word indicating giving at all, as in this example:

Насле́дники, три бра́та и сестра́, переруга́лись, обсужда́я что — *кому́.*
[Heirs-NOM, three brothers-NOM and sister-NOM cussed-each-other-out, discussing what-NOM who-DAT.]
The heirs, three brothers and a sister, cussed each other out while discussing what would go/be given *to whom.*

You will also recognize this verb-less construction in the formulaic phrase Слáва *Бóгу* [Glory-NOM God-DAT] 'Glory *to God*'.

DATIVE: A RECEIVER 2—Indirect objects without direct objects

The remaining uses of the DATIVE: A RECEIVER submeaning are not indirect objects in the classic sense because they don't have any ACCUSATIVE: A DESTINATION direct objects. However, they do involve the transfer of something to a receiver, even if that something is not explicitly named in the accusative case, and for this reason we can think of these uses as being very close relatives to the indirect object. Usually the "missing" direct objects can be found in the meaning of the trigger word; for example, verbs of communication all involve the transfer of a signal to a receiver, and these verbs take the dative case. When you make a contribution to a worthy cause, it is not necessary to specify that you gave them money, we still understand the charitable organization as the receiver even when the money is not mentioned. It is also possible for something to bring itself to a receiver, in which case the "missing" direct object is the subject of the sentence. Each of these types of indirect objects will be taken up below.

There is quite a selection of words that express delivering signals to receivers. For convenience they can be broken down into two groups: those that involve talking and those that do not. In most instances you can easily recover the "missing" direct object by restating these words as 'give a signal to X', where the signal is the direct object and X is the DATIVE: A RECEIVER. Because the signal is already implicit in the word, we can skip right over it and go directly to the receiver. This table contains some of the communication words associated with the dative that you are likely to encounter:

DATIVE: A RECEIVER can express the indirect object without a direct object.

"Missing" direct objects include signals, money and gifts, and the self.

DATIVE: A RECEIVER in the context of giving signals.

Expressions of communication associated with DATIVE: A RECEIVER

communication: talking

'thanks to' благодаря́	'call' звони́ть/позвони́ть звонóк 'call'	'explain' объясня́ть/объясни́ть
'order' веле́ть/повеле́ть	'flatter' льстить/польсти́ть	'answer' отвеча́ть/отве́тить отве́т 'answer'
'say вы to' вы́кать вы́кание 'saying вы to'	'pray' моли́ться/помоли́ться моли́тва 'prayer' моле́бен 'prayer service' моля́щийся 'person who is praying'	'say yes to' подда́кивать/подда́кнуть подда́кивание 'saying yes to'
'speak, tell' говори́ть/сказа́ть		'order' прика́зывать/приказа́ть приказа́ние 'order'
'threaten' грози́ть/пригрози́ть угрóза 'threat'	'remind' напомина́ть/напóмнить напомина́ние 'reminder'	'protest' протестова́ть проте́ст 'protest'
	'promise' обеща́ть	

Expressions of communication associated with DATIVE: A RECEIVER (continued)

communication: talking

'report, inform'
сообща́ть/сообщи́ть
сообще́ние 'report, communication'

'advise'
сове́товать/посове́товать
сове́т 'advice'

'say ты to'
ты́кать
ты́кание 'saying ты to'

'read (out loud) to'
чита́ть/прочита́ть (вслух)

communication: other signals

'applaud'
аплоди́ровать

'nod'
кива́ть/кивну́ть

'bow'
кла́няться/поклони́ться
покло́н 'bow'

'wave'
маха́ть/помаха́ть

'blink, wink'
морга́ть/моргну́ть

'write'
писа́ть/написа́ть
письмо́ 'letter'

'wink'
подми́гивать/подмигну́ть
подми́гивание 'winking'

'message, epistle'
посла́ние

'radio'
ради́ровать

'applaud, clap'
рукоплеска́ть
рукоплеска́ние 'applause'

'signal'
сигна́лить
сигнализи́ровать(ся)
сигна́л 'signal'

'laugh'
смея́ться/посмея́ться

'telegraph'
телеграфи́ровать

'smile'
улыба́ться/улыбну́ться

'grin'
усмеха́ться/усмехну́ться

The following three examples illustrate how communication words involving talking are used with the dative:

Сего́дня он напомина́ет *мне*: в январе́ испыта́ния но́вого стеклопла́стика должны́ быть зако́нчены.

[Today he-NOM reminds me-DAT: in January-LOC tests-NOM new plexiglass-GEN should-NOM be finished-NOM.]

Today he reminds *me*: the tests on the new plexiglass should be finished in January.

Я позвони́л *заве́дующему* спорти́вной ка́федрой.

[I-NOM called head-DAT athletic department-INST.]

I called *the head* of the athletic department.

А я отвеча́ю *ему́*, что я тра́чу то́лько на еду́.

[And I-NOM answer him-DAT, that I-NOM spend only on food-ACC.]

And I answer *him* that I only spend money on food.

There are some communication verbs that do not use the dative case. Благодари́ть/поблагодари́ть 'thank' has an accusative direct object, but it used to take the dative, and the preposition благодаря́ 'thanks to' still does:

Населе́ние Се́рбской Респу́блики благодаря́ *свои́м поли́тикам* уже́ раско́лото ме́жду Па́ле и Ба́ня-Лу́кой.

[Population-NOM Serbian Republic-GEN thanks own politicians-DAT already split-NOM between Pale-INST and Banja-Luka-INST.]

Thanks to *its politicians* the population of the Republic of Serbia is already split between Pale and Banja-Luka.

As you see in the table above, communication through bodily gestures and electrical signals is likewise directed to DATIVE: A RECEIVER. Here is an example so you can see the parallel with verbs of verbal communication:

Он поклони́лся *актри́се.*

[He-NOM bowed actress-DAT.]

He bowed *to the actress.*

In both Russian and English there are some verbs that mean 'give money or a gift', such as *pay* and *donate.* Because the idea that money or a gift is involved is already part of the word, it doesn't need to appear as an accusative direct object, just like the signals above. Here are some of the words you can expect to see with DATIVE: A RECEIVER, along with an example to illustrate:

> DATIVE: A RECEIVER in the context of giving money or gifts.

Expressions of giving money associated with DATIVE: A RECEIVER

'donate'	'compensate'	'pay'
же́ртвовать/поже́ртвовать	компенси́ровать	плати́ть/заплати́ть
поже́ртвование 'donation'	компенса́ция 'compensation'	пла́та, зарпла́та 'pay, wages'
		'change (money back)'
		сда́ча

Я в состоя́нии заплати́ть *гра́жданам* за грехи́ предыду́щих прави́телей.

[I-NOM in condition-LOC pay citizens-DAT for sins-ACC previous rulers-GEN.]

I am in a position to pay *the citizens* for the sins of their previous rulers.

DATIVE: A RECEIVER 3—Giving the self

As an alternative to presenting something to a DATIVE: A RECEIVER, the subject can simply present itself, and this can impact the receiver in two ways. The subject can physically bring itself to the receiver, or it can bring itself merely to the perception of the receiver, usually with verbs meaning 'appear (in a dream)', 'seem', 'make an impression'. Here are some words that commonly indicate the giving of the self to a DATIVE: A RECEIVER:

> DATIVE: A RECEIVER in the context of giving the self.

Expressions of appearance and manifestation associated with DATIVE: A RECEIVER

'appear to in a dream'	'come to; allow oneself to be caught by'	'go to, fall to one's lot, be inherited by'
гре́зиться/пригре́зиться	дава́ться/да́ться	достава́ться/доста́ться

Expressions of appearance and manifestation associated with DATIVE: A RECEIVER (contin-

'become fixed in one's memory' запо́мниться	'seem to' каза́ться/показа́ться	'introduce oneself to' представля́ться/предста́виться представле́ние 'introduction'
'known to' изве́стный	'appear to, haunt' мере́щиться/помере́щиться	'go in front of, precede' предше́ствовать
'impress' импони́ровать	'toward' навстре́чу	'appear to in a dream' сни́ться/присни́ться

Money presents itself to receivers in two situations in this example. In the first instance the receiver is an individual on a payroll (who pays attention to how much is in his check), whereas in the second one it is an anonymous firm (that will sign off on any amount of money):

Ведь зарпла́та достаётся *коне́чному потреби́телю*, кото́рый допо́длинно зна́ет, получи́л он миллио́н и́ли полмиллио́на, в то вре́мя как инвестицио́нные де́ньги ухо́дят *фи́рме*, кото́рая за́просто мо́жет расписа́ться за любо́е коли́чество де́нег.
[After-all salary-NOM goes end user-DAT, who-NOM for-certain knows, received he-NOM million-ACC or half-million-ACC, in that time-ACC as investment money-NOM goes firm-DAT, which-NOM simply can sign for any amount-ACC money-GEN.]
After all a salary goes *to the end user*, who knows for certain whether he received a million or half a million, whereas investment money goes *to a firm* which can simply sign for any amount of money.

Ultimately many verbs of motion can be used to bring the subject to a receiver; the preposition навстре́чу 'toward, to meet' is often used to enhance this meaning:

Навстре́чу *мне* спеши́т экономи́ческий обозрева́тель.
[Toward me-DAT hurries economic reviewer-NOM.]
The economic reviewer comes hurrying toward *me*.

'Seeming' and 'appearing' function as metaphorical extensions of giving the self.

The following three examples are of the metaphoric type. In all cases the subject is presenting itself to the perception of the receiver, by making an appearance (to waking or dreaming consciousness) or by making an impression.

До сего́дняшнего дня моя́ лаборато́рия каза́лась *мне* святы́м ме́стом.
[Until today's day-GEN my laboratory-NOM seemed me-DAT holy place-INST.]
Up to the present day my laboratory has seemed *to me* to be a holy place.

Недáвно *емý* снúлась дéвушка из сосéдней квартúры.
[Recently him-DAT appeared-in-dream girl-NOM from next-door apartment-GEN.]
Recently the girl from the apartment next door appeared *to him* in a dream.

Я замéтил, что на Тáсю обращáют внимáние. Э́то импонúровало *мне*.
[I-NOM noticed, that on Tasya-ACC turn attention-ACC. That-NOM impressed me-DAT.]
I noticed that people were paying attention to Tasya. That impressed *me*.

DATIVE: AN EXPERIENCER 1—Benefit

Something happens to a DATIVE: AN EXPERIENCER, and the dative item absorbs that experience. You can think of this as a diluted version of DATIVE: A RECEIVER; here the dative doesn't get something, instead it gets just an experience of something. Words meaning 'show' and 'appear to' are transitional examples, demonstrating the link between DATIVE: A RECEIVER and DATIVE: AN EXPERIENCER. We use the dative case for experiences because the DATIVE: AN EXPERIENCER is capable of appreciating the impact of whatever action or state it is exposed to. Experiences can be good and bad, thus benefiting or harming the DATIVE: AN EXPERIENCER. Possession and need are also common experiences, and then there are many miscellaneous experiences that don't fit into neat categories. Let's start with the good experiences that bring benefit to the DATIVE: AN EXPERIENCER.

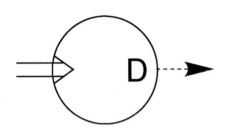

A force (arrow) acts on a DATIVE:: AN EXPERIENCER (circle labeled D), which has the potential to exert a force (dotted arrow)

Kindness comes in many forms, and there is a wealth of ways in which something or someone can bring benefit. Here is a table of words that you can expect to see accompanied by DATIVE: AN EXPERIENCER:

DATIVE: AN EXPERIENCER expresses an item exposed to benefit/harm, possession/need, external forces, ease/difficulty, or obligation/desire.

DATIVE: AN EXPERIENCER in the context of benefit.

Expressions of benefit associated with DATIVE:: AN EXPERIENCER

'thankful to' благодáрный	'please' нрáвиться/понрáвиться	'help' помогáть/помóчь пóмощь 'help'
'favor' благоприя́тствовать	'allow, permit' позволя́ть/позвóлить позвóленный 'permitted'	'forgive, pardon' прощáть/простúть
'be lucky' везтú/повезтú	'patronize, support' покровúтельствовать покровúтельствующий 'patron' покровúтельство 'patronage'	'sympathize' симпатизúровать симпатúчен 'nice'
'be good for' годúться гóдный		симпáтия 'sympathy' симпатизúрующий 'supporter'
	'become attractive to' полюбúться	
'suit, become' идтú		

Expressions of benefit associated with DATIVE:: AN EXPERIENCER (continued)

'serve' служи́ть/послужи́ть слу́жба/служе́ние 'service'	'sympathize' сочу́вствовать сочу́вственный 'sympathetic' сочу́вствие 'sympathy'	'useful' поле́зный по́льза 'use'
'sympathize, condole' соболе́зновать соболе́знование 'sympathy, condolence'	'assist, facilitate' спосо́бствовать спосо́бствование 'assistance'	'pleasant' прия́тный 'convenient' удо́бный
'assist, help' соде́йствовать соде́йствие 'assistance'	'please' угожда́ть/угоди́ть	

Here are some examples of relatively concrete assistance given to a DATIVE: AN EXPERIENCER:

Он позво́лит *на́шей нефтяно́й промы́шленности* реши́ть свои́ пробле́мы.
[He-NOM will-allow our oil industry-DAT solve own problems-ACC.]
He will allow *our oil industry* to solve its own problems.

С э́того моме́нта президе́нт покрови́тельствовал *на́шему мэ́ру.*
[From that moment-GEN president-NOM supported our mayor-DAT.]
From that moment on, the president supported *our mayor.*

The next two examples illustrate 'serving' in a relatively metaphorical sense:

О́ба бо́льше жи́зни люби́ли литерату́ру и ка́ждый по-сво́ему, но одина́ково пре́данно служи́ли *ей.*
[Both-NOM more life-GEN loved literature-ACC and each-NOM in-own-way, but equally devotedly served it-DAT.]
They both loved literature more than life itself and each one did so in their own way, but they served *it* with equal devotion.

Телевизио́нный коммента́тор заме́тил, что духо́вного совершенства мо́жно дости́чь про́сто ве́рой и служе́нием *добру́.*
[Television commentator-NOM remarked, that spiritual perfection-GEN possible attain simply faith-INST and serving-INST good-DAT.]
The television commentator remarked that it is possible to attain spiritual perfection simply through faith and by serving *good.*

DATIVE: AN EXPERIENCER with нра́виться/ понра́виться 'like'.

To express 'like' (any attraction weaker than full-blown love), Russian uses the verb meaning 'please' нра́виться/понра́виться with the dative, and the logical structure of the sentence is the inverse of what we have in English, so you-NOM please me-DAT, really means 'I like you'. Here's an example of how this works in Russian:

Мне нра́вяться те, *кому́* нра́влюсь я.
[Me-DAT please those-NOM, who-DAT please I-NOM.]
I like people *who* like me.

The use of the verb идти́ with the dative to mean 'suit, become' is idiomatic, but then so is the use of English *go* in phrases like *go well with*. In this example, age goes well with Shurochka's looks:

Idiomatic use of
DATIVE: AN
EXPERIENCER with
идти́ to express
'suit, become'.

У Шу́рочки был тот тип вне́шности, *кото́рому* идёт во́зраст.
[By Shurochka-GEN was that type-NOM appearance-GEN, which-DAT suits age-NOM.]
Shurochka had the type of appearance *that* is improved by age.

DATIVE: AN EXPERIENCER 2—Harm

Russian has a rich variety of expressions for harm inflicted upon a DATIVE: AN EXPERIENCER. Some of the most common ones are in this table. You will notice that грози́ть 'threaten' shows up both here and under verbs of communication above. This verb is just as ambiguous in Russian as it is in English; a threat can be construed either as a message delivered to a DATIVE: A RECEIVER or as a physical reality endured by a DATIVE: AN EXPERIENCER.

DATIVE: AN
EXPERIENCER in
the context of
harm.

Expressions of harm associated with DATIVE:: AN EXPERIENCER

'oppose, object' возража́ть/возрази́ть возраже́ние 'objection'	'annoy' досажда́ть/досади́ть	'bore' наску́чить
'in spite of, against, contrary to' вопреки́	'envy' зави́довать	'grow hateful to' опосты́леть
'hostile' враждебный	'forbid' запреща́ть/запрети́ть	'bore, repel' осточерте́ть
'injure, harm' вреди́ть/повреди́ть вре́дный 'harmful' вред 'harm'	'betray' изменя́ть/измени́ть изме́на 'betrayal'	'contradict' пере́чить
'threaten' грози́ть/пригрози́ть	'hinder, annoy' меша́ть/помеша́ть поме́ха 'hinder, annoy'	'prefer (something else) over' предпочита́ть/ предпоче́сть
'be rude to' груби́ть/нагруби́ть	'take revenge' мсти́ть/отомсти́ть месть 'revenge'	'hinder, interfere' препя́тствовать
'be impertinent to' дерзи́ть/надерзи́ть	'get on nerves of' надоеда́ть/надое́сть	'oppose' проти́виться/ воспроти́виться проти́вный 'opposite, contrary' противле́ние 'opposition'
		'oppose, fight against' противобо́рствовать

Expressions of harm associated with DATIVE:: AN EXPERIENCER (continued)

'oppose, counteract' противодействовать	'resist, oppose' сопротивляться сопротивляемость 'resistance, opposition'	'difficult' трудный
'oppose, contrast' противопоставлять/ противопоставить противопоставление 'opposing, contrasting'	'threaten' угрожать угроза 'threat'	'alien' чуждый 'opposition' оппозиция
'contradict' противоречить противоречие 'contradiction'	'offensive' обидный	'detriment' ущерб

Here is an example of a physical threat to a DATIVE: EXPERIENCER, that of AIDS:

И если все "прелести" наркомании грозят *конкретному человеку, самому принимающему* решение "быть или не быть", то СПИД, разносимый грязными шприцами ловцов грёз, грозит *нам всем*.
[And if all "charms"-NOM drug-abuse-GEN threaten concrete person-DAT, self receiving-DAT decision-ACC "be or not be", then AIDS-NOM, spread-NOM dirty syringes-INST catchers-GEN dreams-GEN, threatens us all-DAT.]
And if all the "charms" of drug abuse threaten *a concrete person who himself makes* the decision "to be or not to be", then AIDS, spread by dream-seekers' dirty needles, threatens *us all*.

In the context of an amorous relationship, изменять/изменить refers more specifically to betrayal:

И тут жена стала *ему* изменять. Причём неразборчиво и беспрерывно.
[And here wife-NOM began him-DAT betray. Moreover promiscuously and continually.]
And then his wife began to cheat *on him*. And she did it promiscuously and continually.

Showing a preference for one thing over another causes some harm to that second thing. In Russian the item that is negatively impacted by preference appears in the dative:

Современный зритель часто *пышному зрелищу*, где герои декламируют монологи из классических пьес, предпочитает сладкое пение поп-звёзд из Гонконга.
[Contemporary viewer-NOM often lavish spectacle-DAT, where heroes-NOM recite monologues-ACC from classical plays-GEN, prefers sweet singing-ACC pop-stars-GEN from Hong Kong-GEN.]

The contemporary viewer often prefers the sweet singing of pop-stars from Hong Kong *over the lavish spectacle* of heroes reciting monologues from classical plays.

The following two examples show harm expressed by an adjective and a noun, both triggering the use of the dative:

> *Ей* проти́вен сам звук твоего́ го́лоса.
> [Her-DAT repulsive-NOM self sound-NOM your voice-GEN.]
> The very sound of your voice is repulsive *to her*.

> Трамва́и бы́ли отменены́ почти́ 40 лет наза́д, поско́льку, по мне́нию власте́й, они́ создава́ли поме́хи *тра́нспортным пото́кам*.
> [Trams-NOM were abolished-NOM almost 40-ACC years-GEN ago, since, according opinion-DAT authorities-GEN, they-NOM created hindrances-ACC transportation streams-DAT.]
> Trams were abolished almost 40 years ago because according to the authorities they were a hindrance *to the flow of transportation*.

The preposition вопреки́ 'in spite of, against, contrary to' is used with the dative for adversarial relationships; here is an example of how it works:

> В после́дние ме́сяцы вопреки́ *свои́м идеологи́ческим устано́вкам* он позво́лил провести́ лёгкую экономи́ческую либерализа́цию в стране́.
> [In last months-ACC contrary own ideological aims-DAT he-NOM allowed carry-out light economic liberalization-ACC in country-LOC.]
> Contrary to *his ideological aims*, he allowed a mild economic liberalization to be carried out in the country in recent months.

DATIVE: AN EXPERIENCER 3—Having and needing

Remember that we started our discussion of the dative with verbs meaning 'give'. The final state that the dative ultimately reaches as a result of "giving" is "having". In this use of the DATIVE: AN EXPERIENCER, the dative item experiences possession and related states of having, such as availablility, having knowledge of, and need (the state when having is desired).

DATIVE: AN EXPERIENCER in the contexts of possession, availability, and necessity.

Expressions of having and needing associated with DATIVE:: AN EXPERIENCER

'belong to' принадлежа́ть	'suffice' хвата́ть	'known to' изве́стный изве́стно 'known to'
'be necessary to' тре́боваться/потре́боваться	'sufficient' доста́точный доста́точно 'sufficient(ly)'	'possible' мо́жно

Expressions of having and needing associated with DATIVE:: AN EXPERIENCER (continued)

'impossible' невозмо́жно	'required' обяза́тельный обяза́тельно 'required'	'characteristic of' сво́йственный сво́йственно 'characteristic of'
'need' ну́жный/ну́жен 'needed' ну́жно; на́до 'need to'	'inherent, characteristic' прису́щий	

Here are some examples using the trigger words in the table to express states of having:

> *Вам*, скоре́е всего́, потре́буются бо́льшие су́ммы, чем обы́чно.
> [You-DAT, rather all-GEN, will-be-needed larger sums-NOM, than usual.]
> *You* will probably need larger sums of money than usual.

> *Ему́* для равнове́сия с ми́ром доста́точно два-три бли́зких челове́ка.
> [Him-DAT for balance-GEN with world-INST sufficient two-three close people-NOM.]
> To keep his balance with the world *he* needs only two or three people to be close to.

> *Ему́* изве́стны литерату́рные та́йны про́шлого и бу́дущего.
> [Him-DAT known-NOM literary secrets-NOM past-GEN and future-GEN.]
> *He* knows the literary secrets of the past and the future.

In English we can say that people *have it in them* or that they *have a tendency* to do something, and this tendency that they have is a characteristic; here is a Russian example that uses this kind of logic:

> *Лю́дям* сво́йственно наде́яться и ве́рить в хоро́шее.
> [People-DAT characteristically hope and believe in good-ACC.]
> *People* tend to hope and to believe in good.

The most common way to express need and necessity is with ну́жный/ну́жен 'needed' or ну́жно/на́до 'need to', and similar to нра́виться/понра́виться 'like', the grammatical force of the construction is the opposite of what we have in English. Instead of our needing things, in Russian things are needed to *us*:

> А мо́жет, она́ вообще́ не нужна́ *мне* бо́льше, э́та любо́вь?
> [And perhaps, it-NOM at-all not needed-NOM me-DAT further, this love-NOM?]
> And perhaps *I* don't need it at all anymore, this love?

> *Нам* на́до рабо́тать так, что́бы был и́збран президе́нт, спосо́бный гаранти́ровать разви́тие Росси́и по демократи́ческому пути́.
> [Us-DAT needed work thus, so-that was chosen-NOM president-NOM, capable-NOM guarantee development-ACC Russia-GEN along democratic path-DAT.]

We have to work so that a president is chosen who is capable of guaranteeing Russia's development along the path to democracy.

The DATIVE: AN EXPERIENCER can express possession even without a trigger word like those in the table. Most frequently this happens with body parts which (barring catastrophic accident) belong to the person who inhabits the body. The grammatical logic of the following three sentences is as follows. Russian 'the soldier broke *to him* the head' is equivalent to 'the soldier broke *his* head' because *he* experiences having the head (and the damage thereto). In the same way, 'the old woman looks *to me* into the mouth' is equivalent to 'the old woman looks at *my* mouth', and 'the woman places *to me* onto shoulder hand' is equivalent to 'the woman places her hand on *my* shoulder'.

> Солда́т проломи́л *ему́* го́лову бля́хой.
> [Soldier-NOM broke him-DAT head-ACC name-plate-INST.]
> The soldier broke *his* head with the name-plate.

(By the way, the soldier broke someone else's head, not his own. If it had been his own head, we would see *себе́* [self-DAT] '*himself*' instead of *ему́.*)

> Стару́ха смо́трит *мне* пря́мо в рот и ждёт разу́много сове́та.
> [Old-woman-NOM looks me-DAT straight into mouth-ACC and waits reasonable advice-GEN.]
> The old woman looks right at *my* mouth and waits for reasonable advice.

> Же́нщина кладёт *мне* на плечо́ ру́ку худу́ю, как пти́чья ла́па.
> [Woman-NOM places me-DAT onto shoulder-ACC hand thin-ACC, like bird's foot-NOM.]
> The woman places her hand on *my* shoulder, and it is thin, like a bird's foot.

> Води́тель останови́л маши́ну, отре́зал *зве́рю* хвост, и уе́хал.
> [Driver-NOM stopped vehicle-ACC, cut-off animal-DAT tail-ACC, and rode-away.]
> The driver stopped his vehicle, cut off the *animal's* tail, and drove away.

The only significant exception to the rule that this kind of possession involves body parts is the use of the DATIVE: AN EXPERIENCER with the word конéц; note that this is parallel to our use in English of *to* with this word as in the translation of this example:

> Конца́ *беспоко́йству* не ви́дно.
> [End-GEN upset-DAT not visible.]
> There's no end *to the upset* in sight.

In English when we want to talk about the lack of an opportunity, we can say that someone *has no one to turn to, has nowhere to go, has nothing to hope for.* Russian can express this state of not having a choice by putting the prefix не- on the missing item and using the DATIVE: AN EXPERIENCER, as in these examples:

Margin notes:

DATIVE: AN EXPERIENCER expresses possession of body parts.

DATIVE: AN EXPERIENCER expresses having an end with конéц.

DATIVE: AN EXPERIENCER expresses not having any options with не-.

Я прошу́ проще́ния за изли́шние подро́бности в описа́нии, но *мне* про́сто не́кому об э́том рассказа́ть.
[I-NOM beg forgiveness-GEN for excessive details-ACC in description-LOC, but me-DAT simply no-one-DAT about this-LOC tell.]
I beg your forgiveness for the excessive detail in my description, but *I* simply *don't have* anyone to tell this to.

Обеща́ли, что *че́стным лю́дям* не́чего боя́ться.
[Promised, that honest people-DAT nothing-GEN fear.]
They promised that *honest people have* nothing to fear.

Dative: an experiencer 4—Age, environment, and emotions

This use is the grab-bag for all kinds of other experiences encountered by a DATIVE: AN EXPERIENCER. The logic here is that something is happening in the outside world that is causing a change or a feeling in the DATIVE: AN EXPERIENCER. A constant force exerted by external reality is the unrelenting march of time. As a result we age, and in Russian we experience this process in the dative case. This is why we ask Ско́лько *вам* лет? [How-many you-DAT years-GEN?] 'How old are *you*?' and we reply *Мне* два́дцать лет [Me-DAT twenty-NOM years-GEN] '*I* am twenty years old'. The verb исполня́ться/испо́лниться 'complete' is also associated with the accumulation of birthdays, as in this example:

Легенда́рному Ва́ну Кли́берну, завоева́вшему в 1958 году́ в Москве́ пе́рвую пре́мию на ко́нкурсе и́мени П. И. Чайко́вского, исполня́ется 60 лет.
[Legendary Van Cliburn-DAT, won-DAT in 1958 year-LOC in Moscow-LOC first prize-ACC at competition-LOC name-GEN P. I. Tchaikovsky, completes 60-NOM years-GEN.]
The legendary Van Cliburn, who won first prize at the P. I. Tchaikovsky competition in Moscow in 1958, is 60 years old.

Environmental conditions can induce feelings of heat and cold, as in *ей* хо́лодно/жа́рко [her-DAT cold/hot] '*she feels* cold/hot', as well as a host of emotions, as in these examples:

Мне ве́село оттого́, что день со́лнечный.
[Me-DAT happily from-that, that day-NOM sunny-NOM.]
I'm happy because it's a sunny day.

В тюре́мных ка́мерах они́ жи́ли дру́жно. На во́ле *им* ста́ло тесновато́.
[In prison cells-LOC they-NOM lived harmoniously. At freedom-LOC them-DAT became rather-constrained.]
They lived harmoniously in their prison cells. In freedom *they* began *to feel* constrained.

A common idiom is the use of всё равно́, literally 'all equal', with the dative case to express the feeling of indifference, as in this example:

Предполо́жим, я его́ убью, *ему́* бу́дет всё равно́, где я и что со мной.
[Suppose, I-NOM him-ACC kill, him-DAT will-be all equal, where I-NOM and what-NOM with me-INST.]
Suppose I kill him, then *he* won't care where I am or how I'm doing.

DATIVE: AN EXPERIENCER expresses indifference with всё равно́.

Another idiom for apathy is the use of the dative with не до [not to], meaning 'isn't interested in/doesn't want':

Быва́ет, ты разгова́риваешь с же́нщиной, приво́дишь красноречи́вые до́воды и убеди́тельные аргуме́нты. А *ей* не до аргуме́нтов.
[Happens, you-NOM converse with woman-INST, present eloquent reasons-ACC and convincing arguments-ACC. But her-DAT not to arguments-GEN.]
It happens that you are conversing with a woman, presenting eloquent reasons and convincing arguments. But *she* is not interested in/doesn't care about arguments.

DATIVE: AN EXPERIENCER expresses apathy with не до.

The dative can also be used for feelings of overall well-being, and the verb станови́ться/ стать 'become' frequently appears when there is a change in feeling:

Наро́дному арти́сту Ю́рию Влади́мировичу Нику́лину у́тром 20-ого а́вгуста ста́ло ху́же.
[National artist Yuri Vladimirovich Nikulin-DAT morning-INST 20th-GEN August-GEN became worse.]
National artist Yuri Vladimirovich Nikulin began *feeling* worse on the morning of August 20th.

DATIVE: AN EXPERIENCER expresses changes in well-being with станови́ться/ стать.

От э́той сде́ланной улы́бки *мне* стано́вится не по себе́.
[From that artificial smile-GEN me-DAT becomes not along self-DAT.]
That artificial smile makes *me feel* uneasy.

DATIVE: AN EXPERIENCER 5—Modal meanings

Experiences of difficulty or ease, as in *нам э́то тру́дно/легко́* [us-DAT that-NOM hard/easily] 'that's hard/easy *for us*' belong here, as do experiences of comprehensibility, which overlap somewhat with the concepts of possession and availability discussed above:

DATIVE: AN EXPERIENCER expresses difficulty, ease, obligation, and desire.

Вам э́то не поня́тно? А *мне* э́то абсолю́тно я́сно.
[You-DAT that-NOM not understandable? But me-DAT that-NOM absolutely clear.]
You don't understand it? But it's absolutely clear *to me*.

With an infinitive the dative expresses mild compulsion, something on the order of English *should* or *ought*. Here is an example to illustrate:

Я не знал, идти *мне* за ней сле́дом и́ли в противополо́жную сто́рону.
[I-NOM not knew, go me-DAT behind her-INST or in opposite side-ACC.]
I didn't know whether *I* should follow her or go in the opposite direction.

The various experiences that people can have doing things — feeling like it, having to do it, succeeding at it — can likewise be expressed with the dative case, often by verbs that have no subject. Here are some common verbs used this way, followed by some examples (note that when these verbs have no subjects, they appear with the "default" agreement of neuter singular):

Expressions of feeling like or having to associated with DATIVE::AN EXPERIENCER

'remain, be necessary' оставáться/остáться	'have to, happen to' приходи́ться/прийти́сь	'feel like, want to' хотéться/захотéться
'lie ahead, be destined to, have to' предстоя́ть	'succeed' удавáться/удáться	

И *врачáм* ничего́ не остаётся, как совершéнствовать свои́ познáния в ми́ре захлёстывающих ры́нок ужé совремéнных, синтети́ческих наркóтиков.
[And doctors-DAT nothing-GEN not remains, how perfect own knowledge-ACC in world-LOC overflowing markets-ACC already modern synthetic narcotics-GEN.]
And *doctors* have no choice but to perfect their knowledge of the world where markets are overflowing with modern synthetic narcotics.

Росси́йские и францу́зские инженéры продемонстри́ровали автомати́ческий вездехóд, *котóрому* предстои́т исслéдовать повéрхность Мáрса.
[Russian-NOM and French engineers-NOM demonstrated automatic landrover-ACC, which-DAT is-destined explore surface-ACC Mars-GEN.]
Russian and French engineers demonstrated an automatic landrover *which* is destined to explore the surface of Mars.

По мнéнию экспéртов, рáно и́ли пóздно *прави́тельству, дéлающему* стáвку на сближéние с НАТО, придётся реши́ться уничтóжить ракéты и́ли продáть их.
[Along opinion-DAT experts-GEN, early or late government-DAT, making-DAT stake-ACC on rapprochement-ACC with NATO-INST, must decide destroy missiles-ACC or sell them-ACC.]
According to the experts, sooner or later *a government that is counting* on rapprochement with NATO will have to decide either to destroy its missiles or to sell them.

В пéрвые три мéсяца *вам* удáстся испóльзовать весь свой потенциáл.
[In first three months-ACC you-DAT will-succeed use all own potential-ACC.]
In the first three months *you* will succeed in making the most of all your potential.

Вйжу, что *мáльчику* не хóчется идтй в шкóлу.
[See, that boy-DAT not wants go to school-ACC.]
I see that *the boy* doesn't want to go/doesn't feel like going to school.

DATIVE: AN EXPERIENCER 6—Victims and beneficiaries

In Russian you can add -ся/-сь to many ordinary verbs and use the DATIVE: AN EXPERIENCER to describe how the subject is experiencing an action. The grammatical implication here is that instead of the subject performing the action, the action is something that is happening to the subject. So you can say both он икáет [he-NOM hiccups] 'he is hiccupping' and *емý* икáется [him-DAT hiccups] '*he* has the hiccups'; in the latter case hiccupping is something that is happening to the person. In the next example it would certainly be possible to say instead нéкоторые эмигрáнты живýт плóхо [some emigrants-NOM live badly] 'some emigrants live badly', but by adding -ся/-сь to the verb and putting the logical subject in the dative case, the author of this sentence implies that the emigrants are victims rather than masters of their fate:

> Мы слýшали, что *нéкоторым эмигрáнтам* живётся плóхо.
> [We-NOM heard, that some emigrants-DAT lives badly.]
> We heard that *some emigrants* are living badly.

Ultimately anything can happen to us or for us, and the dative case can be inserted into sentences just to explain who was affected by some event. In both of the examples below, the dative items could easily be removed and the sentences would be perfectly normal and grammatical. The dative items are there to provide some extra information, telling us who was impacted by the event.

> Футбóл и хоккéй заменяют *рýсским людям* релйгию и культýру.
> [Soccer-NOM and hockey-NOM replace Russian people-DAT religion-ACC and culture-ACC.]
> *For Russians*, soccer and hockey take the place of religion and culture.

> Мы перегородйли *всем* дорóгу.
> [We-NOM blocked everyone-DAT road-ACC.]
> We blocked *everyone's* way.

DATIVE: AN EXPERIENCER suggests that an activity is happening to a person.

DATIVE: AN EXPERIENCER indicates who is affected by an event.

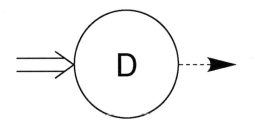

A force (arrow) arrives at a
DATIVE:: A COMPETITOR (circle labeled D), which
has the potential to exert a force (dotted arrow)

DATIVE: A COMPETITOR 1— Matching forces

Remember that the hallmark of the dative is that a dative item has the potential to do something. Grammatically, this means that it can potentially be the subject of a sentence, a role that is usually marked with the nominative

DATIVE: A COMPETITOR compares the actual nominative subject with the dative as the potential subject of a further action.

DATIVE: A
COMPETITOR
matches or
exceeds the
nominative
subject in the
force it exerts.

DATIVE: A
COMPETITOR can
indicate an equal
competitor.

case. The fact that a dative item is potentially a nominative item implies a comparison between the dative and the nominative. The uses of the DATIVE: A COMPETITOR exploit this comparison, for here we see the dative item in competition with a nominative item. In some instances the two items are evenly matched and participate in a symmetrical relationship as equal competitors. In other instances the dative item exerts a force to which the nominative item submits, giving the dative an advantage over the nominative.

In identifying an equal competitor, the meaning of the DATIVE: A COMPETITOR overlaps somewhat with the benefit meaning of DATIVE: AN EXPERIENCER, particularly if the two parties are equally engaged in a harmonious activity. Here are some words that typcially trigger the meaning of roughly equally matched forces, as well as examples of how they are used:

Expressions of equal or matching forces associated with DATIVE:: A COMPETITOR

'accompany (music)' аккомпани́ровать аккомпани́рование 'accompaniment'	'withstand; be opposite (of stars)' противостоя́ть	'akin to' сродни́
'agreeing with' согла́сно	'equal' равня́ться ра́вный 'equal' равноси́льный '(equally) matched'	'identical' иденти́чный 'identical' иденти́чность 'indenticalness'
'correspond, be responsible to' отвеча́ть	'correspond' соотве́тствовать соотве́тствующий 'corresponding, appropriate' соотве́тствие 'correspondence'	'isomorphic' изомо́рфный изомо́рфность 'isomorphism'
'sing along' подпева́ть подпева́ние 'singing along'		'orthogonal' ортогона́лный 'orthogonal'
'precede' предше́ствовать 'precede' предше́ствие 'precession'	'accompany' сопу́тствовать сопу́тствие 'accompaniment'	'similar' подо́бный 'similar' 'in harmony with' созву́чный 'in harmony with'

Систе́ма безопа́сности на авиали́ниях э́тих стран не отвеча́ет *междунаро́дным стандáртам.*
[System-NOM security-GEN on airlines-LOC those countries-GEN not corresponds international standards-DAT.]
The security system used by the airlines of those countries does not correspond *to international standards* .

Отноше́ния ме́жду стра́нами не соотве́тствуют *возмо́жностям.*
[Relations-NOM between countries-INST not correspond possibilities-DAT.]
The relations between the countries are not *what they could be* .

Его́ эсте́тика созву́чна *железнодоро́жной катастро́фе.*
[His aesthetics-NOM in-harmony-with-NOM railroad catastrophe-DAT.]
He has the aesthetics of *a train wreck* .

DATIVE: A COMPETITOR 2—Submission to a greater force

Submission has many entailments, among them belief and obedience. If you submit yourself to someone, you will trust this person, you will fall under the influence of this person, being surprised and amazed at their acts, and you will follow where they lead, possibly to the point of imitating them. In Russian, you will surrender yourself to a dative item, a competitor with an advantage.

DATIVE: A COMPETITOR can indicate a competitor with an advantage.

Expressions of submission associated with DATIVE:: A COMPETITOR

'believe'
ве́рить/пове́рить
ве́рный 'loyal'
ве́рность 'faithfulness, loyalty'

'marvel at'
диви́ться

'trust'
доверя́ть(ся)/ дове́ритъ(ся)
дове́рие 'trust'

'owe, be obligated to'
до́лжен

'obey'
повинова́ться
повинове́ние 'obedience'

'undergo, be subject to'
подверга́ться/подве́ргнуться
подве́рженный 'subject to'
подверже́ние 'liability to'

'give in to'
поддава́ться/подда́ться

'be subject to'
подлежа́ть
подлежа́щий 'subject to'

'imitate'
подража́ть
подража́ние 'imitation'

'submit to, obey'
подчиня́ться/подчини́ться
подчинённый 'subordinate to'
подчине́ние 'subordination, subjection'

'worship'
поклоня́ться
поклоне́ние 'worship'

'submit to, obey'
покоря́ться/покори́ться
поко́рный 'obedient to'

'rejoice at'
ра́доваться/обра́доваться

'surrender, yield to'
сдава́ться/сда́ться

'follow'
сле́довать/после́довать
сле́дование 'movement, proceeding'

'be surprised at'
удивля́ться/удиви́ться

'be similar, assimilate'
уподобля́ться/уподо́биться
подо́бный 'similar'
уподобле́ние 'likening, comparison'

'yield to'
уступа́ть/уступи́ть
усту́пка 'concession, compromise'

'study'
учи́ться/научи́ться
уча́щийся 'student'

These first three examples illustrate subordination in its more ordinary aspects:

Поли́тика президе́нта подве́рглась вновь *ре́зкой кри́тике* на про́шлой неде́ле.
[Policy-NOM president-GEN subjected again sharp criticism-DAT on last week-LOC.]
The president's policy was subjected *to sharp criticism* again last week.

То́лько здоро́вые лю́ди в состоя́нии вы́йти из душе́вного потрясе́ния, а психи́чески больны́е поддаю́тся *э́тому*, дохо́дят до безу́мия и ... проявля́ют себя́ в тво́рчестве.
[Only healthy people-NOM in condition-LOC come-out from emotional shock-GEN, but emotionally ill-NOM give-in this-DAT, reach to insanity-GEN and ... express self-ACC in artwork -LOC.]

Only healthy people have the capacity to overcome emotional shock, but the mentally ill give in *to it*, go insane, and ... express themselves in works of art.

Я подчини́лся *есте́ственному хо́ду* жи́зни.
[I-NOM gave-in natural course-DAT life-GEN.]
I gave in *to the natural course* of life.

Yielding one's beliefs and emotions is specifically illustrated in the following two examples:

Ба́бушка ра́достно кива́ет, она́ ве́рит *ка́ждому моему́ сло́ву*.
[Grandmother-NOM joyously nods, she-NOM believes every my word-DAT.]
Grandmother nods joyously, she believes *my every word*.

Она́ никогда́ не удивля́лась *тому́*, что он почти́ не нужда́ется во сне.
[She-NOM never not surprised that-DAT, that he-NOM almost not need in sleep-LOC.]
She was never surprised *by the fact* that he hardly needed any sleep.

DATIVE: A COMPETITOR 3—к 'to, toward'

к and по describe motion subordinate to DATIVE: A COMPETITOR.

к + DATIVE: A COMPETITOR 'to, toward'.

к + DATIVE: A COMPETITOR is used with human destinations.

The two prefixes most commonly associated with the dative case, к 'to, toward' and по 'along, according to', both use the DATIVE: A COMPETITOR. In both instances, the preposition points us toward something that can exert influence, guiding the nominative subject's action. Approach, as opposed to arrival, implies some level of subordination. When you reach a destination by means of к + DAT, you will have to interact with it rather than just arriving at it. Remember that the primary use of к is to indicate an approach to a human destination, as opposed to arrival at a non-human destination, for which we use в or на and the accusative case. Compare the three sentences in the table below:

some non-human destinations require в *+ ACC*

Дочь пошла́	в	шко́лу.
[Daughter-NOM went	in	school-ACC.]
My daughter went	to	school.

some non-human destinations require на *+ ACC*

Дочь пошла́	на	по́чту.
[Daughter-NOM went	on	post-office-ACC.]
My daughter went	to	the post-office.

all human destinations require к *+ DAT*

Дочь пошла́	к	*врачу́.*
[Daughter-NOM went	to	doctor-DAT.]
My daughter went	to	*the doctor.*

Here is a naturally-occurring use of к with a human destination:

> Он делови́то подходи́л ко *мне*.
> [He-NOM in-business-like-manner approached to me-DAT.]
> He approached *me* in a business-like manner.

Cities and countries are often personified or used to represent the people that live there, and in these instances they will trigger the use of к as well. Notice how Washington and Russia serve this purpose in the following two examples:

Personification of non-human destinations with к + DATIVE: A COMPETITOR.

> Росси́йский президе́нт ещё мо́жет обрати́ться к *Вашингто́ну* с тре́бованием доплати́ть за Аля́ску.
> [Russian president-NOM still can turn to Washington-DAT with demand-INST additionally-pay for Alaska-ACC.]
> The Russian president can still turn to *Washington* and demand further payment for Alaska.

> Во Фра́нции нараста́ет интере́с к *Росси́и.*
> [In France-LOC grows interest-NOM to Russia-DAT.]
> In France there is a growing interest in *Russia*.

One of the important distinctions between a non-human destination and a human one is that when we arrive at a person, we do not enter or otherwise physically encroach upon them, we just come nearer, going in that person's direction. This idea can be extended to physical locations in both space and time, as the following two examples attest:

к + DATIVE: A COMPETITOR with non-human destinations means 'toward, in the direction of'.

> Пала́у, архипела́г, состоя́щий из двухсо́т ме́лких острово́в, располо́женный в 800 киломе́трах к *юго-восто́ку* от Филиппи́н, стал 185-м чле́ном ООН.
> [Palau-NOM, archipelago-NOM, consisting-NOM from two hundred small islands-GEN, located-NOM in 800 kilometers-LOC to south-east-DAT from Philippines-GEN, became 185th member-INST UN-GEN.]
> Palau, an archipelago consisting of two hundred small islands located 800 kilometers to *the southeast* of the Philippines, became the 185th member of the UN.

> К *оди́ннадцати часа́м* я бо́лее и́ли ме́нее разобра́лся в ситуа́ции.
> [To eleven hours-DAT I-NOM more or less understood in situation-LOC.]
> Toward *eleven o'clock* I more or less came to understand the situation.

As we have already seen with the accusative case, a destination can be conceived of in the metaphorical realm of purpose, as in this example:

The metaphorical use of к + DATIVE: A COMPETITOR with non-human destinations to express 'to, for'.

> В предисло́вии к *его́ сбо́рнику* говори́лось, что он рабо́тает фрезеро́вщиком на заво́де.
> [In foreword-LOC to his collected-works-DAT said, that he-NOM works milling-machine-operator-INST at factory-LOC.]

In the foreword to *his collected works* it said that he works as a milling-machine operator at a factory.

Events frequently structure our lives, forcing us to interact with them. In the next pair of examples, there are two events involved. One is named directly, the examinations, and another indirectly through its location, the bed, which is where the drama of death is expected to take place.

> Днём она́ гото́вилась к *экза́менам.*
> [Day-INST she-NOM prepared to examinations-DAT.]
> During the day she prepared for *the examinations.*

> В тот же день к *посте́ли* больно́го пригласи́ли родны́х.
> [In that very day-ACC to bed-DAT patient-GEN invited relatives-ACC.]
> That very day they invited relatives to come to the patient's *bedside.*

There are many phenomena that likewise order our existence. In the next two examples к indicates relationships to two particularly powerful phenomena, those of economic forces and substance abuse:

> Был откры́т япо́нский центр, кото́рый бу́дет гото́вить ка́дры для перехо́да к *ры́ночной эконо́мике.*
> [Was opened-NOM Japanese center-NOM, which-NOM will prepare personnel-ACC for transition-GEN to market economy-DAT.]
> A Japanese center was opened to prepare personnel for the transition to *a market economy.*

> По мне́нию враче́й, уже́ пе́рвые про́бы любо́го нарко́тика мо́гут привести́ к *формирова́нию* психи́ческой, а зате́м и физи́ческой зави́симости.
> [Along opinion-DAT doctors-GEN, already first trials-NOM any narcotic-GEN can lead to formation-DAT psychological-GEN and thereupon physical dependence-GEN.]
> In the opinion of doctors, even the first use of any narcotic can lead to *the formation* of psychological, and thereupon physical, dependence.

Emotions are more abstract, but no less influential forces, and here are two examples of how they interact with к. Note that the second one, к *сожале́нию* '*unfortunately*' is so conventional that it is used as an adverb.

> К *у́жасу* туре́цких власте́й же́ртвой всё ча́ще стано́вятся иностра́нцы.
> [To horror-DAT Turkish authorities-GEN victim-INST all more-frequently become foreigners-NOM.]
> To *the horror* of Turkish authorities, the victims are more and more frequently foreigners.

Отобра́ли, к *сожале́нию*, лишь четвёртую часть.
[Removed, to regret-DAT, only fourth part-ACC.]
Unfortunately, they only removed a fourth of it.

DATIVE: A COMPETITOR 4—по 'along'

The preposition по triggers the one use of the dative case that is not particularly associated with human beings. 'Along' is perhaps the translation of по that best captures its nature, since по's job is to indicate paths. When one selects a path, one must then follow it, submitting to its contours; thus the path exerts an influence much like that suggested by the verbs of subordination above. This is why the use of по is classed under the DATIVE: A COMPETITOR. Our first example is of the path taken by someone who is so happy she feels like she is walking on air:

Э́то сча́стье несло́ её по *во́здуху*.
[That good-fortune-NOM carried her-ACC along air-DAT.]
That good fortune carried her through *the air*.

A shorter path is the area of a body part where something happened, often used when a person is hit by something:

Собира́ли све́дения о пожило́й же́нщине, безжа́лостно уби́той че́м-то тяжёлым по *заты́лку*.
[Gathered information-ACC about elderly woman-LOC, ruthlessly murdered-LOC something heavy-INST along back-of-head-DAT.]
They were gathering information about an elderly woman who was ruthlessly murdered when she was hit by some heavy object in *the back of the head*.

Electronic signals flow across telephone wires, making the telephone a path for communication, as in this example:

Ту́т-то незнако́мый же́нский го́лос по *телефо́ну* предложи́л познако́миться.
[Suddenly unfamiliar woman's voice-NOM along telephone-DAT suggested get-acquainted.]
Suddenly an unfamiliar woman's voice on *the telephone* suggested that they get acquainted.

With plural nouns, по often indicates a kind of place frequently visited, or something that regularly happens at a certain time or on a certain day of the week. The following two examples demonstrate how this works in the domains of space and time:

Зараба́тываем бо́льше ты́сячи в неде́лю. Че́рез день по *рестора́нам* хо́дим.
[Earn more thousand-GEN in week-ACC. Across day-ACC along restaurants-DAT go.]
We earn more than a thousand a week. Every other day we go to *restaurants*.

По *утрám* он вмéсто гимнастических упражнéний и чáшки кóфе пил портвéйн.
[Along mornings-DAT he-NOM instead-of gymnastic exercises-GEN and cup-GEN coffee-GEN drank portwine-ACC.]
In *the mornings* instead of calisthenics and a cup of coffee he would drink portwine.

по + DATIVE: A COMPETITOR expresses distribution.

Distribution of one to each also describes a path indicated by по:

Разместили нас в гостинице Хилтон. По *одномý человéку* в нóмере.
[Placed us-ACC in hotel-LOC Hilton. Along one person-DAT in room-LOC.]
They put us in the Hilton hotel. *One person* in each room.

по + DATIVE: A COMPETITOR expresses movement 'along' metaphoric paths.

There are many possible metaphoric paths. Here are two of the intellect. In the first example, solution must follow the contours of the issues, and in the second, an answer should follow the logic of the problem.

Решили создáть межправительственную комиссию по *торгóво-экономическим вопрóсам.*
[Decided create intergovernmental commission-ACC along market-economy issues-DAT.]
They decided to create an intergovernmental commission for *market-economy issues*.

Президéнт уклонился от чётких отвéтов по *этой проблéме.*
[President-NOM avoided from precise answers-GEN along that problem-DAT.]
The president avoided giving any precise answers concerning *that problem* .

по + DATIVE: A COMPETITOR means 'according to' in the domain of reason.

When you follow logical paths, you are thinking or acting according to things, and 'according to' is one of the most frequent meanings of the preposition по. Here are a few examples to illustrate:

По *нáшей информáции,* обсуждáлось ухудшéние состояния больнóго.
[Along our information-DAT, discussed worsening-NOM state-GEN patient-GEN.]
According to *our information* , they discussed the patient's worsening state.

По *официáльным дáнным,* пропáло бéз вéсти óколо 10 тысяч человéк.
[Along official data-DAT, lost without news-GEN around 10 thousand people-GEN.]
According to *official data* , around 10 thousand people are missing.

По *заявлéнию* врачéй, мáльчик психически совершéнно здорóв.
[Along statement-DAT doctors-GEN, boy-NOM psychologically completely healthy-NOM.]
According to the doctors' *statement* , psychologically the boy is completely healthy.

Following a certain path can also cause things to happen, as we see in this example:

>То ли по *ле́ни*, то ли по *гениа́льной свое́й интуи́ции*, наш режиссёр э́того избежа́л.
>[That whether along laziness-DAT, that whether along ingenious own intuition-DAT, our director-NOM that-GEN avoided.]
>Whether it was due to *laziness* or due to *his own ingenious intuition* , our director managed to avoid that.

По participates in its share of idioms, such as по *всей ви́димости* [along all appearance-DAT] 'to *all appearances* '. Two of the most important idioms are по-*сво́ему* [along-own-DAT] 'in *one's own way*', and сам по *себе́* [self-NOM along self-DAT] 'in *itself*/on its *own*', illustrated in this example:

>Сама́ по *себе́* ха́ртия не име́ет юриди́ческой си́лы.
>[Self-NOM along self-DAT charter-NOM not has legal force-GEN.]
>In *itself*, the charter has no legal force.

EPILOGUE

Our human capacity to perceive, appreciate, and react to the world around us is the foundation upon which the whole of the dative case is built. It should not surprise you that the name *dative* comes from the Latin word for 'give', since giving is the defining concept of human interaction, be it the presentation of gifts, the giving of good and evil, or the give and take of competition. We are never entirely passive: we take money, understand messages, interpret dreams, and struggle against the forces imposed upon us, matching or submitting to them. In Russian, as opposed to English, people see themselves as subject to atmospheric, temporal, and emotional factors in their environment, since being hot, twenty years old, and sad are all things that happen to people as DATIVE: EXPERIENCERS, rather than characteristics of them (as in English). Russian insists on treating people differently from all other items that serve as destinations, since people require the use of к + DATIVE: A COMPETITOR rather than в or на + ACCUSATIVE: A DESTINATION. Surrender can take place on a variety of levels, entailing yielding one's behavior, beliefs, intellect, and sense of awe. The dative case seems to dwell on the negative, for with the dative case we find more words expressing harm than benefit, more words for relationships of submission than harmony, many ways to express imposed obligations, and a tendency for body parts to incur damage. Perhaps as human beings we are more adept at noticing and expressing our fustrations than our delights.

ПО + DATIVE: A COMPETITOR means 'due to' in the domain of causation.

GENITIVE Forms

Feminine declension nouns	hard type: 'room'		soft type: 'week'	

Feminine declension nouns			
hard type: 'room'		**soft type: 'week'**	
singular	plural	singular	plural
ко́мнаты	ко́мнат	неде́ли	неде́ль
-ь: 'talent'			
singular	plural		
спосо́бности	спосо́бностей		

Masculine declension nouns			
hard type: 'courtyard'		**soft type: 'nail'**	
singular	plural	singular	plural
двора́	дворо́в	гвоздя́	гвозде́й

Neuter declension nouns			
hard type: 'body'		**soft type: 'schedule'**	
singular	plural	singular	plural
те́ла	тел	расписа́ния	расписа́ний

Adjectives

hard type: 'first'			
feminine	masculine	neuter	plural
пе́рвой	пе́рвого	пе́рвого	пе́рвых

soft type: 'last'			
feminine	masculine	neuter	plural
после́дней	после́днего	после́днего	после́дних

Pronouns

'I'	'we'	'you' informal	'you'
меня́	нас	тебя́	вас
'she'	'he'	'it'	'they'
(н)её	(н)его́	(н)его́	(н)их
'who'	'what'	'oneself'	
кого́	чего́	себя́	

'this'			
feminine	masculine	neuter	plural
э́той	э́того	э́того	э́тих

'all, every'			
feminine	masculine	neuter	plural
всей	всего́	всего́	всех

Possessives

feminine	masculine	neuter	plural
'my'			
мое́й	моего́	моего́	мои́х
'our'			
на́шей	на́шего	на́шего	на́ших

Numerals

'one'			
feminine	masculine	neuter	plural
одно́й	одного́	одного́	одни́х

'two'	'three'	'four'	'five'
дву́х	трёх	четырёх	пяти́

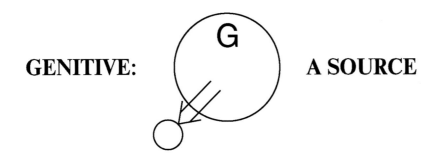

GENITIVE: A SOURCE

The genitive network:

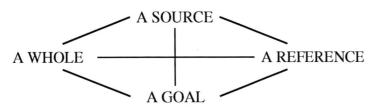

PROLOGUE

Let's start by looking at an example:

> Фиде́ль Ка́стро на пя́том съе́зде *свое́й компа́ртии* говори́л без *умо́лку* шесть *часо́в* и со́рок три мину́ты, что досто́йно *реко́рдов Кни́ги Ги́ннесса.*
> [Fidel Castro-NOM at fifth congress-LOC own communist-party-GEN spoke without pause-GEN six-ACC hours-GEN and forty-three minutes-ACC, that worthy records-GEN Book-GEN Guinness-GEN.]
> At the fifth congress *of his communist party*, Fidel Castro spoke without *pause* for six *hours* and forty-three minutes, an accomplishment worthy *of the Guinness Book of Records.*

Here we see six uses of the genitive case in a single sentence, one that is not even particularly long or unusual. If there were an entry for Russian case use in the Guinness Book of World Records, the genitive case would walk off with multiple honors, among them:

- The genitive is the most used case in Russian. The likelihood of finding sentences with six uses of any other case is relatively small.
- The genitive is used with over one hundred prepositions (about 40 simple prepositions and 70 complex ones), vastly more than all the other cases combined.
- The genitive is the only case that forms chains of consecutive uses, as in our example above: досто́йно *реко́рдов Кни́ги Ги́ннесса* [worthy records-GEN Book-GEN Guinness-GEN], literally 'worthy *of the records of the Book of Guinness*'.
- The genitive is probably the most complex case in Russian, and the basic idea of the gentive is perhaps the hardest to grasp.

The genitive case is the most frequent case, has the most prepositions, forms chains, and has the most complex meaning.

An overview of
the genitive case.

The genitive
case diverts
attention to
another item.

An abstract
definition of the
genitive.

These might look like formidable hurdles, but our strategy is to tackle the last item on the list, the meaning of the genitive. After that, all the other "problems" will become opportunities for easy success.

The uses of the genitive will be described in terms of four categories: GENITIVE: A SOURCE, GENITIVE: A GOAL, GENITIVE: A WHOLE, and GENITIVE: A REFERENCE. The four labels used here hint at both what the basic meaning of the genitive is and why it is so hard to make sense of it. The genitive is by nature an elusive beast, a sort of "back-seat driver" that is always handing off the responsibility of focusing attention to something else. When we say that something comes from a source, we generally aren't as interested in the source as we are in the something that comes from it. The same goes for goals; while a goal is important, what we really care about is the person or thing that is headed for it. In the GENITIVE: A WHOLE use, there is always another item that plays the role of the "part", and of course when we are talking about something that is part of a whole, we are focusing our attention on the part more than on the whole. A reference point is something that we use to locate something else, and in its GENITIVE: A REFERENCE use, the genitive serves as a mental address for other things. Rather than turning focus to the item it marks, the genitive deflects our focus away from it. It is this habit of retreating into the background that makes the genitive so hard to pin down. Passing the buck, by the way, also makes the chaining of genitives possible, allowing focus to bounce from one item to the next.

Looking at the labels, however, it is at first hard to understand what they have in common. After all, a source and a goal seem to be opposites, and both involve movement, whereas whole and reference are static. If we compare the diagrams of the four uses, we see that the GENITIVE: A GOAL is really the same as the GENITIVE: A SOURCE, just run in reverse, and furthermore the GENITIVE: A WHOLE and GENITIVE: A REFERENCE are simply the two endpoints of GENITIVE: A SOURCE. More abstractly, we could say that all of the diagrams support the following definition:

The genitive is a backgrounded item (big circle) that yields focus of attention to something else (small circle) which exists or maneuvers in its proximity.

In order to make sense of this definition we will have to examine the many faces of the genitive in action.

GENITIVE: A SOURCE 1—Going to > coming from

The GENITIVE: A SOURCE meaning is always triggered by a preposition or word indicating removal or withdrawal from the genitive item. All three of the prepositions particularly important in expressing this meaning are often translated as 'from': из, с, and от. These three prepositions reverse the direction of motion described by the prepositions в, на, к in their meaning 'to, toward'. Here again is the table comparing в, на, к, this time adding the reverse direction:

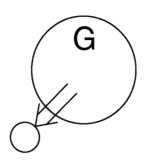

An item (small circle) departs from a
GENITIVE: A SOURCE
(circle labeled G)

GOING TO

some non-human destinations require в *+ ACC*

Дочь пошла	в	шко́лу.
[Daughter-NOM went	in	school-ACC.]
My daughter went	to	school.

some non-human destinations require на *+ ACC*

Дочь пошла	на	по́чту.
[Daughter-NOM went	on	post-office-ACC.]
My daughter went	to	the post-office.

all human destinations require к *+ DAT*

Дочь пошла	к	врачу́.
[Daughter-NOM went	to	doctor-DAT.]
My daughter went	to	the doctor.

Comparison of three GENITIVE: A SOURCE prepositions meaning 'from': из, с, and от.

COMING FROM

non-human destinations that require в *+ ACC use* из *+ GEN when they are sources*

Дочь пришла	из	*шко́лы.*
[Daughter-NOM came	from	school-GEN.]
My daughter came (home)	from	*school.*

non-human destinations that require на *+ ACC use* с *+ GEN when they are sources*

Дочь пришла	с	*по́чты.*
[Daughter-NOM came	from	post-office-GEN.]
My daughter came (home)	from	*the post-office.*

all human destinations require к *+ DAT and use* от *+ GEN when they are sources*

Дочь пришла	от	*врача́.*
[Daughter-NOM came	from	doctor-GEN.]
My daughter came (home)	from	*the doctor.*

GENITIVE: A SOURCE 2—из 'from'

Here are some examples of the use of из to indicate a container or location from which something is removed:

из + GENITIVE: A SOURCE 'from'.

На сту́льях и крова́ти лежа́ли ве́щи, вы́нутые из *сундука́.*
[On chairs-LOC and bed-LOC lay things-NOM, taken-NOM from trunk-GEN.]
On the chairs and bed lay things that had been taken out *of the trunk.*

Из *сара́я* вы́бежал ма́льчик.
[From barn-GEN ran-out boy-NOM.]
A boy ran out *of the barn.*

Он архео́лог, неда́вно верну́лся из *Яку́тии.*
[He-NOM archeologist-NOM, recently returned from Yakutia-GEN.]
He's an archeologist, and he's recently returned from *Yakutia.*

Из can also be used metaphorically to indicate abstract objects and refer to domains other than space. In the first of these two examples Hitchcock's films are the source of horrors, and in the second charity (shown by a very self-important hairdresser) is the source (and thereby the motive) for giving the person a seat in the beauty parlor. Note the use of English *from* and *out of* in these examples; the metaphorical extension of the source concept is something we share with Russian.

Иногда́ Ва́дик зарисо́вывал свои́ сны, похо́жие на у́жасы из *фи́льмов* Хичко́ка.
[Sometimes Vadik-NOM drew his dreams-ACC, similar-ACC on horrors-ACC from films-GEN Hitchcock-GEN.]
Sometimes Vadik drew pictures of his dreams, similar to horrors from Hitchcock's *films.*

Я понима́ю, что поса́жена в кре́сло из *ми́лости* и вообще́ по сравне́нию с парикма́хершей ничего́ не сто́ю.
[I-NOM understand, that seated-NOM to chair-ACC from charity-GEN and in-general along comparison-DAT with hairdresser-INST nothing-GEN not be-worth.]
I understand that I have been given a seat out *of charity* and that in general in comparison with the hairdresser I am worthless.

из + GENITIVE: A
SOURCE in fixed
phrases
исходи́ть из
'proceed from',
оди́н из
'one of'.

Из appears in numerous fixed phrases. Perhaps the two most common ones are исходи́ть из 'proceed from; base one's assumptions on' and оди́н из 'one of [a group of things]'. Here is an example for each of these uses:

Исходя́ из *про́шлого о́пыта,* дога́дываюсь, что ...
[Proceeding from past experience-GEN, guess, that...]
Based on *past experience*, I guess that...

Оди́н из ча́сто *встреча́емых моти́вов* его́ произведе́ний — сон.
[One-NOM from frequently encountered motifs-GEN his works-GEN — sleep-NOM.]
One *of the* frequently *encountered motifs* of his work is sleep.

Из forms two secondary prepositions, both of which can be used in concrete and metaphorical contexts. Из-за, literally means 'from beyond'. The first example below illustrates a concrete use, из-за *рубежа́* [from-beyond border-GEN] 'from *abroad*', whereas the second is metaphorical, indicating a cause:

У э́той фи́рмы то́же есть ресу́рсы из-за *рубежа́.*
[By this firm-GEN also are resources-NOM from-beyond border-GEN.]
This firm also has resources from *abroad.*

Вре́мя от вре́мени она́ перестава́ла кра́ситься, из-за *хандры́*, и́ли из-за *того́*, что пропада́ла кра́ска, и́ли лень бы́ло е́хать в магази́н.
[Time-NOM from time-GEN she-NOM stopped dye from-beyond depression-GEN, or from-beyond that-GEN, that lost dye-NOM, or laziness-NOM was ride to store-ACC.]
From time to time she would stop dyeing her hair, whether from *depression*, or from *the fact* that there was no dye in the store, or because she just felt too lazy to go to the store.

Из-под is the other complex preposition, literally 'from beneath'. The first example is of a concrete use, whereas the second is idiomatic:

из-под + GENITIVE: A SOURCE 'from beneath'.

Гла́вную опо́ру выбива́ют у него́ из-под *ног*.
[Main support-ACC knock-out by him-GEN from-beneath feet-GEN.]
They are knocking his main support out from under *his feet*.

Сковорода́ свали́лась на буты́лки из-под *кефи́ра*, кото́рые стоя́т во́зле плиты́.
[Frying pan-NOM fell on bottles-ACC from-beneath kefir-GEN, which-NOM stand next-to burner-GEN.]
The frying pan fell onto the *kefir* bottles that are next to the burner.

GENITIVE: A SOURCE 3—c 'from'

Just as из takes us on the path reversing the direction of в + ACC for something that is conceived of as a container, so c takes us on the path reversing на + ACC for something that is conceived of as a surface. The bee house was *on* the tree, the pinecone was *on* the ground, and the friends were *at* the language department, all using на for locations, and consequently c for removal from these locations.

c + GENITIVE: A SOURCE 'from'.

Он снял пчели́ный до́мик с *де́рева*.
[He-NOM removed bee house-ACC from tree-GEN.]
He removed the bee house from *the tree*.

Она́ подняла́ с *земли́* ши́шку.
[She-NOM picked-up from ground-GEN pinecone-ACC.]
She picked up a pinecone from *the ground*.

Прия́тели с *филфа́ка* не внуша́ли дове́рия.
[Friends-NOM from language-department-GEN not inspired confidence-GEN.]
Our friends from *the language department* did not inspire confidence.

Although the GENITIVE: A SOURCE preposition that is usually used with human beings is от, we do occasionally see human beings with c, particularly when they are viewed as a source of money, as in the common phrase Ско́лько с *меня́*? [How-much from me-GEN?] 'How much *do I owe you*?', or the following example:

c + GENITIVE: A
SOURCE with
human beings
when they serve
as the source of
funds.

Прави́тельство не собира́ет нало́г с *проститу́ток.*
[Government-NOM not collects tax-ACC from prostitutes-GEN.]
The government does not collect a tax from *prostitutes.*

c + GENITIVE: A
SOURCE in the
domain of time.

With time expressions, c can be used to indicate the time when something begins. Common examples are months and ages, as well as the fixed expression c *mex nop* [from those times-GEN] 'from *that time on*'. Here are three examples to illustrate:

Ра́йса с *пяти́ лет* кле́ила коро́бочки для пилю́ль.
[Raisa-NOM from five years-GEN glued boxes-ACC for pills-GEN.]
Raisa started gluing pill boxes *when she was five years old.*

С *января́* по май вы бу́дете в олимпи́йской фо́рме.
[From January-GEN along May-ACC you-NOM will-be in olympic form-LOC.]
From *January* through May you will be in olympic form.

Я с *де́тства* мечта́л о литерату́ре.
[I-NOM from childhood-GEN dreamed about literature-LOC.]
I have dreamed about literature since *childhood.*

Like any other preposition, c has its metaphorical uses. Here are a couple of examples to whet your appetite, one involving the source serving as a motive (the hangover causing the gloomy mood), and the other referring to an abstract numerical realm:

Ты явля́ешься, когда́ Дудко́ с *похме́лья* — мра́чный.
[You-NOM appear, when Dudko-NOM from hangover-GEN — gloomy-NOM.]
You keep showing up when Dudko is gloomy because *he's got a hangover.*

Сла́ва Бо́гу, мы начина́ли не с *нуля́.*
[Glory-NOM God-DAT, we-NOM started not from zero-GEN.]
Thank God we weren't starting from *zero.*

GENITIVE: A SOURCE 4—от 'from'

As our table above indicates, when a human being serves as GENITIVE: A SOURCE, you can usually expect to see the preposition от. The following example serves to illustrate both the use of от with human sources and the fact that от is frequently used with non-human sources as well:

По его́ лицу́ я по́нял, с каки́м удово́льствием уе́хал бы он на юг от *кри́ка,* от *тёщи,* и от *жены́.*
[Along his face-DAT I-NOM understood, with what pleasure-INST leave would he-NOM to south-ACC from yell-GEN, from mother-in-law-GEN, and from wife-GEN.]
From his face I understood how glad he would be to go south, away from *the yelling*, away from *his mother-in-law*, and away from *his wife.*

Whenever location is expressed in terms of y 'by' + GEN (see below under GENITIVE: A REFERENCE), removal from that place is expressed with от. In Russian a person can stand y *окна́* [by window-GEN] 'by *the window*', and removal from this position is achieved by от:

> Почти́ четы́ре шага́ мо́жно сде́лать в прогу́лке от *окна́* до двери́.
> [Almost four steps-ACC possible do in walk-LOC from window-GEN to door-GEN.]
> One can take almost four steps in walking from *the window* to the door.

от indicates removal 'from' a location marked as y + GENITIVE: A REFERENCE.

The use of от with expressions of time is not particularly common, but here is an example:

> В отве́тном письме́ Луто́хину от *пе́рвого* ма́я 1926 г. Го́рький дал бо́лее развёрнутую оце́нку поэ́зии Цвета́евой.
> [In answer letter-LOC Lutokhin-DAT from first-GEN May-GEN 1926-GEN Gorky-NOM gave more extensive evaluation-ACC poetry-GEN Tsvetaeva-GEN.]
> In his letter of response written to Lutokhin on *the first* of May, 1926, Gorky gave a more extensive evaluation of Tsvetaeva's poetry.

от + GENITIVE: A SOURCE in the domain of time.

In Russian dependence is expressed using the verb зави́сеть (or the noun зави́симость or the adjective зави́симый) от + GEN, as in this example:

> Западноевропе́йские госуда́рства смо́гут уме́ньшить свою́ зави́симость от *стран-чле́нов* ОПЕК.
> [West-European states-NOM can reduce their dependence-ACC from countries-members-GEN OPEC-GEN.]
> West European states can reduce their dependence on *the* OPEC *member-countries.*

от + GENITIVE: A SOURCE in the fixed phrase зави́сеть от 'depend on'.

Just like из and с, от can identify a metaphorical source in terms of a cause. In the case of от, this is usually the cause of illness or death, although other causes can also come into play:

> Её муж у́мер от *разры́ва* се́рдца.
> [Her husband-NOM died from rupture-GEN heart-GEN.]
> Her husband died from a heart *attack.*

от + GENITIVE: A SOURCE in metaphorical domains.

> Утвержда́ют, что Микела́нджело та́кже страда́л от *безу́мных мы́слей.*
> [Claim, that Michelangelo-NOM also suffered from crazy thoughts-GEN.]
> They claim that Michelangelo also suffered from *crazy thoughts.*

> От *зажжённого* за окно́м *фонаря́* на полу́ коса́я зы́бкая тень ра́мы.
> [From lighted-GEN beyond window-INST lamp-GEN on floor slanting flickering shadow-NOM windowframe-GEN.]
> From *the lighted lamp* outside the window there is a slanting, flickering shadow of the windowframe on the floor.

GENITIVE: A SOURCE 5—Withdrawal

In addition to prepositions, some other words trigger the use of GENITIVE: A SOURCE. Like the prepositions, they all indicate motions of withdrawal from the genitive item, whether due to fear or disgust. Here is a table of the words you are likely to encounter, followed by a few examples:

Expressions of fear and avoidance associated with GENITIVE: A SOURCE

'fear' боя́ться	'avoid' избега́ть/избежа́ть	'be shy' стесня́ться/постесня́ться
'abhor, have aversion' гнуша́ться/погнуша́ться	'beware' остерега́ться/остере́чься	'shun, avoid' сторони́ться/посторони́ться
'shy away from' дичи́ться	'be frightened' пуга́ться/испуга́ться	'be ashamed' стыди́ться/постыди́ться
		'shun, stand aloof' чужда́ться

Она́ предава́лась удово́льствиям, разу́мно избега́я *неприя́тностей*.
[She yielded pleasures-DAT, judiciously avoiding unpleasant-things-GEN.]
She abandoned herself to pleasure, judiciously avoiding *unpleasant things*.

Они́ соверше́нно не стесня́лись *прису́тствия* люде́й.
[They-NOM completely not were-shy presence-GEN people-GEN.]
They were not the least bit shy *of the presence* of people.

Они́ не владе́ли англи́йским языко́м и стыди́лись *э́того*.
[They-NOM not commanded English language-INST and were-ashamed this-GEN.]
They did not know English and were ashamed *of this*.

GENITIVE: A GOAL 1—до 'to'

As its name suggests, GENITIVE: A GOAL identifies an item that is approached. Like GENITIVE: A SOURCE, GENITIVE: A GOAL is always triggered by a preposition or other word. By far the most common is the preposition до 'to', which can be applied to the domains of space and time, as well as to metaphorical realms. Here are two examples of how до defines an approach in terms of physical space:

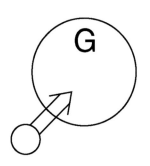

An item (small circle) reaches a
GENITIVE:: A GOAL
(circle labeled G)

До *трамвая* я дошёл благополучно, неся чемодан то в правой, то в левой руке.
[To tram-GEN I-NOM went successfully, carrying suitcase-ACC that in right-LOC, that in left hand-LOC.]
I made my way to *the tram* successfully, carrying my suitcase first in my right hand and then in my left.

Ступеньки моего вагона не доходят до *земли*.
[Steps-NOM my train-car-GEN not go to ground-GEN.]
The steps of my train car do not reach *the ground*.

When used with time expressions, до can mean 'before', as in до *войны* [before war-GEN] 'before *the war*', but more frequently has a meaning very similar to English 'until', as in до *свидания* [until seeing-GEN] 'goodbye (lit: until *we see each other again*)'. Here are a couple of examples to show how this works in sentences:

После тридцати шести лет разлуки, отец и сын беседовали до *утра*.
[After thirty-six years-GEN separation-GEN, father-NOM and son-NOM talked until morning-GEN.]
After being separated for thirty-six years, father and son talked until *morning*.

Выкупавшись в реке, он ложился на траву и спал до *обеда*.
[Having-swum in river-LOC, he-NOM lay-down on grass-ACC and slept until lunch-GEN.]
After taking a swim in the river, he would lie on the grass and sleep until *lunch*.

In relation to points in time, до performs the inverse of с, treating the point as a surface. Thus, as in the following example, one stretches a time line (of devotion to children's literature) from one point (the end of the twenties) to another (the end of life) by using с and до in tandem:

Детская литература с конца 20-х годов до *конца* жизни была его лицом, его визитной карточкой, именем наконец.
[Children's literature-NOM from end-GEN 20's years-GEN until end-GEN life-GEN was his face-INST, his calling card-INST, name-INST in-the-end.]
From the late twenties until *the end* of his life, children's literature was his face, his calling card, his name really.

This pairing of с and до motivates the use of до with the fixed expression до *сих/тех пор* [up-to this/that time-GEN] 'until *this/that time*':

Очевидно, до *сих пор* я казался ей воплощением здоровья и наивности.
[Obviously, until this time-GEN I-NOM seemed her-DAT incarnation-INST health-GEN and naivete-GEN.]
Obviously until *then* I had seemed to her to be health and naivete incarnate.

ДО + GENITIVE: A
GOAL means 'to,
up to' in
metaphorical
domains.

Metaphorically до can describe movement into various states, such as the politico-economic states in the first example below, and states of mind in the second one:

Не ва́жно, что режи́м довёл страну́ до *междунаро́дной изоля́ции,* до *ма́ссового исхо́да* интере́сов, до *безде́нежья.*
[Not important, that regime-NOM led country-ACC to international isolation-GEN, to mass exodus-GEN interests-GEN, to pennilessness-GEN.]
It's not important that the regime led the country to *a state of international isolation*, *mass exodus* of interests, and *pennilessness*.

Гоге́на му́чили ма́ния пресле́дования и депре́ссия, доведя́ его́ до *мы́слей* о самоуби́йстве.
[Gaugin-ACC tormented mania-NOM persecution-GEN and depression-NOM, leading him-ACC to thoughts-GEN about suicide-LOC.]
Gaugin was tormented by persecution mania and depression, leading him to *thoughts* of suicide.

Similar to the time line illustrated above, до can be used to reach points on all kinds of scales, be they numerical or otherwise (extent of persecution, spectrum of painting styles), as in the following examples:

До *двухсо́т ты́сяч тури́стов* ежего́дно приезжа́ют сюда́ полюбова́ться на живо́тных, живу́щих в есте́ственных усло́виях.
[Up-to two hundred thousand tourists-GEN yearly come here admire on animals-ACC, living-ACC in natural conditions-LOC.]
Up to *two hundred thousand tourists* a year come here to admire the animals living in natural conditions.

Но она́ реши́ла пресле́довать своего́ му́жа до *конца́.*
[But she-NOM decided persecute own husband-ACC to end-GEN.]
But she decided to persecute her husband to *the end*.

Карти́ны от сверхреали́зма до *демони́зма* рожда́ются та́м.
[Pictures-NOM from super-realism-GEN to demonism-GEN are-born there.]
Pictures from super-realism to *demonism* are born there.

The idiom
не до +
GENITIVE: A GOAL
means 'not in
the mood for'.

До also participates in an idiomatic phrase used to indicate that someone is not in the mood for something, namely DAT + не до + GEN:

Но Пу́шкину бы́ло не до *дете́й.*
[But Pushkin-DAT was not up-to children-GEN.]
But Pushkin wasn't in the mood for *children*.

Genitive: a goal 2—для 'for' and против 'against'

In the domain of purpose, the approach involved in Genitive: a goal mades a gesture toward the genitive item, usually offering it some kind of benefit, and this is done with the preposition для 'for'. Here are some examples to illustrate:

> Я пишу́ не для *славистов*. Я пишу́ для *норма́льных люде́й*.
> [I-NOM write not for Slavists-GEN. I-NOM write for normal people-GEN.]
> I don't write for *Slavists* . I write for *normal people* .

> Санато́рий был закры́того ти́па, для *высокопоста́вленных люде́й*.
> [Sanatorium-NOM was closed type-GEN, for highly-placed people-GEN.]
> It was an exclusive sanatorium, for *highly-placed people* .

> Придётся обраща́ться за по́мощью к друзья́м и знако́мым для *реше́ния* не́которых пробле́м.
> [Is-necessary turn for help-INST to friends-DAT and acquaintances-DAT for solution-GEN certain problems-GEN.]
> It is necessary to turn to friends and acquaintances in order *to solve* certain problems.

Similar to для is the preposition ра́ди, usually translated as 'for the sake of':

> Что с ва́ми? Я же здесь ра́ди *вас*.
> [What-NOM with you-INST? I-NOM after-all here for-the-sake-of you-GEN.]
> What's with you? After all, I'm here for *your* sake.

An approach in the immediate vicinity of some person or thing can also be an act of aggression directed *against* Genitive: a goal, and this is expressed by means of the preposition против 'against':

> Когда́ была́ кампа́ния про́тив *взя́точничества*, И́горь рисова́л краснорожего взя́точника.
> [When was campaign-NOM against bribery-GEN, Igor-NOM drew red-faced bribe-taker-ACC.]
> When there was a campaign against *bribery* , Igor drew a picture of a red-faced bribe-taker.

> Они́ и́щут сре́дства не то́лько про́тив *ви́руса*, но и для упроще́ния защи́тных фу́нкций на́шего органи́зма.
> [They-NOM seek means-GEN not only against virus-GEN, but also for simplification-GEN defense functions-GEN our body-GEN.]
> They are looking for something not only to fight *the virus* , but also to simplify our body's defense functions.

для + Genitive: a goal means 'for' in the domain of purpose.

ра́ди + Genitive: a goal means 'for the sake of' in the domain of purpose.

про́тив + Genitive: a goal means 'against' in the domain of purpose.

Less frequently про́тив can be interpreted concretely as mere location opposite rather than actual opposition, as in this example:

Про́тив *ко́рпуса* жгли костёр, наве́рное, сжига́ли нену́жный хлам.
[Opposite building-GEN burned bonfire-ACC, probably, burned unneeded trash-ACC.]
Opposite *the building* they burned a bonfire; they were probably burning unneeded trash.

Finally, жаль/жа́лко 'regret, pity' that can be used in impersonal expressions with the genitive (or accusative):

Я люблю́ де́тские голоса́, и мне при э́том быва́ет невырази́мо жаль *свое́й уходя́щей жи́зни*.
[I-NOM love children's voices-ACC, and me-DAT at this-LOC is inexpressibly regret own slipping-away life-GEN.]
I love children's voices, and when I hear them I feel inexpressible regret *for my own life which is slipping away*.

GENITIVE: A GOAL 3—Actual approach

There are two groups of words associated with GENITIVE: A GOAL. For the first group, the goal is actual, and it is touched, held to, acquired, desired, or deserved, in which case the use of the genitive case is obligatory. For the second group, the goal is potential, and it is sought, expected, or hoped for, in which case the use of the genitive is optional. We will look at each group in turn.

Words meaning 'get', 'approach', 'desire' associated with GENITIVE:: A GOAL

'hold to' держа́ться	'worthy' досто́йный	'touch; concern' каса́ться/косну́ться
'get, obtain' добива́ться/доби́ться	'desire, wish' жела́ть/пожела́ть	'listen to; obey' слу́шаться/послу́шаться
'attain, reach' достига́ть/дости́гнуть/дости́чь	'deserve, merit' заслу́живать/заслужи́ть	'be worth, deserve' сто́ить
		'receive, be awarded' удоста́ивать/удосто́ить

Here are a few examples to whet your appetite:

Как вы дости́гли *тако́го нра́вственного соверше́нства*?
[How you-NOM attained such moral perfection-GEN?]
How have you attained *such moral perfection*?
Он встаёт, отхо́дит к окну́. Ка́жется, я доби́лась *своего́* — ему́ неприя́тно.

[He-NOM gets-up, walks to window-DAT. Seems, I-NOM got own-GEN — him-DAT unpleasant.]

He gets up and goes to the window. It seems that I have gotten *what I want* — he is uncomfortable.

Зада́ча литерату́ры состои́т в том, что́бы пока́зывать всех, кого́ обы́чно презира́ют, людьми́, досто́йными *уваже́ния и жа́лости.*

[Task-NOM literature-GEN consists in that-LOC, in-order show everyone-ACC, who-ACC usually despise, people-INST, worthy-INST respect-GEN and pity-GEN.]

Literature's task consists of depicting all people who are despised as people who are worthy of *respect* and *pity*.

As the table suggests, каса́ться/косну́ться can indicate both physical 'touching', as in the first example below, as well as touching in the intellectual realm, usually rendered in English as 'concerning', as in the second example:

Они́ как бу́дто танцева́ли како́й-то ме́дленный та́нец в кра́сной ко́мнате и не каса́лись *по́ла.*

[They-NOM as if danced some slow dance-ACC in red room-LOC and not touched floor-GEN.]

It was as if they were dancing some slow dance in a red room and were not touching *the floor* .

Други́е протоко́лы каса́ются *сотру́дничества* в о́бласти я́дерной энерге́тики и безопа́сности.

[Other protocols-NOM touch collaboration-GEN in area-LOC nuclear energy-GEN and security-GEN.]

Other protocols concern *collaboration* in the area of nuclear energy and security.

The verb жела́ть/пожела́ть 'wish' is an essential but often invisible ingredient in many salutations. A complete sentence such as Я жела́ю вам *успе́ха* [I-NOM wish you-DAT success-GEN] 'I wish you *success* ' shows the underlying structure of these expressions. Usually this formula is abbreviated, leaving only the thing being wished in the genitive case. Here are some common phrases that are built this way:

The invisible role of жела́ть/ пожела́ть 'wish' in salutations using GENITIVE: A GOAL.

Всего́ до́брого/лу́чшего!	[All good/best-GEN!]	*All the best* !
Прия́тного аппети́та!	[Pleasant appetite-GEN!]	*Bon appetit* !
Споко́йной но́чи!	[Calm night-GEN!]	*Good night* !
Счастли́вого пути́!	[Happy trip-GEN!]	Have *a good trip* !

GENITIVE: A GOAL 4—Hypothetical approach

The difference between the words that require the GENITIVE: A GOAL, and those that can use either the genitive or the accusative boils down to a difference between the status of the item that might be marked with the genitive. The verbs that require the genitive also tend to

GENITIVE: A GOAL
is used for
hypothetical
items, and
ACCUSATIVE: A
DESTINATION is
used for specific
items.

require that their object be something we know exists or can identify. You cannot attain a non-existent goal, nor can you touch something that isn't there. But you can look for something or wait for something regardless of whether the object of your quest exists. Snow White sang "Some day my prince will come" before she ever met him, and indeed before she even knew that such a person really existed. She was waiting for a dream, and got lucky. The words that can take either the genitive or the accusative leave the door open for this possibility. When the item being sought is relatively non-specific, the genitive is used; when a specific item is sought, it will appear in the accusative.

Words that can govern GENITIVE:: A GOAL or ACCUSATIVE: A DESTINATION

'wait for' ждáть	'expect' ожидáть	'demand, require' трéбовать/потрéбовать
'seek' искáть	'request' просúть/попросúть	'want; feel like' хотéть/захотéть хотéться/захотéться

The following table should give you some insight into how these verbs are used. Boris is a dreamer like Snow White; he knows that he wants some things, but doesn't necessarily know exactly what they are. His brother Gleb is after specific items he can positively identify.

Comparison of GENITIVE:: A GOAL and ACCUSATIVE: A DESTINATION

Борúс ждёт *автóбуса*.   [Boris-NOM waits bus-GEN.]   Boris is waiting for *a bus*.
(Boris isn't picky. He needs to get away from where he is. He'll take any bus that comes.)

Глеб ждёт автóбус.   [Gleb-NOM waits bus-ACC.]   Gleb is waiting for the bus.
(Gleb knows which bus he wants to take and is waiting for that one.)

Борúс úщет *мéста*.   [Boris-NOM seeks place-GEN.]   Boris is looking for *a job*.
(Boris is unemployed; any job commensurate with his qualifications will do.)

Глеб úщет своё мéсто в зáле.   [Gleb-NOM seeks own place-ACC in hall-LOC.]   Gleb is looking for his seat.
(Gleb has a ticket, and he is trying to find the seat that matches the number printed on it.)

Of course, real examples aren't ordinarily so clear-cut. Here are a couple to illustrate:

Чегó я жду кáждый раз, окáзываясь в незнакóмом мéсте?
[What-GEN I-NOM wait every time-ACC, finding-self in unfamiliar place-LOC?]
What is it that I wait for every time I find myself in an unfamiliar place?

Жизнь, котóрую мы велú, трéбовала *значúтельных расхóдов*.
[Life-NOM, which-ACC we-NOM led, required considerable expenditures-GEN.]
The life we led required *considerable expenditures* .

GENITIVE: A WHOLE 1—'Of', possession, and color

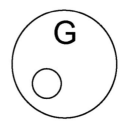

An item (small circle) is a part of a
GENITIVE:: A WHOLE (circle labeled G)

In this submeaning the genitive is a whole of which something else is a part. This accounts for all the uses of the genitive that can be translated as 'of', as well as numerical quantifications indicating amounts of things.

By far the most common use of the genitive is what we call its "bare case" usage, where it is not triggered by any other word. In this pristine state the genitive can indicate possessors, wholes (in relation to parts), and other kinds of 'having' relationships that can motivate a meaning of 'of'.

Perhaps the most basic use of GENITIVE: A WHOLE is to identify wholes that parts belong to. In the physical realm we have parts of discrete objects (floors of buildings), as in the first example below. More abstractly one could say that realities are parts of the world, as in the second example. In the domain of time, hours are parts of the morning, day, evening, or night, motivating the use of утра́ [morning-GEN] 'in the morning', дня [day-GEN] 'in the afternoon', ве́чера [evening-GEN] 'in the evening', and но́чи [night-GEN] 'in the night', as illustrated in the third example.

Мы́ занима́ем це́лый эта́ж *гига́нтского небоскрёба* "Корве́т."
[We-NOM occupy whole floor-ACC giant skyscraper-GEN "Corvette".]
We occupy a whole floor *of the giant* Corvette *skyscraper* .

Дава́йте тре́зво взгля́нем на реа́лии *совреме́нного ми́ра*.
[Let's soberly glance on realities-ACC modern world-GEN.]
Let's take a sober look at the realities *of the modern world* .

В семь часо́в *ве́чера* она́ стоя́ла во́зле его́ до́ма.
[In seven-ACC hours-GEN evening-GEN she-NOM stood next-to his house-GEN.]
At seven o'clock *in the evening* she was standing next to his house.

Since a part belongs to a whole, it can also be thought of as a possession of the whole, and GENITIVE: A WHOLE is often used for this meaning, translatable into English with either the possessive form in *'s*, or with *of*, as in these examples:

Не повтори́те оши́бку *президе́нта*.
[Not repeat error-ACC president-GEN.]
Don't repeat *the president' s* error.

Я вообще́ люблю́ уча́ствовать в жи́зни *други́х люде́й*: сва́тать, сове́товать, лечи́ть.
[I-NOM in-general love participate in life-LOC other people-GEN: do-match-making, advise, heal.]
In general I love to participate in *other people' s* lives/in the life *of other people* : match-making, advising, and healing.

Он нашёл позвонок *ма́монта* в райо́не *ве́чной мерзлоты́.*
[He-NOM found vertebra-ACC mammoth-GEN in region-LOC eternal frost-GEN.]
He found the vertebra *of a mammoth* in the *permafrost* region.

The second use of the genitive in last example above, literally translatable as 'the region *of eternal frost* ', demonstrates another meaning of 'of', namely belonging to a category, being of a type. Here are some examples:

GENITIVE: A WHOLE expresses membership in a category.

Неда́ром я испы́тывал чу́вство *стра́ха.*
[Not-without-reason I-NOM experienced feeling-ACC fear-GEN.]
It is not without reason that I experienced a feeling *of fear* .

Наде́юсь, ты вы́растешь челове́ком *большо́й души́.*
[Hope, you-NOM grow-up person-INST big soul-GEN.]
I hope that you grow up to be a person *with a big soul* .

Был за́пах *дорого́го одеколо́на* в ли́фте.
[Was smell-NOM expensive eau-de-cologne-GEN in elevator-LOC.]
There was the smell *of expensive eau-de-cologne* in the elevator.

GENITIVE: A WHOLE describes color.

Russian characteristically uses the GENITIVE: A WHOLE to describe colors of objects, using the logic of the English phrase *a horse of a different color* :

Он носи́л га́лстук *бе́лого цве́та.*
[He-NOM wore tie-ACC white color-GEN.]
He wore a *white* tie.

GENITIVE: A WHOLE 2—Events, idioms, and chains

GENITIVE: A WHOLE expresses participation in an event.

The items that participate in an event (subject, object, action) are related to each other; in English this relationship is expressed by *of*, and in Russian by the GENITIVE: A WHOLE. In this first example, the event is *a man is planning to publish some books* . This event links the publication to the books:

Он плани́ровал изда́ние *съедо́бных де́тских книг.*
[He-NOM planned publication-ACC edible children's books-GEN.]
He planned the publication *of edible children' s books* .

In this next example the event is *unofficial literature exists* , with the entailment that existence is an attribute of unofficial literature:

Я уже́ тогда́ знал о существова́нии *неофициа́льной литерату́ры.*
[I-NOM already then knew about existence-LOC unofficial literature-GEN.]
At that time I already knew about the existence *of unoffical literature* .

The event *mentally ill people have produced creations*   likewise links the creations to the people:

> Всё бо́льше хозя́ев музе́ев, галере́й и кри́тиков гото́вы рассма́тривать творе́ния психи́чески *больны́х люде́й* как иску́сство.
> [All-NOM more proprietors-GEN museums-GEN, galleries-GEN and critics-GEN ready-NOM consider creations-ACC mentally ill people-GEN as art-ACC.]
> More and more proprietors of museums and galleries, as well as critics, are ready to consider the creations *of* mentally *ill people* as art.

The bare use of GENITIVE: A WHOLE appears in some idiomatic expressions, such as *чего́* [what-GEN] 'why', *всего́* [all-GEN] '*in all, altogether , just, only*', *своего́ ро́да* [own type-GEN] '*in it's own way , all to itself*', and что *но́вого/интере́сного*, etc. [what-NOM new/interesting, etc.-GEN] 'what's/is anything *new/interesting* , etc.', as illustrated in the following examples (the first of which laments the dangers of narcotics):

GENITIVE: A WHOLE in idiomatic expressions.

> Смерть ко́сит и́менно их, молоды́х и здоро́вых, *всего́* лишь раз попро́бовавших забы́ться и уже́ неспосо́бных жить без э́того забытья́.
> [Death-NOM mows precisely them-ACC, young-ACC and healthy-ACC, all-GEN only time-ACC tried-ACC forget-self and already incapable-ACC live without this oblivion-GEN.]
> They are precisely the ones that death mows down, the young and the healthy, who tried *just* once to forget their worries and were no longer capable of living without that oblivion.

> Бо́кс, э́то, в о́бщем-то, *своего́ ро́да* иску́сство.
> [Boxing-NOM, that-NOM, in general-LOC, own type-GEN art-NOM.]
> Boxing is actually an art *all to itself* .

> Кого́ интересу́ют призна́ния литерату́рного неуда́чника? Что́ *поучи́тельного* в его́ и́споведи?
> [Who-ACC interest admissions-NOM literary failure-GEN? What-NOM enlightening-GEN in his confession-LOC?]
> Who is interested in the admissions of a literary failure? Is there anything *enlightening* in his confession?

As mentioned in the introduction to this chapter, the genitive is the one case that can be repeated to form chains. It is specifically the GENITIVE: A WHOLE in its bare case usage that makes this posible. Here is a chain of three consecutive genitive items:

The chaining capacity of GENITIVE: A WHOLE.

> Они́ боевики́ "*Па́ртии исла́мского еди́нства Афганиста́на.*"
> [They-NOM revolutionary-fighters-NOM "Party-GEN Islamic unity-GEN Afghanistan-GEN.]
> They are revolutionary fighters *of the "Islamic unity party of Afghanistan* ".

GENITIVE: A WHOLE 3—Prepositions and prepositional phrases

GENITIVE: A WHOLE
with the
prepositions
среди́ 'among',
посреди́ 'in the
middle of', and
внутри́ 'inside'.

GENITIVE: A WHOLE is also used with the prepositions среди́ 'among', посреди́ 'in the middle of', and внутри́ 'inside'. Here are some examples:

В переры́ве среди́ *уча́стников* на́чали циркули́ровать докуме́нты.
[In break-LOC among participants-GEN began circulate documents-ACC.]
During the break documents began circulating among *the participants* .

Одна́жды мы с ма́чехой бежа́ли по у́лице, торопи́лись в кино́, а посреди́
доро́ги лежа́л райо́нный алкого́лик, но не дя́дя Ко́ля, а друго́й.
[Once we-NOM with step-mother-INST ran along street-DAT, hurried to cinema-ACC, and in-the-middle road-GEN lay regional alcoholic-NOM, but not uncle Kolya-NOM, but other-NOM.]
Once my step-mother and I were running down the street, hurrying to the cinema, and in the middle *of the road* lay a local alcoholic, but it wasn't uncle Kolya, it was someone else.

Самолёт взвы́л, пото́м ста́л набира́ть отча́яние внутри́ *себя́*.
[Airplane-NOM howled, then began gather despair-ACC inside self-GEN.]
The airplane howled and then began gathering despair within *itself* .

There are dozens of prepositional phrases in Russian that function as complex prepositions followed by the GENITIVE: A WHOLE with the meaning 'of'. The following table displays some of the more typical phrases, and is followed by a couple of examples:

Prepositional phrases meaning 'of' associated with GENITIVE:: A WHOLE

в а́дрес	'directed toward'	в тече́ние	'in the course of'
в ви́де	'in the form of'	в усло́виях	'in the conditions of'
в грани́цах	'within the bounds of'	в честь	'in honor of'
в де́ле	'in the case of'	в числе́	'in the number of, among'
в знак	'as a mark/token of'	во вре́мя	'in the time of, during'
в ка́честве	'in the capacity of'	во и́мя	'in the name of'
в направле́нии	'in the direction of'	вне преде́лов	'beyond the limits of'
в о́бласти	'in the area of'	вне ра́мок	'beyond the bounds/framework/ context of'
в отноше́нии	'in the relation of, with respect to'		
в по́льзу	'in favor of, on behalf of'	за счёт	'at the expense of'
в преде́лах	'within the limits/bounds of'	на основа́нии	'on the basis of'
в продолже́нии	'in the course of'	на пути́	'on the path of'
в ра́мках	'within the limits/framework of'	по ме́ре	'according to the measure of, as far as'
в результа́те	'as a result of'	по по́воду	'on the occasion of, concerning'
в ро́ли	'in the role of'	по причи́не	'by reason of'
в смы́сле	'in the sense of, as regards'	по слу́чаю	'by reason of'
в слу́чае	'in case of'	под ви́дом	'under the guise of'
в сфе́ре	'in the realm of'	под и́менем	'in the name of'

Prepositional phrases meaning 'of' associated with GENITIVE:: A WHOLE (continued)			
под назва́нием	'under the title of'	с по́мощью	'with the help of'
под предло́гом	'on the pretext of'	с це́лью	'with the goal of'
при по́мощи	'with the help of'	с то́чки зре́ния	'from the point of view of'
при посре́дстве	'by means of'	со стороны́	'from the side of'
при усло́вии	'on the condition of'	че́рез посре́дство	'by means of'

В ра́мках *рабо́чего визи́та* в Тегера́н состоя́лась встре́ча на́шего специали́ста с представи́телями бази́рующейся в Ира́не афга́нской оппози́ции.
[In frames-LOC working visit-GEN to Tehran-ACC took-place meeting-NOM our specialist-GEN with representatives-INST based-GEN in Iran-LOC Afghan opposition-GEN.]
In the context *of a working visit* to Tehran our specialist met with representatives of the Afghan opposition based in Iran.

Впервы́е в ка́честве *полнопра́вных уча́стников* междунаро́дного соглаше́ния вы́ступили пятна́дцать бы́вших сове́тских респу́блик.
[For-the-first-time in capacity-LOC full-fledged participants-GEN international agreement-GEN acted fifteen-NOM former Soviet republics-GEN.]
For the first time the fifteen former Soviet republics acted in the capacity *of full-fledged participants* in an international agreement.

GENITIVE: A WHOLE 4—Numerals and quantifiers

A part of a whole can also be interpreted as an amount of the whole. In this use, the gentive is viewed as a set of objects or as a substance, and portions of the genitive item are measured out. This accounts for the use of GENITIVE: A WHOLE with numerals, with words meaning 'add', 'subtract', 'full', 'enough', as well as partitive uses.

Numerals come in many types. There are integers, fractions, and indefinite numerals such as ско́лько 'how many', не́сколько 'some', сто́лько 'so many', мно́го 'many/much', немно́го 'not many/much', ма́ло 'few/little', бо́льше 'more', ме́ньше 'fewer/less' нема́ло 'not a few', and many other words indicating amounts. In this sampling of quantifiers with GENITIVE: A WHOLE, note that the quantifier and the quantified (in the genitive) do not have to appear next to each other in a sentence; in the third and fourth examples the genitive item quantified is the first word, whereas the quantifier is the last:

Я опозда́ла на пятна́дцать *мину́т.*
[I-NOM got-late on fifteen-ACC minutes-GEN.]
I was fifteen *minutes* late.

GENITIVE: A WHOLE expresses quantification with numerals, quantifiers, and in partitive expressions.

Он пел про́сто, гро́мко, моното́нно, но в э́том бы́ло сто́лько *прямоты́*, сто́лько *мужско́й и́скренности, беззащи́тности*.
[He-NOM sang simply, loudly, in-monotone, but in that-LOC was so-much-NOM straightforwardness-GEN, so-much-NOM masculine sincerity-GEN, vulnerability-GEN.]
His singing was simple, loud, and monotonous, but in it there was so much *straightforwardness* , so much *masculine sincerity* and *vulnerability* .

Жела́ющих обуча́ться в япо́нском це́нтре оказа́лось чрезвыча́йно мно́го.
[Desiring-GEN study in Japanese center-LOC turned-out exceedingly many-NOM.]
The number of people desiring to study at the Japanese center turned out to be exceedingly large.

Наро́ду станови́лось всё бо́льше.
[People-GEN became all-NOM more.]
More and more *people* were there.

The inversion of a numeral and GENITIVE: A WHOLE expresses approximation.

Although Russian does have words like приблизи́тельно 'approximately', you can achieve a similar effect merely by inverting a numeral and the quantified genitive item. An approximate number of items is cited in the example below:

Их бы́ло *штук* пятьдеся́т.
[They-GEN was items-GEN fifty-NOM.]
There were approximately fifty *of them* .

GENITIVE: A WHOLE 5—'Some'

The partitive use of GENITIVE: A WHOLE means 'some'.

It is not uncommon for the genitive to signal quantification without a numeral or other word to express the amount. The "default" amount is usually equivalent to English *some* (often called the "partitive" meaning in textbooks), and with perfective verbs and certain nouns referring to substances the so-called "second genitive" ending (in -у/-ю) is used, as in the first example below.

Я вы́пил *ча́ю*, кото́рый заказа́л по телефо́ну.
[I-NOM drank-up tea-GEN, which-NOM ordered along telephone-DAT.]
I drank up *the tea* that I ordered by phone.

—А во́дка есть там? —Есть. —Дава́й лу́чше *во́дки* вы́пьем.
[—And vodka-NOM is there? —Is. —Give better vodka-GEN drink-up.]
—And do they have vodka there? —Yes. —Let's drink *(some) vodka* instead.

—А у́тром она́ говори́т, без тебя́ не могу́. —А ты что? —Ну, успоко́ил, *де́нег* дал...
[—And morning-INST she-NOM says, without you-GEN not can. —And you-NOM what-ACC? —Well, calmed, money-GEN gave...]
—And in the morning she says, I can't go on without you. —And what did you say?
—Well, I calmed her down, gave her *some money* .

The genitive can have a quantitative meaning in the presence of a variety of words that express having or manipulating an amount of something. Some of these words are listed in the table and illustrated in the examples below:

Words expressing quantities associated with GENITIVE:: A WHOLE		
'sufficent quantity' доста́ток доста́точно 'enough'	'collect, pick up' набира́ться/набра́ться	'increase, add' прибавля́ть(ся)/приба́вить(ся)
'become filled' исполня́ться/испо́лниться испо́лненный 'full'	'eat/have one's fill' наеда́ться/нае́сться 'full' по́лный	'decrease, subtract' убавля́ть(ся)/уба́вить(ся) 'be enough' хвата́ть/хвати́ть

Она́ броса́ла непоня́тные, зага́дочные фра́зы, испо́лненные *како́го-то потайно́го смы́сла*.
[She-NOM flung incomprehensible, mysterious phrases-ACC, filled-ACC some secret meaning-GEN.]
She flung incomprehensible, mysterious phrases, filled *with some secret meaning* .

Он набра́лся *хра́брости* и спроси́л: почему́?
[He-NOM collected courage-GEN and asked: Why?]
He collected *his courage* and asked: Why?

Буква́льно два дня наза́д я запусти́л ка́рточку в банкома́т и обнару́жил, что на моём счету́ за́ год не то́лько не приба́вилось *причита́ющихся* мне *проце́нтов*, но да́же *мои́х кро́вных* суще́ственно уба́вилось.
[Literally two days-ACC ago I-NOM put card-ACC in automated-teller-ACC and discovered, that on my account-LOC in year-ACC not only not increased owed-GEN me-DAT percents-GEN, but even my own-GEN significantly decreased.]
Just two days ago I put my card into the automated teller and discovered that in the course of a year not only had *the percentage owed* me on my account not been added, but even *my own money* had significantly decreased.

Она́ никогда́ не заду́мывалась над тем, хва́тит ли у неё *сил* и *здоро́вья* на осуществле́ние свои́х пла́нов и что бу́дет пото́м.
[She-NOM never not thought above that-INST, is-enough whether by her-GEN strengths-GEN and health-GEN on realization-ACC own plans-GEN and what-NOM will-be afterward.]
She never thought about whether she had enough *strength* and *health* to realize her plans and what would happen afterward.

GENITIVE: A REFERENCE 1—Dates and other reference points

In the fourth and final meaning of the genitive, the focus of our attention is located near the genitive item, from which it is separated. This combination of proximity and separation allows the genitive to serve as a reference point in the domains of time and space and on scales of qualitative and quantitative assessment. In the domain of time, the most frequent use of the GENITIVE: A REFERENCE is with dates. Note that the genitive is only used for a date when something happens, in other words here the genitive item serves as a temporal reference point for an event:

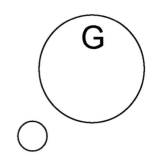

An item (small circle) is in the proximity of a GENITIVE:: A REFERENCE (circle labeled G)

На пресс-конфере́нции, состоя́вшейся *тре́тьего* декабря́, шла речь о ме́рах, предпринима́емых прави́тельством Росси́и для ускоре́ния экономи́ческих рефо́рм.
[On press-conference-LOC took-place-LOC third-GEN December-GEN, went talk-NOM about measures-LOC undertaken-LOC government-INST Russia-GEN for acceleration-GEN economic reforms-GEN.]
At the press conference which took place *on the third* of December, they talked about the measures that the Russian government has undertaken to accelerate economic reforms.

Восьмо́го а́вгуста 1927 г. М. Цвета́ева писа́ла свое́й знако́мой С. Н. Андро́никовой-Гальпе́рн.
[Eighth-GEN August-GEN 1927 year-GEN M. Tsvetaeva-NOM wrote own acquaintance S. N. Andronikova-Galpern-DAT.]
On the eighth of August 1927 M. Tsvetaeva wrote to her acquaintance S. N. Andronikova-Galpern.

A large number of prepositions locate items in both time and space with reference to GENITIVE: A REFERENCE as being without, after, before, behind, near, etc.[56] A few of these prepositions operate in other domains, such as similarity (наподо́бие 'in the likeness of') or concepts (ввиду́ 'in view of', насчёт 'on the matter of'). In many instances (those marked with asterisks) these prepositions clearly derive from earlier prepositional phrases (now written as one word), originally with a following GENITIVE: A WHOLE meaning 'of'; compare these with the prepositional phrases that appear in the section on GENITIVE: A WHOLE above. These complex prepositions can be thought of as belonging to both GENITIVE: A WHOLE and GENITIVE: A REFERENCE.

Prepositions associated with GENITIVE:: A REFERENCE ·

(Items marked with asterisks derive from earlier preposi-tional phrases, now written as one word.)		кро́ме	'except, besides, aside from'
		ми́мо	'by, past'
без	'without'	накану́не*	'on the eve of'
близ	'near'	наподо́бие*	'in the likeness of'
вблизи́*	'nearby'	напро́тив	'opposite'
ввиду́*	'in view of'	насчёт*	'on the matter of'
вдоль*	'along'	о́коло	'around; approximately'
взаме́н*	'in place of'	по́дле	'beside'
вме́сто*	'in place of'	позади́*	'behind'
вне	'outside of'	поми́мо	'aside from'
во́зле	'near'	попере́к*	'across'
вокру́г*	'around'	по́сле	'after'
впереди́*	'in front of'	пре́жде	'before'
вро́де*	'like'	сверх*	'over, above'
		у	'near, at, by'

The following examples display some of these prepositions:

Но без *ри́ска* ничего́ це́нного не сде́лаешь.
[But without risk-GEN nothing valuable-GEN not do.]
But you can't do anything of value without *risk*.

Прави́тельстом Украи́пы при́нято реше́ние о проведе́нии регистра́ции верну́вшихся по́сле *эвакуа́ции* 1986 го́да люде́й и их пропи́ске в населённых пу́нктах, располо́женных вблизи́ *зо́ны.*
[Government-INST Ukraine-GEN taken-NOM decision-NOM about carrying-out-LOC registration-GEN returned-GEN after evacuation-GEN 1986 year-GEN people-GEN and their residence-registration-LOC in settled points-LOC, located-LOC near zone-GEN.]
A decision has been made by the government of Ukraine about registering people who returned afer the 1986 *evacuation* and awarding them residence in settlements near *the zone*.

По бульва́ру вдо́ль *жёлтых скаме́ек*, мимо *ги́псовых урн* шага́ет небольшо́го ро́ста челове́к.
[Along boulevard-DAT along yellow benches-GEN, past plaster urns-GEN strides small stature-GEN person-NOM.]
Down the boulevard, along *the yellow benches* , past *the plaster urns* , strides a person of small stature.

"Жизнь прекра́сна и удиви́тельна!" — как восклица́л това́рищ Маяко́вский накану́не *самоуби́йства.*
["Life-NOM wonderful-NOM and amazing-NOM!" — as exclaimed comrade Mayakovsky-NOM on-the-eve suicide-GEN.]
"Life is wonderful and amazing!" — as comrade Mayakovsky was exclaiming on the eve *of his suicide* .

The idiomatic
expression меж
двух жерновóв
'between a rock
and a hard
place'.

The genitive appears in an idiomatic expression that belongs among the GENITIVE: A REFERENCE prepositions, меж *двух жерновóв*, literally 'between *two millstones* ':

Когдá сам ужé нáчал попи́сывать, попáл я меж *двух жерновóв* — мéжду прáвдой и лóжью.
[When self-NOM already began write, fell I-NOM between two millstones-GEN — between truth-INST and falsehood-INST.]
When I myself began to write, I fell between *a rock and a hard place* — between truth and falsehood.

GENITIVE: A REFERENCE 2—у 'by'

у + GENITIVE: A
REFERENCE means
'by, near' in the
domain of space.

The use of the preposition у could be a subchapter to itself. У can be variously deployed in the domains of space, possession, and causation. In its basic spatial use, у simply means 'by' or 'near':

У *дверú* сиди́т мисс Фи́ллипс и вя́жет.
[By door-GEN sits Miss Phillips-NOM and knits.]
Miss Phillips sits by *the door* and knits.

у + GENITIVE: A
REFERENCE
expresses
possession.

By far the most common use of у is in the Russian construction that expresses 'have', у possessor-GEN + (есть) + possession-NOM, literally 'by *the possessor* is a possession', usually understood as '*the possessor* has a possession'. Here is an example:

Крóме вас, у *семьú* уби́той бы́ли друзья́ и́ли хорóшие знакóмые?
[Aside-from you-GEN, by family-GEN deceased-GEN were friends-NOM or good acquaintances-NOM?]
Aside from you, did *the family* of the deceased have any friends or close acquaintances?

A similar constuction is used for pain and other sensations coming from body parts (which are our inalienable possessions):

Вдруг я замéтил, что у *меня́* трясу́тся ру́ки.
[Suddenly I-NOM noticed, that by me-GEN shake hands-NOM.]
Suddenly I noticed that *my* hands were shaking.

у + GENITIVE: A
REFERENCE with
people expresses
'at so-and so's
place'.

When the genitive item is a person, у + GENITIVE: A REFERENCE can mean 'at *so-and so's place* ', as in this example:

Мéсяц назáд я забы́ла у *негó* очки́ от сóлнца.
[Month-ACC ago I-NOM forgot by him-GEN glasses-ACC from sun-GEN.]
A month ago I forgot my sunglasses at *his place* .

This construction can also be used to express causation, in other words, having someone do something for you. In this example: 'doing my hair y someone-GEN' = 'having *someone* do my hair':

The causative use of y + GENITIVE: A REFERENCE with people.

Мне безразли́чно, у *кого́* причёсываться, я пото́м всё равно́ переде́лаю по-сво́ему.
[Me-DAT indifferent, by who-GEN do-hair, I-NOM afterward all same redo in-own-way.]
I don't care *who* does my hair, afterward I redo it my own way anyway.

GENITIVE: A REFERENCE 3—Lack

As we have already seen above under GENITIVE: A WHOLE, the genitive case in Russian is associated with quantification. The separation aspect of GENITIVE: A REFERENCE is here interpreted as negative quantification, or lack, a use commonly called the "genitive of negation". Note that separation does not necessarily imply non-existence, it just means that the genitive item isn't available. In the first example below there is of course no denial that the American way of life exists, but the hearer is separated from it by a lack of experience:

GENITIVE: A REFERENCE with negation expresses lack.

Вы про́сто не зна́ете *америка́нской жи́зни.*
[You-NOM simply not know American life-GEN.]
You simply don't know *(anything about) life in America* .

Here are a few more typical examples of the GENITIVE: A REFERENCE with negated verbs. Notice that the genitive item can be either the subject of the sentence (as in the first two examples) or the direct object (as in the last two):

В то же вре́мя в ча́стном се́кторе *никаки́х забасто́вок* не́ было.
[In that same time-ACC in private sector-LOC no-kind strikes-GEN not was.]
At the same time there were *no strikes* in the private sector.

Когда́ я добра́лся до угла́ — *её* нигде́ не́ было.
[When I-NOM reached to corner-GEN — she-GEN nowhere not was.]
When I reached the corner — *she* wasn't anywhere.

Мо́жно бы́ло догада́ться, что *си́льного впечатле́ния* я не произвёл.
[Possible was surmise, that strong impression-GEN I-NOM not made.]
One could surmise that I did not make *a strong impression* .

Остана́вливаюсь перед рису́нками, *ничего́* не ви́жу, кро́ме чёрно-бе́лых пя́тен.
[Stop in-front drawings-INST, nothing-GEN not see, aside-from black-white spots-GEN.]
I stop in front of the drawings, but I don't see *anything* except black and white spots.

The following table lists some words in Russian that express the concept 'lack' and are associated with the use of the GENITIVE: A REFERENCE:

Expressions of lacking associated with GENITIVE:: A REFERENCE

'deficit' дефици́т	'be deprived' лиша́ться/лиши́ться лишённый 'deprived'	'be lacking' недостава́ть/недоста́ть недоста́ток 'lack'
'deprive' лиша́ть/лиши́ть		'shortage' нехва́тка

Here are a couple of examples for orientation:

Обы́чная на́ша жизнь была́ лишена́ *всей э́той ро́скоши, каза́вшейся* театра́льной, предназна́ченой исключи́тельно для счастли́вой мину́ты.
[Ordinary our life-NOM was deprived-NOM all this luxury-GEN, seeming-GEN theatrical-INST, set-aside-INST exclusively for happy minute-GEN.]
Our ordinary life was deprived *of all this luxury , which seemed* theatrical, and was set aside exclusively for a happy time.

38 проце́нтов (бо́льше тре́ти!) москвиче́й се́туют на нехва́тку не *магази́нов* и *рестора́нов*, а *городски́х туале́тов*.
[38-NOM percent-GEN (more third-GEN!) Muscovites-GEN complain on shortage-ACC not stores-GEN and restaurants-GEN, but municipal toilets-GEN.]
38 percent (more than a third!) of Muscovites complain of a lack not *of stores* and *restaurants* , but *of municipal toilets* .

GENITIVE: A REFERENCE 4—Comparison

GENITIVE: A REFERENCE in making comparisons.

Finally, distance gives you a perspective for comparing items separated along various scales of measure. GENITIVE: A REFERENCE allows you to examine the difference between the genitive item (which is held as the standard) and another item in a comparison. This motivates the use of the genitive with comparative adjectives and adverbs in constructions of the type: other item + comparative + standard-GEN, meaning 'the other item is better/longer/stronger, etc. *than the genitive item* '. Here are some examples:

О́бщее де́ло должно́ быть вы́ше *ли́чных интере́сов*.
[Common cause-NOM should be higher personal interests-GEN.]
The common cause should be higher (priority) *than personal interests* .

Глу́по держа́ть в помеще́нии бо́льше *одно́й карти́ны* Рембра́ндта.
[Stupid keep in room-LOC more one picture-GEN Rembrandt-GEN.]
It is stupid to keep more *than one of* Rembrandt's *pictures* in the room.

Пел он, возмо́жно, и ху́же *за́падных певцо́в,* но тря́сся сильне́е.
[Sang he-NOM, perhaps, even worse Western singers-GEN, but shook stronger.]
Perhaps he did sing worse *than Western singers*, but he shook more.

Год бу́дет лу́чше *предыду́щего.*
[Year-NOM will-be better previous-GEN.]
This year will be better *than the previous one.*

Epilogue

The word *genitive* is related to *generation* and *genesis*, and all these words are derived from the Latin and Greek roots meaning 'give birth'. Indeed giving birth is the means by which living creatures such as ourselves serve as sources for more of our kind. The genitive case continues the theme of the role of human beings that was so prominent in our discussion of the dative case. People get special treatment in the system of preposition and case combinations to express 'going to', 'being at', and 'coming from'. Not only do we humans require к + DAT when we are destinations, but as locations we demand у + GEN and when we are places of departure we are the objects of от + GEN. Location у + GEN 'at' a person can motivate a variety of interpretations, among them possession, being at someone's place, or having that someone do something. Physical movement from and to items can be metaphorically extended to express human beings' emotional withdrawal from and attraction to things through fear, disgust, desire, or expectation. Russian even asks us whether we can identify the object of our desire, thus grammatically capturing that very human dilemma of knowing that we want something but not knowing exactly what that something is. The genitive case is also very concerned with quantity in terms of amounts, deficiency, and comparison. In the current age of quantification, when we are all threatened with being reduced to statistics and identification numbers, it is curious to note that the Russian genitive integrates an appreciation of our distinctive human qualities with a focus on numerical concepts.

LOCATIVE Forms

Feminine declension nouns				
hard type: 'room'		**soft type: 'week'**	
singular	plural	singular	plural
ко́мнате	ко́мнатах	неде́ле	неде́лях

-ь: 'talent'				
singular	plural		
спосо́бности	спосо́бностях		

Masculine declension nouns

hard type: 'courtyard'		**soft type: 'nail'**	
singular	plural	singular	plural
дворе́	двора́х	гвозде́	гвоздя́х

Neuter declension nouns

hard type: 'body'		**soft type: 'schedule'**	
singular	plural	singular	plural
те́ле	тела́х	расписа́нии	расписа́ниях

Adjectives

hard type: 'first'			
feminine	masculine	neuter	plural
пе́рвой	пе́рвом	пе́рвом	пе́рвых

soft type: 'last'			
feminine	masculine	neuter	plural
после́дней	после́днем	после́днем	после́дних

Pronouns

'I'	'we'	'you' informal	'you'
мне	нас	тебе́	вас

'she'	'he'	'it'	'they'
(н)ей	(н)ём	(н)ём	(н)их

'who'	'what'	'oneself'	
ком	чём	себе́	

'this'			
feminine	masculine	neuter	plural
э́той	э́том	э́том	э́тих

'all, every'			
feminine	masculine	neuter	plural
всей	всём	всём	всех

Possessives

feminine	masculine	neuter	plural
'my'			
мое́й	моём	моём	мои́х

'our'			
на́шей	на́шем	на́шем	на́ших

Numerals

'one'			
feminine	masculine	neuter	plural
одно́й	одно́м	одно́м	одни́х

'two'	'three'	'four'	'five'
дву́х	трёх	четырёх	пяти́

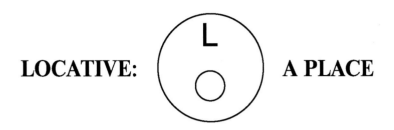

LOCATIVE: A PLACE

Prologue

An overview of the locative case.

LOCATIVE: A PLACE is a setting, locating an item in space, time, or a metaphorical domain. The locative is the only case in Russian that always requires a preposition, and is therefore often called the "prepositional case". Five prepositions are associated with LOCATIVE: A PLACE: в 'in', на 'on', при 'at', о 'about', and по 'upon, after'. The uses of в, на, and при are based upon human experience of physical location in the domain of our three-dimensional environment. The domain of the preposition о is topics of thought or discourse, things that we think, talk, and write about. The use of the preposition по with the locative is relatively rare.

LOCATIVE: A PLACE 1—в 'in'

B 'in' is by far the most common preposition used with the locative, and in its basic sense it identifies an enclosed place in three-dimensional space, a container. This place can be defined by boundaries, such as the walls of apartments, houses, an elevator, or even a plastic bag (as in the examples below), or it can be an enveloping substance (in this case, manure):

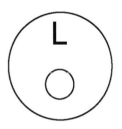

An item (small circle) is in a LOCATIVE: A PLACE (circle labeled L)

в + LOCATIVE: A PLACE means 'in' a container.

Он счита́ет, что в *кварти́рах* москвиче́й зимо́й тепле́е, чем в *токи́йских дома́х*, где нет центра́льного отопле́ния.
[He-NOM thinks, that in apartments-LOC Muscovites-GEN winter-INST warmer, than in Tokyo houses-LOC, where not central heating-GEN.]
He thinks that in winter it is warmer in Muscovites' *apartments* than it is in *Tokyo houses*, where there is no central heating.

Он не переноси́л е́здить в *ли́фте* компа́нией, остава́ться в *за́мкнутом простра́нстве* с незнако́мым челове́ком.
[He-NOM not endured ride in elevator-LOC group-INST, stay in closed space-LOC with uknown person-INST.]
He could not endure riding in *an elevator* with others, staying in *a closed space* with an unknown person.

Он промёрз, как свежеморо́женый о́вощ в *целлофа́не*.
[He-NOM froze, like fresh-frozen vegetable-NOM in cellophane-LOC.]
He was frozen, like a flash-frozen vegetable in *cellophane*.

Бы́ло очеви́дно, что он занима́ется у́мственным трудо́м, и очеви́дно, что его́ дед привы́к стоя́ть по коле́но в *наво́зе* и шурова́ть лопа́той.
[Was obvious, that he-NOM is-occupied intellectual work-INST, and obvious, that his grandfather-NOM accustomed stand up-to knee-ACC in manure-LOC and heave shovel-INST.]
It was obvious that he does intellectual work, and obvious that his grandfather is used to standing in *manure* up to his knees and heaving a shovel.

The container referred to by в in physical space need not have physical or fixed boundaries. Consider the political boundaries we project upon cities and countries, or the temporary container created by folding the fingers toward the palm, as in the following examples:

Ма́льчики во *всех стра́нах* одина́ково не хотя́т ходи́ть в шко́лу.
[Boys-NOM in all countries-LOC equally not want go to school-ACC.]
Boys in *all countries* equally dislike going to school.

До трамва́я я дошёл благополу́чно, нося́ чемода́н то в *пра́вой*, то в *ле́вой руке́*.
[To tram-GEN I-NOM went successfully, carrying suitcase-ACC that in right-LOC, that in left hand-LOC.]
I made my way to the tram successfully, carrying my suitcase first in *my right hand* and then in *my left*.

В + LOCATIVE: A PLACE expresses wearing.

Clothing serves as a container for the body, inspiring the use of в to express wearing, which can be extended even to other worn items, such as glasses and beards. Here's a typical example with clothing, one with a clear parallel in English:

Она́ стоя́ла в стороне́, в *коро́тком пальто́*, из кото́рого давно́ вы́росла.
[She-NOM stood in side-LOC, in short coat-LOC, from which-GEN long-ago outgrew.]
She stood to one side, in *a short coat* which she had long ago outgrown.

The idiomatic use of в + LOCATIVE: A PLACE meaning 'at a distance of'.

The preposition в followed by a unit of distance constitutes an idiomatic expression translatable as 'at a distance of'. Here is an example:

Пала́у, архипела́г, состоя́щий из двухсо́т ме́лких острово́в, располо́женный в *800 киломе́трах* к ю́го-восто́ку от Филиппи́н, стал 185-м чле́ном ООН.
[Palau-NOM, archipelago-NOM, consisting-NOM from two-hundred small islands-GEN, located-NOM in 800 kilometers-LOC to south-east from Philippines-GEN, became 185th member-INST UN-GEN.]
Palau, an archipelago consisting of two hundred small islands located at *a distance of 800 kilometers* to the south-east of the Philippines, became the 185th member of the UN.

When implemented in the domain of time, в + LOCATIVE: A PLACE tends to be associated with extended periods of time 'in' which events can be located, and the use is indeed very similar to the temporal use of 'in' in English:

> Ка́жется маловероя́тным, что́бы он плани́ровал в *бу́дущем* боро́ться за президе́нтское кре́сло.
> [Seems unlikely-INST, that he-NOM planned in future-LOC fight for president's seat-ACC.]
> It seems unlikely that he was planning in the *future* to fight for the president's seat.

> В *де́тстве* она́ утвержда́ла, что её мать не убо́рщица в магази́не, а киноактри́са.
> [In childhood-LOC she-NOM claimed, that her mother-NOM not cleaning-lady-NOM in store-LOC, but movie-actress-NOM.]
> In *her childhood* she claimed that her mother was not a cleaning lady in a store, but a movie actress.

> Ещё оди́н центр был откры́т в *ноябре́* в Хаба́ровске.
> [Yet one center-NOM was opened-NOM in November-LOC in Khabarovsk-LOC.]
> Another center was opened in *November* in Khabarovsk.

В + LOCATIVE: A PLACE can operate in many other domains, all of which are understood as metaphorical spaces. Marriage is a state of being which one can be 'in', as seen in the first example below. The numerical domain locates the position of inflation in the second example. The third sentence contains two examples of abstract locations, one is an emotional state of passion, and the other is a group of people constituting the diplomatic corps.

> Печа́льно, но тех, кто сча́стлив в *бра́ке*, по́лностью игнори́руют.
> [Unfortunately, but those-ACC, who-NOM happy-NOM in marriage-LOC completely ignore.]
> It's unfortunate, but those who are happy in *marriage* are completely ignored.

> Инфля́ция в *годово́м исчисле́нии* дости́гла 120 проце́нтов.
> [Inflation in annual calculation-LOC reached 120 percent-GEN.]
> In *the annual calculation* inflation reached 120 percent.

> В *пристра́стии* к му́зыке он, пожа́луй, лиди́рует в *дипломати́ческом ко́рпусе*.
> [In passion-LOC to music-DAT he-NOM, probably, leads in diplomatic corps-LOC.]
> In *his passion* for music he is probably the leader in *the diplomatic corps*.

In the chapter on the accusative case it was noted that certain nouns referring to people with verbs meaning 'go, join, play the role of' have a special idiomatic accusative plural that looks just like the nominative plural, such as пойти́ в го́сти [go in guests-ACC] 'go for a visit', пойти́ в солда́ты [go in soldiers-ACC] 'become a soldier'. There are parallel idioms for expressing the state of being a guest, a soldier, etc. that use the locative plural; the most common of these is быть в *гостя́х* [be in guests-LOC] 'be *visiting*' (literally 'be *a guest*' at someone's place).

LOCATIVE: A PLACE 2—Words that trigger в; the 2nd locative

A large number of words in Russian are typically followed by the preposition в + LOCA-TIVE: A PLACE. Some of them have obvious parallels to English phrases, but many do not and some might seem altogether counter-intuitive. Here is a list of в + LOC phrases you can expect to encounter:

Words that can trigger в + LOCATIVE: A PLACE

'assure of'
заверя́ть/заве́рить в
завере́ние в 'assurance of'

'consist, lie in'
заключа́ться/заключи́ться в

'get tangled up in, get involved in'
запу́тываться/запу́таться в

'confusion'
пу́таница в

'excel in'
изощря́ться/изощри́ться в
изощре́ние в 'refinement in'

'clever at'
ло́вкий в
ло́вкость в 'cleverness in'

'need'
нужда́ться в
нужда́ в 'need of'

'accuse of, charge with'
обвиня́ть/обвини́ть в
обвине́ние в 'accusation of'

'be deceived, disappointed in'
обма́нываться/обману́ться в

'find oneself in'
ока́зываться/оказа́ться в

'experienced in'
о́пытный в
о́пыт в 'experience in'

'refuse, deny'
отка́зывать/отказа́ть в
отка́з в 'refusal of'

'give an account of, report on'
отчи́тываться/отчита́ться в
отчёт в 'account of, report on'

'suspect of'
подозрева́ть/заподо́зрить в
подозре́ние в 'suspicion of'

'need of'
потре́бность в

'confess to'
признава́ться/призна́ться в
призна́ние в 'confession of'

'understand'
разобра́ться/разбира́ться в

'be disappointed in'
разочаро́вываться/
разочарова́ться в
разочарова́ние в 'disappointment in'

'confess to'
сознава́ться/созна́ться в

'doubt'
сомнева́ться в
сомне́ние в 'doubt of'

'consist in, lie in, be'
состоя́ть в

'lucky with'
счастли́вый в
сча́стье в 'luck with'

'convince (oneself) of'
убежда́ть(ся)/убеди́ть(ся) в
убежде́ние в 'conviction'

'certainty about'
уве́ренность в
уве́рен в 'certain of'

'successful with'
уда́чливый в
уда́ча в 'success with'

'assure oneself of'
удостоверя́ться/удостове́риться в
удостовере́ние в 'attestation of'

'reproach because of'
упрека́ть/упрекну́ть в
упрёк в 'reproach for'

'succeed, make progress in'
успева́ть/успе́ть в
успева́ние в 'progress in'

'success in'
успе́х(и) в

'participate in'
уча́ствовать в
уча́ствующий в 'participant in'
уча́стие в 'participation in'

'be counted among'
чи́слиться в

Here are some examples of how these phrases work in real sentences:

Она́ никогда́ не удивля́лась тому́, что он почти́ не нужда́ется во *сне*.
[She-NOM never not be-surprised that-DAT, that he-NOM almost not need in sleep-LOC.]
It never surprised her that he hardly needed any *sleep*.

Ка́ждый день я обвиня́л её в *сме́ртных греха́х*.
[Every day-ACC I-NOM accused her-ACC in mortal sins-LOC.]
Every day I accused her of *mortal sins*.

Снача́ла над ним смея́лись, пото́м ста́ли отмеча́ть успе́хи в *психиатри́и* и *иску́сстве*, а в конце́ концо́в позво́лили откры́ть "Дом худо́жников".
[At-first above him-INST laughed, then started notice successes-ACC in psychiatry-LOC and art-LOC, and in end-LOC ends-GEN allowed open "House-ACC artists-GEN".]
At first people laughed at him, but then they started to notice his successes in *psychiatry* and in *art*, and finally they allowed him to open a "House of Artists".

Го́рький оказа́лся в весьма́ *нело́вком положе́нии*: Пастерна́к мог заподо́зрить его́ в *неи́скренности*.
[Gorky-NOM found-self in very awkward position-LOC: Pasternak-NOM could suspect him-ACC in insincerity-LOC.]
Gorky found himself in *a* very *awkward position*: Pasternak could suspect him of *insincerity*.

About 150 masculine nouns in Russian have an alternate locative singular ending in -у́/-ю́ (always stressed), sometimes called the "second locative". The second locative only occurs with the prepositions в and на, but it spans the domains of space, time, and metaphorical space, as we see in these three examples:

The second locative ending -у́/-ю́ with в + LOCATIVE: A PLACE.

Смех выраба́тывает в *мозгу́* челове́ка эндорфи́ны — вещества́, кото́рые посыла́ют свои́ сигна́лы лимфоци́там, противостоя́щим ви́русам и инфе́кциям.
[Laughter-NOM produces in brain-LOC person-GEN endorphines-ACC — substances-ACC, which-NOM send their signals-ACC lymphocytes-DAT, resisting-DAT viruses-DAT and infections-DAT.]
Laughter creates in a person's *brain* endorphines — substances which send their signals to the lymphocytes that resist viruses and infections.

Вся э́та рабо́та должна́ быть завершена́ в *теку́щем году́*.
[All this work-NOM should-NOM be completed-NOM in current year-LOC.]
All this work should be completed in *the current year*.

Я перека́тывала го́лову по поду́шке как в *бреду́*.
[I-NOM turned head-ACC along pillow-DAT as in delirium-LOC.]
I turned my head from side to side on the pillow as if in *a delirium*.

LOCATIVE: A PLACE 3—на 'on, at'

In its basic spatial meaning, на 'on' + LOCATIVE: A PLACE refers to a two-dimensional surface where something is located.

На *сту́льях* и *крова́ти* лежа́ли ве́щи, вы́нутые из сундука́, а сундука́ нигде́ не́ было.
[On chairs-LOC and bed-LOC lay things-NOM, taken-out from chest-GEN, but chest-GEN nowhere not was.]
There were things that had been taken out of the chest lying on *the chairs* and *bed*, but the chest was nowhere to be found.

Ма́ма говори́т, что когда́-то я просыпа́лся с улы́бкой на *лице́*.
[Mom-NOM says, that once I-NOM woke-up with smile-INST on face-LOC.]
Mom says that I used to wake up with a smile on *my face*.

Since attachment is something that happens on a surface, на + LOCATIVE: A PLACE can also be used to express an attachment or connection to something; notice that English 'on' shares this capacity in this example and its translation below:

Их соба́ка, ма́ленькая, похо́жая на лиси́цу, мета́лась на *цепи́*, захлёбываясь ла́ем.
[Their dog-NOM, small-NOM, similar-NOM on vixen-ACC, dashed-about on chain-LOC, choking bark-INST.]
Their small, vixen-like dog dashed about on *its chain*, choking on its barks.

The fact that на does not require boundaries (whereas в does), makes на the natural candidate for locations that are events or phenomena, or anything else that does not have defined limits; in this use the meaning of на is often better translated as 'at'. However, because there is not a perfect fit between Russian на and English 'at', students are often told to assume that all locations use в + LOC, and that they must memorize a list of exceptions that use на instead. This is good advice, but it might also help to look at some of the categories that the so-called "на-words" tend to fall into. Here is a list representing common на-words (other than surfaces) that might make the task of mastering their use a bit easier:

A categorization of common "на words"

Locations that are islands, peninsulas, mountain ranges, clearings:

на *Аля́ске* 'in *Alaska*'
на *Гава́йях* 'in *Hawaii*'
на *Кавка́зе* 'in *the Caucasus*'
на *Ки́пре* 'in *Cyprus*'
на *о́строве* 'on *an island*'

на *пло́щади* 'in *a square*'
на *полуо́строве* 'on *a peninsula*'
на *поля́не* 'in *a clearing*'
на *стадио́не* 'at/in *a stadium*'

на *у́лице* 'in *the street*'
на *Ура́ле* 'in *the Urals*'
на *фе́рме* 'at/on *a farm*'

Points of embarcation for travel (passenger, freight, or mail):

на *аэродро́ме* 'at *an aerodrome*'
на *ба́зе* 'at *a base*'

на *вокза́ле* 'at *a train station*'
на *остано́вке* 'at *a stop* (for buses or trams)'

на *по́чте* 'at/in *a post office*'
на *ста́нции* 'at/in *a station*'

Events

на *балу́* 'at *a ball*'
на *вы́ставке* 'at *an exhibition*'
на *заседа́нии* 'at/in *a meeting*'
на *конфере́нции* 'at *a conference*'

на *конце́рте* 'at *a concert*'
на *собра́нии* 'at/in *a meeting*'
на *спекта́кле* 'at *a show*'

на *съе́зде* 'at *a congress*'
на *экску́рсии* 'on *an excursion*'
на *я́рмарке* 'at *a fair*'

Compass points and other generalized locations:

на *во́здухе* 'in *the open air, outside*'
на *восто́ке* 'in *the east*'
на *за́паде* 'in *the west*'

на *ме́сте* 'in *place*'
на *све́те* 'in *the world*'
на *се́вере* 'in *the north*'

на *со́лнце* 'in *the sunshine*'
на *целине́* 'in *the virgin lands*'
на *ю́ге* 'in *the south*'

Certain buildings, work/trade environments, and academic units:

на *би́рже* 'at *the exchange*'
на *да́че* 'at/in *a cottage*'
на *заво́де* 'at/in *a factory*'

на *ка́федре* 'in *a department* (of university)'
на *предприя́тии* 'at *an enterprise*'
на *ры́нке* 'at *the market*'

на *скла́де* 'at/in *a warehouse*'
на *фа́брике* 'at/in *a factory*'
на *факульте́те* 'in *a department/ school* (of university)'

Upper floors of buildings:

на *балко́не* 'in *the balcony* (of a theater); on *a balcony*'

на *пе́рвом, второ́м,... этаже́* 'on *the first, second, ...floor*'

на *чердаке́* 'in *the attic*'

There are a few words that can use either на or в without much difference in meaning; here are the most common ones:

Words that can use both на and в + LOCATIVE: A PLACE

на/в *душе́* 'in *one's soul*'
на/в *кварти́ре* 'in *an apartment*'

на/в *ку́хне* 'in *the kitchen*'
на/в *не́бе* 'in *the sky*'

на/в *по́ле* 'in *a field*'
на/в *се́рдце* 'in *one's heart*'
на/в *суде́* 'at *a trial*'

Here are some examples of на used with "на-words":

На *Моско́вской межба́нковской валю́тной би́рже* курс до́ллара США в пя́тницу не́сколько сни́зился.

[At Moscow inter-bank currency exchange-LOC exchange-rate-NOM dollar-GEN USA-GEN in Friday-ACC somewhat declined.]

At *the Moscow inter-bank currency exchange* the exchange rate for the US dollar declined somewhat on Friday.

На *заседа́нии* прави́тельственных делега́ций в Москве́ возросли́ тре́ния по фина́нсово-экономи́ческим вопро́сам ме́жду Украи́ной и Росси́ей.
[At meeting-LOC government delegations-GEN in Moscow-LOC increased friction-NOM along financial-economic issues-DAT between Ukraine-INST and Russia-INST.]

At *the meeting* of government delegations in Moscow there was increased friction between Ukraine and Russia concerning financial and economic issues.

Ви́дно, на *по́чте* что́-то перепу́тали.
[Apparently, at post-office-LOC something-ACC mixed-up.]

Apparently they got something mixed up at *the post office*.

На *суде́* уже́ шла о нём речь.
[At trial-LOC already went about it-LOC talk-NOM.]

They already talked about it at *the trial*.

<table>
<tr><td>на + LOCATIVE: A PLACE in the domain of time.</td><td>The use of на + LOCATIVE: A PLACE in the domain of time is restricted, being commonly used only with weeks and with the transitional times between day and night, as in the representative phrases in the table below:</td></tr>
</table>

на + LOCATIVE: A PLACE in time expressions

на *про́шлой/э́той/бу́дущей неде́ле* 'last/this/next week'		на *заре́/рассве́те*	'at *dawn*'
на *восхо́де*	'at *sunrise*'	на *зака́те*	'at *sunset*'

<table>
<tr><td>на + LOCATIVE: A PLACE in metaphorical domains.</td><td>The use of на + LOCATIVE: A PLACE in the domain of abstract locations is also relatively uncommon; here is an example of how an abstract point is conceived of as a location *on* or *at* rather than *in*:</td></tr>
</table>

Мне вдруг превы́ше всего́ захоте́лось косну́ться пра́вым плечо́м своего́ отца́, а ле́вым — своего́ сы́на: спра́ва — про́шлое, сле́ва — бу́дущее, а я на *живо́м сты́ке* двух времён.
[Me-DAT suddenly above all-GEN wanted touch right shoulder-INST own father-GEN, and left-INST — own son-GEN: on-right — past-NOM, on-left — future-NOM, and I-NOM at live juncture-LOC two times-GEN.]

Suddenly I wanted above all else to touch my father with my right shoulder and my son with my left shoulder: on the right is the past, on the left, the future, and I am at *the live juncture* between the two times.

Locative: a place 4   147

LOCATIVE: A PLACE 4—Words that trigger на; the 2nd locative

The number of words associated with на + LOC is fewer than those for в. Many of the resulting phrases involve means of transportation or abilities such as speaking various languages or playing musical instruments. The words you are most likely to encounter are in this table:

Words that can trigger на + LOCATIVE: A PLACE

'ride in (*a train/a bus, etc.*)' ездить/éхать на (*пóезде/автóбусе*) поéздка на (*пóезде/автóбусе*) 'trip by (*train/bus, etc.*)'	'sail on (*a steamboat/a canoe, etc.*)' плáвать/плы́ть на (*парохóде/ челнé*)	'be based on' осно́вываться/основáться на
'play (*the piano/flute/guitar, etc.*)' игрáть на (*роя́ле/флéйте/гитáре*) игрá на (*роя́ле/флéйте/гитáре*) 'playing (*the piano/flute/guitar, etc.*)'	'speak (*Russian/English, etc.*)' говори́ть/сказáть на (*ру́сском/ англи́йском языкé*) говоря́щий на (*ру́сском/ англи́йском языкé*) 'speaker of (*Russian/English, etc.*)'	'affect, have impact on' отражáться/отрази́ться на отражéние на 'affect, impact on' 'concentrate on' сосредото́чиваться/ сосредото́читься на
'go (*ice-skating/boating, etc.*)' катáться на (*конькáх/лóдке*) катáние на (*конькáх/лóдке*) 'going (*ice-skating/boating, etc.*)'	'get married to (when man takes *a wife*)' жени́ться на жени́тьба на 'marriage to (when man takes *a wife*)'	'go (*skiing/sailing, etc.*)' ходи́ть на (*лы́жах/парусáх*) ходьбá на (*лы́жах/парусáх*) 'going (*skiing/sailing, etc.*)'
'fly in (*a plane, etc.*)' летáть/летéть на (*самолёте*) полёт на (*самолёте*) 'flight in (*a plane, etc.*)'	'insist on' настáивать/настоя́ть на настáивание на 'insistence on'	'economize on, save on' эконо́мить/сэконо́мить на эконо́мия на 'economizing on'

Here are a couple of sentences to demonstrate these phrases in action:

> Éсли в Япóнии произойдёт смéна приоритéтов, не отрази́тся ли э́то отрицáтельно на *отношéниях* мéжду нáшими стрáнами?
> [If in Japan-LOC happens change-NOM priorities-GEN, not affect whether this-NOM negatively on relations-LOC between our countries-LOC?]
> If there is a change in priorities in Japan, won't this have a negative impact on *relations* between our countries?

> Ро́дственники поги́бшего настáивали на *том*, что он был заби́т камня́ми.
> [Relatives-NOM deceased-GEN insisted on that-LOC, that he-NOM was killed-NOM stones-INST.]
> The relatives of the deceased insisted that he had been stoned to death.

Some idiomatic phrases also employ на + LOC; a representative sample of these phrases is in the following table:

на + LOC: a place in idimatic phrases.

на + LOCATIVE: A PLACE in idiomatic expressions

'(be) *outside*'
(быть) на *дворе́*

'(be) on *pension, retired*'
(быть) на *пе́нсии*

'(be) worn around *one's neck*'
(быть) на *ше́е*

'(happen) *the other day*'
(случи́ться) на *днях*

'*actually*'
на *са́мом де́ле*

Words that can trigger на or в + LOCATIVE: A PLACE.

A few words can combine with either на or в + LOC, such as специализи́роваться на/в 'specialize in' and сходи́ться/сойти́сь на/в 'agree on', both of which are illustrated with на in the two examples below:

И́горь специализи́руется на *де́тской ве́рхней оде́жде*.
[Igor-NOM specializes on children's outer wear-LOC.]
Igor specializes in *children's outer wear*.

Схо́димся на *том*, что брю́ки гла́жу я, а он чита́ет мне вслух.
[Come-together on that-LOC, that pants-ACC iron I-NOM, and he-NOM reads me-DAT out-loud.]
We agree that I'm to iron the pants and he's to read to me out loud.

The second locative ending -ý/-ю́ with на + LOCATIVE: A PLACE.

Like в, на can appear with the so-called second locative ending in stressed -ý/-ю́ to express locations in various domains and in the idiom на *ходу́* [on gait-LOC] 'while on *the move*'. Here are some examples:

Ми́ша вопи́л пе́сню про шика́рный го́род Я́лту на *ю́жном берегу́*.
[Misha-NOM wailed song-ACC about splendid town Yalta-ACC on southern coast-LOC.]
Misha wailed a song about the splendid town of Yalta on *the southern coast*.

Лётчик огляде́лся по сторона́м, как бы мы́сленно проща́ясь со все́м, с по́лем, с просты́м деревя́нным сру́бом на *краю́* по́ля.
[Pilot-NOM looked-around along sides-DAT, as if mentally saying-farewell with everything-INST, with field-INST, with simple wooden cabin-INST on edge-LOC field-GEN.]
The pilot looked about from side to side, as if mentally saying farewell to everything, the field, the simple wooden cabin at *the edge* of the field.

Ма́льчик уса́живается на *полу́* с ку́биками.
[Boy-NOM seats-self on floor-LOC with blocks-INST.]
The boy seats himself on *the floor* with the blocks.

LOCATIVE: A PLACE 5—при 'by, at'

The sense of association that allows us to use на to describe a dog on a chain is the central idea of the preposition при 'at', and this idea of association gets extended to space, time, and metaphorical domains. In the domain of space, the meaning of при is usually best translated as 'by' or 'at', as in the following example:

при + LOCATIVE: A PLACE means 'by, at' in the domain of space.

> В Брюссе́ле открыва́ется постоя́нное представи́тельсто Росси́и при *НАТО*.
> [In Brussels-LOC opens permanent representation-NOM Russia-GEN at NATO-LOC.]
> Permanent representation for Russia is being established at *NATO* in Brussels.

If an item is permanently connected to another item, then при can have a meaning closer to 'with', 'given', or 'having', as in this example, where пе́чка refers to the traditional Russian stove that serves as a furnace and is attached to an exterior wall:

при + LOCATIVE: A PLACE means 'with, having'.

> До мои́х шестна́дцати лет мы жи́ли в полубара́ке на сва́ях, в гну́сной коммуна́лке, в одно́й ко́мнате втроём, при *пе́чке*, но без ва́нны и горя́чей воды́.
> [To my sixteen years-GEN we-NOM lived in semi-barrack-LOC on piles-LOC, in disgusting communal-apartment-LOC, in one room-LOC three-together, at stove-LOC, but without bathtub-GEN and hot water-GEN.]
> Until I was sixteen we lived in a semi-barrack built on pilings, in a disgusting communal apartment, all three of us in one room, with *a stove*, but without a bathtub or hot water.

This use of при is most commonly encountered in the phrase при *себе́* [with self-LOC], which you can use to say whether you have a given thing with *you* at the present moment.

A condition is something that can be attached to an item in metaphoric space, as in this example:

при + LOCATIVE: A PLACE in metaphorical domains.

> Федера́льная казна́ выделя́ет рабо́тникам полови́ну де́нег в фо́рме бюдже́тной ссу́ды, при *усло́вии*, е́сли регина́льная казна́ выпла́чивает другу́ю полови́ну.
> [Federal treasury-NOM allots workers-DAT half-ACC money-GEN in form-LOC budgetary grant-GEN, at condition-LOC, if regional treasury-NOM pays-off other half-ACC.]
> The federal treasury allots half of the money to the workers in the form of a budgetary loan, on *the condition* that the regional treasury pays off the other half.

Here is another example of the 'with/given' meaning of при in a metaphoric domain:

> Установи́ть конта́кт с други́ми мира́ми при *ны́нешнем отноше́нии* к космона́втике не уда́стся.

[Establish contact-ACC with other worlds-INST at current attitude-LOC to space-exploration-DAT not succeed.]

We won't succeed in establishing contact with other worlds given *the current attitude* toward space exploration.

при + LOCATIVE: A PLACE means 'at, while, when' in the domain of time.

By far the most common use of при is, however, in the domain of time, where this preposition temporally connects two items, giving us to understand that they are simultaneous. In the first two examples below, we see that English 'at' can serve the same purpose as при, but often this preposition is translated with words such as 'while' or 'when', as in our third example:

При *слóве* "óчень", мой глазá напóлнились непролѝвшимися слезáми.
[At word-LOC "very" my eyes-NOM filled unshed tears-INST.]
At *the word* "very", my eyes filled with unshed tears.

Я отвечáю и при *этом* ищý в её глазáх вторóй смы́сл.
[I-NOM respond and at this-LOC search in her eyes-LOC other meaning-ACC.]
I respond and at *the same time* search for some other meaning in her eyes.

Собирáемся перерегистрѝровать телефóн при *наслéдовании* квартѝры.
[Intend re-register telephone-ACC at inheritance-LOC apartment-GEN.]
We intend to change the registration of the telephone when *we inherit* the apartment.

при + LOCATIVE: A PLACE in idiomatic phrases.

При participates in two important idiomatic expressions: при *чём* [at what-LOC] '*why*' and не при *чём* [not at what-LOC] '*irrelevant*'.

LOCATIVE: A PLACE 6—о 'about'

о + LOCATIVE: A PLACE means 'about' in the domain of topics of conversation or thought.

The primary domain of the preposition о 'about' is topics for oral and written communication and thought. As we see in the four examples below, this preposition introduces items that we hear, talk, write, and think about:

Недéлю назáд я слы́шала по рáдио передáчу о *счáстье.*
[Week-ACC ago I-NOM heard along radio-DAT program-ACC about happiness-LOC.]
A week ago I heard a radio program about *happiness.*

Áся расскáзывает о *Серёже* печáльные, трóгательные истóрии.
[Asya-NOM tells about Seryozha-LOC sad, touching stories-ACC.]
Asya tells sad, touching stories about *Seryozha.*

— Вот, — усмехáется он, — написáл ромáн о *рабóчем клáссе,* как все.
["Here," grins he-NOM, "wrote novel-ACC about working class-LOC, like everyone-NOM."]
" Here," he grins, "I've written a novel about *the working class,* like everyone else."

Я реши́л подписа́ться на газе́ту <<Изве́стия>>, не ду́мая ни о *како́й лотере́е*
— про́сто потому́ что понра́вилась газе́та.
[I-NOM decided subscribe on newspaper-ACC "Izvestia"-NOM, not thinking not
about what lottery-LOC — simply because pleased newspaper-NOM.]
I decided to subscribe to the newspaper "Izvestia" without thinking about *any lot-*
tery — simply because I liked the newspaper.

Like при, о can mean 'with'. This use is restricted to describing how many things an item
has, and it appears only in formulaic phrases such as стол о *трёх но́жках* [table-NOM
about three legs-LOC] 'a *three-legged* table', до́мик о *двух этажа́х* [house-NOM about
two stories-LOC] 'a *two-story* house'.

о + LOCATIVE: A PLACE means 'with' in the domain of space.

LOCATIVE: A PLACE 7—по 'after'

As mentioned in the introduction to this chapter, the locative case can be used with the
preposition по to mean 'after, upon'. The combination of по + LOCATIVE: A PLACE is a historical left-over in modern Russian, limited to the domains of time and of emotional longing. In
the domain of time, по + LOC tends to have a bureaucratic flavor, as in the following
phrases:

по + LOCATIVE: A PLACE means 'after, upon' in the domain of time.

по + LOCATIVE: A PLACE in the domain of time

'after the deadline *is passed*' по *истече́нии* сро́ка	'after/upon *arrival*' по *прибы́тии*	'upon *examination*' по *рассмотре́нии*
'after (*the end* of) work' по *оконча́нии* рабо́ты		

In the domain of emotional longing, the locative is an alternative ending in the two phrases
скуча́ть по 'miss (a person, place, thing)' and тоска́ по 'longing for', which can be followed with either the dative or the locative case.

по + LOCATIVE: A PLACE expresses the object of emotional longing.

The Russian Academy Grammar offers the following quote from Turgenev, demonstrating
the use of по + LOC in the domain of time:

По *возвраще́нии* в дере́вню бурми́стр повёл нас посмотре́ть ве́ялку.
[After return-LOC to village-ACC bailiff-NOM led us-ACC look winnowing-ma-
chine-ACC.]
After his *return* to the village, the bailiff took us to look at the winnowing machine.

Epilogue

Russian views most locations as containers (with в) or as surfaces (with на). However, since even in physical space many locations are not unambiguously either containers or surfaces, Russian uses conceptual conventions to choose between these two options. Thus any location that is understood as bounded is a potential container. Any location that is unbounded and/or has some vertical elevation can be construed as a surface. Time is usually understood as a container, whereas events are surfaces (at least when we attend them — however, we can talk about their contents with в). With the preposition при we see that the concept of physical contiguity is translated into the domain of time as simultaneity. Thinking and talking have their own domain, with topics serving as locations for pondering and discussing. The locative case demonstrates very clearly how agile Russian is in taking locational concepts derived from spatial relations and implementing them in other domains. Indeed, this is a recurrent theme all through the case system.

APPENDIX

This Appendix is intended to serve as a general orientation tool for identifying the endings associated with the six cases. The paradigms, along with the notes and exceptions, should enable you to identify virtually all the case endings you are likely to encounter. These paradigms will not, however, provide you with a comprehensive guide to other features of Russian inflection, such as placement of stress and mobile vowels (some other books that will give you this information are listed among our suggestions for Further Reading; Levin 1978 is particularly recommended).

Russian Spelling Rules

In order to properly interpret the paradigms, you need to keep in mind the spelling rules that apply to combining consonant and vowel letters and the spelling of [j] (which sounds like the *y* in *yes*). Note that these are rules for spelling case endings; they are not a complete guide to Russian spelling. Most Russian consonants can be hard or soft (and are therefore called "paired"), but instead of having separate consonant letters to show this, Russian uses vowel letters and the soft sign, ь. Here is how it is done:

Spelling rules for case endings.

The use of hard and soft vowel letters to spell hard and soft paired consonants.

---

in order to spell a hard paired consonant:

a consonant letter:	is combined with	a hard vowel letter:
б, в, з, л, м, н, п, р, с, т, ф		а, э, ы, о, у

---

in order to spell a soft paired consonant:

a consonant letter:	is combined with	a soft vowel letter:
б, в, з, л, м, н, п, р, с, т, ф		я, е, и, ё, ю ог ь

As a rule, if the last consonant in a word is hard, it will generally stay that way throughout its paradigm, and if it is soft it will stay soft. The only major exception will be in the LOC singular, which is -e and softens the final consonant for all hard type nouns (although a few hard masculine nouns can have a LOC singular of -y, which of course does not soften). Note also that ё is just e when it is not stressed, and both these letters stand in for o in position after a soft paired consonant.

Spelling rules are different for the consonants that are not paired. These consonants come in four types, and here are the rules that apply:

The use of hard and soft vowel letters with unpaired consonants.

---

the velars г, к, х:

a velar consonant letter:	is combined with	only the following vowel letters:
г, к, х		а, е, и, о, у

---

the hushers ж, ч, ш, щ:

a husher consonant letter:	is combined with	only the following vowel letters:
ж, ч, ш, щ		а, е, и, у, ó (if stressed)/e (if unstressed)

ц:

the consonant letter: ц	is combined with	only the following vowel letters: а, е, ы, у, ó (if stressed)/е (if unstressed)

[j] (which sounds like y in yes) can be spelled in three ways:

1) when there is no vowel following it or at the end of a word it has its own letter: й

2) after a consonant, the soft sign: ь	is combined with	a soft vowel letter: я, е, и, ё, ю
3) after a vowel	you simply add	a soft vowel letter: я, е, и, ё, ю

If an ending has an o after a hard paired consonant, this vowel will appear after a husher or ц as ó if it is stressed, or as e if it is not stressed. Compare these examples of INST singular forms for двор 'courtyard', нож 'knife', and месяц 'month'.

o after hard paired consonant двором	ó if stressed after husher or ц ножóм	e if unstressed after husher or ц месяцем

Understanding the spelling of [j] should make it easier for you to spell endings on words that have stems ending in [j]. For example, the NOM singular and GEN singular endings are the same for 'courtyard': NOM singular двор, GEN singular дворá as they are for 'genius': NOM singular гéний, GEN singular гéния ([j] is the final consonant of гéний, and it is still there even when the ending is added, so the ending is actually -a). There are also noun stems that end in [j] after a consonant. Compare for example тюрьмá 'prison' (a hard type feminine) with семья́ 'family' (a soft type feminine with [j] as its final consonant):

NOM singular	NOM plural	GEN plural
тюрьмá	тю́рьмы	тю́рем
семья́	сéмьи	семéй

Both nouns have the same stem structure, since both stems end in two consonants: the stem of тюрьмá ends in soft рь + м, and the stem of семья́ ends in soft мь + [j]. And both nouns have the same ending for the GEN plural: a zero ending (the removal of the vowel represented by a or я), which also motivates an inserted e for both words. Семья́ spells й in the GEN plural because [j] is at the end of the word.

Declension of Nouns

Nouns come in three genders: feminine, masculine, and neuter. For each gender we will list the endings for both a stem ending in a hard paired consonant ("hard" type) and for a stem ending in a soft paired consonant ("soft" type). Using the spelling rules above, you can determine which ending (hard type or soft type) you will need for the unpaired consonants. Although all of the information you really need is in the paradigms and the special notes attached to them, there are a couple of global issues that are worth mentioning at the outset: animacy and the formation of the GEN plural.

All animate nouns (nouns referring to living beings of the animal kingdom, including ourselves) substitute the GEN plural form for the ACC plural. Masculine animate nouns make this substitution in the singular as well, using the GEN singular form for the ACC singular. This is mentioned in the paradigms (except in the case of neuter nouns, where animacy is rare), but here are some concrete examples for good measure. Note that for inanimates the ACC forms are the same as the NOM forms, but for animates the ACC forms are the same as the GEN forms:

The role of animacy in the declension of nouns.

	feminine inanimate 'room'	animate 'actress'	masculine inanimate 'courtyard'	animate 'actor'	neuter inanimate 'cemetery'	animate 'monster'
NOMsg	ко́мната	актри́са	двор	актёр	кла́дбище	чудо́вище
NOMpl	**ко́мнаты**	**актри́сы**	**дворы́**	актёры	**кла́дбища**	чудо́вища
ACCpl	**ко́мнаты**	**актри́с**	**дворы́**	**актёров**	**кла́дбища**	**чудо́вищ**
GENpl	ко́мнат	**актри́с**	дворо́в	**актёров**	кла́дбищ	**чудо́вищ**

For masculine nouns, note also animacy in the singular:

NOMsg	**двор**	актёр
ACCsg	**двор**	**актёра**
GENsg	двора́	**актёра**

The GEN plural has three endings: zero (the removal of a final vowel), -ов/-ев (spelling rules apply), and -ей. With very few exceptions, the choice of GEN plural ending can be decided by looking at the NOM singular form:

Rules for the distribution of the three genitive plural endings: zero, *-ов/-ев*, and *-ей*.

zero

If the NOM singular ends in a vowel, remove that vowel to get a zero ending. There are examples of this GEN plural ending for feminine and neuter nouns in the table directly above. Be sure to use ь or й to spell a soft paired consonant or [j] left at the end: NOM singular неде́ля 'week' gives GEN plural неде́ль; NOM singular фами́лия 'last name' gives GEN plural фами́лий.

-ов/-ев

If the NOM singular ends in a hard paired consonant (б, в, з, л, м, н, п, р, с, т, ф), a velar (г, к, х), ц, or й, spell -ов/-ев. This gives us not only the GEN plural дворо́в above, but also the GEN plural не́мцев 'Germans' from NOM singular не́мец and GEN plural слоёв 'layers' from NOM singular слой.

-ей

If the NOM singular ends in a soft paired consonant (in other words б, в, з, л, м, н, п, р, с, т, ф + ь) or a husher (ж, ч, ш, щ), the ending is -ей. For example: NOM singular автомоби́ль 'automobile' has GEN plural автомоби́лей and NOM singular нож 'knife' has GEN plural ноже́й.

Feminine Declension Nouns

	hard type: 'room'		soft type: 'week'		-ь: 'talent'	
	singular	plural	singular	plural	singular	plural
NOM	кóмната	кóмнаты	недéля	недéли	спосóбность	спосóбности
INST	кóмнатой	кóмнатами	недéлей	недéлями	спосóбностью	спосóбностями
ACC	кóмнату	кóмнаты	недéлю	недéли	спосóбность	спосóбности
		= GEN if animate		= GEN if animate		
DAT	кóмнате	кóмнатам	недéле -ия > -ии	недéлям	спосóбности	спосóбностям
GEN	кóмнаты	кóмнат	недéли	недéль	спосóбности	спосóбностей
LOC	кóмнате	кóмнатах	недéле -ия > -ии	недéлях	спосóбности	спосóбностях

The INST singular of hard type and soft type nouns has a variant (archaic/poetic) ending -ою/-ею. Soft type nouns ending in -ия use -ии in both the DAT singular and the LOC singular, so истóрия 'history' has the form истóрии for both. It is not uncommon for soft type feminine nouns ending in -ня to harden their final consonant in the GEN plural form: NOM singular пéсня 'song' has GEN plural пéсен.

Not all feminine declension nouns are feminine. There are many nouns of both the hard and soft type that refer to male human beings, such as дéдушка 'grandfather', дя́дя 'uncle', and nicknames like Кóстя from Константи́н or Гри́ша from Григóрий. Although these nouns and names decline as animate feminine declension nouns, any adjective that agrees with them uses masculine endings, which gives us стáрый дéдушка 'old grandfather'. There is also one masculine noun which follows the feminine type in -ь, путь 'way'; it asserts its masculinity only in the INST singular, which is путём.

Exceptions:

1) Мáть 'mother' and дóчь 'daughter' follow the declension of спосóбность, but add -ер- before all endings: INST singular мáтерью/дóчерью, DAT/GEN/LOC singular and NOM plural мáтери/дóчери, etc. For the word 'daughter', the INST plural has two variants: дочеря́ми/дочерьми́.

2) Лóшадь 'horse' has the exceptional INST plural лошадьми́ alongside the expected лошадя́ми.

3) Some soft type nouns and some nouns with stem in husher + a have a GEN plural in -ей instead of zero: вожжá 'rein' has GEN plural вожжéй, тётя 'aunt' has GEN plural тётей, and the same goes for дя́дя 'uncle' with GEN plural дя́дей.

Masculine Declension Nouns

	hard type: 'courtyard'		soft type: 'nail'	
	singular	plural	singular	plural
NOM	двор	дворы́	гвоздь	гвóзди
INST	дворóм	дворáми	гвоздём	гвоздя́ми
ACC	двор	дворы́	гвоздь	гвóзди
	= GEN if animate	= GEN if animate	= GEN if animate	= GEN if animate
DAT	дворý	дворáм	гвоздю́	гвоздя́м
GEN	дворá	дворóв	гвоздя́	гвоздéй
LOC	дворé	дворáх	гвоздé	гвоздя́х

Some masculine declension nouns can also have the ending -**у**/-**ю** in the GEN singular and/or LOC singular, for example ча́ю '(some) tea' and в снегу́ 'in the snow'. This is discussed in the chapters on the genitive and locative cases. There are also many masculine declension nouns that use the ending -**а́**/-**я́** for the NOM plural: NOM singular дом 'house' has NOM plural дома́, and NOM singular учи́тель has NOM plural учителя́. Inanimates use this ending for the ACC plural as well, so we have ACC plural дома́.

Exceptions:

1) Some words have a hard type declension in the singular, but a soft type declension throughout the plural, adding a [j] (spelled **ь** + soft vowel letter) to the stem. Compare the NOM singular and plural forms in these examples:

	NOM singular	NOM plural
'man'	муж	мужья́
'chair'	стул	сту́лья
'brother'	брат	бра́тья
'son'	сын	сыновья́
'friend'	друг	друзья́

There are a few nouns that can have both a hard and soft plural of this type, depending upon their meaning: зуб 'tooth' usually has the NOM plural зу́бы, but if it refers to the teeth on a cogged wheel, its NOM plural is зу́бья.

2) A rarer case of a hard type singular and a soft type plural is represented by чёрт 'devil' and сосе́д 'neighbor', which have the NOM plural forms че́рти and сосе́ди and follow the soft type declension throughout the plural.

3) Some nouns have a singular stem in -**ин**, but form their plural by removing -**ин**. All of these nouns refer to human beings, and most of them name members of a nationality. In the plural they continue to follow the hard type declension, but they can have a variety of NOM plural endings. By far the most common NOM plural ending is -**е**, but note variants also:

	NOM singular	NOM plural
'Englishman'	англича́нин	англича́не
'Bulgarian'	болга́рин	болга́ры
'master'	хозя́ин	хозя́ева

All of these nouns have a zero ending in the GEN-ACC plural: англича́н, болга́р, хозя́ев.

4) There are a number of nouns referring to the young of animals that have a singular stem ending in -**онок**/-**ёнок** which follows the masculine hard type declension, but a plural stem ending -**ат**/-**ят** which follows the neuter hard type declension. For example, NOM singular котёнок 'kitten' has the NOM plural котя́та, with an animate GEN-ACC plural of котя́т. Ребёнок 'child' has two plurals: one is the expected NOM plural ребя́та which however means 'fellows', whereas 'children' is expressed by the NOM plural де́ти (which follows the soft type declension and has the unusual INST plural детьми́).

Notes on the masculine declension endings.

5) One very common noun has a completely different stem in the plural than in the singular: человéк 'person' (hard type masculine throughout the singular), with the NOM plural лю́ди **'people'** (soft stem masculine throughout the plural, but note that the GEN plural with numerals is usually человéк instead of людéй).

6) A few nouns have a zero ending in the GEN plural, which is therefore the same as the NOM singular: солдáт 'soldier', сапóг 'boot', глаз 'eye'.

7) The GEN plural of гóд 'year' is usually лéт; годóв is possible only when referring to a special set of years: мóда девянóстых годóв 'fashion of the nineties'.

Neuter Declension Nouns

	hard type: 'body'		soft type: 'schedule'	
	singular	plural	singular	plural
NOM	тéло	телá	расписáние	расписáния
INST	тéлом	телáми	расписáнием	расписáниями
ACC	тéло	телáм	расписáние	расписáния
DAT	тéлу	телáм	расписáнию	расписáниям
GEN	тéла	тел	расписáния	расписáний
LOC	тéле	телáх	расписáнии	расписáниях

Notes on the neuter declension endings.

The vast majority of soft type neuter nouns end in -ие; for those that do not, the LOC singular ending is -е, so NOM singular and LOC singular look alike for мóре 'sea'.

Exceptions

1) A few common neuter nouns do not follow the usual rules for the GEN plural. Мóре 'sea' and пóле 'field' have GEN plural forms морéй and полéй. Плáтье 'dress' and óблако 'cloud' have GEN plural forms плáтьев and облакóв.

2) There are ten neuter nouns that end in -мя: брéмя 'burden', врéмя 'time', вы́мя 'udder', знáмя 'banner', и́мя 'name', плáмя 'flame', плéмя 'tribe', сéмя 'seed', стрéмя 'stirrup', тéмя 'crown (of head)'. All of them decline like врéмя, with the additon of -ен to the stem; the only exceptions are the GEN plural forms for сéмя and стрéмя, which are семя́н and стремя́н.

	singular	plural
NOM	врéмя	временá
INST	врéменем	временáми
ACC	врéмя	временá
DAT	врéмени	временáм
GEN	врéмени	времён
LOC	врéмени	временáх

3) Чу́до 'miracle' and нéбо 'heaven' both add -ес to their stems throughout the plural, giving NOM plural чудесá and небесá. Тéло can use the alternate plural телесá in the special meaning 'heavenly bodies'.

4) A few nouns have a soft stem ending in [j] in the plural; the most common is дéрево 'tree' (with the expected hard type neuter declension throughout the singular), which has NOM plural дерéвья. All such nouns have the unexpected GEN plural -ев.

5) A few nouns, most referring to paired parts of the body, have an unexpected NOM plural in -и:

	NOM singular	NOM plural
'knee'	колéно	колéни
'shoulder'	плечó	плéчи
'ear'	ýхо	ýши
'apple'	я́блоко	я́блоки

Indeclinable nouns.

There are also some borrowed nouns of all genders that do not decline at all, for example сопрáно 'soprano' (feminine in reference to a singer, but neuter in reference to a musical part), and кенгурý 'kangaroo' (masculine).

Adjectives

Adjectives, like nouns, come in hard and soft types, and they match their gender, number, and case to the noun they modify.

	hard type: 'first'		
	feminine	masculine	neuter	plural
NOM	пéрвая	пéрвый -óй if stressed	пéрвое	пéрвые
INST	пéрвой	пéрвым	пéрвым	пéрвыми
ACC	пéрвую	пéрвый = GEN if animate	пéрвое	пéрвые = GEN if animate
DAT	пéрвой	пéрвому	пéрвому	пéрвым
GEN	пéрвой	пéрвого	пéрвого	пéрвых
LOC	пéрвой	пéрвом	пéрвом	пéрвых

	soft type: 'last'		
	feminine	masculine	neuter	plural
NOM	послéдняя	послéдний	послéднее	послéдние
INST	послéдней	послéдним	послéдним	послéдними
ACC	послéднюю	послéдний = GEN if animate	послéднее	послéдние = GEN if animate
DAT	послéдней	послéднему	послéднему	послéдним
GEN	послéдней	послéднего	послéднего	послéдних
LOC	послéдней	послéднем	послéднем	послéдних

Notes on adjectival endings.

Both hard and soft type adjectives have variant (archaic/poetic) endings -ою/-ею for the feminine INST singular. There are short adjectives, but these appear only in the nominative case (NOMINATIVE: AN IDENTITY), for example я готóва, он готóв, мы все готóвы 'I am ready, he is ready, we are all ready'. In addition, there are some soft type adjectives that have short endings in the NOM and ACC; these are possessive adjectives like вóлчий 'wolf's' and the ordinal numeral трéтий 'third'. These adjectives have the following NOM and ACC endings (their endings for other cases contain ь followed by the soft type endings listed above, giving трéтьей, трéтьего, etc.):

	feminine	masculine	neuter	plural
NOM	тре́тья	тре́тий	тре́тье	тре́тьи
ACC	тре́тью	тре́тий	тре́тье	тре́тьи
		тре́тьего		тре́тьих
		if animate		if animate

Pronouns

	'I'	'we'	'you' informal	'you'
NOM	я	мы	ты	вы
INST	мно́й	на́ми	тобо́й	ва́ми
ACC	меня́	нас	тебя́	вас
DAT	мне	нам	тебе́	вам
GEN	меня́	нас	тебя́	вас
LOC	мне	нас	тебе́	вас

	'she'	'he'	'it'	'they'
NOM	она́	он	оно́	они́
INST	(н)ей	(н)им	(н)им	(н)и́ми
ACC	(н)её	(н)его́	(н)его́	(н)их
DAT	(н)ей	(н)ему́	(н)ему́	(н)им
GEN	(н)её	(н)его́	(н)его́	(н)их
LOC	ней	нём	нём	них

	'who'	'what'	'oneself'
NOM	кто	что	
INST	кем	чем	собо́й
ACC	кого́	что	себя́
DAT	кому́	чему́	себе́
GEN	кого́	чего́	себя́
LOC	ком	чём	себе́

'this'

	feminine	masculine	neuter	plural
NOM	э́та	э́тот	э́то	э́ти
INST	э́той	э́тим	э́тим	э́тими
ACC	э́ту	э́тот	э́то	э́ти
		э́того		э́тих
		if animate		if animate
DAT	э́той	э́тому	э́тому	э́тим
GEN	э́той	э́того	э́того	э́тих
LOC	э́той	э́том	э́том	э́тих

'all, every'

	feminine	masculine	neuter	plural
NOM	вся	весь	всё	все
INST	всей	всем	всем	все́ми
ACC	всю	весь	всё	все
		всего́		всех
		if animate		if animate
DAT	всей	всему́	всему́	всем
GEN	всей	всего́	всего́	всех
LOC	всей	всём	всём	всех

Note the variant (archaic/poetic) INST forms **мно́ю, тобо́ю, (н)е́ю, собо́ю**, and feminine **э́тою, все́ю. Сам** 'by oneself' looks exactly like **э́тот** except that it does not add -**от** in the masculine NOM singular. **Тот** 'that' looks just like **э́тот** except that (like **весь**) it uses the vowel **е** everywhere that **э́тот** uses **и** (so the plural is **те, те́ми**, etc.).

Notes on pronouns.

Possessives

'my'

	feminine	masculine	neuter	plural
NOM	моя́	мой	моё	мои́
INST	мое́й	мои́м	мои́м	мои́ми
ACC	мою́	мой	моё	мои́
		моего́		мои́х
		if animate		if animate
DAT	мое́й	моему́	моему́	мои́м
GEN	мое́й	моего́	моего́	мои́х
LOC	мое́й	моём	моём	мои́х

'our'

	feminine	masculine	neuter	plural
NOM	на́ша	наш	на́ше	на́ши
INST	на́шей	на́шим	на́шим	на́шими
ACC	на́шу	наш	на́ше	на́ши
		на́шего		на́ших
		if animate		if animate
DAT	на́шей	на́шему	на́шему	на́шим
GEN	на́шей	на́шего	на́шего	на́ших
LOC	на́шей	на́шем	на́шем	на́ших

Твой 'your (informal)', and **свой** 'one's own' look just like **мой. Ваш** 'your' looks just like **наш**. And of course **её** 'her', **его́** 'his', and **их** 'their' do not decline. Aside from the NOM singular masculine form (which has the vowel е instead of и), **чей** 'whose' looks just like **тре́тий** (for example, feminine forms are **чья, чьей, чью**, etc.). As with adjectives, the feminine INST singular of possessives has a variant ending -**ею**.

Notes on possessives.

Numerals

'one'

	feminine	masculine	neuter	plural
NOM	одна́	оди́н	одно́	одни́
INST	одно́й	одни́м	одни́м	одни́ми
ACC	одну́	оди́н	одно́	одни́
		одного́		одни́х
		if animate		if animate
DAT	одно́й	одному́	одному́	одни́м
GEN	одно́й	одного́	одно́й	одни́х
LOC	одно́й	одно́м	одно́м	одни́х

	'two'	'three'	'four'	'five'
NOM	две (feminine)	три	четы́ре	пять
	два (masc/neut)			
INST	двумя́	тремя́	четырьмя́	пятью́
ACC	две / два	три	четы́ре	пять
	двух	трёх	четырёх	
	if animate	if animate	if animate	
DAT	двум	трём	четырём	пяти́
GEN	двух	трёх	четырёх	пяти́
LOC	двух	трёх	четырёх	пяти́

Notes on
numerals

Note the feminine INST variant одно́ю. О́ба 'both' has the following forms for masculine and neuter: INST обо́ими, ACC о́ба, DAT обо́им, GEN обо́их, LOC обо́их. The feminine forms are the same, but the vowel **e** is substituted for **a**, giving о́бе, обе́ими, etc. When the numbers о́ба/о́бе, два/две, три, and четы́ре (also called the "paucal numerals") are used in the NOM or ACC cases, the adjectives and nouns they modify appear with a variety of endings. Adjectives use an ending that looks like the GEN plural (the only acceptable ending when the noun is masculine or neuter) or the NOM/ACC plural (preferred when the noun is feminine). Nouns use an ending that looks like the GEN singular, but sometimes has a unique stress (for example, in the phrase два часа́ 'two hours', часа́ has no equivalent anywhere in the paradigm for час 'hour'; the GEN singular is ча́са). This book will follow the convention of treating the entire paucal numeral + adjective + noun phrase as NOM when the numeral is NOM, and ACC when the numeral is ACC, thus:

У меня́ *три краси́вых бра́та* и *две краси́вые/краси́вых сестры́*.
[By me-GEN three handsome brothers-NOM and two beautiful sisters-NOM.]
I have *three handsome brothers* and *two beautiful sisters*.

Я ждала́ *четы́ре до́лгих часа́* и *четы́ре до́лгие/до́лгих мину́ты*.
[I-NOM waited four long hours-ACC and four long minutes-ACC.]
I waited *four long hours* and *four long minutes*.

Collective numerals have one form for the NOM and (inanimate) ACC, such as дво́е 'twosome', тро́е 'threesome', че́тверо 'foursome', пя́теро 'fivesome', etc., and form all other cases with adjectival endings, giving for example the INST forms: двои́ми, трои́ми, четверы́ми, пятеры́ми, etc. Ско́лько 'how many' behaves like the collectives (INST: ско́лькими). Со́рок 'forty', девяно́сто 'ninety', сто 'hundred' all have the ending -a in the INST, DAT, GEN, and LOC forms. For numerals from 'two hundred' to 'nine hundred', however, сто is declined like any hard type neuter noun, with the exception that 'two hundred' is две́сти. Ты́сяча 'thousand', миллио́н 'million', and миллиа́рд 'billion' are all declined just like ordinary nouns.

Prepositions

Notes on
prepositions.

Most prepositions that end in a consonant (без 'without', из 'from', над 'above', об 'about, against', от 'from', пе́ред 'before', под 'under') or consist only of a consonant (в 'to', к 'to', с 'with, from, approximately') will frequently add the vowel -о (creating безо, изо, надо, обо, ото, пéредо, подо, во, ко, со) preceding certain consonant clusters, in particular:

мн- (primarily in forms of мнóго/мнóгие 'many' and the pronoun я 'I'): во мнóгом 'in many ways', ко мне 'to me', пéредо мной 'before me'

вс- (primarily in forms of весь 'all'): изо всех сил 'with all one's might', ко всем 'to everyone'.

The addition of -о to prepositions is also common when the consonant cluster of the next word begins with the same (or similar) consonant as the one at the end of the preposition: во втóрник 'on Tuesday', со столá 'from the table', со злóсти 'out of spite', со щáми 'with cabbage soup', со счёта 'from the bill'. Less predictable is the insertion of -о before words with other consonant clusters, such as во рту 'in one's mouth', ко дну 'to the bottom', обо что 'against what', подо льдом 'under the ice'.

The preposition о 'against, about' always adds -б (becoming об) before words beginning in a vowel (а, э, и, о, у), and frequently adds the -б even before consonants when used with the accusative case to indicate 'against', as in об стéнку 'against the wall'. Regardless of the case used, об will further add -о (becoming обо) before most declined forms (containing мн- and вс-) of я and весь: обо мне 'about me', обо всём 'about everything'.

Names

Russian first names and patronymics decline like nouns, but surnames follow a variety of patterns, depending upon their stem shape. There are five types of surnames: 1) Russian surnames ending in -ын, -ин, -ов, -ёв, or -ев; 2) Russian and foreign surnames ending in a consonant; 3) Surnames ending in unstressed -а or-я; 4) Russian surnames with adjectival stems ending in -ый, -ий, or -óй; 5) Russian surnames ending in -ых, -их, -аго, -яго, -ово, Ukrainian surnames ending in -ко, -енко, and all foreign surnames ending in a vowel (other than -а).

1) Russian surnames ending in -ын, -ин, -ов, -ёв, or -ев follow a mixed declension containing both nominal and pronominal endings.

Notes on names.

	feminine singular	masculine singular	plural
NOM	Пýшкина	Пýшкин	Пýшкины
INST	Пýшкиной	Пýшкиным	Пýшкиными
ACC	Пýшкину	Пýшкина	Пýшкиных
DAT	Пýшкиной	Пýшкину	Пýшкиным
GEN	Пýшкиной	Пýшкина	Пýшкиных
LOC	Пýшкиной	Пýшкине	Пýшкиных

2) Russian and foreign surnames ending in a consonant are declined like masculine nouns when they refer to a male person, but are indeclinable when they refer to a female person. Compare: Я люблю́ Дика Лóнга 'I love Dick Long' vs. Я люблю́ Сáру Лонг 'I love Sara Long'.

3) Surnames ending in unstressed -a or-я are declined like feminine nouns regardless of whether they refer to a man or woman: Я люблю́ Була́та/Мари́ю Окуджа́ву 'I love Bulat/Maria Okudzhava'.

4) Russian surnames with adjectival stems ending in -ый, -ий, or -о́й are declined like adjectives and agree in gender and number with the person or persons that they refer to: Я люблю́ Андре́я Бе́лого/Ма́ю Плесе́цкую 'I love Andrej Belyj/Maja Plesetskaja'.

5) Russian surnames ending in -ых, -их, -аго, -яго, -ово, Ukrainian surnames ending in -ко, -енко, and all foreign surnames ending in a vowel (other than -a) are indeclinable (although there is some tendency to decline the Ukrainian surnames ending in -ко, -енко like Russian surnames ending in unstressed -a, cf. 3 above): Я люблю́ До́ктора Жива́го/Шевче́нко (Шевче́нку).

FURTHER READINGS

This is a list of particularly useful reference and theoretical materials that have inspired the *Case Book for Russian*, which interested students might wish to consult, but not a comprehensive bibliography on the topics of case meaning and morphology.

On Russian case meanings:

Brecht, Richard D. and James S. Levine, eds. 1986. *Case in Slavic*. Columbus: Slavica. [*This is a compendium of articles on case in Slavic languages by leading scholars; about half of the articles deal specifically with Russian case usage. In addition to the articles, there is a very useful introduction on Case and Meaning by the editors and a thorough, if now somewhat outdated bibliography.*]

Jakobson, Roman. 1984. "Contribution to the General Theory of Case: General Meanings of the Russian Cases", in *Roman Jakobson. Russian and Slavic Grammar. Studies 1931-1981*, ed. by Waugh, Linda R. and Morris Halle. Berlin/New York/Amsterdam: Mouton, pp. 59-103. [*This is a translation from the German of the original article which was published in 1936 by the Prague Linguistic Circle and then again in 1971 in volume 2 of Jakobson's Selected Writings. This visionary article remains a landmark in the field of Russian case semantics.*]

Wade, Terence. 1992. *A Comprehensive Russian Grammar*, ed. by Michael J. de K. Holman. Oxford/Cambridge, USA: Blackwell. [*This is an excellent reference book, and can be used to supersede previous grammars of Russian by Pulkina and Unbegaun. See particularly the section on Case Usage, pp. 85-110 and the chapter on The Preposition, pp. 416-487.*]

Wierzbicka, Anna. 1980. *The Case for Surface Case*. Ann Arbor: Karoma. [*This book is devoted to the Russian instrumental as an illustration of Wierzbicka's reasons for objecting to certain aspects of Fillmore's theoretical writings — see Fillmore's "The Case for Case" cited below.*]

On Russian case endings:

Leed, Richard and Slava Paperno. 1987. *5000 Russian Words*. Columbus: Slavica. [*This is a dictionary giving the complete stressed paradigms for 5000 of the most common nouns, pronouns, adjectives, and verbs of Russian. Leed's Appendix on Russian Endings at the back of the book is especially useful.*]

Levin, Maurice I. 1978. *Russian Declension and Conjugation: A Structural Description with Exercises*. Columbus: Slavica. [*This book is devoted entirely to a systematic description of endings for nouns, pronouns, adjectives, and verbs. The system also handles stress and fill vowels, and there are enough exercises to enable students to fully master Russian inflection. Doing the exercises is tedious, but worthwhile.*]

On meaning and metaphor in grammar:

Dahl, Osten. 1985. *Case Grammar and Prototypes*. Duisburg: L.A.U.D. [*A brief and insightful work, much ahead of its time.*]

Fillmore, Charles J. 1968. "The Case for Case", in: Emmon Bach and Robert T. Harms (eds.), *Universals in Linguistic Theory*. New York: Reinhart & Winston, pp. 1-88. [*This work is widely regarded as a pathbreaking article on case semantics. Fillmore revisited this topic in 1977, in "The Case for Case Reopened", in: Peter Cole and Jerrold M. Saddock (eds.), Grammatical Relations. Syntax & Semantics 8. New York: Academic Press, pp. 59-81 and also in 1982 in "Frame Semantics", in: Linguistic Society of Korea (eds.), Linguistics in the Morning Calm. Seol: Hanshin, pp. 111-138.*]

Johnson, Mark. 1987. *The Body in the Mind*. Chicago/London: U of Chicago Press. [*This book deals with the way in which perceptual experience serves as source material for deriving abstract relationships in human cognition. Chapters 2, 4, and 5 are particularly relevant to the relationships encoded in case.*]

Lakoff, George. 1987. *Women, Fire, and Dangerous Things*. Chicago/London: U of Chicago Press. [*This book explores the relevance of metaphor, metonymy, and semantic category structure to grammar. It rambles quite a lot, but establishes the principles according to which the Case Book for Russian seeks to explain the cases as coherent semantic wholes.*]

Langacker, Ronald. W. 1987. *Foundations of Cognitive Grammar: Theoretical Prerequisites, Vol. 1*, and 1991. *Foundations of Cognitive Grammar: Descriptive Application, Vol. 2*. Stanford: Stanford University Press. [*This work fleshes out the ideas suggested by Lakoff in serious detail, but is rather difficult to wade through.*]

Talmy, Leonard. 1986. *The Relation of Grammar to Cognition*. Berkeley: Berkeley Cognitive Science Report. [*Also in: Proceedings of TINLAP-2, ed. by D. Waltz. Champaign, Ill: Coordinated Science Laboratory, University of Illinois. This article deals specifically with the distinctions between lexical and grammatical meaning.*]

Sources

The examples in *The Case Book for Russian* have been culled from the following sources:

PERIODICALS:
Аргументы и факты (1998)
Известия (1994, 1995, 1997, 1998)
Итоги (1998)
Коммерсант (1998)
Комсомольская правда (1998)
Красная звезда (1998)
Литературная газета (1997, 1998)
Московская правда (1998)
Московский комсомолец (1998)
Независимая газета (1997, 1998)
Огонек (1998)
Правда (1998)
Российские вести (1998)
Сегодня (1998)

BOOKS:

Баранская, Наталья. 1989. *Неделя как неделя*, ed. by Lora Paperno, Natalie Roklina, and Richard Leed. Columbus: Slavica.

Довлатов, Сергей. 1991. Две повести. Москва: Слово.

Довлатов, Сергей. 1993. Собрание прозы в трех томах. Петербург: Лимбус-пресс.

Маринина, Александра. 1997. *Иллюзия греха*. Москва: Ексмо.

Набатникова, Татьяна. 1995. *Не родись красивой*. Ростов-на-Дону: Изд-во Проф-пресс.

Петрушевская, Людмила. 1996. *Собрание сочинений в пяти томах. Том I*. Москва: ТКО АСТ.

Simes, Natasha and Richard M. Robin. 1992. *Political Russian: An Intermediate Course in Russian Language for International Relations, National Security and Socio-Economics*. Dubuque: Kendall/Hunt.

Токарева, Виктория. 1996. *Летающие качели*. Москва: ЕКСМО.

Щербакова, Галина. 1996. *Вам и не снилось*. Москва: Издательский дом русанова.

Щербакова, Галина. 1996. *Год Алены*. Москва: Вагриус.

WEBSITES:

Хармс, Даниил. http://sunsite.sut.ac.jp/asia/russia/russian-studies/Literature/Harms.

Маканин, Владимир. "Кавказский пленный". Новый мир. http://www.friends-partners.org/~afarber/makanin/index.html

Новодворская, Валерия. *По ту сторону отчаяния.* Москва: Издательство новости, 1993.   http://mech.math.msu.su/~gmk/ds/side088.htm

Солженицын. http://sunsite.sut.ac.jp/asia/russia/russian-studies/Literature/Gulag.

Сорокин, Владимир. "Очередь". http://www.sparc.spb.su/Avz/lit/Sorokin/ochered.html

Notes on the Exercises

Three Levels of Exercises
Exercises for *The Case Book for Russian* are divided into three levels of increasing difficulty. Level I exercises contain short sentences with vocabulary that is common to first-year courses. Level II exercises contain longer, more difficult sentences and vocabulary. Level III exercises contain the most complex sentences and the most difficult vocabulary. Sentences with participles or verbal adverbs are almost exclusively limited to Level III. It is highly recommended that you work through the exercises using the accompanying software package, *The Case Book for Russian INTERACTIVE*, but the exercises are also provided here for easy use in the classroom.

Three Types of Exercises
For each level, there are three different types of exercises. There are separate exercise sets for each case individually, in which the task is to identify the instances of the case in question and explain why the case is used. Following the single-case exercises are mixed-case exercises of the same type. These mixed-case exercises ask the student to identify all the cases in a sentence and explain why the case is used. A second type of mixed case exercise presents all case items in the nominative case and requires the student to reconstruct the original sentence. Translation from Russian to English is also featured in the exercises. For questions on specific constructions in the exercises, consult the index for the relevant section of the book.

The Answer Key
An answer key is available for instructors using *The Case Book for Russian*. However, all answers to the exercises may be found by using *The Case Book for Russian* INTERACTIVE. The answer key contains all the original sentences where the Russian example is given in full followed by the sentence parsing and a smooth English translation. Numbers following each sentence in the exercises correspond to the sentence number in the key.

Additional Activities
In addition to working through these exercises, students may apply the knowledge gained from this book in analyzing any readings, dialogues, or other speech contexts. In order to facilitate active case use, instructors may wish to have students write Russian sentences using selected vocabulary from the various tables throughout the book.

Level I Exercises

Nominative Exercise 1, Level I

Identify the instances of the NOMINATIVE *case in the following sentences and explain why the* NOMINATIVE *is used.*

1 То положе́ние, в кото́ром я находи́лась, бы́ло абсолю́тно просты́м и я́сным.
[That situation-_____ , in which-_____ I-_____ was-found, was absolutely simple-_____ and clear-_____ .] (I-4)

2 Они́ всегда́ бы́ли хулига́нами, то́лько внача́ле ма́ленькие хулига́ны, пото́м ю́ные, а тепе́рь ста́рые.
[They-_____ always were hooligans-_____ , just at-first little hooligans-_____ , then young-_____ , and now old-_____ .] (I-10)

3 В э́том году́ Росси́ю, возмо́жно, посети́т глава́ управле́ния национа́льной оборо́ны Япо́нии.
[In this year-_____ Russia-_____ , possibly, visits head-_____ administration-_____ national defense-_____ Japan-_____ .] (I-17)

4 Вот из тре́тьего подъе́зда выхо́дит с портфе́лем мой сосе́д.
[Here from third doorway-_____ walks-out with briefcase-_____ my neighbor-_____ .] (I-28)

5 —Кто э́то подходи́л? —Убо́рщица...Же́нщина лет шести́десяти пяти́.
[-Who-_____ that-_____ came? -Maid-_____ ...Woman-_____ years-_____ sixty five-_____ .] (I-42)

6 Мой брат — раб своего́ органи́зма.
[My brother-_____ — slave-_____ own body-_____ .] (I-56)

7 Кому́ оно́ ну́жно сейча́с, моё самолю́бие?
[Who-_____ it-_____ needed-_____ now, my narcissism-_____ ?] (I-59)

8 Пото́м из окна́ вы́валилась тре́тья стару́ха, пото́м четвёртая, пото́м пя́тая.
[Then from window-_____ tumbled-out third old-woman-_____ , then fourth-_____ , then fifth-_____ .] (I-72)

9 Интере́сно, попадёт ли в ру́ки мэ́ра Лужко́ва э́тот но́мер "Литгазе́ты"?
[Interesting, fall if in hands-_____ mayor Luzhkov-_____ this issue-_____ "Litgazeta-_____ "?] (I-85)

10 Буква́льно че́рез час к ней прие́дет "расстре́льная брига́да".
[Literally in hour-_____ to her-_____ comes "execution brigade-_____ ". (I-91)

11 Бóлее тогó, по мы́сли áвтора, Солжени́цын вели́к незави́симо от тогó, прав он и́ли не прав в свои́х сужде́ниях.

[More that-_____ , along thought-_____ author-_____ , Solzhenitsyn-_____ great-_____ irrespective from that-_____ , right-_____ he-_____ or not right-_____ in own judgments-_____ .] (I-95)

12 А здесь вообщé здóрово спать. Ую́тный уголóк. Я сто лет на прирóде не спал, а ты?

[And here generally cool sleep. Comfortable corner-_____ . I-_____ hundred-_____ years-_____ in nature-_____ not slept, and you-_____ ?] (I-136)

Nominative
Exercise 2
Level I

Nominative Exercise 2, Level I

Identify the instances of the NOMINATIVE *case in the following sentences and explain why the* NOMINATIVE *is used.*

1 Таки́м óбразом, всё вы́глядело соверше́нно нормáльно, éсли не считáть тогó фáкта, что я ещё не былá женóй Геóргия.

[This image-_____ , all-_____ looked completely normal, if not consider that fact-_____ , that I-_____ still not was wife-_____ Georgij-_____ .] (I-5)

2 Верони́ка вы́лезла из кустóв и стáла так, чтóбы Вади́м её заме́тил.

[Veronika-_____ crawled-out from bushes-_____ and stood so, so-that Vadim-_____ her-_____ noticed.] (I-11)

3 В нáше вре́мя роль испове́дника выполня́ют друзья́ и знакóмые.

[In our time-_____ role-_____ confessor-_____ fill friends-_____ and acquaintances-_____ .] (I-22)

4 Я должнá былá спроси́ть насчёт талáнтов, но воздержáлась.

[I-_____ should-_____ was ask about talents-_____ , but held-back.] (I-30)

5 Круг её знакóмых составля́ли адвокáты, врачи́, журнали́сты, худóжники.

[Circle-_____ her acquaintances-_____ composed lawyers-_____ , doctors-_____ , journalists-_____ , artists-_____ . (I-43)

6 Я сочиня́ю стихи́. Э́то моё основнóе заня́тие в жи́зни.

[I-_____ compose verses-_____ . That-_____ my principle occupation-_____ in life-_____ .] (I-57)

7 Я дал ей лáпу, как собáка, и так же посмотре́л в глазá.

[I-_____ her-_____ gave paw-_____ , like dog-_____ , and thus also looked in eyes-_____ .] (I-64)

8 Он прóсит меня́ к себе́, спрáшивает, как идёт рабóта.

[He-_____ asks me-_____ to self-_____ , asks, how goes work-_____ .] (I-74)

9   Похороны состоялись на следующий день, при участии президента Белоруссии.
    [Funeral-_____ took-place on next day-_____ , at participation-_____ president-_____ Belorussia-_____ .] (I-86)

10 Надо иметь в виду, что она человек глубоко верующий.
    [Necessary have in view-_____ , that she-_____ person-_____ deeply believing-_____ .] (I-92)

11 Что же произошло на самом деле, и каковы мотивы родителей шестнадцатилетней теннисистки?
    [What-_____ EMPH happened in actual matter-_____ , and what-kind-of-_____ motives-_____ parents-_____ sixteen-year-old tennis-player-_____ ?] (I-119)

12 А при Сталине разве творилось такое?
    [And under Stalin-_____ really made such-_____ ?] (I-138)

Nominative Exercise 3, Level I

Identify the instances of the NOMINATIVE *case in the following sentences and explain why the* NOMINATIVE *is used.*

1   Наша первая встреча прошла тем не менее без излишних восторгов.
    [Our first meeting-_____ passed that-_____ not less without excess enthusiasm-_____ .] (I-6)

2   Фигура у неё была как цифра "восемь," один круг на другом.
    [Figure-_____ by her-_____ was like number-_____ "eight"-_____ , one circle-_____ on other-_____ .] (I-14)

3   С первых же страниц в его книге чувствуется проблематика необычная и трудная.
    [From first-_____ very pages-_____ in his book-_____ is-felt problems unusual-_____ and difficult-_____ .] (I-26)

4   Эмиграция есть "лаборатория свободы".
    [Emigration-_____ is "laboratory-_____ freedom-_____ ".] (I-41)

5   Один из моих старых знакомых, работающий в столице, решил сделать мне подарок.
    [One-_____ from my old friends-_____ , working-_____ in capitol-_____ , decided make me-_____ present-_____ .] (I-54)

6   Третью неделю идёт борьба за жизнь.
    [Third week-_____ goes battle-_____ for life-_____ .] (I-58)

7   Только актёры могут играть один спектакль по десять раз. А мы не актёры, а люди. И не играем, а живём.
[Only actors-_____ can play one show-_____ along ten-_____ times-_____ . But we-_____ not actors-_____ , but people-_____ . And not play, but live.] (I-67)

8   Мне вот дадут план, и тогда — прощай моя диссертация!
[Me-_____ look give plan-_____ and then — goodbye my dissertation-_____ !] (I-80)

9   Какое же впечатление на вас производит начало судебного процесса?
[What impression-_____ on you-_____ make initiation-_____ judicial process-_____ ?] (I-90)

10   Известно, что юность доверчива и любопытна, а потому и бесстрашна.
[Known, that youth-_____ gullible-_____ and curious-_____ and for-that-reason also fearless-_____ .] (I-93)

11   Нет, он не пьяный. Просто обалдел от жары.
[No, he-_____ not drunk-_____ . Simply became-woozy from heat-_____ .] (I-135)

12   Вера пела в полный голос, и было слышно по этому голосу, что у неё хорошее настроение.
[Vera-_____ sang in full voice-_____ , and was audible by this voice-_____ , that by her-_____ good mood-_____ .] (I-146)

Instrumental
Exercise 1
Level I

Instrumental Exercise 1, Level I

Identify the instances of the INSTRUMENTAL case in the following sentences and explain why the INSTRUMENTAL is used.

1   И как раз в этот момент с лестницы стали нашу комнату открывать ключом.
[And how time in that moment -_____ from stairwell-_____ began our room-_____ open key-_____ .] (I-1)

2   Наша первая встреча прошла тем не менее без излишних восторгов.
[Our first meeting-_____ passed that-_____ not less without excess enthusiasm-_____ .] (I-6)

3   Чтобы попасть к дяде, надо спуститься ниже этажом.
[So-that arrive to uncle-_____ , necessary descend lower floor-_____ .] (I-24)

4   Мой прадед был русским.
[My great-grandfather-_____ was Russian-_____ .] (I-61)

5   Я éхал в троллéйбусе, а он столкнýлся с автóбусом, и мне пришлóсь идтú пешкóм.
       [I-_____ rode in trolleybus-_____, but it-_____ collided with bus-_____, and me-_____ was-necessary go by-foot-_____.] (I-83)

6   Не бывáть тебé американцем. И не уйтú от своегó прóшлого.
       [Not be you-_____ American-_____ . And not leave from own past-_____.] (I-99)

7   Вчерá я над ним не рабóтала.
       [Yesterday I-_____ over it-_____ not worked.] (I-107)

8   Я открывáю кран и умывáю лицó холóдной водóй.
       [I-_____ open faucet-_____ and wash face-_____ cold water-_____ .] (I-111)

9   Из-за тогó, что он обладáет огрóмными финáнсовыми ресýрсами, он имéет весьмá серьёзное влияние на конгрéсс США.
       [Because-of that-_____, that he-_____ controls huge financial resources-_____, he-_____ has very serious influence-_____ on Congress-_____ USA-_____ .] (I-120)

10   Вóзле рынка должны квáсом торговáть.
       [Alongside market-_____ should-_____ kvass-_____ trade.] (I-137)

11   Мáша босикóм, гóлая, пошлá на кýхню, чтóбы попúть воды.
       [Masha-_____ barefoot-_____, naked-_____, went to kitchen-_____ , in-order-to drink water-_____ .] (I-149)

12   Вся жизнь пóсле сорокá — чем ты занимáешься, что ешь и какýю кнúгу читáешь — всё э́то на лицé и на рукáх.
       [All life-_____ after forty-_____ — what-_____ you-_____ occupy-self, what-_____ eat and what-kind-of book-_____ read — all-_____ this-_____ on face-_____ and on hands-_____ .] (I-158)

Instrumental Exercise 2, Level I

Identify the instances of the INSTRUMENTAL *case in the following sentences and explain why the* INSTRUMENTAL *is used.*

Instrumental
Exercise 2
Level I

1   То положéние, в котóром я находúлась, бы́ло абсолю́тно простым и я́сным.
       [That situation-_____ , in which-_____ I-_____ was-found, was absolutely simple-_____ and clear-_____ .] (I-4)

2   Её кóмната былá огрóмной и темновáтой, с красúвой старúнной мéбелью, с почтú чёрным паркéтом.
       [Her room-_____ was enormous-_____ and rather-dark-_____ , with beautiful antique furniture-_____ , with almost black parquet-floor-_____ .] (I-7)

3   Я сижу́ перед зе́ркалом и рабо́таю над собо́й.
     [I-_____ sit before mirror-_____ and work above self-_____ .] (I-165)

4   Подо мно́й и позади́ меня́ — го́ры.
     [Under me-_____ and behind me-_____ — mountains-_____.] (I-66)

5   Коро́че, я пропуска́л одну́ ле́кцию за друго́й. Лу́чше всего́, таки́м о́бразом, мне запо́мнились университе́тские коридо́ры.
     [Shorter, I-_____ skipped one lecture-_____ beyond another-_____ . Better all-_____ , such form-_____ , me-_____ get-memorized university corridors-_____.] (I-97)

6   Ба́йрон поги́б сравни́тельно молоды́м челове́ком.
     [Byron-_____ died relatively young man-_____ .] (I-101)

7   Сую́ его́ под дива́н со слова́ми <<сиди́ и молчи́>>.
     [I-shove him-_____ under couch-_____ with words-_____ "sit and be-quiet".] (I-109)

8   Ребя́та сра́зу же усе́лись за стол и смо́трят на ого́нь под кастрю́лями.
     [Kids-_____ immediately EMPHATIC sat behind table-_____ and look to fire-_____ under pots-_____ .] (I-114)

9   Она́ предпочита́ла ти́хую жизнь с му́жем и двумя́ детьми́.
     [She-_____ preferred quiet life-_____ with husband-_____ and two children-_____.] (I-122)

10   В ту о́сень Людми́ла Серге́евна бро́сила корми́ть гру́дью сы́на.
     [In that fall-_____ Ludmila Sergeyevna-_____ quit feed breast-_____ son-_____.] (I-143)

11   Ма́ша вообще́ счита́ла себя́ интеллиге́нткой. Она́ ест ле́вой. Хлеб берёт руко́й, а не ви́лкой.
     [Masha-_____ in-general considered self-_____ intellectual-_____ . She-_____ eats left-_____ . Bread-_____ takes hand-_____ , and not fork-_____ .] (I-150)

12   Тала́нт деньга́ми слома́ть нельзя́.
     [Talent-_____ money-_____ break not-allowed.] (I-159)

<table>
<tr><td>Instrumental
Exercise 3
Level I</td><td></td></tr>
</table>

Instrumental Exercise 3, Level I

Identify the instances of the INSTRUMENTAL case in the following sentences and explain why the INSTRUMENTAL is used.

1   Таки́м о́бразом, всё вы́глядело соверше́нно норма́льно, е́сли не счита́ть того́
     фа́кта, что я ещё не была́ жено́й Гео́ргия.
     [This image-_____ , all-_____ looked completely normal, if not consider that fact-
     _____ , that I-_____ still not was wife-_____ Georgij-_____ .] (I-5)

2   Лётчик улыбну́лся како́й-то неопределённой, о́чень ве́жливой улы́бкой и
     пошёл.
     [Pilot-_____ smiled some indefinite-_____ , very polite smile-_____ and went.] (I-
     12)

3   И тепе́рь я тебя́ спрошу́: чем мои́ де́ти ху́же други́х?
     [And now I-_____ you-_____ ask: what-_____ my children-_____ worse others-
     _____ ?] (I-39)

4   Смотрю́ на Лю́сю и де́лаю ей знак глаза́ми — <<вы́йдем>>.
     [Look at Lyusya-_____ and make her-_____ sign-_____ eyes-_____ — "go-
     out".] (I-78)

5   Я помаха́л руко́й знако́мому худо́жнику.
     [I-_____ waived hand-_____ acquaintance artist-_____ .] (I-98)

6   Чем же ты накорми́л дете́й?
     [What-_____ EMPHATIC you-_____ fed children-_____ ?] (I-105)

7   Пото́м отправля́ю дете́й с Ди́мой гуля́ть, а сама́ принима́юсь за дела́.
     [Then send children-_____ with Dima-_____ walk, and self-_____ get-set for
     business-_____ .] (I-110)

8   Э́ти деклара́ции не подтвержда́лись каки́ми-либо фа́ктами.
     [These declarations-_____ not backed-up some-kind-of facts-_____ .] (I-18)

9   Ночно́й клуб по́льзуется популя́рностью, в выходны́е сюда́ прихо́дят по
     две́сти-три́ста челове́к — в том числе́ шахтёры.
     [Night club-_____ enjoys popularity-_____ , in days-off-_____ here come by 200-
     300-_____ people-_____ — in that number-_____ miners-_____ .] (I-131)

10   А ма́ма весёлая, с не́которой изли́шней ли́хостью. Э́то у неё всегда́ от вина́.
     [And mama-_____ happy-_____ , with certain excessive spirit-_____ . This-_____
     by her-_____ always from wine-_____ .] (I-144)

11   Домо́й шёл ночно́й по́езд, мать всегда́ им приезжа́ла, е́сли е́здила в го́род.
     [Homewards went night train-_____ , mother-_____ always it-_____ arrived, if went
     to city-_____ .] (I-152)

Accusative Exercise 1, Level I

Identify the instances of the ACCUSATIVE *case in the following sentences and explain why the* ACCUSATIVE *is used.*

1   И как раз в э́тот моме́нт с ле́стницы ста́ли на́шу ко́мнату открыва́ть ключо́м.
    [And how time in that moment -_____ from stairwell-_____ began our room-_____ open key-_____.] (I-1)

2   Веро́ника вы́лезла из кусто́в и ста́ла так, что́бы Вади́м её заме́тил.
    [Veronika-_____ crawled-out from bushes-_____ and stood so, so-that Vadim-_____ her-_____ noticed.] (I-11)

3   Есть у нас така́я тради́ция — отмеча́ть все сове́тские и церко́вные пра́здники.
    [There-is by us-_____ such tradition-_____ — celebrate all Soviet-_____ and church holidays-_____.] (I-23)

4   За ка́ждый но́мер в оте́ле мы пла́тим бо́льше ста до́лларов.
    [For each room-_____ in hotel-_____ we-_____ pay more hundred dollars-_____.] (I-48)

5   Ка́ждая па́ра должна́ роди́ть двои́х и́ли, ка́жется, да́же трои́х, а у нас то́лько по одному́.
    [Each couple-_____ should-_____ give-birth two-_____ or, seems, even three-_____, but by us-_____ only along one-_____.] (I-79)

6   Белору́сская оппози́ция провела́ в столи́це респу́блики ше́ствие и ми́тинг.
    [Belorussian opposition-_____ led in capital-_____ republic-_____ procession-_____ and meeting-_____.] (I-96)

7   Я открыва́ю кран и умыва́ю лицо́ холо́дной водо́й.
    [I-_____ open faucet-_____ and wash face-_____ cold water-_____.] (I-111)

8   Ра́зве мы мо́жем прожи́ть на твою́ зарпла́ту?
    [Really we-_____ can live-through on your salary-_____?] (I-115)

9   Она́ предпочита́ла ти́хую жизнь с му́жем и двумя́ детьми́.
    [She-_____ preferred quiet life-_____ with husband-_____ and two children-_____.] (I-122)

10 Так бу́дет че́рез час, и че́рез су́тки, и че́рез ме́сяц.
    [Thus will-be in hour-ACC, and in day-ACC, and in month-ACC.] (I-166)

11 Когда́ он приходи́л? ... Ну с неде́лю ... мо́жет, с пять дней...
    [When he-_____ arrived? ... Well about week-_____...maybe about five-_____ days-_____...] (I-141)

12   В дежу́рные иду́т пожилы́е же́нщины, пенсионе́рки.
      [In attendants-_____ go elderly women-_____, pensioners-_____.] (I-156)

Accusative Exercise 2, Level I
   Identify the instances of the ACCUSATIVE *case in the following sentences and explain why the* ACCUSATIVE *is used.*

1   Жить на литерату́рные за́работки тру́дно.
      [Live on literary earnings-_____ hard.] (I-3)

2   В наш век всё мо́жно спроси́ть и узна́ть по телефо́ну.
      [In our era-_____ everything-_____ possible ask and find-out along telephone-_____.] (I-19)

3   Моя́ ма́чеха мечта́ет, что́бы я вы́шла за́муж за пе́рвого встре́чного.
      [My stepmother-_____ dreams, so-that I-_____ went married behind first person-met-_____.] (I-27)

4   Я сочиня́ю стихи́. Э́то моё основно́е заня́тие в жи́зни.
      [I-_____ compose verses-_____. That-_____ my principle occupation-_____ in life-_____.] (I-57)

5   О́чень гру́стную карти́ну про "Росси́йскую Атланти́ду" нарисова́л нам А. Деря́ин.
      [Very sad picture-_____ about "Russian Atlantis-_____" drew us-_____ A. Deryain-_____.] (I-84)

6   Нефть с Ка́спия пойдёт че́рез Ту́рцию, а не Новоросси́йск.
      [Oil-_____ from Caspian-_____ will-go through Turkey-_____, and not Novorossiysk-_____.] (I-103)

7   Я сдаю́сь — отодви́ну свои́ дела́ на по́сле обе́да.
      [I-_____ give-up — put-off own matters-_____ to after lunch-_____.] (I-113)

8   Снаряжа́емся, берём са́нки и отправля́емся на кана́л ката́ться с гор.
      [Get-ready, take sled-_____ and set-off to canal-_____ ride from mountains-_____.] (I-117)

9   Ведь, поми́мо хокке́я на траве́, на но́вом стадио́не мо́жно игра́ть в ре́гби, бейсбо́л, софтбо́л...
      [Know, besides hockey-_____ on grass-_____, on new stadium-___ possible play in rugby-_____, baseball-_____, softball-_____...] (I-124)

10   Неде́лю дождя́ не́ было.
      [Week-_____ rain-_____ not was.] (I-77)

11   В ту о́сень Людми́ла Серге́евна бро́сила корми́ть гру́дью сы́на.
      [In that fall-_____ Ludmila Sergeyevna-_____ quit feed breast-_____ son-_____.]
      (I-143)

12   — Вы ро́дом из Смоле́нска?
      — Да.
      — Е́здите на ро́дину?
      ["You-_____ birth-_____ from Smolensk-_____?"
      " Yes."
      "Go to homeland-_____?"] (I-160)

Accusative
Exercise 3
Level I

Accusative Exercise 3, Level I

Identify the instances of the ACCUSATIVE case in the following sentences and explain why the ACCUSATIVE is used.

1   Вади́м то́же ничего́ не сказа́л, прошёл в ко́мнату и лёг на дива́н лицо́м к стене́.
     [Vadim-_____ also nothing-_____ not said, went in room-_____ and lay on couch-_____ face-_____ to wall-_____.] (I-8)

2   То, что он де́лает, он де́лает хорошо́, но ему́ доста́точно знать э́то одному́.
     [That-_____, which-_____ he-_____ does, he-_____ does well, but him-_____ enough know that-_____ one-_____.] (I-20)

3   Она́ де́ржит зо́нтик при себе́ на слу́чай дождя́ и́ли жары́.
     [She-_____ keeps umbrella-_____ at her-_____ on case-_____ rain-_____ or heat-_____.] (I-32)

4   Тре́тью неде́лю идёт борьба́ за жизнь.
     [Third week-_____ goes battle-_____ for life-_____.] (I-58)

5   По́хороны состоя́лись на сле́дующий день, при уча́стии президе́нта Белору́ссии.
     [Funeral-_____ took-place on next day-_____, at participation-_____ president-_____ Belorussia-_____.] (I-86)

6   Че́рез две мину́ты я сплю.
     [Through two-_____ minutes-_____ I-_____ sleep.] (I-104)

7   Ребя́та сра́зу же усе́лись за стол и смо́трят на ого́нь под кастрю́лями.
     [Kids-_____ immediately EMPHATIC sat behind table-_____ and look to fire-_____ under pots-_____.] (I-114)

8   Лежу́ и вслу́шиваюсь в тишину́.
     [I-lie and listen-intently to silence-_____.] (I-118)

9 Вы по́мните себя́ в шестна́дцать лет?
[You-_____ remember self-_____ in 16-_____ years-_____?] (I-125)

10 Пое́здка в Экспре́ссе дли́тся че́тверо су́ток и сто́ит 4,5 ты́сячи до́лларов.
[Trip-_____ on Express-_____ lasts four-_____ days-_____ and costs 4.5-_____ thousand-_____ dollars-_____.] (I-139)

11 Ве́ра пе́ла в по́лный го́лос, и бы́ло слы́шно по э́тому го́лосу, что у неё хоро́шее настрое́ние.
[Vera-_____ sang in full voice-_____, and was audible by this voice-_____, that by her-_____ good mood-_____.] (I-146)

12 Англича́не со́тню лет оккупи́ровали И́ндию, поги́бла вели́кая инди́йская культу́ра?
[English-_____ hundred-_____ years-_____ occupied India-_____, perished great Indian culture-_____?] (I-163)

Dative Exercise 1, Level I

Identify the instances of the DATIVE case in the following sentences and explain why the DATIVE is used.

Dative
Exercise 1
Level I

1 Ей ещё на́до бы́ло забежа́ть в магази́н, купи́ть проду́кты, пото́м пое́хать в больни́цу к свое́й ма́ме, пото́м верну́ться и взя́ть из де́тского са́да свою́ ма́ленькую до́чку.
[Her-_____ still necessary was run in store-_____, buy groceries-_____, then go in hospital-_____ to own mother-_____, then return and take from childrens' garden-_____ own small daughter-_____.] (I-13)

2 Алёна ста́рше Да́шки на три го́да, зна́чит, ей два́дцать два.
[Alyona-_____ older Dashka-_____ to three-_____ years-_____, means, her-_____ twenty-two-_____.] (I-155)

3 Е́сли я когда́-нибудь кому́-нибудь понра́влюсь, то тако́й челове́к пока́жется мне и у́мным и краси́вым.
[If I-_____ ever anyone-_____ please, then that person-_____ seem me-_____ and smart-_____ and attractive-_____.] (I-29)

4 Га́лка всех подру́г разогна́ла, никто́ ей не ну́жен.
[Galka-_____ all girlfriends-_____ chased-away, no-one-_____ her-_____ not needed-_____.] (I-40)

5 Са́харов вам э́того не прости́т.
[Sakharov-_____ you-_____ that-_____ not forgive.] (I-52)

6   Я дал ей ла́пу, как соба́ка, и так же посмотре́л в глаза́.
     [I-_____ gave her-_____ paw-_____, like dog-_____, and thus also looked in eyes-
     _____.] (I-64)

7   Он про́сит меня́ к себе́, спра́шивает, как идёт рабо́та.
     [He-_____ asks me-_____ to self-_____, asks, how goes work-_____.] (I-74)

8   Смотрю́ на Лю́сю и де́лаю ей знак глаза́ми — <<вы́йдем>>.
     [Look at Lyusya-_____ and make her-_____ sign-_____ eyes-_____ — "go-out".]
     (I-78)

9   О́чень гру́стную карти́ну про "Росси́йскую Атланти́ду" нарисова́л нам А.
     Деря́ин.
     [Very sad picture-_____ about "Russian Atlantis-_____" drew us-_____ A. Deryain-
     _____.] (I-84)

10   Не быва́ть тебе́ америка́нцем. И не уйти́ от своего́ про́шлого.
     [Not be you-_____ American-_____. And not leave from own past-_____.] (I-99)

11   От э́той мы́сли мне стано́вится гру́стно.
     [From this thought-_____ me-_____ becomes sad.] (I-112)

12   Нельзя́ поддава́ться па́нике.
     [Not-allowed give-in panic-_____.] (I-140)

Dative Exercise 2 Level I

Dative Exercise 2, Level I
     *Identify the instances of the DATIVE case in the following sentences and explain why
     the DATIVE is used.*

1   Ве́ра пе́ла в по́лный го́лос, и бы́ло слы́шно по э́тому го́лосу, что у неё
     хоро́шее настрое́ние.
     [Vera-_____ sang in full voice-_____, and was audible by this voice-_____, that by
     her-_____ good mood-_____.] (I-146)

2   С друго́й стороны́, домофо́н то́лько помога́ет кварти́рному во́ру.
     [From other side-_____, intercom-_____ only helps apartment thief-_____.] (I-157)

3   В наш век всё мо́жно спроси́ть и узна́ть по телефо́ну.
     [In our era-_____ everything-_____ possible ask and find-out along telephone-
     _____.] (I-19)

4   Ли́ля смотре́ла по сторона́м с наи́вным и рассе́янным выраже́нием.
     [Lilya-_____ looked along sides-_____ with naive-_____ and absent-minded ex-
     pression-_____.] (I-31)

5   У меня́ не́ было тогда́ влече́ния к литерату́ре.
     [By me-_____ not was then attraction-_____ to literature-_____.] (I-49)

6   Кому́ оно́ ну́жно сейча́с, моё самолю́бие?
     [Who-_____ it-_____ needed-_____ now, my narcissism-_____?] (I-59)

7   И вам её не жа́лко?
     [And you-_____ her-_____ not sorry?] (I-65)

8   От э́той сде́ланной улы́бки мне стано́вится не по себе́.
     [From that fake smile-_____ me-_____ becomes not along self-_____.] (I-75)

9   Ка́ждая па́ра должна́ роди́ть двои́х и́ли, ка́жется, да́же трои́х, а у нас то́лько
     по одному́.
     [Each couple-_____ should-_____ give-birth two-_____ or, seems, even three-_____,
     but by us-_____ only along one-_____.] (I-79)

10   Напряга́юсь — не ве́рю уша́м свои́м.
     [Strain — not believe ears own-_____.] (I-89)

11   Пра́вде вообще́ трудне́е проти́виться, чем лжи́.
     [Truth-_____ generally more-difficult oppose, than-_____ lie-_____.] (I-100)

12   Дим, я тебя́ прошу́, дай мне ко́нчить.
     [Dima-_____, I-_____ you-_____ ask, let me-_____ finish.] (I-116)

Dative Exercise 3, Level I

Identify the instances of the DATIVE case in the following sentences and explain why the DATIVE is used.

1   Че́хова она́ зна́ет то́лько благодаря́ телевизио́нной пропага́нде. Счита́ет
     его́ ну́дным.
     [Chekhov-_____ she-_____ knows only thanks-to television propaganda-_____.
     Considers him-_____ boring-_____.] (I-148)

2   Я ведь жил там лет до шести́, по алле́ям учи́лся ходи́ть!
     [I-_____ after-all lived there years-_____ to six-_____, along paths-_____ learned
     walk!] (I-161)

3   То, что он де́лает, он де́лает хорошо́, но ему́ доста́точно знать э́то одному́.
     [That-_____, which-_____ he-_____ does, he-_____ does well, but him-_____
     enough know that-_____ one-_____.] (I-20)

4   Катери́на всё завеща́ла не́скольким музе́ям.
     [Katerina-_____ everything-_____ bequeathed few museums-_____.] (I-35)

5   Я до́лжен был кому́-то показа́ть свои́ ру́кописи. Но кому́?
[I-_____ should-_____ was someone-_____ show own manuscripts-_____. But whom-_____?] (I-50)

6   Кро́ме того́, он помага́ет ю́ным регби́стам кома́нды из одного́ небольшо́го го́рода Фра́нции.
[Aside that-_____, he-_____ helps young rugby-players-_____ team-_____ from one small city-_____ France-_____.] (I-62)

7   Мы успе́ли привы́кнуть друг к дру́гу.
[We-_____ managed get-used friend-_____ to friend-_____.] (I-68)

8   А вдруг он хо́чет переда́ть ей мою́ рабо́ту?
[And suddenly he-_____ wants transfer her-_____ my work-_____?] (I-76)

9   Мне вот даду́т план, и тогда́ — проща́й моя́ диссерта́ция!
[Me-_____ look give plan-_____ and then — goodbye my dissertation-_____!] (I-80)

10   Зна́ете, вам о́чень э́та причёска идёт.
[Know, you-_____ very this hairdo-_____ goes.] (I-94)

11   Я помаха́л руко́й знако́мому худо́жнику.
[I-_____ waived hand-_____ acquaintance artist-_____.] (I-98)

12   Я зна́ю, ни у кого́ не бу́дет сто́лько дней по боле́зни, как у меня́.
[I-_____ know, not by who-_____ not will-be so-many days-_____ along sickness-_____, as by me-_____.] (I-106)

Genitive Exercise 1, Level I

Identify the instances of the GENITIVE *case in the following sentences and explain why the* GENITIVE *is used.*

1   И как раз в э́тот моме́нт с ле́стницы ста́ли на́шу ко́мнату открыва́ть ключо́м.
[And how time in that moment -_____ from stairwell-_____ began our room-_____ open key-_____.] (I-1)

2   Вокру́г костра́ стоя́ли лю́ди и смотре́ли с заду́мчивыми лица́ми.
[Around campfire-_____ stood people-_____ and looked with pensive faces-_____.] (I-15)

3   Вско́ре рабо́чие принесли́ но́вый ковёр взаме́н испо́рченного.
[Soon workers-_____ brought new carpet-_____ in-place ruined-_____.] (I-34)

4   Мы шли вдоль клéток.
     [We-_____ walked along cages-_____.] (I-46)

5   Грóхот колёс тóтчас же заглушúл джáзовую мелóдию.
     [Clattering-_____ wheels-_____ suddenly drowned-out jazz melody-_____.] (I-53)

6   Когдá я чегó-то жду, я не могý при э́том ни дýмать ни читáть.
     [When I-_____ something-_____ wait, I-_____ not can at this-_____ neither think
     nor read.] (I-63)

7   Чукóвский сохранúл бóлее ста пúсем от Рéпина за 1907-1929 гóды.
     [Chukovsky-_____ kept more hundred letters-_____ from Repin-_____ for 1907-
     1929 years-_____.] (I-73)

8   Я знáю, ни у когó не бýдет стóлько дней по болéзни, как у меня́.
     [I-_____ know, not by who-_____ not will-be so-many days-_____ along sickness-
     _____, as by me-_____.] (I-106)

9   Из-за тогó, что он обладáет огрóмными финáнсовыми ресýрсами, он имéет
     весьмá серьёзное влия́ние на конгрéсс США.
     [Because-of that-_____, that he-_____ controls huge financial resources-_____, he-
     _____ has very serious influence-_____ on Congress-_____ USA-_____.] (I-120)

10   Из Москвы́ мóжно доéхать за день.
     [From Moscow-_____ possible get-to in day-_____.] (I-129)

11   —У них перерыв скóро?
     —Навéрно с чáсу до двух.
     [— By them-_____ break-_____ soon?
     —Probably from hour-_____ to two-_____.] (I-36)

12   А мáма весёлая, с нéкоторой излúшней лúхостью. Э́то у неё всегдá от винá.
     [And mama-_____ happy-_____, with certain excessive spirit-_____. This-_____
     by her-_____ always from wine-_____.] (I-144)

Genitive Exercise 2, Level I
     *Identify the instances of the GENITIVE case in the following sentences and explain why
     the GENITIVE is used.*

1   Политúческого решéния кýрдской проблéмы покá не вúдно.
     [Political solution-_____ Kurdish problem-_____ still not visible.] (I-2)

2   В э́том годý Россúю, возмóжно, посетúт главá управлéния национáльной
     оборóны Япóнии.
     [In this year-_____ Russia-_____, possibly, visits head-_____ administration-_____
     national defense-_____ Japan-_____.] (I-17)

3   У неё нет ро́дственников, кото́рым ей хоте́лось бы оста́вить всё э́то.
[By her-_____ not relatives-_____, who-_____ her-_____ wanted would leave all this-_____.] (I-37)

4   Я по́мню тесноту́ о́коло доски́ с расписа́ниями.
[I-_____ remember crush-_____ around board-_____ with schedules-_____.] (I-47)

5   Оди́н из мои́х ста́рых знако́мых, рабо́тающий в столи́це, реши́л сде́лать мне пода́рок.
[One-_____ from my old friends-_____, working-_____ in capitol-_____, decided make me-_____ present-_____.] (I-54)

6   Подо мно́й и позади́ меня́ — го́ры.
[Under me-_____ and behind me-_____ — mountains-_____.] (I-66)

7   От э́той сде́ланной улы́бки мне стано́вится не по себе́.
[From that fake smile-_____ me-_____ becomes not along self-_____.] (I-75)

8   Я сдаю́сь — отодви́ну свои́ дела́ на по́сле обе́да.
[I-_____ give-up — put-off own matters-_____ to after lunch-_____.] (I-113)

9   С тех пор его́ со́бственные материа́лы, как и статьи́ други́х куби́нских журнали́стов, публикова́лись в разли́чных газе́тах США и Лати́нской Аме́рики.
[From this time-_____ his personal materials-_____, as also articles-_____ other Cuban journalists-_____, publicized in various newspapers-_____ USA-_____ and Latin America-_____.] (I-121)

10   Цена́ бу́лки хле́ба бо́льше до́ллара.
[Price-_____ loaf-_____ bread-_____ more dollar-_____.] (I-130)

11   Неде́лю дождя́ не́ было.
[Week-_____ rain-_____ not was.] (I-77)

12   Я ра́ди тебя́ живу́, а ты говори́шь — учи́сь...
[I-_____ for-sake you-_____ live, and you-_____ say — study...] (I-145)

Genitive Exercise 3 Level I

Genitive Exercise 3, Level I
Identify the instances of the GENITIVE case in the following sentences and explain why the GENITIVE is used.

1   Таки́м о́бразом, всё вы́глядело соверше́нно норма́льно, е́сли не счита́ть того́
    фа́кта, что я ещё не была́ жено́й Гео́ргия.
    [This image-_____, all-_____ looked completely normal, if not consider that fact-
    _____, that I-_____ still not was wife-_____ Georgiy-_____.] (I-5)

2   Вот из тре́тьего подъе́зда выхо́дит с портфе́лем мой сосе́д.
    [Here from third doorway-_____ walks-out with briefcase-_____ my neighbor-
    _____.] (I-28)

3   И тепе́рь я тебя́ спрошу́: чем мои́ де́ти ху́же други́х?
    [And now I-_____ you-_____ ask: what-_____ my children-_____ worse others-
    _____?] (I-39)

4   У меня́ не́ было тогда́ влече́ния к литерату́ре.
    [By me-_____ not was then attraction-_____ to literature-_____.] (I-49)

5   Де́лай как мо́жно бо́льше оши́бок, и ты вы́играешь!
    [Do as possible more mistakes-_____ and you-_____ win!] (I-55)

6   Еди́нственная наде́жда — два косми́ческих корабля́ <<Во́яджер>>, кото́рые
    продолжа́ют путеше́ствие среди́ звёзд Мле́чного пути́.
    [Only hope-_____ — two-_____ space ships-_____ "Voyager-_____", which-_____
    continue travel-_____ among stars-_____ Milky Way-_____.] (I-69)

7   У гро́ба поко́йного президе́нт говори́л в основно́м о себе́.
    [By grave-_____ deceased-_____ president-_____ talked in principle-_____ about
    self-_____.] (I-87)

8   От э́той мы́сли мне стано́вится гру́стно.
    [From this thought-_____ me-_____ becomes sad.] (I-112)

9   Ведь, поми́мо хокке́я на траве́, на но́вом стадио́не мо́жно игра́ть в ре́гби,
    бейсбо́л, софтбо́л...
    [You-know, besides hockey-_____ on grass-_____, on new stadium-_____ possible
    play in rugby-_____, baseball-_____, softball-_____...] (I-124)

10 Нет, он не пья́ный. Про́сто обалде́л от жары́.
    [No, he-_____ not drunk-_____. Simply became-woozy from heat-_____.] (I-135)

11 Сейча́с ча́ю попьём.
    [Now tea-_____ drink.] (I-81)

12 Хо́чется дома́шней еды́, не в том смы́сле, что здесь пло́хо ко́рмят, а в том,
    что хо́чется люби́мой пи́щи.
    [Wants home food-_____, not in that sense-_____, that here poorly feed, but in that-
    _____, that wants favorite food-_____.] (I-153)

Locative Exercise 1, Level I

Identify the instances of the LOCATIVE case in the following sentences and explain why the LOCATIVE is used.

1   То положе́ние, в кото́ром я находи́лась, бы́ло абсолю́тно просты́м и я́сным.
[That situation-_____, in which-_____ I-_____ was-found, was absolutely simple-_____ and clear-_____.] (I-4)

2   В моско́вской жи́зни наш япо́нец чу́вствует себя́ комфо́ртно.
[In Moscow life-_____ our Japanese-_____ feel self-_____ comfortable.] (I-16)

3   Она́ де́ржит зо́нтик при себе́ на слу́чай дождя́ и́ли жары́.
[She-_____ keeps umbrella-_____ at her-_____ on case-_____ rain-_____ or heat-_____.] (I-32)

4   Был за́пах дорого́го одеколо́на в ли́фте.
[Was smell-_____ expensive eau-de-cologne-_____ in elevator-_____.] (I-45)

5   Когда́ я чего́-то жду, я не могу́ при э́том ни ду́мать ни чита́ть.
[When I-_____ something-_____ wait, I-_____ not can at this-_____ neither think nor read.] (I-63)

6   У гро́ба поко́йного президе́нт говори́л в основно́м о себе́.
[By grave-_____ deceased-_____ president-_____ talked in principle-_____ about self-_____.] (I-87)

7   Она́ рабо́тает медсестро́й в той же больни́це, что и муж.
[She-_____ works nurse-_____ in that same hospital-_____, that and husband-_____.] (I-123)

8   А здесь вообще́ здо́рово спать. Ую́тный уголо́к. Я сто лет на приро́де не спал, а ты?
[And here generally great sleep. Comfortable corner-_____. I-_____ hundred-_____ years-_____ in nature-_____ not slept, and you-_____?] (I-136)

9   Хо́чется дома́шней еды́, не в том смы́сле, что здесь пло́хо ко́рмят, а в том, что хо́чется люби́мой пи́щи.
[Wants home food-_____, not in that sense-_____, that here poorly feed, but in that-_____, that wants favorite food-_____.] (I-153)

Locative Exercise 2, Level I

Identify the instances of the LOCATIVE case in the following sentences and explain why the LOCATIVE is used.

1 В мо́лодости не це́нишь то, что у тебя́ есть, и всё вре́мя хо́чется чего́-то друго́го.
[In youth-_____ not value that-_____, what-_____ by you-_____ is, and all time-_____ want something else-_____.] (I-9)

2 В хо́ре я всегда́ стоя́ла в после́днем ряду́.
[In choir-_____ I-_____ always stood in last row-_____.] (I-25)

3 В э́том до́ме она́ жила́ до́льше всех его́ обита́телей.
[In that house-_____ she-_____ lived longer all its inhabitants-_____.] (I-33)

4 За ка́ждый но́мер в оте́ле мы пла́тим бо́льше ста до́лларов.
[For each room-_____ in hotel-_____ we-_____ pay more hundred dollars-_____.] (I-48)

5 Я е́хал в тролле́йбусе, а он столкну́лся с авто́бусом, и мне пришло́сь идти́ пешко́м.
[I-_____ rode in trolleybus-_____, but it-_____ collided with bus-_____, and me-_____ was-necessary go by-foot-_____.] (I-83)

6 Неда́вно в Ве́не откры́ли кру́пную вы́ставку с экспона́тами на те́му "Иску́сство и бред".
[Recently in Vienna-_____ opened major exhibition-_____ with pieces-_____ on theme-_____ "Art-_____ and delirium-_____".] (I-88)

7 Ведь, помимо хокке́я на траве́, на но́вом стадио́не мо́жно игра́ть в ре́гби, бейсбо́л, софтбо́л...
[You know, besides hockey-_____ on grass-_____, on new stadium-_____ possible play in rugby-_____, baseball-_____, softball-_____...] (I-124)

8 А при Ста́лине ра́зве твори́лось тако́е?
[And at Stalin-_____ really made such-_____?] (I-138)

9 Спроси́те у десяти́ челове́к об их люби́мом геро́е, писа́теле и компози́торе.
[Ask by ten people-_____ about their favorite hero-_____, writer-_____ and composer-_____.] (I-162)

Locative Exercise 3, Level I
Identify the instances of the LOCATIVE *case in the following sentences and explain why the* LOCATIVE *is used.*

1   Фигу́ра у неё была́ как ци́фра "во́семь," оди́н круг на друго́м.
[Figure-_____ by her-_____ was like number-_____ "eight"-_____, one circle-_____ on other-_____.] (I-14)

2   С пе́рвых же страни́ц в его́ кни́ге чу́вствуется проблема́тика необы́чная и тру́дная.
[From first-_____ very pages-_____ in his book-_____ is-felt problems unusual-_____ and difficult-_____.] (I-26)

3   Я посыла́л ему́ свои́ заме́тки о лю́дях труда́.
[I-_____ sent him-_____ own observations-_____ about people-_____ labor-_____.] (I-44)

4   В рома́не не упомина́лось и́мени Ста́лина.
[In novel-_____ not mentioned name-_____ Stalin-_____.] (I-51)

5   По́хороны состоя́лись на сле́дующий день, при уча́стии президе́нта Белору́ссии.
[Funeral-_____ took-place on next day-_____, at participation-_____ president-_____ Belorussia-_____.] (I-86)

6   Что же произошло́ на са́мом де́ле, и каковы́ моти́вы роди́телей шестнадцатиле́тней тенниси́стки?
[What-_____ EMPH happened in actual matter-_____, and what-kind-of-_____ motives-_____ parents-_____ sixteen-year-old tennis-player-_____?] (I-119)

7   Тогда́ Я́на начала́ танцева́ть в оде́жде — в купа́льнике.
[Then Jana-_____ began dance in clothes-_____ — in bathing-suit-_____.] (I-132)

8   Да́же ча́йник лежа́л на боку́.
[Even teapot-_____ lay on side-_____.] (I-151)

9   Вся жизнь по́сле сорока́ — чем ты занима́ешься, что ешь и каку́ю кни́гу чита́ешь — всё э́то на лице́ и на рука́х.
[All life-_____ after forty-_____ — what-_____ you-_____ occupy-self, what-_____ eat and what book-_____ read — all this-_____ on face-_____ and on hands-_____.] (I-158)

Mixed Case Exercise 1, Level I

Identify the cases in the sentences below and explain why those cases are used.
Provide your own English translation of the sentence and compare it with the trans-
lation in the key.

1   И как раз в э́тот моме́нт с ле́стницы ста́ли на́шу ко́мнату открыва́ть ключо́м.
    [And how time in that moment -_____ from stairwell-_____ began our room-_____
    open key-_____.] (I-1)

2   Они́ всегда́ бы́ли хулига́нами, то́лько внача́ле ма́ленькие хулига́ны, пото́м
    ю́ные, а тепе́рь ста́рые.
    [They-_____ always were hooligans-_____, just at-first little hooligans-_____, then
    young-_____, and now old-_____.] (I-10)

3   В э́том году́ Росси́ю, возмо́жно, посети́т глава́ управле́ния национа́льной
    оборо́ны Япо́нии.
    [In this year-_____ Russia-_____, possibly, visits head-_____ administration-_____
    national defense-_____ Japan-_____.] (I-17)

4   Смысл э́той жи́зни состоя́л в том, что́бы зарабо́тать как мо́жно бо́льше
    де́нег.
    [Meaning-_____ this life-_____ consisted in that-_____ so-that earn as possible
    more money-_____.] (I-38)

5   Я до́лжен был кому́-то показа́ть свои́ ру́кописи. Но кому́?
    [I-_____ should-_____ someone-_____ show own manuscripts-_____. But whom-
    _____?] (I-50)

6   То́лько актёры мо́гут игра́ть оди́н спекта́кль по де́сять раз. А мы не актёры,
    а лю́ди. И не игра́ем, а живём.
    [Only actors-_____ can play one show-_____ along ten-_____ times-_____. But
    we-_____ not actors-_____, but people-_____. And not play, but live.] (I-67)

7   Интере́сно, попадёт ли в ру́ки мэ́ра Лужко́ва э́тот но́мер "Литгазе́ты"?
    [Interesting, fall if in hands-_____ mayor Luzhkov-_____ this issue-_____
    "Litgazeta-_____"?] (I-85)

8   Коро́че, я пропуска́л одну́ ле́кцию за друго́й. Лу́чше всего́, таки́м о́бразом,
    мне запо́мнились университе́тские коридо́ры.
    [Shorter, I-_____ skipped one lecture-_____ beyond another-_____. Better all-_____,
    such form-_____, me-_____ get-memorized university corridors-_____.] (I-97)

9   Де́нег, кото́рые она́ тут зараба́тывает, ей хвата́ет на шпи́льки.
    [Money-_____, which-_____ she-_____ here earns, her-_____ suffices for hairpins-
    _____.] (I-133)

10   Домóй шёл ночнóй пóезд, мать всегдá им приезжáла, éсли éздила в гóрод.
[Homewards went night train-_____, mother-_____ always it-_____ arrived, if went to city-_____.] (I-152)

Mixed Case Exercise 2, Level I
Identify the cases in the sentences below and explain why those cases are used. Provide your own English translation of the sentence and compare it with the translation in the key.

1   Ей ещё нáдо бы́ло забежáть в магази́н, купи́ть продýкты, потóм поéхать в больни́цу к своéй мáме, потóм вернýться и взять из дéтского сáда свою мáленькую дóчку.
[Her-_____ still necessary was run in store-_____, buy groceries-_____, then go in hospital-_____ to own mother-_____, then return and take from childrens' garden-_____ own small daughter-_____.] (I-13)

2   Есть у нас такáя тради́ция — отмечáть все совéтские и церкóвные прáздники.
[There-is by us-_____ such tradition-_____ — celebrate all Soviet-_____ and church holidays-_____.] (I-23)

3   Гáлка всех подрýг разогнáла, никтó ей не нýжен.
[Galka-_____ all girlfriends-_____ chased-away, no-one-_____ her-_____ not needed-_____.] (I-40)

4   Сáхаров вам э́того не прости́т.
[Sakharov-_____ you-_____ that-_____ not forgive.] (I-52)

5   Оди́н из мои́х стáрых знакóмых, рабóтающий в столи́це, реши́л сдéлать мне подáрок.
[One-_____ from my old friends-_____, working-_____ in capitol-_____, decided make me-_____ present-_____.] (I-54)

6   То положéние, в котóром я находи́лась, бы́ло абсолю́тно просты́м и я́сным.
[That situation-_____, in which-_____ I-_____ was-found, was absolutely simple-_____ and clear-_____.] (I-4)

7   Пóхороны состоя́лись на слéдующий день, при учáстии президéнта Белорýссии.
[Funeral-_____ took-place on next day-_____, at participation-_____ president-_____ Belorussia-_____.] (I-86)

8   Ценá компроми́сса былá непомéрно высóкой.
[Cost-_____ compromise-_____ was inordinately high-_____.] (I-102)

9   У меня́ пря́мо пересо́хло во рту́.
     [By me-_____ right-away dried-up in mouth-_____.] (I-134)

10   У Щербако́вой есть ре́дкий дар — она́ чу́вствует, чем па́хнет ве́тер вре́мени.
     [By Shcherbakova-_____ there-is rare gift-_____ — she-_____ senses, what-_____
     smells wind-_____ time-_____.] (I-164)

11   Алёна ста́рше Да́шки на три го́да, зна́чит, ей два́дцать два.
     [Alyona-_____ older Dashka-_____ to three-_____ years-_____, means, her-_____
     twenty-two-_____.] (I-155)

12   Еди́нственная наде́жда — два косми́ческих корабля́ <<Во́яджер>>, кото́рые
     продолжа́ют путеше́ствие среди́ звёзд Мле́чного пути́.
     [Only hope-_____ — two-_____ space ships-_____ "Voyager-_____", which-_____
     continue travel-_____ among stars-_____ Milky Way-_____.] (I-69)

Mixed Case Exercise 3, Level I
     Put the underlined words and phrases into the correct cases. Provide your own
     English translation of the sentence and compare it with the translation in the key.

1   Тако́й о́браз, всё вы́глядело соверше́нно норма́льно, е́сли не счита́ть тот
     факт, что я ещё не была́ жена́ Гео́ргий. (I-5)

2   Вади́м то́же ничто́ не сказа́л, прошёл в ко́мната и лёг на дива́н лицо́ к стена́.
     (I-8)

3   В моско́вская жизнь наш япо́нец чу́вствует себя́ комфо́ртно. (I-16)

4   Вско́ре рабо́чие принесли́ но́вый ковёр взаме́н испо́рченный. (I-34)

5   Круг её знако́мые составля́ли адвока́ты, врачи́, журнали́сты, худо́жники.
     (I-43)

6   И вы она́ не жа́лко? (I-65)

7   Из толпа́ выделя́ется челове́к сре́дний ро́ст и спра́шивает Петро́в, что он
     записа́л у себя́ в записна́я кни́жечка. (I-70)

8   Мы стоя́ли по ра́зные сто́роны пруд и смотре́ли друг на дру́г. (I-82)

9   Неда́вно в Ве́на откры́ли кру́пная вы́ставка с экспона́ты на те́ма "Иску́сство
     и бред". (I-88)

10   Бо́лее то, по мысль а́втор, Солжени́цын вели́к незави́симо от то, прав он
     и́ли не прав в свой сужде́ния. (I-95)

Mixed Case
Exercise 4
Level I

11   Снаряжа́емся, берём са́нки и отправля́емся на кана́л ката́ться с го́ры. (I-117)

12   И он полюби́л своя́ боле́знь бо́льше себя́, бо́льше Ве́ра, бо́льше сын... (I-142)

Mixed Case Exercise 4, Level I

Put the underlined words and phrases into the correct cases. Provide your own English translation of the sentence and compare it with the translation in the key.

1   На́ша пе́рвая встре́ча прошла́ то не ме́нее без изли́шние восто́рги. (I-6)

2   Вокру́г костёр стоя́ли лю́ди и смотре́ли с заду́мчивые ли́ца. (I-15)

3   У она́ нет ро́дственники, кото́рые она́ хоте́лось бы оста́вить всё э́то. (I-37)

4   И тепе́рь я ты спрошу́: что мой де́ти ху́же други́е? (I-39)

5   Я посыла́л он свой заме́тки о лю́ди труд. (I-44)

6   За ка́ждый но́мер в оте́ль мы пла́тим бо́льше сто до́ллары. (I-48)

7   Предполага́ется, что компенса́ция мо́гут получи́ть пятна́дцать ты́сяча челове́к. (I-60)

8   Одна́жды вы́шел он и́з дом, пошёл в ла́вочка купи́ть столя́рный клей. (I-71)

9   Како́е же впечатле́ние на вы произво́дит нача́ло суде́бный проце́сс? (I-90)

10   Зарпла́та нау́чные сотру́дники со сте́пени была́, наве́рное, раз в пять вы́ше сре́дняя. (I-127)

11   Гото́в ли вы проли́ть своя́ кровь ра́ди сча́стье наро́дный? (I-128)

12   Слу́шай моя табли́ца умноже́ние. Два́жды два бу́дет четы́ре, а три́жды три — де́вять. А я ты люблю́. (I-147)

13   Ма́ша босико́м, го́лая, пошла́ на ку́хня, что́бы попи́ть вода́. (I-149)

Multi-Case Preposition Exercise 1, Level I
Choose the correct preposition and case combinations from the choices below.

1 И как раз <u>в э́тот моме́нт/в э́том моме́нте</u> <u>с ле́стницу/с ле́стницы/с ле́стницей</u> ста́ли на́шу ко́мнату открыва́ть ключо́м.
Just at that moment they began to open our room from the stairwell with a key. (I-1)

2 Её ко́мната была́ огро́мной и темнова́той, <u>с краси́вую стари́нную ме́бель/с краси́вой стари́нной ме́бели/с краси́вой стари́нной ме́белью</u>, <u>с почти́ чёрный парке́т/с почти́ чёрного парке́та/с почти́ чёрным парке́том</u>.
Her room was enormous and rather dark, with beautiful antique furniture, and a nearly black parquet floor. (I-7)

3 Ей ещё на́до бы́ло забежа́ть <u>в магази́н/в магази́не</u>, купи́ть проду́кты, пото́м пое́хать <u>в больни́цу/в больни́це</u> к свое́й ма́ме, пото́м верну́ться и взя́ть из де́тского са́да свою́ ма́ленькую до́чку.
She still had to run by the store and buy groceries, then drive to the hospital to see her mom, then return and get her little girl from day care. (I-13)

4 <u>В хор/В хо́ре</u> я всегда́ стоя́ла <u>в после́дний ряд/в после́днем ряду́</u>.
I always stood in the last row in the choir. (I-25)

5 Вот из тре́тьего подъе́зда выхо́дит <u>с портфе́ль/с портфе́ля/с портфе́лем</u> мой сосе́д.
And here my neighbor walks out of the third doorway with his briefcase. (I-28)

6 Я посыла́л ему́ свои́ заме́тки <u>о люде́й/о лю́дях</u> труда́.
I sent him my observations about working people. (I-44)

7 Тре́тью неде́лю идёт борьба́ <u>за жизнь/за жи́знью</u>.
The battle for life has been going on for three weeks. (I-58)

8 Ка́ждая па́ра должна́ роди́ть двои́х и́ли, ка́жется, да́же трои́х, а у нас то́лько <u>по одного́/по одному́</u>.
Each couple should have two children or perhaps even three, but we only have one each. (I-79)

9 Коро́че, я пропуска́л одну́ ле́кцию <u>за другу́ю/за друго́й</u>. Лу́чше всего́, таки́м о́бразом, мне запо́мнились университе́тские коридо́ры.
In brief, I skipped one lecture after another. Best of all, in this way I memorized the university corridors. (I-97)

10 Сую́ его́ <u>под дива́н/под дива́ном</u> <u>со слова́/со слов/со слова́ми</u> <<сиди́ и молчи́>>.
I shove him under the couch with the words "sit and be quiet". (I-109)

11   С те поры́/С тех пор/С те́ми пора́ми его́ со́бственные материа́лы, как и статьи́ други́х куби́нских журнали́стов, публикова́лись в разли́чные газе́ты/в разли́чных газе́тах США и Лати́нской Аме́рики.
From this point his personal materials, just like the articles of other Cuban journalists, were publicized in various newspapers of the USA and Latin America. (I-121)

12   На́до сказа́ть, что за после́дние не́сколько лет/за после́дними не́сколькими года́ми пла́та за прое́зд/за прое́здом до Москвы́ практи́чески не вы́росла.
One must say that for the last several years, the cost of a trip to Moscow has not really gone up. (I-126)

Multi-Case
Preposition
Exercise 2
Level I

Multi-Case Preposition Exercise 2, Level I

Choose the correct preposition and case combinations from the choices below.

1   Жить на литерату́рные за́работки/на литерату́рных за́работках тру́дно.
It is hard to live on a writer's wages. (I-3)

2   Вади́м то́же ничего́ не сказа́л, прошёл в ко́мнату/в ко́мнате и лёг на дива́н/на дива́не лицо́м к стене́.
Vadim also said nothing, he walked into the room and lay down on the couch with his face towards the wall. (I-8)

3   В моско́вскую жи́знь/В моско́вской жи́зни наш япо́нец чу́вствует себя́ комфо́ртно.
Our Japanese friend feels comfortable in Moscow life. (I-16)

4   С пе́рвые же страни́цы/С пе́рвых же страни́ц/С пе́рвыми же страни́цами в его́ кни́гу/в его́ кни́ге чу́вствуется проблема́тика необы́чная и тру́дная.
From the very first pages of his book one can sense unusual and difficult problems. (I-26)

5   Я по́мню тесноту́ о́коло доски́ с расписа́ния/с расписа́ний/с расписа́ниями.
I remember the crush around the schedule board. (I-47)

6   То́лько актёры мо́гут игра́ть оди́н спекта́кль по де́сять раз/по десяти́ ра́зам. А мы не актёры, а лю́ди. И не игра́ем, а живём.
Only actors can perform the same show ten times. But we aren't actors, we're people. And we aren't performing, we're living. (I-67)

7   Нефть с Ка́спий/с Ка́спия/с Ка́спием пойдёт че́рез Ту́рцию, а не Новоросси́йск.
Oil from the Caspian will go through Turkey, not Novorossiysk. (I-103)

8   Пото́м отправля́ю дете́й с Ди́му/с Ди́мы/с Ди́мой гуля́ть, а сама́ принима́юсь за дела́/за дела́ми.

Then I send the kids off for a walk with Dima, and I myself get ready for business. (I-110)

9   Она́ рабо́тает медсестро́й <u>в ту же больни́цу/в той же больни́це</u>, что и муж. She works as a nurse in the same hospital as her husband. (I-123)

10   Ночно́й клуб по́льзуется популя́рностью, <u>в выходны́е/в выходны́х</u> сюда́ прихо́дят <u>по две́сти-три́ста челове́к/по двумста́м-трёмста́м челове́кам</u> — <u>в то число́/в том числе́</u> шахтёры. The night club enjoys popularity, around two-three hundred people come here on days off, miners among them. (I-131)

11   Ве́чером они́ соберу́тся попи́ть травяно́го ча́ю, и́ли пойду́т <u>в теа́тр/в теа́тре</u>. In the evening they will gather to drink some herbal tea or to go to the theater. (I-154)

12   Спроси́те у десяти́ челове́к <u>об их люби́мого геро́я, писа́теля и компози́тора/об их люби́мом геро́е, писа́теле и компози́торе</u>. Ask ten people about their favorite hero, writer, and composer. (I-162)

Multi-Case Preposition Exercise 3, Level I
Choose the correct preposition and case combinations from the choices below.

1   То положе́ние, <u>в кото́рое/в кото́ром</u> я находи́лась, бы́ло абсолю́тно просты́м и я́сным. The situation in which I found myself was absolutely simple and clear. (I-4)

2   <u>В мо́лодость/В мо́лодости</u> не це́нишь то, что у тебя́ есть, и всё вре́мя хо́чется чего́-то друго́го. In youth you never value what you have, but the whole time you want something else. (I-9)

3   Она́ действи́тельно <u>с не́которые поры́/с не́которых пор/с не́которыми пора́ми</u> переста́ла звони́ть и появля́ться. Come time ago she really had stopped calling and stopping by. (I-21)

4   Моя́ ма́чеха мечта́ет, что́бы я вы́шла за́муж <u>за пе́рвый встре́чный/за пе́рвого встре́чного/за пе́рвым встре́чным</u>. My stepmother's dream is that I will get married to the first man I meet. (I-27)

5   Опа́ де́ржит зо́нтик при себе́ <u>на слу́чай/на слу́чае</u> дождя́ и́ли жары́. She keeps an umbrella with her in case of rain or hot weather. (I-32)

6   <u>За ка́ждый но́мер</u>/<u>За ка́ждым но́мером</u> <u>в оте́ль</u>/<u>в оте́ле</u> мы пла́тим бо́льше ста до́лларов.
For each room in the hotel we are paying more than one hundred dollars. (I-48)

7   Бо́лее того́, <u>по мы́сли</u>/<u>по мы́слям</u> а́втора, Солжени́цын вели́к незави́симо от того́, прав он и́ли не прав <u>в свои́ сужде́ния</u>/<u>в свои́х сужде́ниях</u>.
Furthermore, in the author's opinion, Solzhenitsyn is great irrespective of whether or not he is right in his judgments. (I-95)

8   Позавчера́ положи́ла его́ <u>в свой я́щик</u>/<u>в своём я́щике</u> — <u>под дневни́к</u>/<u>под дневнико́м</u>.
The day before yesterday, I put it in my box under the journal. (I-108)

9   Ребя́та сра́зу же усе́лись <u>за стол</u>/<u>за столо́м</u> и смо́трят <u>на ого́нь</u>/<u>на огне́</u> <u>под кастрю́ли</u>/<u>под кастрю́лями</u>.
The kids immediately sat down at the table and were looking at the fire under the pots. (I-114)

10   Ведь, поми́мо хокке́я <u>на траву́</u>/<u>на траве́</u>, <u>на но́вый стадио́н</u>/<u>на но́вом стадио́не</u> мо́жно игра́ть <u>в ре́гби, бейсбо́л, софтбо́л...</u>/<u>в ре́гби, бейсбо́ле, софтбо́ле...</u>
You know, in addition to field hockey, in the new stadium you can play rugby, baseball, softball... (I-124)

11   Когда́ он приходи́л? ...Ну <u>с неде́лю</u>/<u>с неде́ли</u>/<u>с неде́лей</u>...мо́жет, <u>с пять дней</u>/<u>с пяти́ дней</u>/<u>с пятью́ дня́ми</u>...
When did he come? ...Well about a week...maybe, about five days... (I-141)

Level II Exercises

| Nominative Exercise 1 Level II | Nominative Exercise 1, Level II |

Identify the instances of the NOMINATIVE *case in the following sentences and explain why the* NOMINATIVE *is used.*

1   Для собра́вшихся был устро́ен конце́рт, во вре́мя кото́рого среди́ музыка́нтов появи́лся сам президе́нт.
    [For gathered-_____ was organized-_____ concert-_____, in time-_____ which-_____ among musicians-_____ appeared himself president-_____.] (II-3)

2   Дюк смотре́л на пла́мя, и ему́ каза́лось, что э́то о́гненный оле́нь бежи́т и не мо́жет вы́рваться в не́бо.
    [Duke-_____ looked at flame-_____, and him-_____ seemed, that this-_____ fiery deer-_____ runs and not can tear-away to sky-_____.] (II-17)

3   У неё выраже́ние пти́цы, кото́рой хо́чется пить, ей не даю́т, и похо́же, она́ ско́ро отбу́дет из э́того ми́ра.
    [By her-_____ expression-_____ bird-_____, who-_____ wants drink, her-_____ not give, and appears, she-_____ soon will-leave from this world-_____.] (II-29)

4   И́менно здесь, среди́ э́той стери́льной белизны́, рожда́лись иде́и, приходи́ли разочарова́ния, ста́вились экспериме́нты.
    [Precisely here, among this sterile whiteness-_____, were-born ideas-_____, came disappointments-_____, were-performed experiments-_____.] (II-42)

5   — Я не говорю́ вам — что писа́ть. Я то́лько скажу́ вам — чего́ мы писа́ть категори́чески не должны́.
    [— I-_____ not tell you-_____ what-_____ write. I-_____ only tell you-_____ — what-_____ we-_____ write categorically not should-_____.] (II-55)

6   Моё восприя́тие существова́ло вокру́г меня́, как тума́н, а я сиде́л как бы в це́нтре со́бственного восприя́тия.
    [My perception-_____ existed around me-_____, like fog-_____, and I-_____ sat as if in center-_____ own perception-_____.] (II-78)

7   Соде́йствует ли душе́вная боле́знь разви́тию тво́рческих спосо́бностей, в ча́стности худо́жника?
    [Contribute whether mental illness-_____ development-_____ creative abilities-_____, in particular-_____ artist-_____?] (II-97)

8   Ла́ты нужны́ тем, у кого́ нет фигу́ры.
    [Armor-_____ needed-_____ those-_____, by whom-_____ not figures-_____.] (II-114)

9   Набо́р предлага́емых сообще́ний не о́чень широ́к, к приме́ру <<Пора́ обе́дать>> и́ли <<Я зайду́ за тобо́й в шко́лу>>.
[Set-_____ offered messages-_____, not very broad-_____, to example-_____ "Time eat" or "I-_____ will-drop-by behind you-_____ to school-_____.] (II-131)

10   Се́льские лю́ди вдруг начина́ют понима́ть: их никому́ не ну́жная земля́ на са́мом де́ле име́ет большу́ю це́нность...
[Village people-_____ suddenly begin understand: their no-one-_____ not needed land-_____ in actual fact-_____ has big value-_____...] (II-145)

Nominative Exercise 2, Level II

Nominative Exercise 2 Level II

Identify the instances of the NOMINATIVE case in the following sentences and explain why the NOMINATIVE is used.

1   Она́ действи́тельно была́ горожа́нка, никогда́ не жила́ в дере́вне, никогда́ не спива́лась до боле́зни, и её интересова́ло всё, чего́ она́ не могла́ пости́чь со́бственным о́пытом.
[She-_____ really was city-woman-_____, never not lived in country-_____, never not drunk to illness-_____, a her-_____ interested everything-_____, what-_____ she-_____ not was-able grasp own experience-_____.] (II-6)

2   На его́ жи́зненном столе́, как в кита́йском рестора́не, стоя́ло сто́лько блюд, что смешно́ бы́ло нае́сться че́м-то одни́м и не попро́бовать друго́го.
[On his life table-_____, as in Chinese restaurant-_____, stood so-many-_____ dishes-_____, that absurd was fill-up something one-_____ and not try another-_____.] (II-18)

3   То́мас Ма́нн одна́жды заме́тил, что в исто́рии рома́на ве́хами ча́ще всего́ стано́вятся кни́ги, о кото́рых при их появле́нии осо́бенно уве́ренно говори́лось: э́то не рома́н.
[Thomas Mann-_____ once remarked, that in history-_____ novel-_____ landmarks-_____ more-frequently all-_____ become books-_____, about which-_____ at their appearance-_____ especially confidently said: this-_____ not novel-_____.] (II-30)

4   Меня́ всегда́ угнета́ло противоесте́ственное скопле́ние ре́дкостей.
[Me-_____ always depressed unnatural accumulation-_____ rare-objects-_____.] (II-43)

5   Де́ло в том, что на́ши сре́дства ограни́чены. А зна́чит, ограни́чено число́ на́ших дороги́х госте́й.
[Thing-_____ in that-_____, that our means-_____ limited-_____. But means, limited-_____ number-_____ our dear guests-_____.] (II-57)

6   Де́ти безрабо́тных беру́т приме́р с роди́телей — ка́ждый четвёртый ю́ный
поля́к говори́т о свои́х пла́нах так: <<Бу́ду безрабо́тным>>.
[Children-_____ unemployed-_____ take example-_____ from parents-_____ —
every fourth young Pole-_____ talks about own plans-_____ thus: "Will-be unem-
ployed-_____".] (II-80)

7   К сча́стью, М. Цвета́евой вся э́та запу́танная и неприя́тная исто́рия, ви́димо,
не косну́лась.
[To happiness-_____, M. Tsvetaeva-_____ all that tangled-_____ and unpleasant
story-_____, evidently, not touched.] (II-100)

8   На заня́тия собира́ется вся лаборато́рия — челове́к два́дцать; прохо́дят они́
в большо́й, сосе́дней с на́шей ко́мнате.
[To classes-_____ gathers all laboratory-_____ — people-_____ 20-_____; go-
through they-_____ in big, neighboring-_____ with ours-_____ room-_____.] (II-
118)

9   Вашингто́нская администра́ция опра́вдывается тем, что я́кобы опозда́ла с
пода́чей конгре́ссу на продле́ние злополу́чного зако́на.
[Washington administration-_____ justifies-self that-_____, that supposedly were-
late with sending-_____ Congress-_____ to extension-_____ unfortunate law-_____.]
(II-134)

10   —Ты   са́мая   очарова́тельная   же́нщина   го́рода   Москвы́.
—Ха, ха, ха! Вади́м, вы́пейте лу́чше ещё ча́ю.
[—You-_____ most charming woman-_____ city-_____ Moscow-_____.
— Ha ha ha! Vadim-_____, drink better more tea-_____.] (II-99)

11   Гла́вное — не приотвори́ть на звоно́к дверь, не подда́ться мину́тной
сла́бости.
[Main-thing-_____ — not open to ring-_____ door-_____, not give-in minute's
weakness-_____.] (II-163)

Nominative
Exercise 3
Level II

Nominative Exercise 3, Level II
Identify the instances of the NOMINATIVE *case in the following sentences and explain
why the* NOMINATIVE *is used.*

1   Он встре́тил её взгля́д — сам смути́лся её смуще́нием, и они́ не́сколько
дли́нных, несконча́емых секу́нд смотре́ли друг на дру́га.
[He-_____ met her gaze-_____ — self-_____ was-embarrassed her embarassment-
_____, and they-_____ several-_____ long, endless seconds-_____ looked other-
_____ on other-_____.] (II-7)

2   Посо́л подбро́сил в ками́н берёзовых дров и заме́тил: "А зима́ в Росси́и не
така́я уж зла́я."
[Ambassador-_____ threw-on in fireplace-_____ birch logs-_____ and remarked:
"But winter-_____ in Russia-_____ not such already evil-_____."] (II-19)

3   А сейча́с э́тот арти́ст разжире́л как свинья́, и про́сто ди́ву даёшься, что вре́мя
де́лает с людьми́.
[And now that artist-_____ got-fat like pig-_____, and just marvel-_____ give, what-
_____ time-_____ does with people-_____.] (II-34)

4   В те го́ды я ещё не знал, что де́ньги — бре́мя. Что элега́нтность — ма́ссовая
у́личная фо́рма красоты́. Что ве́чная иро́ния — люби́мое, а гла́вное —
еди́нственное ору́жие беззащи́тных.
[In those years-_____ I-_____ still not knew, that money-_____ — burden-_____.
That elegance-_____ — mass pedestrian form-_____ beauty-_____. That eternal
irony-_____ — favorite-_____, and importantly — only weapon-_____ defense-
less-_____.] (II-44)

5   Не повыша́йте то́на, ми́стер Большако́в.
[Not raise tone-_____, mister Bolshakov-_____.] (II-58)

6   Он то́же бесе́довал со мной, то́лько днём, интересова́лся, каки́е журна́лы,
катало́ги — америка́нские, англи́йские — я просмотре́ла.
[He-_____ also talked with me-_____, only day-_____, interested, what magazines-
_____, catalogs-_____ — American-_____, English-_____ — I-_____ looked-
through.] (II-84)

7   Из о́кон зда́ния Му́рманской областно́й администра́ции ви́ден ры́бный порт.
[From windows-_____ building-_____ Murmansk regional administration-_____
visible-_____ fishing port-_____.] (II-101)

8   "Вот каки́е у нас краси́вые де́ти," говорю́ я и зову́ их на ку́хню накрыва́ть
вме́сте на стол.
["There what-kind-of by us-_____ pretty children-_____," say I-_____ and call them-
_____ to kitchen-_____ cover together on table-_____.] (II-122)

9   Вся семья́ сро́чно занима́ется оформле́нием необходи́мых докуме́нтов, и
Наде́жда Анто́новна бо́льше всего́ бои́тся, что не успе́ет всё офо́рмить до
пое́здки.
[All family-_____ urgently does filling-out-_____ necessary papers-_____, and
Nadezhda Antonovna-_____ more all-_____ is-afraid, that not have-time all-_____
fill-out before trip-_____.] (II-137)

10   Президе́нт подчеркну́л, что Росси́и ну́жно само́й разобра́ться и поня́ть, что происхо́дит в эконо́мике страны́.
[President-_____ emphasized, that Russia-_____ necessary self-_____ understand and understand, what-_____ happens in economics-_____ country-_____.] (II-149)

Instrumental Exercise 1, Level II

Identify the instances of the INSTRUMENTAL *case in the following sentences and explain why the* INSTRUMENTAL *is used.*

1   Обита́тели гнезда́ с серди́тым жужжа́нием набро́сились на оби́дчика це́лым ро́ем и ста́ли жа́лить его́.
[Inhabitants-_____ nest-_____ with angry buzz-_____ threw-selves-on offender-_____ whole swarm-_____ and began sting him-_____.] (II-1)

2   Он закры́л глаза́, что́бы проника́ло как мо́жно ме́ньше раздражи́телей, и тут же уви́дел взгля́д Светла́ны и по́нял, что таки́ми одина́ковыми взгля́дами он мог обменя́ться то́лько со свое́й жено́й, и бо́льше ни с одни́м челове́ком на всём све́те.
[He-_____ closed eyes-_____, so-that penetrated as possible less irritations-_____, and here already saw look-_____ Svetlana-_____ and understood, that such identical looks-_____ he-_____ could exchange only with own wife-_____, and more not with one person-_____ on whole world-_____.] (II-10)

3   Обуче́ние бу́дет идти́ с примене́нием соверше́нной компью́терной и лингафо́нной те́хники.
[Instruction-_____ will go with application-_____ complete computer-_____ and language laboratory technology-_____.] (II-24)

4   Коне́чно, в её во́зрасте смешно́ называ́ть кого́-то дя́дей и́ли тётей, пора́ уже́ переходи́ть на имена́-о́тчества, но Ста́сов всегда́ был для неё дя́дей Вла́диком.
[Of-course, in her age-_____ silly call someone-_____ uncle-_____ or aunt-_____, time already switch-over to names-patronymics-_____, but Stasov-_____ always was for her-_____ uncle Vladik-_____.] (II-40)

5   Студе́нты запаса́ли спиртно́е на ве́чер. Причём держа́ли его́ не в холоди́льниках, а ме́жду око́нными ра́мами.
[Students-_____ stocked-up alcohol-_____ for evening-_____. Moreover kept it-_____ not in refrigerators-_____, but between window frames-_____.] (II-69)

6   Э́то предупрежде́ние принадлежи́т учёному, кото́рый после́дние го́ды акти́вно занима́ется созда́нием нау́чно-популя́рных телепрогра́мм по ко́смосу, пи́шет кни́ги и киносцена́рии.
[This warning-_____ belongs scholar-_____, who-_____ last years-_____ actively

is-occupied creation-_____ scientific-popular television-shows-_____ along space-_____, writes books-_____ and screenplays-_____.] (II-81)

7   Óсенью 1923 гóда в Прáгу приéхал хорошó знáвший Цветáеву поэ́т В. Ф. Ходасéвич.
[Fall-_____ 1923 year-_____ in Prague-_____ arrived well knew-_____ Tsvetaev-_____ poet V. F. Khodasevich-_____.] (II-98)

8   Мы не располагáем такими срéдствами.
[We-_____ not have-at-disposal such means-_____.] (II-116)

9   Вашингтóнская администрáция опрáвдывается тем, что я́кобы опоздáла с подáчей конгрéссу на продлéние злополýчного закóна.
[Washington administration-_____ justifies-self that-_____, that supposedly were-late with sending-_____ Congress-_____ to extension-_____ unfortunate law-_____.] (II-134)

10   К счáстью, óба пилóта успéли катапультировáться за нéсколько секýнд пéред тем, как реактивный самолёт врéзался в зéмлю.
[To fortune-_____, both-_____ pilots-_____ had time eject within several-_____ seconds-_____ before that-_____, as jet airplane-_____ dug-into to ground-_____.] (II-154)

11   Понимáете, тóлько по мóлодости возмóжно с утрá до вéчера занимáться хозя́йством, а вéчером игрáть королéву.
[You-understand, only along youth-_____ possible from morning-_____ to evening-_____ occupy-self domestic-work-_____, and evening-_____ play queen-_____.] (II-164)

Instrumental Exercise 2, Level II

Identify the instances of the INSTRUMENTAL case in the following sentences and explain why the INSTRUMENTAL is used.

1   Э́та странá считáется довóльно бéдной по чáсти прирóдных ископáемых.
[That country-_____ is-considered quite poor-_____ along portion-_____ natural resources-_____.] (II-2)

2   И вдруг ýтро напóлнилось мя́укающими звýками электрогитáры.
[And suddenly morning-_____ filled mewing sounds-_____ electric-guitar-_____.] (II-12)

3   Балкóн был мáленький, заснéженный, весь застáвлен хлáмом.
[Balcony-_____ was small-_____, snow-covered-_____, all-_____ crammed-_____ trash-_____.] (II-26)

4   Не успе́л профе́ссор зако́нчить, как в прохо́д ме́жду ряда́ми шагну́ла
    америка́нка сре́дних лет.
    [Not managed professor-_____ finish, how in aisle-_____ between rows-_____
    stepped American-_____ middle years-_____.] (II-45)

5   В ми́ре есть нема́ло ли́деров, кото́рые не мо́гут искупи́ть пе́ред наро́дами
    свое́й со́бственной вины́.
    [In world-_____ is not-few-_____ leaders-_____, who-_____ not can redeem be-
    fore nations-_____ own own guilt-_____.] (II-70)

6   Он то́же бесе́довал со мной, то́лько днём, интересова́лся, каки́е журна́лы,
    катало́ги — америка́нские, англи́йские — я просмотре́ла.
    [He-_____ also talked with me-_____, only day-_____, interested, what magazines-
    _____, catalogs-_____ — American-_____, English-_____ — I-_____ looked-
    through.] (II-84)

7   Я предлага́ю вам посмотре́ть на мир и мои́ми глаза́ми, глаза́ми ру́сской
    же́нщины из бли́жнего зарубе́жья.
    [I-_____ suggest you-_____ look at world-_____ also my eyes-_____, eyes-_____
    Russian woman-_____ from near abroad-_____.] (II-104)

8   Вы́палив э́то, она́ хло́пает две́рью.
    [Having-blurted-out this-_____, she-_____ slams door-_____.] (II-117)

9   Вся семья́ сро́чно занима́ется оформле́нием необходи́мых докуме́нтов, и
    Наде́жда Анто́новна бо́льше всего́ бои́тся, что не успе́ет всё офо́рмить до
    пое́здки.
    [All family-_____ urgently does filling-out-_____ necessary papers-_____, and
    Nadezhda Antonovna-_____ more all-_____ is-afraid, that not have-time all-_____
    fill-out before trip-_____.] (II-137)

10 Э́то обы́чная пра́ктика — дели́ть счёт за телефо́н по́ровну ме́жду
    прожива́ющими в но́мере.
    [This-_____ usual practice-_____ — divide bill-_____ for telephone-_____ evenly
    between living-together-_____ in room-_____.] (II-155)

11 Росси́ей всегда́ пра́вила аристокра́тия, и он по своему́ о́бразу мышле́ния
    аристокра́т до мо́зга косте́й.
    [Russia-_____ always ruled aristocracy-_____, and he-_____ along own form-_____
    thinking-_____ aristocrat-_____ to marrow-_____ bones-_____.] (II-165)

Instrumental Exercise 3, Level II

> *Identify the instances of the* INSTRUMENTAL *case in the following sentences and explain why the* INSTRUMENTAL *is used.*

1   По мне́нию специали́стов, пока́ нельзя́ счита́ть япо́нское лека́рство препара́том, спосо́бным помо́чь больны́м рассе́янным склеро́зом в тяжёлом состоя́нии.
[Along opinion-_____ specialists-GEN, at-present must-not consider Japanese medicine-_____ preparation-_____, capable-_____ help patients-_____ multiple sclerosis-_____ in serious condition-_____.] (II-4)

2   Режиссёр пил чай и звони́л по телефо́ну, приде́рживая тру́бку плечо́м.
[Director-_____ drank tea-_____ and called along telepone-_____, holding receiver-_____ shoulder-_____.] (II-14)

3   Когда́ челове́к испы́тывает стресс и́ли сре́дней си́лы неприя́тность, в кровь выбра́сывается гормо́н под назва́нием адренали́н.
[When person-_____ expereinces stress-_____ or average force-GEN annoyance-_____, in blood-_____ is-released hormone-_____ under name-_____ adrenaline-_____.] (II-27)

4   Газе́тная рабо́та поны́не явля́ется для меня́ исто́чником существова́ния.
[Newspaper work-_____ up-to-present is for me-GEN source-_____ livelihood-GEN.] (II-46)

5   Слу́чай э́тот специали́сты до сих пор счита́ют небыва́лым.
[Case this-_____ specialists-_____ to this time-GEN consider unprecedented-_____.] (II-72)

6   Каки́м-то не свои́м, охри́пшим, го́лосом прошу́ я извини́ть меня́, обеща́ю стать со́браннее и выска́киваю в коридо́р.
[Some not own, hoarse, voice-_____ ask I-_____ excuse me-_____, promise become more-organized and jump-out in hall-_____.] (II-87)

7   Стара́лся отвеча́ть бана́льным идеа́лам му́жества, кото́рыми руково́дствовался в те го́ды.
[Tried answer banal ideals-_____ courage-GEN, which-_____ was-guided in those years-_____.] (II-111)

8   Я чуть прикаса́юсь к её руке́ щеко́й.
[I-_____ hardly touch to her hand-_____ cheek-_____.] (II-120)

9   Когда́ в пятидеся́тые го́ды создава́лось телеви́дение, туда́ шли неуда́чники кино́ и теа́тра, а та́кже лю́ди, кото́рые чу́вствовали: за э́тим де́лом — бу́дущее.

[When in fifties years-_____ created television-_____, there went unfortunate-ones-_____ movies-GEN and theater-GEN, but also people-_____, which-_____ felt: beyond this thing-_____ — future-_____.] (II-142)

10   Я сама́ себе́ каза́лась проти́вной оттого́, что когда́-то с ним целова́лась.

[I-_____ self-_____ self-_____ seemed nasty-_____ from-that, that sometime with him-_____ kissed.] (II-156)

Accusative
Exercise 1
Level II

Accusative Exercise 1, Level II

Identify the instances of the ACCUSATIVE *case in the following sentences and explain why the* ACCUSATIVE *is used.*

1   Обита́тели гнезда́ с серди́тым жужжа́нием набро́сились на оби́дчика це́лым ро́ем и ста́ли жа́лить его́.

[Inhabitants-_____ nest-_____ with angry buzz-_____ threw-selves-on offender-_____ whole swarm-_____ and began sting him-_____.] (II-1)

2   Дюк смотре́л на пла́мя, и ему́ каза́лось, что э́то о́гненный оле́нь бежи́т и не мо́жет вы́рваться в не́бо.

[Duke-_____ looked at flame-_____, and him-_____ seemed, that this-_____ fiery deer-_____ runs and not can tear-away to sky-_____.] (II-17)

3   Владисла́в вы́пил свой чай в три больши́х глотка́ и реши́тельно подня́лся.

[Vladislav-_____ drank own tea-_____ in three-_____ big gulps-_____ and decisively got-up.] (II-38)

4   Ми́стер Хи́ггинс дал нам всевозмо́жные инстру́кции.

[Mister Higgins-_____ gave us-_____ all-kinds instructions-_____.] (II-51)

5   Э́то предупрежде́ние принадлежи́т учёному, кото́рый после́дние го́ды акти́вно занима́ется созда́нием нау́чно-популя́рных телепрогра́мм по ко́смосу, пи́шет кни́ги и киносцена́рии.

[This warning-_____ belongs scholar-_____, who-_____ last years-_____ actively is-occupied creation-_____ scientific-popular television-shows-_____ along space-_____, writes books-_____ and screenplays-_____.] (II-81)

6   Душевнобольны́е худо́жники продаю́т свои́ карти́ны за пятьдеся́т ты́сяч ма́рок и бо́лее.

[Mentally-ill artists-_____ sell own pictures-_____ for fifty-_____ thousands-_____ marks-_____ and more.] (II-93)

7   Подобра́л во́ин с земли́ недозре́лую фи́гу, ки́нул её в певца́, и угоди́л ему́ пря́мо в рот.
[Picked-up warrior-_____ from earth-_____ unripe fig-_____, threw it-_____ in singer-_____, and hit him-_____ straight in mouth-_____.] (II-110)

8   Дим, дава́й не бу́дем обсужда́ть э́то, прошу́ тебя́, погла́дь сего́дня свои́ брю́ки сам, мне на́до доши́ть.
[Dima-_____, let's not will discuss this-_____, ask you-_____, iron today own pants-_____ self-_____, me-_____ need finish-up-sewing.] (II-123)

9   Соба́к ко́рмят посторо́нние же́нщины, на свои́ де́ньги покупа́ют им еду́, поэ́тому соба́ки их лю́бят и признаю́т.
[Dogs-_____ feed outside women-_____, to own money-_____ buy them-_____ food-_____, therefore dogs-_____ them-_____ love and recognize.] (II-132)

10 Зимо́й из-за поля́рной но́чи невозмо́жно просну́ться, ле́том невозмо́жно усну́ть по друго́й причи́не: в три часа́ но́чи в окно́ лу́пит со́лнце.
[Winter-_____ because-of polar night-_____ impossible wake-up, summer-_____ impossible fall-asleep along other reason-_____: in three-_____ hours-_____ night-_____ to window-_____ thrashes sun-_____.] (II-146)

11 Был слу́чай, когда́ престу́пника нашли́ по отпеча́ткам зубо́в — он был голо́дный и надку́сил кусо́к ма́сла.
[Was incident-_____, when criminal-_____ found along imprints-_____ teeth-_____ — he-_____ was hungry-_____ and took-bite piece-_____ butter-_____.] (II-162)

Accusative Exercise 2, Level II
Identify the instances of the ACCUSATIVE case in the following sentences and explain why the ACCUSATIVE is used.

Accusative
Exercise 2
Level II

1   Гео́ргий сел и написа́л письмо́, и я не сказа́ла ему́ в отве́т ничего́, про́сто взяла́ э́тот листо́к и ушла́ к себе́ на ку́хню.
[Georgi-_____ sat-down and wrote letter-_____, and I-_____ not said him-_____ in answer-_____ nothing-_____, just took that paper-_____ and went to self-_____ to kitchen-_____.] (II-5)

2   Росси́я должна́ игра́ть бо́лее заме́тную роль в динами́чном азиа́тском регио́не, и Япо́ния мо́жет оказа́ть ей в э́том соде́йствие.
[Russia-_____ should play more noticeable role-_____ in dynamic Asian region-_____, and Japan-_____ can give her-_____ in this-_____ assistance-_____.] (II-22)

3   Му́жа она́ то́же не по́мнила, но понима́ла, что раз у неё бы́ло че́тверо дете́й, то, наве́рное, и муж был.
[Husband-_____ she-_____ also not remembered, but understood, that if by her-_____ was foursome-_____ children-_____, then, surely, and husband-_____ was.]
(II-39)

4   Свою́ речь он посвяти́л тво́рчеству Достое́вского.
[His speech-_____ he-_____ dedicated works-_____ Dostoevsky-_____.] (II-59)

5   Муж чита́ет письмо́ и волну́ется до тако́й сте́пени, что роня́ет из рук стака́н с водо́й, кото́рый па́дает на́ пол и разбива́ется.
[Husband-_____ reads letter-_____ and gets-upset to such level-_____, that drops from hands-_____ glass-_____ with water-_____, which-_____ falls on floor-_____ and breaks.] (II-83)

6   Психиа́тр причисля́ет себя́ то́же к худо́жникам, его́ гига́нтские пла́стиковые фигу́ры украша́ют мно́гие америка́нские па́рки.
[Psychiatrist-_____ counts self-_____ also to artists-_____, his gigantic sculptural figures-_____ decorate many American parks-_____.] (II-95)

7   Стара́лся отвеча́ть бана́льным идеа́лам му́жества, кото́рыми руково́дствовался в те го́ды.
[Tried answer banal ideals-_____ courage-_____, which-_____ was-guided in those years-_____.] (II-111)

8   О Го́споди, он, ка́жется, ду́мает, что ра́ди э́той встре́чи я реши́ла укороти́ть ю́бку!
[O Lord-_____, he-_____, it-seems, thinks, that for this date-_____ I-_____ decided shorten skirt-_____!] (II-124)

9   Прави́тельство Еги́пта, опира́ясь на старода́вний и полузабы́тый зако́н, реши́ло ликвиди́ровать в стране́ слу́жбу телохрани́телей.
[Government-_____ Egypt-_____, relying on ancient and half-forgotten law-_____, decided liquidate in country-_____ service-_____ bodyguards-_____.] (II-135)

10   Живёт она́ на сре́дства "спо́нсора" — жена́того бизнесме́на, кото́рый снима́ет для неё кварти́ру и периоди́чески про́сит её бро́сить э́ту дура́цкую рабо́ту в клу́бе и вари́ть до́ма пельме́ни.
[Lives she-_____ on means-_____ "sponsor"-_____ — married businessman-_____, who-_____ rents for her-_____ apartment-_____ and periodically asks her-_____ quit this foolish work-_____ in club-_____ and cook at-home pelmeni-_____.] (II-147)

11 Гла́вное — не приотвори́ть на звоно́к дверь, не подда́ться мину́тной сла́бости.
[Main-thing-_____ — not open to ring-_____ door-_____, not give-in minute's weakness-_____.] (II-163)

Accusative Exercise 3, Level II
Identify the instances of the ACCUSATIVE *case in the following sentences and explain why the* ACCUSATIVE *is used.*

1 Он встре́тил её взгля́д — сам смути́лся её смуще́нием, и они́ не́сколько дли́нных, несконча́емых секу́нд смотре́ли друг на дру́га.
[He-_____ met her gaze-_____ — self-_____ was-embarrassed her embarassment-_____, and they-_____ several-_____ long, endless seconds-_____ looked other-_____ on other-_____.] (II-7)

2 Я задохну́лась в пе́рвое мгнове́ние, как бу́дто меня́ столкну́ли с моста́ в холо́дную ре́чку в октябре́ ме́сяце.
[I-_____ gasped in first moment-_____, as if me-_____ pushed-off from bridge-_____ to cold river-_____ in October month-_____.] (II-25)

3 Он люби́л здесь рабо́тать, и вообще́, была́ бы его́ во́ля, проводи́л бы здесь бо́льшую часть вре́мени.
[He-_____ loved here work, and in-general, was would his will-_____, spend would here larger part-_____ time-_____.] (II-41)

4 И че́рез мину́ту гре́ческий певе́ц сконча́лся от уду́шья.
[And across minute-_____ Greek singer-_____ died from asphyxiation-_____.] (II-60)

5 Он то́же бесе́довал со мной, то́лько днём, интересова́лся, каки́е журна́лы, катало́ги — америка́нские, англи́йские — я просмотре́ла.
[He-_____ also talked with me-_____, only day-_____, interested, what magazines-_____, catalogs-_____ — American-_____, English-_____ — I-_____ looked-through.] (II-84)

6 Он оста́лся врачо́м, а не преврати́лся в мецена́та от иску́сства.
[He-_____ remained doctor-_____, and not turned into patron-_____ art-_____.] (II-96)

7 И́нна огляде́ла цветы́, верну́ла их ба́бке, востре́бовала де́ньги обра́тно и купи́ла на них я́блоки у сосе́дней стару́хи.
[Inna-_____ examined flowers-_____, returned them-_____ woman-_____, demanded money-_____ back and bought for them-_____ apples-_____ by neighboring old-woman-_____.] (II-8)

8   Ребя́та пьют молоко́, две мину́ты мы реша́ем, идти́ ли ещё гуля́ть, и — отка́зываемся.
    [Kids-_____ drink milk-_____, two-_____ minutes-_____ we-_____ decide, go whether still walk, and — decline.] (II-126)

9   Три трудне́йших го́да я прожи́л в хо́лоде и темноте́.
    [Three-_____ quite-difficult year-_____ I-_____ lived-through in cold-_____ and dark-_____.] (II-136)

10 Вон у нас во дворе́ за три го́да — два уби́йства бы́ло. С ограбле́нием.
    [There by us-_____ in courtyard-_____ in three-_____ years-_____ — two-_____ murders-_____ were. With robbery-_____.] (II-79)

Dative Exercise 1, Level II

Identify the instances of the DATIVE case in the following sentences and explain why the DATIVE is used.

1   Э́та страна́ счита́ется дово́льно бе́дной по ча́сти приро́дных ископа́емых.
    [That country-_____ is-considered quite poor-_____ along portion-_____ natural resources-_____.] (II-2)

2   Режиссёр пил чай и звони́л по телефо́ну, приде́рживая тру́бку плечо́м.
    [Director-_____ drank tea-_____ and called along telepone-_____, holding receiver-_____ shoulder-_____.] (II-14)

3   У него́ я́зва желу́дка, и она́ дикту́ет ему́ свой режи́м, а режи́м навя́зывает положи́тельный о́браз жи́зни.
    [By him-_____ ulcer-_____ stomach-_____, and it-_____ dictates him-_____ own regime-_____, and regime-_____ imposes positive mode-_____ life-_____.] (II-28)

4   Свою́ речь он посвяти́л тво́рчеству Достое́вского.
    [His speech-_____ he-_____ dedicated works-_____ Dostoevsky-_____.] (II-59)

5   Э́то предупрежде́ние принадлежи́т учёному, кото́рый после́дние го́ды акти́вно занима́ется созда́нием нау́чно-популя́рных телепрогра́мм по ко́смосу, пи́шет кни́ги и киносцена́рии.
    [This warning-_____ belongs scholar-_____, who-_____ last years-_____ actively is-occupied creation-_____ scientific-popular television-shows-_____ along space-_____, writes books-_____ and screenplays-_____.] (II-81)

6   К сча́стью, М. Цвета́евой вся э́та запу́танная и неприя́тная исто́рия, ви́димо, не косну́лась.
    [To happiness-_____, M. Tsvetaeva-_____ all that tangled-_____ and unpleasant story-_____, evidently, not touched.] (II-100)

7 Все мы по очереди делились новой информацией.
[All we-_____ along turn-_____ shared new information-_____.] (II-115)

8 Оплачивает компания иногородним студентам и приезд в Москву на вручение стипендии, два дня проживания в столице.
[Pays-for company-_____ out-of-town students-_____ and trip-_____ to Moscow-_____ to handing-out-_____ stipend-_____, two-_____ days-_____ stay-_____ in capital-_____.] (II-127)

9 Президент подчеркнул, что России нужно самой разобраться и понять, что происходит в экономике страны.
[President-_____ emphasized, that Russia-_____ necessary self-_____ understand and understand, what-_____ happens in economics-_____ country-_____.] (II-149)

10 Мне сказали, что в январе было совершено 435 квартирных краж.
[Me-_____ told, that in January-_____ was committed 435-_____ apartment robberies-_____.] (II-161)

Dative Exercise 2, Level II
Identify the instances of the DATIVE *case in the following sentences and explain why the* DATIVE *is used.*

1 По мнению специалистов, пока нельзя считать японское лекарство препаратом, способным помочь больным рассеянным склерозом в тяжёлом состоянии.
[Along opinion-_____ specialists-_____, at-present must-not consider Japanese medicine-_____ preparation-_____, capable-_____ help patients-_____ multiple sclerosis-_____ in serious condition-_____.] (II-4)

2 Всё сидели тихо и смотрели на Дюка, и начинали верить Нине Георгиевне в том, что Дюк действительно нуль, пустое место.
[All-_____ sat quietly and looked at Duke-_____, and started believe Nina Georgievna-_____ in that-_____, that Duke-_____ really zero-_____, empty place-_____.] (II-15)

3 У неё выражение птицы, которой хочется пить, ей не дают, и похоже, она скоро отбудет из этого мира.
[By her-_____ expression-_____ bird-_____, who-_____ wants drink, her-_____ not give, and appears, she-_____ soon will-leave from this world-_____.] (II-29)

4   Двáдцать шесть процéнтов опрóшенных не смоглú отвéтить на вопрóс: "Какúе из скульптýрных пáмятников вам бóльше всегó нрáвятся?" Не смóтрят чéтверть москвичéй по сторонáм, дáже по выходнúм дням, не до монумéнтов им.
[Twenty six-_____ percent-_____ questioned-_____ not could answer on question-_____: "Which-_____ from sculptural monuments-_____ you-_____ more all-_____ please?" Not look fourth-_____ Muscovites-_____ along sides-_____, even along weekend days-_____, not to monuments-_____ them-_____.] (II-61)

5   Тетрáдка, в котóрой мы распúсываемся в лаборатóрии по утрáм, лежáла тогдá у негó на столé, и он посмáтривал на неё, но ничегó не сказáл.
[Notebook-_____, in which-_____ we-_____ log-in in laboratory-_____ along mornings-_____, lay then by him-_____ on table-_____, and he-_____ looked at it-_____, but nothing-_____ not said.] (II-85)

6   Я предлагáю вам посмотрéть на мир и мойми глазáми, глазáми рýсской жéнщины из блúжнего зарубéжья.
[I-_____ suggest you-_____ look at world-_____ also my eyes-_____, eyes-_____ Russian woman-_____ from near abroad-_____.] (II-104)

7   Я чуть прикасáюсь к её рукé щекóй.
[I-_____ hardly touch to her hand-_____ cheek-_____.] (II-120)

8   Вице-президéнт попросúл меня, чтóбы я отпрáвился в Срéднюю Áзию для укреплéния нáших двухсторóнних свя́зей и демонстрáции нáшей поддéржки стрáнам э́того региóна.
[Vice-president-_____ asked me-_____, in-order-to I-_____ set-off to Central Asia-_____ for strengthening-_____ our bilateral ties-_____ and demonstration-_____ our support-_____ countries-_____ this region-_____.] (II-128)

9   Верхóвная власть должнá принадлежáть президéнту, считáют трúдцать три процéнта россúйских грáждан.
[Supreme power-_____ should-_____ belong president-_____, consider 33-_____ percent-_____ Russian citizens-_____.] (II-150)

10   Был слýчай, когдá престýпника нашлú по отпечáткам зубóв — он был голóдный и надкýсил кусóк мáсла.
[Was incident-_____, when criminal-_____ found along imprints-_____ teeth-_____ — he-_____ was hungry-_____ and took-bite piece-_____ butter-_____.] (II-162)

Dative Exercise 3, Level II

Identify the instances of the DATIVE *case in the following sentences and explain why the* DATIVE *is used.*

1   Гео́ргий сел и написа́л письмо́, и я не сказа́ла ему́ в отве́т ничего́, про́сто взяла́ э́тот листо́к и ушла́ к себе́ на ку́хню.
[Georgi-_____ sat-down and wrote letter-_____, and I-_____ not said him-_____ in answer-_____ nothing-_____, just took that paper-_____ and went to self-_____ to kitchen-_____.] (II-5)

2   Дюк смотре́л на свой по́яс, и ему́ бы́ло так его́ жаль, бу́дто он расстава́лся не с ве́щью, а с бли́зким дру́гом.
[Duke-_____ looked at own belt-_____, and him-_____ was so him-_____ sorry, as-if he-_____ parted not with thing-_____, but with close friend-_____.] (II-16)

3   Я мечта́ю, что́бы мои́ роди́тели постаре́ли и растолсте́ли, тогда́ — кому́ они́ бу́дут нужны́?
[I-_____ dream, so-that my parents-_____ got-old and got-fat, then — who-_____ they-_____ will-be needed-_____?] (II-36)

4   Э́то сле́дующая по зна́чимости зада́ча по́сле вы́платы пе́нсий и зарпла́т учителя́м.
[That-_____ next-_____ along significance-_____ task-_____ after payment-_____ pensions-_____ and wages-_____ teachers-_____.] (II-68)

5   Мы впра́ве наде́яться, что вы бу́дете дорожи́ть дове́рием, кото́рое мы ока́зываем молодо́му специали́сту.
[We-_____ have-right hope, that you-_____ will value trust-_____, that-_____ we-_____ give young specialist-_____.] (II-86)

6   По да́нным Министе́рства здравоохране́ния Росси́йской Федера́ции, 20,3 проце́нта ма́льчиков-подро́стков про́бовали нарко́тики, ка́ждый пя́тый.
[Along data-_____ Ministry-_____ health-_____ Russian Federation-_____, 20.3-_____ percent-_____ boys-adolescents-_____ tried narcotics-_____, every fifth-_____.] (II-105)

7   Для ребя́т э́то поздно́вато, но на́до же им хоть в выходно́й погуля́ть как сле́дует.
[For kids-_____ this-_____ late, but necessary EMPHATIC them-_____ even to day-off-_____ walk as follows.] (II-121)

8   Вашингто́нская администра́ция опра́вдывается тем, что я́кобы опозда́ла с пода́чей конгре́ссу на продле́ние злополу́чного зако́на.
[Washington administration-_____ justifies-self that-_____, that supposedly were-late with sending-_____ Congress-_____ to extension-_____ unfortunate law-_____.] (II-134)

9   Свéжую чернику, к примéру, принимáют по 3-4 рубля за килогрáмм, сушёную — от 20 до 40 рублéй (в кáждом райóне свои цéны).
[Fresh bilberry-_____, to example-_____, takes around 3-4-_____ rubles-_____ for kilogram-_____, dried-_____ — from 20-_____ to 40-_____ rubles-_____ (in each region-_____ own prices-_____).] (II-151)

10   Глáвное — не приотворить на звонóк дверь, не поддáться минýтной слáбости.
[Main-thing-_____ — not open to ring-_____ door-_____, not give-in minute's weakness-_____.] (II-163)

Genitive
Exercise 1
Level II

Genitive Exercise 1, Level II
Identify the instances of the GENITIVE *case in the following sentences and explain why the* GENITIVE *is used.*

1   Эта странá считáется довóльно бéдной по чáсти прирóдных ископáемых.
[That country-_____ is-considered quite poor-_____ along portion-_____ natural resources-_____.] (II-2)

2   Он закрыл глазá, чтóбы проникáло как мóжно мéньше раздражителей, и тут же увидел взгляд Светлáны и пóнял, что такими одинáковыми взглядами он мог обменяться тóлько со своéй женóй, и бóльше ни с одним человéком на всём свéте.
[He-_____ closed eyes-_____, so-that penetrated as possible less irritations-_____, and here already saw look-_____ Svetlana-_____ and understood, that such identical looks-_____ he-_____ could exchange only with own wife-_____, and more not with one person-_____ on whole world-_____.] (II-10)

3   Прави́тельство Япóнии до сих пор окáзывало поддéржку уси́лиям президéнта в проведéнии экономи́ческих и полити́ческих рефóрм.
[Government-_____ Japan-_____ to this time-_____ gave support-_____ efforts-_____ president-_____ in conducting-_____ economic and political reforms-_____.] (II-23)

4   У неё выражéние пти́цы, котóрой хóчется пить, ей не даю́т, и похóже, онá скóро отбýдет из этого ми́ра.
[By her-_____ expression-_____ bird-_____, who-_____ wants drink, her-_____ not give, and appears, she-_____ soon will-leave from this world-_____.] (II-29)

5   Владислáв выпил свой чай в три больши́х глоткá и реши́тельно подня́лся.
[Vladislav-_____ drank own tea-_____ in three-_____ big gulps-_____ and decisively got-up.] (II-38)

6   Не успéл профéссор закóнчить, как в прохóд мéжду рядáми шагнýла
    америкáнка срéдних лéт.
    [Not managed professor-_____ finish, how in aisle-_____ between rows-_____
    stepped American-_____ middle years-_____.] (II-45)

7   Актёр, бýдучи с гастрóлями во Фрáнкфурте, добѝлся там политѝческого
    убéжища.
    [Actor-_____, being with tour-_____ in Frankfurt-_____, got there political asy-
    lum-_____.] (II-52)

8   Дéло в том, что нáши срéдства ограничены. А знáчит, ограничено числó
    нáших дорогѝх гостéй.
    [Thing-_____ in that-_____, that our means-_____ limited-_____. But means, lim-
    ited-_____ number-_____ our dear guests-_____.] (II-57)

9   Бýдем писáть так же гениáльно — но без егó нелéпостей и ошѝбок.
    [Will write thus brilliantly — but without his absurdities-_____ and errors-_____.]
    (II-64)

10 Слýчай этот специалѝсты до сих пор считáют небывáлым.
    [Case this-_____ specialists-_____ to this time-_____ consider unprecedented-
    _____.] (II-72)

11 Я не вѝжу ничегó плохóго в том, что Щербакóвой удаётся угадáть желáние
    читáтеля рóвно за минýту до тогó, как сам читáтель это желáние чётко
    осознаёт.
    [I-_____ not see nothing-_____ bad-_____ in that-_____, that Shcherbakova-_____
    is-successful guess desire-_____ reader-_____ exactly to minute-_____ until that-
    _____, as self-_____ reader-_____ this desire-_____ clearly realizes.] (II-167)

Genitive Exercise 2, Level II

*Identify the instances of the GENITIVE case in the following sentences and explain why
the GENITIVE is used.*

1   Для собрáвшихся был устрóен концéрт, во врéмя котóрого средѝ музыкáнтов
    появѝлся сам президéнт.
    [For gathered-_____ was organized-_____ concert-_____, in time-_____ which-
    _____ among musicians-_____ appeared himself president-_____.] (II-3)

2   Эти лунá, рекá, плакýчая ѝва бѝли всегдá в её жѝзни, и никогдá нé было
    так, чтóбы их нé было.
    [These moon-_____, river-_____, weeping willow-_____ always in her life-_____,
    and never not been so, so-that they-_____ not was.] (II-11)

3   Обуче́ние бу́дет идти́ с примене́нием соверше́нной компью́терной и лингафо́нной те́хники.
[Instruction-_____ will go with application-_____ complete computer-_____ and language laboratory technology-_____.] (II-24)

4   От ни́х ве́ет тако́й убеди́тельной ску́кой, что э́та ску́ка достига́ет седьмо́го этажа́, проника́ет че́рез стекло́ и каса́ется моего́ лица́.
[From them-_____ blows such convincing boredom-_____, that this boredome-_____ reaches seventh floor-_____, penetrates through glass-_____ and touches my face-_____.] (II-31)

5   Му́жа она́ то́же не по́мнила, но понима́ла, что раз у неё бы́ло че́тверо дете́й, то, наве́рное, и муж был.
[Husband-_____ she-_____ also not remembered, but understood, that if by her-_____ was foursome-_____ children-_____, then, surely, and husband-_____ was.] (II-39)

6   Певе́ц облада́л краси́вым ни́зким барито́ном удиви́тельного те́мбра.
[Singer-_____ possessed beautiful deep baritone-_____ amazing timbre-_____.] (II-47)

7   Любо́й из них мог разгорячи́ться безо вся́кого по́вода.
[Any-_____ from them-_____ could get-excited without any reason-_____.] (II-53)

8   Не повыша́йте то́на, ми́стер Большако́в.
[Not raise tone-_____, mister Bolshakov-_____.] (II-58)

9   Тогда́ литерату́ру преподава́ли хорошо́, и мы нае́лись вели́ких писа́телей уже́ в шко́ле.
[Then literature-_____ taught well, and we-_____ got-fed-up great writers-_____ already in school-_____.] (II-65)

10   — Ну пока́, — вдруг соглаша́ется Ми́ша. — Счастли́вого о́тдыха.
[—Well so-long, — suddenly acquieses Misha-_____. — Happy vacation-_____.] (II-74)

11   Обита́тели э́того до́ма — лауреа́ты разли́чных пре́мий, представля́ли свои́ карти́ны в Кёльне, Пари́же и Сан-Па́уло.
[Residents-_____ this house-_____ — laureates-_____ various prizes-_____, exhibited own pictures-_____ in Cologne-_____, Paris-_____ and San Paulo-_____.] (II-94)

Genitive Exercise 3, Level II

Identify the instances of the GENITIVE case in the following sentences and explain why the GENITIVE is used.

1 Она́ действи́тельно была́ горожа́нка, никогда́ не жила́ в дере́вне, никогда́ не спива́лась до боле́зни, и её интересова́ло всё, чего́ она́ не могла́ пости́чь со́бственным о́пытом.
[She-_____ really was city-woman-_____, never not lived in country-_____, never not drunk to illness-_____, a her-_____ interested everything-_____, what-_____ she-_____ not was-able grasp own experience-_____.] (II-6)

2 Тогда́ она́ наде́ла ю́бку-ми́ни, босоно́жки на платфо́рме и вы́шла и́з дому.
[Then she-_____ put-on mini-skirt-_____, sandals-_____ on platform-_____ and left from house-_____.] (II-13)

3 Я задохну́лась в пе́рвое мгнове́ние, как будто меня́ столкну́ли с моста́ в холо́дную ре́чку в октябре́ ме́сяце.
[I-_____ gasped in first moment-_____, as if me-_____ pushed-off from bridge-_____ to cold river-_____ in October month-_____.] (II-25)

4 Её вы́везли из Испа́нии в три́дцать шесто́м году́, и она́ тут жила́ и росла́, что́бы одна́жды встре́тить ру́сского па́рня и в звёздный час зача́ть сы́на.
[Her-_____ brought from Spain-_____ in thirty sixth year-_____, and she-_____ here lived and grew, so-that once meet Russian guy-_____ and in star hour-_____ conceive son-_____.] (II-32)

5 Коне́чно, в её во́зрасте смешно́ называ́ть кого́-то дя́дей и́ли тётей, пора́ уже́ переходи́ть на имена́-о́тчества, но Ста́сов всегда́ был для неё дя́дей Вла́диком.
[Of-course, in her age-_____ silly call someone-_____ uncle-_____ or aunt-_____, time already switch-over to names-patronymics-_____, but Stasov-_____ always was for her-_____ uncle Vladik-_____.] (II-40)

6 Среди́ эмигра́нтских писа́телей я занима́ю како́е-то ме́сто.
[Among emigrant writers-_____ I-_____ occupy some place-_____.] (II-49)

7 Фина́нсовой подде́ржки её роди́телей стыди́лся.
[Financial support-_____ her parents-_____ was-ashamed.] (II-54)

8 И че́рез мину́ту гре́ческий певе́ц сконча́лся от уду́шья.
[And across minute-_____ Greek singer-_____ died from asphyxiation-_____.] (II-60)

9 Без преувеличе́ния, мо́жно сказа́ть, что сейча́с вся росси́йская медици́на рабо́тает на президе́нта.
[Without exaggeration-_____, possible say, that now all Russian medical-profession-_____ works on president-_____.] (II-67)

10   Еле́не звони́ть бы́ло не́куда: они́ с му́жем жи́ли за́ городом без телефо́на и про́чих удо́бств.
[Elena-_____ call was nowhere: they-_____ with husband-_____ lived beyond city-_____ without telephone-_____ and other comforts-_____.] (II-76)

Locative
Exercise 1
Level II

Locative Exercise 1, Level II

Identify the instances of the LOCATIVE case in the following sentences and explain why the LOCATIVE is used.

1   По мне́нию специали́стов, пока́ нельзя́ счита́ть япо́нское лека́рство препара́том, спосо́бным помо́чь больны́м рассе́янным склеро́зом в тяжёлом состоя́нии.
[Along opinion-_____ specialists-_____, at-present must-not consider Japanese medicine-_____ preparation-_____, capable-_____ help patients-_____ multiple sclerosis-_____ in serious condition-_____.] (II-4)

2   Тогда́ она́ наде́ла ю́бку-ми́ни, босоно́жки на платфо́рме и вы́шла и́з дому.
[Then she-_____ put-on mini-skirt-_____, sandals-_____ on platform-_____ and left from house-_____.] (II-13)

3   Прави́тельство Япо́нии до сих пор ока́зывало подде́ржку уси́лиям президе́нта в проведе́нии экономи́ческих и полити́ческих рефо́рм.
[Government-_____ Japan-_____ to this time-_____ gave support-_____ efforts-_____ president-_____ in conducting-_____ economic and political reforms-_____.] (II-23)

4   Бо́льше всего́ на све́те он лю́бит ходи́ть в похо́ды, спать в пала́тках, вари́ть уху́ в закопчённом котелке́.
[More everything-_____ on world-_____, he-_____ loves go in hikes-_____, sleep in tents-_____, cook fish-soup-_____ in sooty pot-_____.] (II-33)

5   Недаром же среди́ моско́вских журнали́стов хо́дят слу́хи о баснословных зарпла́тах рабо́тников э́того печа́тного о́ргана.
[Not-without-reason among Moscow journalists-_____ go rumors-_____ about legendary wages-_____ workers-_____ that press organ-_____.] (II-62)

6   Тетра́дка, в кото́рой мы распи́сываемся в лаборато́рии по утра́м, лежа́ла тогда́ у него́ на столе́, и он посма́тривал на неё, но ничего́ не сказа́л.
[Notebook-_____, in which-_____ we-_____ log-in in laboratory-_____ along mornings-_____, lay then by him-_____ on table-_____, and he-_____ looked at it-_____, but nothing-_____ not said.] (II-85)

7   Обита́тели э́того до́ма — лауреа́ты разли́чных пре́мий, представля́ли свои́
    карти́ны в Кёльне, Пари́же и Сан-Па́уло.
    [Residents-_____ this house-_____ — laureates-_____ various prizes-_____, ex-
    hibited own pictures-_____ in Cologne-_____, Paris-_____ and San Paulo-_____.]
    (II-94)

8   Свою́ борьбу́ про́тив Ка́стро фонд целико́м прово́дит в ра́мках
    пропаганди́стской войны́.
    [Own struggle-_____ against Castro-_____ fund completely leads in frames-_____
    propaganda war-_____.] (II-133)

9   Я уча́ствовал в пяти́ во́йнах, ходи́л в ата́ку, так что бы́ло мо́ре кро́ви.
    [I-_____ participated in five wars-_____, went in attack-_____, so that was sea-
    _____ blood-_____.] (II-144)

10 Президе́нт подчеркну́л, что Росси́и ну́жно само́й разобра́ться и поня́ть, что
    происхо́дит в эконо́мике страны́.
    [President-_____ emphasized, that Russia-_____ necessary self-_____ understand
    and understand, what-_____ happens in economics-_____ country-_____.] (II-149)

11 А по́вести Гали́ны Щербако́вой где́-то посереди́нке: на полпути́ от
    мелодра́мы к бытово́й дра́ме.
    [But stories-_____ Galina Shcherbakova-_____ somewhere in-middle: on half-path-
    _____ from melodrama-_____ to domestic drama-_____.] (II-166)

Locative Exercise 2, Level II

*Identify the instances of the LOCATIVE case in the following sentences and explain
why the LOCATIVE is used.*

1   Она́ действи́тельно была́ горожа́нка, никогда́ не жила́ в дере́вне, никогда́
    не спива́лась до боле́зни, и её интересова́ло всё, чего́ она́ не могла́ пости́чь
    со́бственным о́пытом.
    [She-_____ really was city-woman-_____, never not lived in country-_____, never
    not drunk to illness-_____, a her-_____ interested everything-_____, what-_____
    she-_____ not was-able grasp own experience-_____.] (II-6)

2   На его́ жи́зненном столе́, как в кита́йском рестора́не, стоя́ло сто́лько блюд,
    что смешно́ бы́ло нае́сться чём-то одни́м и не попро́бовать друго́го.
    [On his life table-_____, as in Chinese restaurant-_____, stood so-many-_____
    dishes-_____, that absurd was fill-up something one-_____ and not try another-
    _____.] (II-18)

3   Я задохну́лась в пе́рвое мгнове́ние, как бу́дто меня́ столкну́ли с моста́ в холо́дную ре́чку в октябре́ ме́сяце.
[I-_____ gasped in first moment-_____, as if me-_____ pushed-off from bridge-_____ to cold river-_____ in October month-_____.] (II-25)

4   Éсли мы и говори́ли о Бо́ге, то в состоя́нии по́зы, коке́тства.
[If we-_____ even spoke about God-_____, then in state-_____ pose-_____, coquetry-_____.] (II-48)

5   Цыга́нка заме́тила следы́ борьбы́ на моём лице́.
[Gypsy-woman-_____ noticed traces-_____ struggle-_____ on my face-_____.] (II-66)

6   Мы на свобо́де! Мы ды́шим по́лной гру́дью! Говори́м всё, что ду́маем! Уве́ренно смо́трим в бу́дущее!
[We-_____ on freedom-_____! We-_____ breathe full chest-_____! Say everything-_____, that-_____ think! Confidently look in future-_____!] (II-89)

7   Тру́дно бы́ло разобра́ться в том дыму́.
[Difficult was understand in that smoke-_____.] (II-107)

8   Три трудне́йших го́да я прожи́л в хо́лоде и темноте́.
[Three-_____ quite-difficult year-_____ I-_____ lived-through in cold-_____ and dark-_____.] (II-136)

9   Се́льские лю́ди вдруг начина́ют понима́ть: их никому́ не ну́жная земля́ на са́мом де́ле име́ет большу́ю це́нность...
[Village people-_____ suddenly begin understand: their no-one-_____ not needed land-_____ in actual fact-_____ has big value-_____...] (II-145)

10   Заме́тно уху́дшилось самочу́вствие, вплоть до того́, что врачи́ наста́ивают на скоре́йшем ухо́де в о́тпуск не ме́нее чем на 30 дней.
[Noticeably worsened condition-_____, right-up to that-_____, that doctors-_____ insist on immediate departure-_____ to leave-_____ not less than to 30-_____ days-_____.] (II-153)

Loctive
Exercise 3
Level II

Locative Exercise 3, Level II
Identify the instances of the LOCATIVE *case in the following sentences and explain why the* LOCATIVE *is used.*

1   Он закры́л глаза́, что́бы проника́ло как мо́жно ме́ньше раздражи́телей, и тут же уви́дел взгля́д Светла́ны и по́нял, что таки́ми одина́ковыми взгля́дами он мог обменя́ться то́лько со свое́й жено́й, и бо́льше ни с одни́м челове́ком на всём све́те.

[He-_____ closed eyes-_____, so-that penetrated as possible less irritations-_____, and here already saw look-_____ Svetlana-_____ and understood, that such identical looks-_____ he-_____ could exchange only with own wife-_____, and more not with one person-_____ on whole world-_____.] (II-10)

2   Он признаёт, что в усло́виях внутриполити́ческой обстано́вки в Росси́и тру́дно говори́ть о реше́нии за́втра и́ли послеза́втра.
[He-_____ admits, that in conditions-_____ internal-political situation-_____ in Russia-_____ hard talk about solution-_____ tomorrow or day-after-tomorrow.] (II-20)

3   То́мас Ма́нн одна́жды заме́тил, что в исто́рии рома́на ве́хами ча́ще всего́ стано́вятся кни́ги, о кото́рых при их появле́нии осо́бенно уве́ренно говори́лось: э́то не рома́н.
[Thomas Mann-_____ once remarked, that in history-_____ novel-_____ landmarks-_____ more-frequently all-_____ become books-_____, about which-_____ at their appearance-_____ especially confidently said: this-_____ not novel-_____.] (II-30)

4   Поро́ки его́ заключа́лись в отсу́тствии недоста́тков.
[Flaws his-_____ consisted in absence-_____ shortcomings-_____.] (II-56)

5   Студе́нты запаса́ли спиртно́е на ве́чер. Причём держа́ли его́ не в холоди́льниках, а ме́жду око́нными ра́мами.
[Students-_____ stocked-up alcohol-_____ for evening-_____. Moreover kept it-_____ not in refrigerators-_____, but between window frames-_____.] (II-69)

6   Семь мину́т профе́ссор обвиня́л молодо́го писа́теля в хулига́нстве, порногра́фии и забве́нии ру́сских гуманисти́ческих тради́ций.
[Seven-_____ minutes-_____ professor-_____ accused young writer-_____ in hooliganism-_____, pornography-_____ and neglect-_____ Russian humanistic traditions-_____.] (II-90)

7   Э́то была́ радиопереда́ча о му́жественном хорео́графе, кото́рый сохрани́л на За́паде ве́рность люби́мой профе́ссии.
[This was radio-broadcast-_____ about courageous choreographer-_____, who-_____ preserved in West-_____ faithfulness-_____ beloved profession-_____.] (II-109)

8   Все производи́тели това́ров на вы́ставке утвержда́ли, что ввози́ть това́ры из-за грани́цы намно́го про́ще, чем выпуска́ть их в Росси́и.
[All producers-_____ goods-_____ at exhibition-_____ confirmed, that import goods-_____ from-beyond border-_____ much simpler, than-_____ produce them-_____ in Russia-_____.] (II-138)

9   Вон у нас во дворе́ за три го́да — два уби́йства бы́ло. С огgrabле́нием.
[There by us-_____ in courtyard-_____ in three-_____ years-_____ — two-_____
murders-_____ were. With robbery-_____.] (II-79)

10   О ро́ли домофо́на в жи́зни моско́вского подъе́зда мы говори́ли с
сотру́дниками Отде́ла по борьбе́ с кра́жами чужо́го иму́щества.
[About role-_____ intercom-_____ in life-_____ Moscow entryway-_____ we-_____
spoke with employee-_____ Department-_____ along struggle-_____ with robber-
ies-_____ other's property-_____.] (II-160)

Mixed Case Exercise 1 Level II

Mixed Case Exercise 1, Level II
Identify the cases in the sentences below and explain why those cases are used.
Provide your own English translation of the sentence and compare it with the trans-
lation in the key.

1   И́нна всё вре́мя ждала́, что Ада́м прояви́т каки́е-то зна́ки
заинтересо́ванности: коснётся ло́ктем ло́ктя и́ли мизи́нцем мизи́нца.
[Inna-_____ all time-_____ waited, that Adam-_____ show some signs-_____ in-
terest-_____ : touches elbow-_____ elbow-_____ or pinky-finger-_____ pinky-
finger-_____.] (II-9)

2   Когда́ че́рез полтора́ часа́ труп увезли́, сле́дственная гру́ппа отпра́вилась во
Дворе́ц молодёжи, где накану́не зако́нчился ко́нкурс красоты́.
[When after one-and-a-half-_____ hour-_____ corpse-_____ took-away, investiga-
tion team-_____ headed to Palace-_____ youth-_____, where day-before finished
contest-_____ beauty-_____.] (II-37)

3   Газе́тная рабо́та поны́не явля́ется для меня́ исто́чником существова́ния.
[Newspaper work-_____ up-to-present is for me-_____ source-_____ livelihood-
_____.] (II-46)

4   В том же году́ америка́нский журна́л <<Пипл>> избира́ет францу́за
<<челове́ком го́да>>.
[In that year-_____ American magazine-_____ "People-_____" chooses French-
man-_____ "Man-_____ year-_____" .] (II-73)

5   Муж Лю́си — до́ктор нау́к, неда́вно постро́или большу́ю кооперати́вную
кварти́ру, де́нег хвата́ет, у пятиле́тнего Ми́ши есть ня́ня.
[Husband-_____ Lyusya-_____ — doctor-_____ sciences-_____, recently built large
cooperative apartment-_____, money-_____ is-enough, by five-year-old Misha-
_____ is nanny-_____.] (II-88)

6   О́сенью 1923 го́да в Пра́гу прие́хал хорошо́ зна́вший Цвета́еву поэ́т В. Ф.
Ходасе́вич.

[Fall-_____ 1923 year-_____ in Prague-_____ arrived well knew-_____ Tsvetaev-_____ poet V. F. Khodasevich-_____.] (II-98)

7   Все мы по óчереди делúлись нóвой информáцией.
[All we-_____ along turn-_____ shared new information-_____.] (II-115)

8   Ребя́та пьют молокó, две минýты мы решáем, идтú ли ещё гуля́ть, и — откáзываемся.
[Kids-_____ drink milk-_____, two-_____ minutes-_____ we-_____ decide, go whether still walk, and — decline.] (II-126)

9   Когдá в пятидеся́тые гóды создавáлось телевúдение, тудá шли неудáчники кинó и теáтра, а тáкже лю́ди, котóрые чýвствовали: за э́тим дéлом — бýдущее.
[When in fifties years-_____ created television-_____, there went unfortunate-ones-_____ movies-_____ and theater-_____, but also people-_____, which-_____ felt: beyond this thing-_____ — future-_____.] (II-142)

10   Я самá себé казáлась протúвной оттогó, что когдá-то с ним целовáлась.
[I-_____ self-_____ self-_____ seemed nasty-_____ from-that, that sometime with him-_____ kissed.] (II-156)

Mixed Case Exercise 2, Level II

Identify the cases in the sentences below and explain why those cases are used. Provide your own English translation of the sentence and compare it with the translation in the key.

1   Вáжно, напримéр, довестú до свéдения россия́н тот факт, что до трéтьего сентября́ 1945 гóда Россúя никогдá не владéла э́тими четырьмя́ островáми.
[Important, for-example, bring to attention-_____ Russians-_____ that fact-_____, that until third-_____ September-_____ 1945 year-_____ Russia-_____ never owned those four islands-_____.] (II-21)

2   Мýжа онá тóже не пóмнила, но понимáла, что раз у неё бы́ло чéтверо детéй, то, навéрное, и муж был.
[Husband-_____ she-_____ also not remembered, but understood, that if by her-_____ was foursome-_____ children-_____, then, surely, and husband-_____ was.] (II-39)

3   Певéц обладáл красúвым нúзким баритóном удивúтельного тéмбра.
[Singer-_____ possessed beautiful deep baritone-_____ amazing timbre-_____.] (II-47)

4   Выраже́ние лица́ тако́е, бу́дто ей рассказа́ли что́-то интере́сное и проси́ли бо́льше никому́ не передава́ть.
[Expression-_____ face-_____ such-_____, as-if her-_____ told something interesting-_____ and asked more no-one-_____ not pass-on.] (II-75)

5   Семь мину́т профе́ссор обвиня́л молодо́го писа́теля в хулига́нстве, порногра́фии и забве́нии ру́сских гуманисти́ческих тради́ций.
[Seven-_____ minutes-_____ professor-_____ accused young writer-_____ in hooliganism-_____, pornography-_____ and neglect-_____ Russian humanistic traditions-_____.] (II-90)

6   Она́ покупа́ла на э́ти де́ньги и нефть, и истреби́тели, и мно́гое друго́е, что́бы получи́ть при́быль.
[She-_____ bought for that money-_____ and oil-_____, and fighter-planes-_____, and many other-_____, so-that receive profit-_____.] (II-103)

7   Я чуть прикаса́юсь к её руке́ щеко́й.
[I-_____ hardly touch to her hand-_____ cheek-_____.] (II-120)

8   Опла́чивает компа́ния иногоро́дним студе́нтам и прие́зд в Москву́ на вруче́ние стипе́ндии, два дня прожива́ния в столи́це.
[Pays-for company-_____ out-of-town students-_____ and trip-_____ to Moscow-_____ to handing-out-_____ stipend-_____, two-_____ days-_____ stay-_____ in capital-_____.] (II-127)

9   Туда́ оди́н-два ра́за в неде́лю приезжа́ла автола́вка, исто́чник всех благ в ви́де еды́ и питья́.
[There one-two-_____ occasions-_____ in week-_____ came lunch-wagon-_____, source-_____ all blessings-_____ in form-_____ food-_____ and drink-_____.] (II-143)

10   "Ты мно́гого доби́лась свое́й парти́йной че́стностью?" с сарка́змом спро́сит её Ма́ша.
["You-_____ much-_____ got own party honesty-_____?," with sarcasm-_____ asks her-_____ Masha-_____.] (II-158)

Mixed Case Exercise 3 Level II

Mixed Case Exercise 3, Level II
Identify the cases in the sentences below and explain why those cases are used. Provide your own English translation of the sentence and compare it with the translation in the key.

1   Коне́чно, в её во́зрасте смешно́ называ́ть кого́-то дя́дей и́ли тётей, пора́ уже́ переходи́ть на имена́-о́тчества, но Ста́сов всегда́ был для неё дя́дей Вла́диком.

[Of-course, in her age-_____ silly call someone-_____ uncle-_____ or aunt-_____, time already switch-over to names-patronymics-_____, but Stasov-_____ always was for her-_____ uncle Vladik-_____.] (II-40)

2   Я ви́жу его́ издалека́, с угла́ у́лицы Войно́ва, где был тогда́ Дом писа́телей и где все мы тогда́ пыта́лись заня́ть сту́лья.
[I-_____ see him-_____ from-afar, from corner-_____ street-_____ Voinov-_____, where was then House-_____ writers-_____ and where all we-_____ then tried occupy seats-_____.] (II-63)

3   Ты ничего́ не отдаёшь. Ты чемпио́н эгои́зма, и в э́том твоя́ тво́рческая индивидуа́льность.
[You-_____ nothing-_____ not give. You-_____ champion-_____ egotism-_____, and in that-_____ your artistic individuality-_____.] (II-77)

4   А "пода́рок"-то, ока́зывается, мне устро́ил банк, в кото́ром я име́л глу́пость откры́ть счёт и получи́ть пла́стиковую ка́рточку.
[But "gift-_____", turns-out, me-_____ arranged bank-_____, in which-_____ I-_____ had stupidity-_____ open account-_____ and received plastic card-_____.] (II-91)

5   По да́нным Министе́рства здравоохране́ния Росси́йской Федера́ции, 20,3 проце́нта ма́льчиков-подро́стков про́бовали нарко́тики, ка́ждый пя́тый.
[Along data-_____ Ministry-_____ health-_____ Russian Federation-_____, 20.3-_____ percent-_____ boys-adolescents-_____ tried narcotics-_____, every fifth-_____.] (II-105)

6   Ла́ты нужны́ тем, у кого́ нет фигу́ры.
[Armor-_____ needed-_____ those-_____, by whom-_____ not figures-_____.] (II-114)

7   Вашингто́нская администра́ция опра́вдывается тем, что я́кобы опозда́ла с пода́чей конгре́ссу на продле́ние злополу́чного зако́на.
[Washington administration-_____ justifies-self that-_____, that supposedly were-late with sending-_____ Congress-_____ to extension-_____ unfortunate law-_____.] (II-134)

8   Эпо́ха монетари́зма в Росси́и зака́нчивается. Тру́дно сказа́ть, когда́ она́ зако́нчится совсе́м, но игра́ть в де́ньги в Росси́и бо́льше не бу́дут.
[Epoch-_____ monetarianism-_____ in Russia-_____ ends. Difficult say, when it-_____ will-end completely, but play in money-_____ in Russia-_____ more not will-be.] (II-140)

9   О ро́ли домофо́на в жи́зни моско́вского подъе́зда мы говори́ли с сотру́дниками Отде́ла по борьбе́ с кра́жами чужо́го иму́щества.
[About role-_____ intercom-_____ in life-_____ Moscow entryway-_____ we-_____ spoke with employees-_____ Department-_____ along struggle-_____ with robberies-_____ other's property-_____.] (II-160)

10 Межрелигио́зная рознь мо́жет способствовать распа́ду Росси́и.
[Interreligious disagreement-_____ may assist break-up-_____ Russia-_____.] (II-112)

<table>
<tr><td>Mixed Case
Exercise 4
Level II</td></tr>
</table>

Mixed Case Exercise 4, Level II

Put the underlined words and phrases into the correct cases. Provide your own English translation of the sentence and compare it with the translation in the key.

1   <u>Обита́тели</u> <u>гнездо́</u> с <u>серди́тое жужжа́ние</u> набро́сились на <u>оби́дчик</u> <u>це́лый</u> <u>рой</u> и ста́ли жа́лить <u>он</u>. (II-1)

2   У <u>она́</u> <u>выраже́ние</u> <u>пти́ца</u>, <u>кото́рая</u> хо́чется пить, <u>она́</u> не даю́т, и похо́же, <u>она́</u> ско́ро отбу́дет из <u>э́тот мир</u>. (II-29)

3   <u>Он</u> люби́л здесь рабо́тать, и вообще́, была́ бы его́ <u>во́ля</u>, проводи́л бы здесь <u>бо́льшая часть</u> <u>вре́мя</u>. (II-41)

4   <u>Цыга́нка</u> заме́тила <u>следы́</u> <u>борьба́</u> на <u>моё лицо́</u>. (II-66)

5   <u>По́двиг</u> состоя́л в <u>тот</u>, что у <u>мы</u> снача́ла на́до бы́ло ненави́деть <u>зе́ки</u>, а пото́м — <u>охра́нники</u>. А <u>Довла́тов</u> знал и люби́л и <u>те</u>, и <u>други́е</u>. (II-92)

6   <u>Моя́ ба́бушка</u> счита́ет, что <u>дискоте́ка</u> сро́дни <u>танцплоща́дка</u> — <u>что-то</u> <u>тро́гательное и не́жное</u>. (II-106)

7   "Вот <u>каки́е</u> у <u>мы</u> <u>краси́вые де́ти</u>," говорю́ <u>я</u> и зову́ <u>они́</u> на <u>ку́хня</u> накрыва́ть вме́сте на <u>стол</u>. (II-122)

8   <u>Вся семья́</u> сро́чно занима́ется <u>оформле́ние</u> <u>необходи́мые докуме́нты</u>, и <u>Наде́жда Анто́новна</u> бо́льше <u>всё</u> бойтся, что не успе́ет <u>всё</u> офо́рмить до <u>пое́здка</u>. (II-137)

9   Вон у <u>мы</u> во <u>двор</u> за <u>три</u> <u>год</u> — <u>два</u> <u>уби́йство</u> бы́ло. С <u>ограбле́ние</u>. (II-79)

10 А тепе́рь <u>дочь</u> живёт отде́льно, <u>влюблён</u> до <u>умопомраче́ние</u> в <u>свой му́ж</u>. (II-159)

11 Росси́я всегда́ пра́вила <u>аристокра́тия</u>, и <u>он</u> по <u>свой о́браз мышле́ние</u> <u>аристокра́т</u> до <u>мозг ко́сти</u>. (II-165)

Mixed Case Exercise 5, Level II

Put the underlined words and phrases into the correct cases. Provide your own English translation of the sentence and compare it with the translation in the key.

1 По <u>мне́ние специали́сты</u>, пока́ нельзя́ счита́ть <u>япо́нское лека́рство препара́т</u>, <u>спосо́бный</u> помо́чь <u>больны́е рассе́янный склеро́з</u> в <u>тяжёлое состоя́ние</u>. (II-4)

2 От <u>они́</u> ве́ет <u>така́я убеди́тельная ску́ка</u>, что <u>эта ску́ка</u> достига́ет <u>седьмо́й эта́ж</u>, проника́ет че́рез <u>стекло́</u> и каса́ется <u>моё лицо́</u>. (II-31)

3 И́менно здесь, среди́ <u>эта стери́льная белизна́</u>, рожда́лись <u>иде́и</u>, приходи́ли <u>разочарова́ния</u>, ста́вились <u>экспериме́нты</u>. (II-42)

4 <u>Студе́нты</u> запаса́ли <u>спиртно́е</u> на <u>ве́чер</u>. Причём держа́ли <u>он</u> не в <u>холоди́льники</u>, а ме́жду <u>око́нные ра́мы</u>. (II-69)

5 <u>Де́ти безрабо́тные</u> беру́т <u>приме́р</u> с <u>роди́тели</u> — <u>ка́ждый четвёртый юный поля́к</u> говори́т о <u>свой пла́ны</u> так: <<Бу́ду <u>безрабо́тный</u>>>. (II-80)

6 <u>Душевнобольны́е худо́жники</u> продаю́т <u>свой карти́ны</u> за <u>пятьдеся́т ты́сячи ма́рки</u> и бо́лее. (II-93)

7 <u>Она́</u> набира́ла для <u>изда́тельства все мой произведе́ния</u>. А зна́чит, чита́ть <u>мой расска́зы</u> <u>она́</u> уже́ не обяза́тельно. (II-108)

8 <u>Ди́ма</u>, дава́й не бу́дем обсужда́ть <u>это</u>, прошу́ <u>ты</u>, погла́дь сего́дня <u>свой брю́ки</u> <u>сам</u>, <u>я</u> на́до доши́ть. (II-123)

9 С <u>торго́вые наце́нки</u> в <u>магази́н подо́бные тетра́дки</u> подни́мутся до <u>шесть ты́сячи рубли́</u>. (II-139)

10 Отны́не при <u>утра́та води́тельское удостовере́ние автомобили́сты</u> не ну́жно бу́дет сдава́ть <u>но́вый экза́мен</u>. (II-148)

11 Был <u>слу́чай</u>, когда́ <u>престу́пник</u> нашли́ по <u>отпеча́тки зу́бы</u> — <u>он</u> был <u>голо́дный</u> и надку́сил <u>кусо́к ма́сло</u>. (II-162)

Mixed Case Exercise 6, Level II
Put the underlined words and phrases into the correct cases. Provide your own English translation of the sentence and compare it with the translation in the key.

1   <u>Гео́ргий</u> сел и написа́л <u>письмо́</u>, и <u>я</u> не сказа́ла <u>он</u> в <u>отве́т</u> <u>ничто́</u>, про́сто взяла́ <u>э́тот листо́к</u> и ушла́ к <u>себя́</u> на <u>ку́хня</u>. (II-5)

2   <u>Она́</u> вы́везли из <u>Испа́ния</u> в <u>три́дцать шесто́й год</u>, и <u>она́</u> тут жила́ и росла́, что́бы одна́жды встре́тить <u>ру́сский па́рень</u> и в <u>звёздный час</u> зача́ть <u>сы́н</u>. (II-32)

3   В <u>те го́ды</u> я ещё не знал, что <u>де́ньги</u> — <u>бре́мя</u>. Что <u>элега́нтность</u> — <u>ма́ссовая у́личная фо́рма красота́</u>. Что <u>ве́чная иро́ния</u> — <u>люби́мое</u>, а <u>гла́вное</u> — <u>еди́нственное ору́жие беззащи́тные</u>. (II-44)

4   В <u>ми́р</u> есть нема́ло <u>ли́деры</u>, <u>кото́рые</u> не мо́гут искупи́ть пе́ред <u>наро́ды</u> <u>своя́ со́бственная вина́</u>. (II-70)

5   <u>Тетра́дка</u>, в <u>кото́рая</u> <u>мы</u> распи́сываемся в <u>лаборато́рия</u> по <u>у́тра</u>, лежа́ла тогда́ у <u>он</u> на <u>стол</u>, и <u>он</u> посма́тривал на <u>она́</u>, но <u>ничто́</u> не сказа́л. (II-85)

6   <u>Обита́тели э́тот дом</u> — <u>лауреа́ты разли́чные пре́мии</u>, представля́ли <u>свои карти́ны</u> в <u>Кёльн</u>, <u>Пари́ж</u> и <u>Сан-Па́уло</u>. (II-94)

7   Подобра́л <u>во́ин</u> с <u>земля́</u> <u>недозре́лая фи́га</u>, ки́нул <u>она́</u> в <u>певе́ц</u>, и угоди́л <u>он</u> пря́мо в <u>рот</u>. (II-110)

8   О <u>Госпо́дь</u>, <u>он</u>, ка́жется, ду́мает, что ра́ди <u>э́та встре́ча</u> я реши́ла укороти́ть <u>ю́бка</u>! (II-124)

9   Живёт <u>она́</u> на <u>сре́дства</u> "<u>спо́нсор</u>" — <u>жена́тый бизнесме́н</u>, <u>кото́рый</u> снима́ет для <u>она́</u> <u>кварти́ра</u> и периоди́чески про́сит <u>она́</u> бро́сить <u>э́та дура́цкая рабо́та</u> в <u>клуб</u> и вари́ть до́ма <u>пельме́ни</u>. (II-147)

10   <u>Президе́нт</u> подчеркну́л, что <u>Росси́я</u> ну́жно <u>сама́</u> разобра́ться и поня́ть, <u>что</u> происхо́дит в <u>эконо́мика страна́</u>. (II-149)

11   Понима́ете, то́лько по <u>мо́лодость</u> возмо́жно с <u>у́тро</u> до <u>ве́чер</u> занима́ться <u>хозя́йство</u>, а <u>ве́чер</u> игра́ть <u>короле́ва</u>. (II-164)

Mixed Case Exercise 7, Level II
Put the underlined words and phrases into the correct cases. Provide your own English translation of the sentence and compare it with the translation in the key.

1 Йнна оглядéла <u>цветы́</u>, вернýла <u>они́</u> <u>бáбка</u>, вострéбовала <u>дéньги</u> обрáтно и купи́ла на <u>они́</u> <u>я́блоки</u> у <u>сосéдняя старýха</u>. (II-8)

2 Когдá <u>онá</u> нет дóма, в <u>двéри</u> <u>запи́ска</u>: "Ключи́ под <u>кóврик</u>. Едá на <u>плитá</u>. Бýду в <u>шесть</u>. Целýю, <u>мáма</u>." (II-35)

3 Не успéл <u>профéссор</u> закóнчить, как в <u>прохóд</u> мéжду <u>ряды́</u> шагнýла <u>америкáнка</u> <u>срéдние лéта</u>. (II-45)

4 <<<u>Кислорóд</u>>> — диск никтó неизвéстный композитор óколо <u>мéсяц</u> держáл тогдá <u>пéрвое мéсто</u> в <u>мировы́е хит-парáды</u>. (II-71)

5 <u>Какóй-то не свой, охри́пший, гóлос</u> прошý <u>я</u> извини́ть <u>я</u>, обещáю стать сóбраннее и выскáкиваю в <u>коридóр</u>. (II-87)

6 <u>Психиáтр</u> причисля́ет <u>себя́</u> тóже к <u>худóжники</u>, <u>егó гигáнтские плáстиковые фигýры</u> украшáют <u>мнóгие америкáнские пáрки</u>. (II-95)

7 Для <u>ребя́та</u> <u>э́то</u> поздновáто, но нáдо же <u>они́</u> хоть в <u>выходнóй</u> погуля́ть как слéдует. (II-121)

8 <u>Я</u> шью и расскáзываю <u>Ди́ма</u>, что подсчитáли <u>нáши дни</u> <<по <u>болéзнь</u>>>, что у <u>я</u> <u>сéмьдесят вóсемь дни</u> — почти́ <u>цéлый квартáл</u>. (II-125)

9 <u>Кýчер-мужи́к</u> вслепýю гнал <u>лóшади</u>, но <u>врéмя</u> от <u>врéмя</u> оборáчивался и кричáл сквозь <u>пургá</u>: "Ничтó, <u>бáрин</u>! Ничтó, вы́беремся!" (II-141)

10 За <u>мимóзовый "сезóн"</u>, а <u>э́то</u>, примéрно, <u>две недéля</u> с <u>двадцáтое феврáль</u> по <u>седьмóе март</u>, мóжно заработáть óколо <u>пятьсóт рубли́</u>. (II-152)

Multi-Case Preposition Exercise 1, Level II
Choose the correct preposition and case combinations from the choices below.

1 Обитáтели гнездá <u>с серди́тое жужжáние/с серди́того жужжáния/с серди́тым жужжáнием</u> набрóсились <u>на оби́дчика/на оби́дчике</u> цéлым рóем и стáли жáлить егó.
With an angry buzz, the nest's inhabitants attacked the offender as a whole swarm and began to sting him. (II-1)

2   Я задохну́лась <u>в пе́рвое мгнове́ние/в пе́рвом мгнове́нии</u>, как будто меня́ столкну́ли <u>с моста́/с мосто́м</u> <u>в холо́дную ре́чку/в холо́дной ре́чке</u> <u>в октя́брь ме́сяц/в октябре́ ме́сяце</u>.
For an instant I was gasping for air as if I had been pushed off a bridge into a cold river in the month of October. (II-25)

3   Е́сли мы и говори́ли <u>о Бо́га/о Бо́ге</u>, то <u>в состоя́ние/в состоя́нии</u> по́зы, коке́тства.
If we even spoke about God, then it was in the guise of a pose, coquetry. (II-48)

4   Неда́ром же среди́ моско́вских журнали́стов хо́дят слу́хи <u>о баснословные зарплаты/о баснословных зарпла́тах</u> работников э́того печа́тного о́ргана.
It is not without reason that among Moscow journalists rumours circulate about the legendary wages of people who work for that organ of the press. (II-62)

5   Студе́нты запаса́ли спиртно́е <u>на ве́чер/на ве́чере</u>. Причём держа́ли его́ не <u>в холоди́льники/в холоди́льниках</u>, а ме́жду око́нными ра́мами.
The students stocked up on alcohol for the party. Moreover, they didn't keep it in refrigerators, but between the window frames. (II-69)

6   Тетра́дка, <u>в кото́рую/в кото́рой</u> мы распи́сываемся <u>в лаборато́рию/в лаборато́рии</u> <u>по у́тра/по утра́м</u>, лежа́ла тогда́ у него́ <u>на стол/на столе́</u>, и он посма́тривал <u>на неё/на ней</u>, но ничего́ не сказа́л.
The notebook that we logged into in the laboratory in the mornings lay on his table and he would look at it occasionally, but he didn't say anything. (II-85)

7   <u>На заня́тия/На заня́тиях</u> собира́ется вся лаборато́рия — челове́к два́дцать; прохо́дят они́ <u>в большу́ю, сосе́днюю с на́шей ко́мнату/в большо́й, сосе́дней с на́шей ко́мнате</u>.
The whole laboratory, around 20 people, gathers at the classes which are held in the big room neighboring ours. (II-118)

8   Впервы́е <u>за мно́гие го́ды/за мно́гими года́ми</u> без по́мощи студе́нтов реши́ли убра́ть урожа́й земледе́льцы на́шей о́бласти.
For the first time in many years, the farmers of our province have decided to gather the harvest without the help of students. (II-129)

9   Все производи́тели това́ров <u>на вы́ставку/на вы́ставке</u> утвержда́ли, что ввози́ть това́ры из-за грани́цы намно́го про́ще, чем выпуска́ть их <u>в Росси́ю/в Росси́и</u>.
All the producers of goods at the exhibition confirmed that it is much simpler to import goods from abroad than to produce them in Russia. (II-138)

10 К счáстью, óба пилóта успéли катапульти́роваться <u>за нéсколько секýнд</u>/<u>за нéсколькими секýндами</u> пéред тем, как реакти́вный самолёт врéзался <u>в зéмлю</u>/<u>в землé</u>.

Fortunately, both pilots had time to eject within seconds before the jet plane crashed into the ground. (II-154)

Multi-Case Preposition Exercise 2, Level II

Choose the correct preposition and case combinations from the choices below.

Multi-Case
Preposition
Exercise 2
Level II

1 Геóргий сел и написáл письмó, и я не сказáла емý <u>в отвéт</u>/<u>в отвéте</u> ничегó, прóсто взялá э́тот листóк и ушлá к себé <u>на кýхню</u>/<u>на кýхне</u>.

Georgi sat down and wrote out a letter, and I said nothing to him in response; I just took the piece of paper and went to my place in the kitchen. (II-5)

2 Когдá человéк испы́тывает стресс и́ли срéдней си́лы неприя́тность, <u>в кровь</u>/<u>в крови́</u> выбрáсывается гормóн <u>под назвáние</u>/<u>под назвáнием</u> адреналúн.

When a person experiences stress or some average-sized annoyance, the hormone called adrenaline is released into the blood. (II-27)

3 <u>За час</u>/<u>За чáсом</u> до э́того мы <u>с негó</u>/<u>с ним</u> расстáлись вóзле пивнóго бáра.

An hour before this we had parted with him at the beer bar. (II-50)

4 Цыгáнка замéтила следы́ борьбы́ <u>на моё лицó</u>/<u>на моём лицé</u>.

The gypsy woman noticed the traces of struggle on my face. (II-66)

5 Дéти безрабóтных берýт примéр <u>с роди́телей</u>/<u>с роди́телями</u> — кáждый четвёртый ю́ный поля́к говори́т <u>о свой плáны</u>/<u>о свои́х плáнах</u> так: <<Бýду безрабóтным>>.

Children of people who are unemployed take their example from their parents — one in four young Poles says the following about his plans: "I will be unemployed". (II-80)

6 Мы <u>на свобóду</u>/<u>на свобóде</u>! Мы ды́шим пóлной грýдью! Говори́м всё, что дýмаем! Увéренно смóтрим <u>в бýдущее</u>/<u>в бýдущем</u>!

We are free! We breathe freely! We say everything that we think! We look confidently into the future! (II-89)

7 Э́то былá радиопередáча <u>о мýжественного хореóграфа</u>/<u>о мýжественном хореóграфе</u>, котóрый сохрани́л <u>на Зáпад</u>/<u>на Зáпаде</u> вéрность люби́мой профéссии.

This was a radio program about a courageous choreographer, who remained faithful to his beloved profession in the West. (II-109)

8   Сейчáс ся́ду <u>за свóдный грáфик</u>/<u>за свóдным грáфиком</u>, нáдо сдéлать так, чтóбы остáлось внестú <u>в негó</u>/<u>в нём</u> тóлько нóвые испытáния.
Right now I'll sit down with the combined graph; it needs to be done so that only the new tests remain to be added to it. (II-119)

9   Президéнт Таджикистáна убедúтельно продемонстрúровал, что ситуáцию <u>в респýблику</u>/<u>в респýблике</u> он контролúрует.
The president of Tajikistan convincingly demonstrated that he controls the situation in the republic. (II-130)

10   Свéжую чернúку, к примéру, принимáют <u>по 3-4 рубля́</u>/<u>по 3-4 рубля́м</u> <u>за килогрáмм</u>/<u>за килогрáммом</u>, сушёную — от 20 до 40 рублéй (<u>в кáждый райóн</u>/<u>в кáждом райóне</u> свои́ цéны).
For example, they take fresh bilberries for 3-4 rubles per kilogram, dried ones from 20 to 40 rubles (each region has its own prices). (II-151)

11   Э́то обы́чная прáктика — делúть счёт <u>за телефóн</u>/<u>за телефóном</u> пóровну мéжду проживáющими <u>в нóмер</u>/<u>в нóмере</u>.
This is the usual practice, to divide the bill evenly between those sharing the room. (II-155)

Multi-Case Preposition Exercise 3, Level II
Choose the correct preposition and case combinations from the choices below.

1   Онá действúтельно былá горожáнка, никогдá не жилá <u>в дерéвню</u>/<u>в дерéвне</u>, никогдá не спивáлась до болéзни, и её интересовáло всё, чегó онá не моглá постúчь сóбственным óпытом.
She was truly a city woman: she had never lived in the country, had never drunk until she was sick, and she was interested in everything that she wasn't able to perceive via her own experience. (II-6)

2   Бóльше всегó <u>на свет</u>/<u>на свéте</u> он лю́бит ходúть <u>в похóды</u>/<u>в похóдах</u>, спать <u>в палáтки</u>/<u>в палáтках</u>, варúть ухý <u>в закопчённый котелóк</u> /<u>в закопчённом котелкé</u>.
More than anything else in the world, he loves going on hikes, sleeping in tents, and cooking fish soup in a sooty pot. (II-33)

3   Актёр, бýдучи <u>с гастрóли</u>/<u>с гастрóлей</u>/<u>с гастрóлями</u> <u>во Фрáнкфурт</u>/<u>во Фрáнкфурте</u>, добúлся там политúческого убéжища.
While on tour in Frankfurt, the actor obtained political asylum there. (II-52)

4   Без преувеличéния, мóжно сказáть, что сейчáс вся российская медицúна рабóтает <u>на президéнта</u>/<u>на президéнте</u>.
One can say without exaggeration that the whole of the Russian medical profession is working on the president now. (II-67)

5   Режиссёр встаёт <u>с кре́сла</u>/<u>с кре́сел</u>/<u>с кре́слами</u>, огля́дывает актри́су <u>с го́лову</u>/ <u>с головы́</u>/<u>с голово́й</u> до ног и ме́дленно ухо́дит.

Seryozhka and I stay in the kitchen all evening, he really misses me during the day so he won't even go away from me. (II-82)

6   Свою́ борьбу́ про́тив Ка́стро фонд целико́м прово́дит <u>в ра́мки</u>/<u>в ра́мках</u> пропаганди́стской войны́.

The fund carries on the struggle against Castro completely within the framework of a propaganda war. (II-133)

7   <u>За мимо́зовый "сезо́н"</u>/<u>За мимо́зовым "сезо́ном"</u>, а э́то, приме́рно, две неде́ли <u>с двадца́тый</u>/<u>с двадца́того</u>/<u>с двадца́тым</u> февраля́ <u>по седьмо́е</u>/<u>по седьмо́му</u> ма́рта, мо́жно зарабо́тать о́коло пятисо́т рубле́й.

During the mimosa "season", this is about two weeks from the twentieth of February to the seventh of March, it is possible to earn around 500 rubles. (II-152)

8   Ма́ша поду́мала, что, когда́ она́ нако́пит де́нег, она́ <u>с мать</u>/<u>с ма́тери</u>/<u>с ма́терью</u> жить не бу́дет.

Masha thought that when she got got together enough money, she wouldn't live with her mother anymore. (II-157)

Multi-Case Preposition Exercise 4, Level II
Choose the correct preposition and case combinations from the choices below.

Multi-Case
Preposition
Exercise 4
Level II

1   Он закры́л глаза́, чтобы проника́ло как мо́жно ме́ньше раздражи́телей, и тут же уви́дел взгляд Светла́ны и по́нял, что таки́ми одина́ковыми взгля́дами он мог обменя́ться то́лько <u>со свою́ жену́</u>/<u>со свое́й жены́</u>/<u>со свое́й жено́й</u>, и бо́льше ни <u>с одного́ челове́ка</u>/<u>с одни́м челове́ком</u> <u>на весь свет</u>/<u>на всём све́те</u>.

He closed his eyes so that the least amount of irritation would penetrate, and just then he saw Svetlana's look and he understood that he could only exchange identical looks like that with his wife and with no other person in the entire world. (II-10)

2   Когда́ её нет до́ма, <u>в две́ри</u>/<u>в дверя́х</u> запи́ска: "Ключи́ <u>под ко́врик</u>/<u>под ко́вриком</u>. Еда́ <u>на плиту́</u>/<u>на плите́</u>. Бу́ду <u>в шесть</u>/<u>в шести́</u>. Целу́ю, ма́ма."

When she isn't at home there is a note on the door: "The key is under the mat. Food is on the stove. I will be back at six. Kisses, mom." (II-35)

3   Два́дцать шесть проце́нтов опро́шенных не смогли́ отве́тить <u>на вопро́с</u>/<u>на вопро́се</u>: "Каки́е из скульпту́рных па́мятников вам бо́льше всего́ нра́вятся?" Не смо́трят че́тверть москвиче́й <u>по сто́роны</u>/<u>по сторона́м</u>, да́же <u>по выходы́е дни</u>/<u>по выходны́м дням</u>, не до монуме́нтов им.

Twenty-six percent of those asked could not answer the question: "Which sculptural monuments do you like the best?"   A quarter of all Muscovites don't look around, even on weekends. They aren't into monuments. (II-61)

4   Муж чита́ет письмо́ и волну́ется до тако́й сте́пени, что роня́ет из рук стака́н <u>с во́ду</u>/<u>с воды́</u>/<u>с водо́й</u>, кото́рый па́дает <u>на́ пол</u>/<u>на полу́</u> и разбива́ется.
The husband reads the letter and becomes so upset that he drops glass of water from his hands and it falls on the floor and breaks. (II-83)

5   Одна́ко незадо́лго до переда́чи де́ла <u>в суд</u>/<u>в суде́</u> Соловьёва отказа́лась от услу́г обо́их свои́х защи́тников.
However shortly before the case was brought to court Soloveva refused the services of both of her defense lawyers. (II-102)

6   Журна́л "Столи́ца" реши́л преуспе́ть <u>за счёт</u>/<u>за счето́м</u> махина́ций. Ему́ спосо́бствовал банк "СБС-А́гро."
Capital magazine decided to be successful at the expense of machination. The SBS-Agro bank assisted it. (II-113)

7   Опла́чивает компа́ния иногоро́дним студе́нтам и прие́зд <u>в Москву́</u>/<u>в Москве́</u> <u>на вруче́ние</u>/<u>на вруче́нии</u> стипе́ндии, два дня прожива́ния <u>в столи́цу</u>/<u>в столи́це</u>.
The company is even paying the out-of-town students for the trip to Moscow to get their stipends and for a two-day stay in the capital. (II-127)

8   Прави́тельство Еги́пта, опира́ясь <u>на старода́вний и полузабы́тый зако́н</u>/<u>на старода́внем и полузабы́том зако́не</u>, реши́ло ликвиди́ровать <u>в страну́</u>/<u>в стране́</u> слу́жбу телохрани́телей.
The government of Egypt, relying on an ancient and half-forgotten law, decided to liquidate bodyguard service in the country. (II-135)

9   Заме́тно уху́дшилось самочу́вствие, вплоть до того́, что врачи́ наста́ивают <u>на скоре́йший ухо́д</u>/<u>на скоре́йшем ухо́де</u> <u>в о́тпуск</u>/<u>в о́тпуске</u> не ме́нее чем <u>на 30 дней</u>/<u>на 30 днях</u>.
The condition had noticeably worsened right up to the point of the doctors' insisting on an immediate departure for a leave of no less than 30 days. (II-153)

10   Я не ви́жу ничего́ плохо́го <u>в то</u>/<u>в том</u>, что Щербако́вой удаётся угада́ть жела́ние чита́теля ро́вно <u>за мину́ту до того́</u>/<u>за мину́той до того́</u>, как сам чита́тель э́то жела́ние чётко осознаёт.
I don't see anything bad in Shcherbakova's success in figuring out the desire of the reader exactly a minute before the reader himself clearly realizes the desire. (II-167)

Level III Exercises

Nominative Exercise 1, Level III

Identify the instances of the NOMINATIVE case in the following sentences and explain why the NOMINATIVE is used.

1   Он ме́льком взгляну́л на мать, глаза́ у него́ смотре́ли утомлённо, как будто он не держа́л как сле́дует ве́ки.
[He-_____ cursorily glanced on mother-_____, eyes-_____ by him-_____ looked wearily, as if he-_____ not held as should eyelids-_____.] (III-1)

2   Полице́йский счёл себя́ оскорблённым и привлёк оби́дчика.
[Policeman-_____ considered self-_____ offended-_____ and sued offender-_____.] (III-9)

3   А́ня всерьёз купи́ла биле́т на пра́здник Но́вого го́да, не подозрева́я о том, что на э́том пра́зднике должны́ быть таки́е же одино́чки, как она́ сама́, те, кого́ не при́няли, отве́ргли студе́нческие вечери́нки.
[Anya-_____ seriously bought ticket-_____ on party-_____ New Year-_____, not suspecting about that-_____, that at this party-_____ should-_____ be such just lonely-women-_____, like she-_____ herself-_____, those-_____, who-_____ not accepted, spurned student parties-_____.] (III-15)

4   У неё лицо́ соверше́нно ма́ленькой де́вочки, и э́то де́тское ли́чико нале́плено на ме́лкую, как ты́ковка, голо́вку.
[By her-_____ face-_____ completely small girl-_____, and that child's face-_____ stuck-_____ on small-_____, like little-pumpkin-_____, little-head-_____.] (III-23)

5   Вообще́ лицо́ есть, но черты́ не свя́заны одно́й те́мой и как бы взя́ты с не́скольких лиц.
[In-general face-_____ is, but features-_____ not connected-_____ one theme-_____ and as it taken-_____ from several faces-_____.] (III-31)

6   В кулуа́рах писа́теля окружи́ла толпа́ единомы́шленников и почита́телей.
[In entrance-hall-_____ writer-_____ swarmed crowd-_____ like-minded-people-_____ and admirers-_____.] (III-45)

7   Мой вид испуга́л мои́х сле́дователей. Они́ устыди́лись, сапоги́ приказа́ли верну́ть, хотя́ я ничего́ у них не проси́ла.
[My appearance-_____ frightened my interrogators-_____. They-_____ were-ashamed, boots-_____ ordered return, although I-_____ nothing-_____ by them-_____ not asked.] (III-58)

8   В стране́ нахо́дятся деся́тки ты́сяч бе́женцев из Либе́рии, испы́тывающих кра́йнюю нужду́ в продово́льствии и предме́тах пе́рвой необходи́мости.
[In country-_____ are tens-_____ thousands-_____ refugees-_____ from Liberia-_____, experiencing-_____ extreme need-_____ in food-_____ and items-_____ first aid-_____.] (III-77)

9   Одна́ко далеко́ не все фи́льмы, предста́вленные на пари́жском фестива́ле, окра́шены траги́ческим и́ли драмати́ческим па́фосом.
[However far not all films-_____, shown-_____ at Paris festival-_____, tinged-_____ tragic-_____ or dramatic pathos-_____.] (III-92)

10   И тут на её горизо́нте возни́к знамени́тый эстра́дный певе́ц.   Сейча́с его́ и́мя забы́то, но в шестидеся́тые го́ды он был популя́рнее Сина́тры.
[And here on her horizon-_____ appeared famous stage singer-_____.   Now his name-_____ forgotten-_____, but in sixty years-_____ he-_____ was more-popular Sinatra-_____.] (III-106)

11   Хозя́йка ланчоне́та ми́ссис Бо́но с гро́хотом поднима́ет желе́зную решётку.
[Owner-_____ luncheonette-_____ Mrs. Bono-_____ with crash-_____ lifts iron grill-_____.] (III-130)

12   Под землёй че́рез не́сколько сантиме́тров лёд, ве́чная мерзлота́, све́рху снег.
[Under ground-_____ through several-_____ centimeters-_____ ice-_____, eternal frost-_____, on-top snow-_____.] (III-161)

Nominative Exercise 2, Level III

Identify the instances of the NOMINATIVE *case in the following sentences and explain why the* NOMINATIVE *is used.*

1   Брази́лия явля́ется крупне́йшим в ми́ре производи́телем и продавцо́м ко́фе, выра́щивая о́коло тридцати́ проце́нтов всего́ мирово́го урожа́я аром́атных бобо́в.
[Brazil-_____ is biggest-_____ in world-_____ producer-_____ and seller-_____ coffee-_____, growing around thirty percent-_____ entire world harvest-_____ aromatic beans-_____.] (III-2)

2   Он всегда́ приноси́л с собо́й буты́лку вина́, выпива́л её оди́н, вдова́ те́м вре́менем укла́дывала ребёнка спать, наре́зала како́й-то просто́й сала́т, что бы́ло под руко́й, то ли вари́ла яйцо́ вкруту́ю, коро́че, хлопота́ла, но не о́чень.
[He-_____ always brought with self-_____ bottle-_____ wine-_____, drank-up it-_____ one-_____, widow-_____ that time-_____ put-down child-_____ sleep, cut-up some simple salad-_____, what-_____ was under hand-_____, that or boil egg-_____ hard-boiled, in-short, fussed, but not very.] (III-16)

3   Тре́тий претенде́нт на ру́ку мое́й до́чери оказа́лся взро́слый, тридцатипятиле́тний мужи́к, кото́рый вообще́ понача́лу не мог определи́ться, за кем ему́ уха́живать — за ней и́ли за мной.
[Third aspirant-_____ to hand-_____ my daughter-_____ turned-out adult-_____, thirty-five-year-old fellow-_____, who-_____ in-general at-first not could determine, behind who-_____ him-_____ court — behind her-_____ or behind me-_____.] (III-24)

4   При взгля́де на э́ту ко́мнату с лежа́щим посреди́не на полу́ тру́пом ста́рой же́нщины почему́-то возника́ла ассоциа́ция с Достое́вским.
[At sight-_____ on that room-_____ with lying-_____ in-middle on floor-_____ corpse-_____ old woman-_____ somehow sprung-up association-_____ with Dostoevsky-_____.] (III-34)

5   Слон был похо́ж на грома́дную копну́ се́на.
[Elephant-_____ was resembling-_____ on enormous stack-_____ hay-_____.] (III-47)

6   По слова́м враче́й, они́ де́лают всё возмо́жное и невозмо́жное, что́бы вы́вести на́шего президе́нта из тяжеле́йшего состоя́ния, но перенесённые им боле́зни осложня́ют зада́чу.
[Along words-_____ doctors-_____, they-_____ do everything possible-_____ and impossible-_____, so-that lead-out our president-_____ from most-serious condition-_____, but endured-_____ him-_____ diseases-_____ complicate task-_____.] (III-66)

7   Оттого́, что я был влюблён, я как бы прикосну́лся к бессме́ртию и стал немно́жечко моло́же.
[Because, that I-_____ was in-love-_____, I-_____ as if touched to immortality-_____ and became somewhat younger.] (III-80)

8   Я по́днял ру́ку и потяну́л на себя́ чемода́н. Све́рху лежа́ли раке́ты для бадминто́на. Они́ пое́хали и упа́ли на́ пол.
[I-_____ raised arm-_____ and pulled on self-_____ suitcase-_____. On-top lay rackets-_____ for badminton-_____. They-_____ slipped-out and fell on floor-_____.] (III-86)

9   Не́когда процвета́вший жанр пеки́нской о́перы не выде́рживает зако́нов ры́нка.
[Once having-blossomed genre-_____ Peking opera-_____ not withstand laws-_____ market-_____.] (III-96)

10   Я не то́лько не сторо́нник, но и акти́вный проти́вник разли́чных тео́рий "мирово́го за́говора."
[I-_____ not only not supporter-_____, but and active opponent-_____ various theories-_____ "worldwide conspiracy-_____".] (III-114)

11   Жа́лость и тёплая вода́ де́лают своё де́ло — из-под ду́ша я выхожу́ подобре́вшая и освежённая.
[Pity-_____ and warm water-_____ do own matter-_____ — from-under shower-_____ I-_____ exit made-kinder-_____ and refreshed-_____.] (III-134)

12 Свя́занные сза́ди посине́вшие ру́ки при э́том задира́лись кве́рху; каза́лось,
он мо́лится каки́м-то необы́чным спо́собом.
[Bound-_____ from-behind turned-blue hands-_____ in this-_____ broke upwards;
seemed, he-_____ prays some unusual means-_____.] (III-163)

Nominative Exercise 3, Level III

*Identify the instances of the NOMINATIVE case in the following sentences and explain
why the NOMINATIVE is used.*

1 Постановле́ние о подписа́нии соглаше́ния ме́жду прави́тельством Ру́сской
Федера́ции и прави́тельством Респу́блики Кипр о безви́зовом режи́ме въе́зда
и вы́езда подпи́сано премье́р-мини́стром.
[Resolution-_____ about signing-_____ agreement-_____ between government-
_____ Russian Federation-_____ and government-_____ Republic-_____ Cyprus-
_____ about visa-less procedure-_____ entering-_____ and leaving-_____ signed-
_____ prime-minister-_____.] (III-6)

2 Соба́ка шара́хнулась от кри́ка и оберну́ла к ней удивлённую мо́рду.
[Dog-_____ was-startled from scream-_____ and turned to her-_____ surprised
muzzle-_____.] (III-17)

3 Светла́на сиде́ла перед Дю́ком, её пле́чи бы́ли легко́ присы́паны пе́рхотью,
а шко́льная фо́рма име́ла тако́й вид, бу́дто она́ спала́, не раздева́ясь, на
ме́льнице на мешка́х с муко́й.
[Svetlana-_____ sat before Duke-_____, her shoulders-_____ were lightly sprinkled-
_____ dandruff-_____, and school uniform-_____ had such look-_____, as-if she-
_____ slept, not getting-undressed, at mill-_____ on bags-_____ with flour-_____.]
(III-19)

4 Вхо́дит мой аспира́нт, на его́ лице́ напи́сано отвраще́ние к жи́зни: то ли
перепи́л, то ли недоспа́л.
[Enters my graduate-student-_____, on his face-_____ written-_____ disgust-_____
toward life-_____, that either over-drank, that either underslept.] (III-25)

5 Мно́го говори́тся о том, что журнали́стика для литера́тора — заня́тие
па́губное.
[A-lot-_____ is-said about that-_____, that journalism-_____ for writer-_____ —
profession pernicious-_____.] (III-39)

6 Гениа́льная иде́я! Принесёт нам три миллио́на до́лларов! Успе́х на сто
проце́нтов гаранти́руется. Никако́го ри́ска. Че́рез три неде́ли мы открыва́ем
фа́брику.
[Brilliant idea-_____! Will-bring us-_____ three-_____ million-_____ dollars-
_____! Success-_____ on hundred-_____ percent-_____ is-guaranteed. No risk-
_____. In three-_____ weeks-_____ we-_____ open factory-_____.] (III-50)

7   Президе́нт це́нтра хирурги́и на́звал чу́дом то, что семидесятишестиле́тний челове́к, перенёсший сорокомину́тную клини́ческую смерть, живёт уже́ две неде́ли.
[President-_____ center-_____ surgery-_____ named miracle-_____ that-_____, that seventy-six-year-old man-_____, experienced-_____ forty-minute clinical death-_____, lives already two-_____ weeks-_____.] (III-67)

8   Мне каза́лось, что, поми́мо любви́ ко мне, у тебя́ должно́ быть чу́вство до́лга, но ты счита́л, что ничего́ не до́лжен, тогда́ и я тебе́ ничего́ не должна́.
[Me-_____ seemed, that in-addition love-_____ to me-_____, by you-_____ should-_____ be feeling-_____ obligation-_____, but you-_____ thought, that nothing-_____ not obliged-_____, then and I-_____ you-_____ nothing-_____ not obliged-_____.] (III-83)

9   Вме́сте с гла́вным геро́ем мо́жно посочу́вствовать совреме́нной исто́рии не о́чень счастли́вой семе́йной па́ры, расска́занной в фи́льме <<Му́зыка для декабря́>>.
[Together with main hero-_____ possible sympathize modern story-_____ not very happy family pair-_____, told-_____ in film-_____ "Music-_____ for December-_____."] (III-99)

10 Моше́нничество — э́то ли́бо завладе́ние ли́чным иму́ществом гра́ждан, ли́бо приобрете́ние пра́ва на завладе́ние иму́ществом путём обма́на и́ли злоупотребле́ния дове́рием.
[Swindling-_____ — that-_____ either taking-possession-_____ personal property-_____ citizens-_____, or acqustion-_____ right-_____ on taking-possession-_____ property-_____ way-_____ deceit-_____ or abuse-_____ trust-_____.] (III-118)

11 Есть, по-мо́ему, уда́чное реше́ние пробле́мы захороне́ния те́ла Ле́нина, кото́рая сего́дня столь боле́зненно воспринима́ется разли́чными круга́ми росси́йского о́бщества.
[There-is, in-my-opinion, successful solution-_____ problem-_____ preservation-_____ body-_____ Lenin-_____, which-_____ today quite sickly is-received vari-ous circles-_____ Russian society-_____.] (III-141)

12 А два дня наза́д в Ленингра́дском вое́нном о́круге был заде́ржан офице́р, у кото́рого бы́ли обнару́жены пистоле́т с двумя́ обо́ймами, оди́н килогра́мм троти́ла в ша́шках по три́ста гра́ммов, о́коло 50 патро́нов кали́бра 7,62 и 5,6, пять сигна́льных раке́т и бо́лее шести́ ты́сяч до́лларов.
[But two-_____ day-_____ ago in Leningrad military district-_____ was detained-_____ officer-_____, at which-_____ were discovered-_____ pistol-_____ with two clips-_____, one kilogram-_____ TNT-_____ in charges-_____ along three-hun-dred-_____ grams-_____, around 50 cartridges-_____ caliber-_____ 7.62 and 5.6, five-_____ signal rockets-_____ and more six thousands-_____ dollars-_____.] (III-169)

Instrumental Exercise 1, Level III

Identify the instances of the INSTRUMENTAL *case in the following sentences and explain why the* INSTRUMENTAL *is used.*

1   Брази́лия явля́ется крупне́йшим в ми́ре производи́телем и продавцо́м ко́фе, выра́щивая о́коло тридцати́ проце́нтов всего́ мирово́го урожа́я арома́тных бобо́в.
[Brazil-_____ is biggest-_____ in world-_____ producer-_____ and seller-_____ coffee-_____, growing around thirty percent-_____ entire world harvest-_____ aromatic beans-_____.] (III-2)

2   Постановле́нием No. 315 глава́ областно́й администра́ции учреди́л ежеме́сячные стипе́ндии студе́нтам ву́зов, око́нчившим шко́лу с золото́й меда́лью.
[Decree-_____ No. 315 head-_____ regional administration-_____ established monthly stipends-_____ students-_____ institutions-of-higher-education-_____, graduated-_____ school-_____ with gold medal-_____.] (III-11)

3   Светла́на сиде́ла перед Дю́ком, её пле́чи бы́ли легко́ присы́паны пе́рхотью, а шко́льная фо́рма име́ла тако́й вид, бу́дто она́ спала́, не раздева́ясь, на ме́льнице на мешка́х с муко́й.
[Svetlana-_____ sat before Duke-_____, her shoulders-_____ were lightly sprinkled-_____ dandruff-_____, and school uniform-_____ had such look-_____, as-if she-_____ slept, not getting-undressed, at mill-_____ on bags-_____ with flour-_____.] (III-19)

4   При взгля́де на э́ту ко́мнату с лежа́щим посреди́не на полу́ тру́пом ста́рой же́нщины почему́-то возника́ла ассоциа́ция с Достое́вским.
[At sight-_____ on that room-_____ with lying-_____ in-middle on floor-_____ corpse-_____ old woman-_____ somehow sprung-up association-_____ with Dostoevsky-_____.] (III-34)

5   С не́которых пор мой почто́вый я́щик ста́ли зава́ливать разли́чного ро́да макулату́рой.
[From some time-_____ my mail box-_____ started stuff various kind-_____ pulp-fiction-_____.] (III-53)

6   Предста́вьте, что вы договори́лись зае́хать ве́чером за свое́й возлю́бленной и отпра́виться с ней в шика́рный рестора́н, а накану́не вас одоле́ли головны́е бо́ли.
[Imagine, that you-_____ agreed go evening-_____ for your beloved-_____ and go with her-_____ to fancy restaurant-_____, but night-before you-_____ overcame head aches-_____.] (III-74)

7 Активизи́руя диафра́гмы, смех углубля́ет дыха́ние, обогаща́ет кислоро́дом кровь и вентили́рует лёгкие.

[Activating diaphragms-_____, laughter-_____ deepens breathing-_____, enriches oxygen-_____ blood-_____ and ventilates lungs-_____.] (III-94)

8 Что каса́ется само́й Мари́ны Цвета́евой, то она́ была́ до глубины́ души́ тро́нута забо́той и внима́нием, проя́вленными Го́рьким к её сестре́.

[What-_____ touches self-_____ Marina Tsvetaeva-_____, that she-_____ was to depth-_____ soul-_____ touched-_____ concern-_____ and attention-_____, shown-_____ Gorky-_____ to her sister-_____.] (III-109)

9 Мо́жет, возьмёт тебя́ на рабо́ту литсотру́дником и́ли хотя́ бы корре́ктором.

[May, will-take you-_____ to work-_____ literary-assistant-_____ or although would proof-reader-_____.] (III-129)

10 Фонд Раджи́ва Га́нди, осно́ванный е́ю, помога́ет де́тям, же́нщинам и бе́дным и стал са́мой влия́тельной неправи́тельственной организа́цией в И́ндии.

[Fund-_____ Rajiva Gandi-_____, founded-_____ her-_____, helps children-_____, women-_____ and poor-_____ and became most influential non-governmental organization-_____ in India-_____.] (III-146)

11 Боковы́м зре́нием она́ отме́тила, что на друго́й доро́жке оста́лись стоя́ть о́чень то́лстая тётенька, килогра́ммов на сто, и высо́кий ма́льчик.

[Side vision-_____ she-_____ noticed, that on other road-_____ stopped stand very fat lady-_____, kilograms-_____ to 100-_____, and tall boy-_____.] (III-171)

12 Геро́иню Щербако́вой вы легко́ мо́жете встре́тить в о́череди за дешёвыми ту́флями на распрода́же, в авто́бусе в час пик, в магази́не (то́лько не в блестя́щем суперма́ркете).

[Heroine-_____ Shcherbakova-_____ you-_____ easily may meet in line-_____ behind cheap shoes-_____ on sale-_____, in bus-_____ to time peak-_____, in store-_____ (only not in sparkling supermarket-_____.] (III-185)

Instrumental Exercise 2, Level III

Identify the instances of the INSTRUMENTAL case in the following sentences and explain why the INSTRUMENTAL is used.

1 Предприя́тие вы́пустит шестна́дцать ты́сяч маши́н, оди́ннадцать ты́сяч из кото́рых реализу́ются за грани́цей.

[Enterprise-_____ will-produce sixteen-_____ thousand-_____ cars-_____, eleven-_____ thousand-_____ from which-_____ will-be-sold beyond border-_____.] (III-3)

2   Полити́ческая поли́ция располага́ет богате́йшим архи́вом, в кото́ром, как
    утвержда́ют, соде́ржатся досье́ на полмиллио́на францу́зов.
    [Political police-_____ have-at-disposal most-rich archive-_____, in which-_____,
    as claim, are-kept files-_____ on half-million-_____ French-_____.] (III-12)

3   Тре́тий претенде́нт на ру́ку мое́й до́чери оказа́лся взро́слый,
    тридцатипятиле́тний мужи́к, кото́рый вообще́ понача́лу не мог
    определи́ться, за кем ему́ уха́живать — за ней и́ли за мной.
    [Third aspirant-_____ to hand-_____ my daughter-_____ turned-out adult-_____,
    thirty-five-year-old fellow-_____, who-_____ in-general at-first not could deter-
    mine, behind who-_____ him-_____ court — behind her-_____ or behind me-_____.]
    (III-24)

4   Уби́тая же, говори́ли, была́ победи́тельницей ко́нкурса красоты́.
    [Dead-_____, said, was winner-_____ contest-_____ beauty-_____.] (III-35)

5   Они́ втя́гивают животы́, расставля́ют ло́кти, коро́че, изнемога́ют под ремнём
    физи́ческого соверше́нства.
    [They-_____ suck-in stomachs-_____, hold-out elbows-_____, in-short, wear-out
    under strap-_____ physical perfection-_____.] (III-42)

6   Она́ была́ тогда́ гора́здо знамени́тее Серге́я, кото́рый глу́хо пребыва́л в
    а́рмии, ниче́м никого́ осо́бенно не занима́я; пью́щие ге́нии, вылета́ющие из
    институ́тов, бы́ли тогда́ в на́ших круга́х скоре́е но́рмой, чем собы́тием.
    [She-_____ was then much more-famous Sergei-_____, who-_____ quietly spent-
    time in army-_____ nothing-_____ no-one-_____ particularly not interesting; drink-
    ing geniuses-_____, flying-out-_____ from institutes-_____, were then in our circles-
    _____ rather norm-_____, what-_____ event-_____.] (III-55)

7   Мы стои́м с ней по ра́зные концы́ го́рода, как два бара́на на мо́стике
    горба́том, ка́ждый со свое́й пра́вдой.
    [We-_____ stand with her-_____ along various ends-_____ town-_____, like two-
    _____ ram-_____ on bridge hump-backed-_____, each-_____ with own truth-_____.]
    (III-79)

8   Двойно́й станда́рт в поли́тике облада́ет сво́йством бумера́нга.
    [Double standard-_____ in politics-_____ has property-_____ boomerang-_____.]
    (III-95)

9   Да, он мо́жет быть немно́жко смешны́м, ма́лость неле́пым, чуть торопли́вым
    и да́же, суди́ его́ Бог, хамова́тым.
    [Yes, he-_____ may be somewhat silly-_____, bit absurd-_____, trifle hasty-_____
    and even, judge him-_____ God-_____ rather-loutish-_____.] (III-113)

10   Я перепи́сываю в дневни́к результа́ты вчера́шнего о́пыта, укла́дываю в коро́бку бро́шенные вчера́ образцы́, рву и выки́дываю черновики́ с расчётами.
[I-_____ rewrite in journal-_____ results-_____ yesterday's experiment-_____, pack-away in box-_____ thrown-away-_____ yesterday samples-_____, shred and toss-out rough-drafts-_____ with calculations-_____.] (III-132)

11   Он по́льзуется всео́бщим внима́нием и призна́нием по сию́ по́ру, когда́ не оста́лось в его́ жи́зни уже́ ни одно́й официа́льной подпо́рки, когда́ почти́ забы́то, что он был председа́телем правле́ния Сою́за компози́торов, когда́ не упомина́ют о его́ зва́ниях и награ́дах.
[He-_____ enjoys universal attention-_____ and recognition-_____ along this time-_____, when not remained in his life-_____ already not one official support-_____, when almost forgotten-_____, that he-_____ was representative-_____ board-_____ Union-_____ composers-_____, when not remind about his titles-_____ and awards-_____.] (III-156)

12   Он уда́рился гру́дью о водопрово́дную трубу́, кото́рая проходи́ла по газо́ну.
[He-_____ hit chest-_____ against water pipe-_____, which-_____ ran along lawn-_____.] (III-175)

Instrumental
Exercise 3
Level III

Instrumental Exercise 3, Level III
Identify the instances of the INSTRUMENTAL *case in the following sentences and explain why the* INSTRUMENTAL *is used.*

1   В Росси́и сейча́с из-за спа́да произво́дства сокраща́ется потребле́ние электроэне́ргии, так что изли́шки мы с удово́льствием продади́м на За́пад.
[In Russia-_____ now from-beyond fall-_____ production-_____ declines use-_____ electricity-_____, so that surplus-_____ we-_____ with pleasure-_____ will-sell to West-_____.] (III-4)

2   Эсто́нские роя́листы восхищены́ англи́йской мона́рхией и, в ча́стности, при́нцем Эдва́рдом, явля́ющимся, с их то́чки зре́ния, превосхо́дным и соверше́нным во всех отноше́ниях при́нцем.
[Estonian royalists-_____ delighted-_____ English monarchy-_____ and, in particular-_____, prince Edward-_____, being-_____, from their point-_____ view-_____, superb-_____ and perfect-_____ in all relations-_____ prince-_____.] (III-13)

3   Ра́ньше он приходи́л к нам с жа́лобами на сосе́дей, отравля́ющих из-за сте́нки пи́щу и обжига́ющих его́ че́рез потоло́к неви́димыми луча́ми.
[Earlier he-_____ came to us-_____ with complaints-_____ on neighbors-_____, poisoning-_____ from-beyond wall-_____ food-_____ and burning-_____ him-_____ through ceiling-_____ invisible rays-_____.] (III-26)

4   Ты мóжешь быть гéнием и провúдцем. Велúким еретúком и герóем трудá.
Это не имéет значéния.   Материáльные плодú человéческих усúлий
неминýемо станóвятся объéктом рúночной торгóвли.
[You-_____ can be genius-_____ and prophet-_____. Great heretic-_____ and hero-
_____ labor-_____. This-_____ not have meaning-_____. Material fruits-_____
human efforts-_____ inevitably become object-_____ market trade-_____.] (III-
37)

5   Во мне шла борьбá тёмного со свéтлым, подозрúтельности с вéрой в
человéчество.
[In me-_____ went battle-_____ dark-_____ with light-_____, suspicion-_____ with
faith-_____ in humanity-_____.] (III-61)

6   Президéнт цéнтра хирургúи нáзвал чýдом то, что семидесятишестилéтний
человéк, перенёсший сорокоминýтную клинúческую смерть, живёт ужé две
недéли.
[President-_____ center-_____ surgery-_____ named miracle-_____ that-_____, that
seventy-six-year-old man-_____, experienced-_____ forty-minute clinical death-
_____, lives already two-_____ weeks-_____.] (III-67)

7   Я увéренно подошёл и постучáл в дверь костáшками пáльцев.
[I-_____ confidently went-up and knocked on door-_____ knuckles-_____ fingers-
_____.] (III-85)

8   Почýвствуете себя брóшенным и непóнятым.
[Feel self-_____ thrown-_____ and not-understood-_____.] (III-97)

9   Мошéнничество — это лúбо завладéние лúчным имýществом грáждан, лúбо
приобретéние прáва на завладéние имýществом путём обмáна úли
злоупотреблéния довéрием.
[Swindling-_____ — that-_____ either taking-possession-_____ personal property-
_____ citizens-_____, or acqusition-_____ right-_____ on taking-possession-_____
property-_____ way-_____ deceit-_____ or abuse-_____ trust-_____.] (III-118)

10   Сейчáс он живёт вмéсте с женóй и сыновьями в Монáко, однáко склоняется
к томý, чтóбы перебрáться в Швéцию.
[Now he-_____ lives together with wife-_____ and sons-_____ in Monaco-_____,
however yielding to that-_____, in-order-to move to Sweden-_____.] (III-137)

11   Под землёй чéрез нéсколько сантимéтров лёд, вéчная мерзлотá, свéрху снег.
[Under ground-_____ through several-_____ centimeters-_____ ice-_____, eternal
frost-_____, on-top snow-_____.] (III-161)

12   Потом каждый раз, где бы они ни были, он её глазом зацепит и держит,
как кошка цыплю.
[Then each time-_____, where would they-_____ not were, he-_____ her-_____
eye-_____ hook and holds, like cat-_____ chick-_____.] (III-176)

Accusative Exercise 1 Level III

Accusative Exercise 1, Level III
Identify the instances of the ACCUSATIVE *case in the following sentences and explain why the* ACCUSATIVE *is used.*

1   Он мельком взглянул на мать, глаза у него смотрели утомлённо, как будто
он не держал как следует веки.
[He-_____ cursorily glanced on mother-_____, eyes-_____ by him-_____ looked
wearily, as if he-_____ not held as should eyelids-_____.] (III-1)

2   Аня всерьёз купила билет на праздник Нового года, не подозревая о том,
что на этом празднике должны быть такие же одиночки, как она сама, те,
кого не приняли, отвергли студенческие вечеринки.
[Anya-_____ seriously bought ticket-_____ on party-_____ New Year-_____, not
suspecting about that-_____, that at this party-_____ should-_____ be such just
lonely-women-_____, like she-_____ herself-_____, those-_____, who-_____ not
accepted, spurned student parties-_____.] (III-15)

3   Врач, не снимая ботинок, даже не вытерев ноги, двинется прямо в комнату.
[Doctor-_____, not removing shoes-_____, even not having-wiped feet-_____, moves
straight in room-_____.] (III-32)

4   Тогда почему же я ощущаю себя на грани физической катастрофы? Откуда
у меня чувство безнадёжной жизненной непригодности? В чём причина
моей тоски?
[Then why I-_____ feel self-_____ on edge-_____ physical catastrophe-_____?
From-where by me-_____ feeling-_____ hopeless life uselessness-_____? In what-
_____ cause-_____ my melancholy-_____?] (III-48)

5   Спецслужбы зарубежного государства арестовывают и бросают в тюрьму
российских граждан, не совершивших никакого преступления.
[Special-services-_____ foreign government-_____ arrest and throw in jail-_____
Russian citizens-_____ not having-committed-_____ no crime-_____.] (III-64)

6   Мы стоим с ней по разные концы города, как два барана на мостике
горбатом, каждый со своей правдой.
[We-_____ stand with her-_____ along various ends-_____ town-_____, like two-
_____ ram-_____ on bridge hump-backed-_____, each-_____ with own truth-_____.]
(III-79)

7   Меня́ в четы́рнадцать лет понесло́ в комсомо́л, в кото́ром я не нашла́
    никако́й револю́ционной рома́нтики.
    [Me-_____ in fourteen-_____ years-_____ brought to communist-youth-league-
    _____, in which-_____ I-_____ not found any revolutionary romance-_____.] (III-
    88)

8   Почу́вствуете себя́ бро́шенным и непо́нятым.
    [Feel self-_____ thrown-_____ and not-understood-_____.] (III-97)

9   Коро́че говоря́, речь идёт о норма́льном проце́ссе борьбы́ мировы́х сил за
    влия́ние и за выжива́ние.
    [Shorter speaking, speech-_____ goes about normal process-_____ struggle-_____
    world's powers-_____ for influence-_____ and for survival-_____.] (III-115)

10 Ко́стя сбил одея́ло, Гу́лька съе́хала с поду́шки, вы́сунула но́жку из крова́ти.
    [Kostya-_____ dislodged blanket-_____, Gulka-_____ came-down from pillow-
    _____, stuck-out little-leg-_____ from bed-_____.] (III-135)

11 Э́то гене́тик Ри́чард Сид, заяви́вший, что уже́ че́рез три ме́сяца начнёт
    клони́ровать челове́ка.
    [This-_____ geneticist Richard Seed-_____, announced-_____, that already through
    three-_____ month-_____ begins clone man-_____.] (III-158)

12 Э́тот идио́т режиссёр заста́вил меня́ сле́довать заду́манному пла́ну.
    [This idiot-_____ director-_____ forced me-_____ follow proposed plan-_____.]
    (III-170)

Accusative Exercise 2, Level III

*Identify the instances of the ACCUSATIVE case in the following sentences and explain
why the ACCUSATIVE is used.*

1   Но́вых слу́чаев распростране́ния холе́ры на други́е террито́рии Росси́и не
    обнару́жено.
    [New-_____ cases-_____ spread-_____ cholera-_____ to other areas-_____ Rus-
    sia-_____ not discovered.] (III-5)

2   Он всегда́ приноси́л с собо́й бутылку вина́, выпива́л её оди́н, вдова́ тем
    вре́менем укла́дывала ребёнка спать, нареза́ла како́й-то просто́й сала́т, что
    бы́ло под руко́й, то ли вари́ла яйцо́ вкруту́ю, коро́че, хлопота́ла, но не о́чень.
    [He-_____ always brought with self-_____ bottle-_____ wine-_____, drank-up it-
    _____ one-_____, widow-_____ that time-_____ put-down child-_____ sleep, cut-
    up some simple salad-_____, what-_____ was under hand-_____, that or boil egg-
    _____ hard-boiled, in-short, fussed, but not very.] (III-16)

3   Два́дцать лет наза́д она́ то́же была́ влюблена́ в одного́ арти́ста до поте́ри
пу́льса, и весь их класс сходи́л с ума́.
[Twenty-_____ years-_____ ago she-_____ also was in-love-_____ in one artist-
_____ to loss-_____ pulse-_____, and all their class-_____ was-going from mind-
_____.] (III-33)

4   Он носи́л га́лстук цве́та ру́хнувшей наде́жды.
[He-_____ wore tie-_____ color-_____ dashed hope-_____.] (III-49)

5   По слова́м враче́й, они́ де́лают всё возмо́жное и невозмо́жное, что́бы вы́вести
на́шего президе́нта из тяжеле́йшего состоя́ния, но перенесённые им боле́зни
осложня́ют зада́чу.
[Along words-_____ doctors-_____, they-_____ do everything possible-_____ and
impossible-_____, so-that lead-out our president-_____ from most-serious condi-
tion-_____, but endured-_____ him-_____ diseases-_____ complicate task-_____.]
(III-66)

6   Мы сбежа́ли на на́бережную и пошли́ вдоль мо́ря.
[We-_____ ran-down on embankment-_____ and walked along sea-_____.] (III-
81)

7   Тут спра́ва из сара́я вы́бежал молодо́й челове́к и, перепры́гнув через коры́то,
на кото́ром среди́ помо́ев лежа́ла свинья́, с кри́ком побежа́л к воро́там.
[Here on-right from barn-_____ ran-out young man-_____ and, having jumped over
trough-_____, on which-_____ among slop-_____ lay pig-_____, with shout-_____
ran to gate-_____.] (III-101)

8   Когда́ в тридца́тые го́ды возни́кла нужда́ в духоподъёмной, спла́чивающей
наро́д геро́ике, власть испо́льзовала для э́того и́менно Се́вер.
[When in thirty years-_____ arose need-_____ in spiritually-uplifting-_____, gal-
vanizing-_____ nation-_____ heroics-_____, regime-_____ used for this-_____ precisely North-_____.] (III-116)

9   Япо́нская компа́ния пе́йджинговой свя́зи выпуска́ет в прода́жу недороги́е
пе́йджеры, специа́льно предназна́ченные для переда́чи коди́рованных
сообще́ний де́тям.
[Japanese company-_____ paging network-_____ puts-out to sale-_____ inexpen-
sive pagers-_____ especially intended-_____ for transmission-_____ coded mes-
sages-_____ children-_____.] (III-140)

10   Возмущённым роди́телям дире́ктор обеща́л вско́ре найти́ учителе́й, но в
середи́не го́да призна́лся в своём бесси́лии и предложи́л призва́ть на по́мощь
ча́стную фи́рму.
[Upset parents-_____ director-_____ promised soon find teachers-_____, but in
middle-_____ year-_____ acknowledged in own powerlessness-_____ and proposed
summon to help-_____ private firm-_____.] (III-155)

11 Лет пятна́дцать наза́д, идя́ по сне́жной лесно́й целине́ на лы́жах, мо́жно бы́ло наткну́ться и на за́ячьи, и да́же на ли́сьи следы́.
[Years-_____ fifteen-_____ ago, going along snowy forest virgin-soil-_____ on skis-_____, may was stumble-upon and on rabbit-_____, and even on fox tracks-_____.] (III-159)

12 Ко́стик, две неде́ли до того́ пролежа́вший с радикули́том, в три метро́вых шага́ перема́хивает че́рез газо́н, а на асфа́льте, сцепи́в зу́бы от презре́ния, стои́т Людми́ла.
[Kostik-_____, two-_____ weeks-_____ to that-_____ laid-up-_____ with radiculitis-_____, in three-_____ meter steps-_____ leaps through lawn-_____, and on asphalt-_____, having-clinched teeth-_____ from disdain-_____ stands Ludmila-_____.] (III-172)

Accusative Exercise 3, Level III

Identify the instances of the ACCUSATIVE case in the following sentences and explain why the ACCUSATIVE is used.

Accusative
Exercise 3
Level III

1 Прое́кт соглаше́ния предусма́тривает, что гра́ждане обо́их госуда́рств, име́ющие де́йствующие заграндокуме́нты, мо́гут въезжа́ть на террито́рию друго́го госуда́рства без виз на срок до девяно́ста дней.
[Draft-_____ agreement-_____ stipulates, that citizens-_____ both states-_____, having-_____ valid international-documents-_____ can enter territory-_____ other state-_____ without visas-_____ for period-_____ to ninety days-_____.] (III-7)

2 Соба́ка шара́хнулась от кри́ка и оберну́ла к ней удивлённую мо́рду.
[Dog-_____ was-startled from scream-_____ and turned to her-_____ surprised muzzle-_____.] (III-17)

3 О́пытный престу́пник снача́ла подгото́вит себе́ кана́л бы́строго сбы́та, найдёт переку́пщиков, кото́рые суме́ют спла́вить карти́ны и украше́ния.
[Experienced criminal-_____ first prepare self-_____ channel-_____ quick sale-_____, finds second-hand-dealers-_____, who-_____ know-how get-rid pictures-_____ and decorations-_____.] (III-36)

4 Гениа́льная иде́я! Принесёт нам три миллио́на до́лларов! Успе́х на сто проце́нтов гаранти́руется. Никако́го ри́ска. Че́рез три неде́ли мы открыва́ем фа́брику.
[Brilliant idea-_____! Will-bring us-_____ three-_____ million-_____ dollars-_____! Success-_____ on hundred-_____ percent-_____ is-guaranteed. No risk-_____. In three-_____ weeks-_____ we-_____ open factory-_____.] (III-50)

5   Президе́нт це́нтра хирурги́и на́звал чу́дом то, что семидесятишестиле́тний челове́к, перенёсший сорокомину́тную клини́ческую смерть, живёт уже́ две неде́ли.
[President-_____ center-_____ surgery-_____ named miracle-_____ that-_____, that seventy-six-year-old man-_____, experienced-_____ forty-minute clinical death-_____, lives already two-_____ weeks-_____.] (III-67)

6   О́чень мо́жет ста́ться, что жизнь заду́мана, как доро́га к верши́не. Дойду́ ли я до свое́й верши́ны и́ли уста́ну и верну́сь, чтобы лечь на дива́н?
[Very can happen, that life-_____ planned-_____, like road-_____ to summit-_____. Reach if I-_____ to own summit-_____ or get-tired and return, so-that lie-down on couch-_____?] (III-82)

7   Активизи́руя диафра́гмы, смех углубля́ет дыха́ние, обогаща́ет кислоро́дом кровь и вентили́рует лёгкие.
[Activating diaphragms-_____, laughter-_____ deepens breathing-_____, enriches oxygen-_____ blood-_____ and ventilates lungs-_____.] (III-94)

8   Взяв меня́ в свою́ гру́ппу и поручи́в мне, полго́да наза́д, испыта́ния но́вого материа́ла, дире́ктор, коне́чно, рискова́л.
[Having-taken me-_____ in own group-_____ and entrusted me-_____, half-year-_____ ago, experiments-_____ new material-_____, director-_____, of-course, risked.] (III-102)

9   Она́ нашла́ ме́сто для му́жа, пропа́вшего в те го́ды в глуши́.
[She-_____ found place-_____ for husband-_____, who-had-disappeared-_____ in those years-_____ in backwoods-_____.] (III-122)

10   Форма́льный по́вод для закры́тия ми́ссии тако́в: конгре́сс США ушёл на кани́кулы, так и не продли́в де́йствие зако́на, разреша́ющего Соединённым Шта́там име́ть дипломати́ческие конта́кты с ООН.
[Formal cause-_____ for closing-_____ mission-_____ such-_____: Congress-_____ USA-_____ left for vacation-_____, so even not extended action-_____ law-_____, allowing-_____ United States-_____ have diplomatic contacts-_____ with UN-_____.] (III-150)

11   Под землёй че́рез не́сколько сантиме́тров лёд, ве́чная мерзлота́, све́рху снег.
[Under ground-_____ through several-_____ centimeters-_____ ice-_____, eternal frost-_____, on-top snow-_____.] (III-161)

12   Он уда́рился гру́дью о водопрово́дную трубу́, кото́рая проходи́ла по газо́ну.
[He-_____ hit chest-_____ against water pipe-_____, which-_____ ran along lawn-_____.] (III-175)

Dative Exercise 1, Level III

Identify the instances of the DATIVE case in the following sentences and explain why the DATIVE is used.

1   Постановле́нием No. 315 глава́ областно́й администра́ции учреди́л ежеме́сячные стипе́ндии студе́нтам ву́зов, око́нчившим шко́лу с золото́й меда́лью.
[Decree-_____ No. 315 head-_____ regional administration-_____ established monthly stipends-_____ students-_____ institutions-of-higher-education-_____, graduated-_____ school-_____ with gold medal-_____.] (III-11)

2   Ра́ньше он приходи́л к нам с жа́лобами на сосе́дей, отравля́ющих из-за сте́нки пи́щу и обжига́ющих его́ че́рез потоло́к неви́димыми луча́ми.
[Earlier he-_____ came to us-_____ with complaints-_____ on neighbors-_____, poisoning-_____ from-beyond wall-_____ food-_____ and burning-_____ him-_____ through ceiling-_____ invisible rays-_____.] (III-26)

3   Плани́ровал изда́ние съедо́бных де́тских кни́г. Зате́м вына́шивал прое́кт съедо́бных ша́хмат. Наконе́ц, пришёл к волну́ющей иде́е съедо́бных да́мских тру́сиков.
[Planned publication-_____ edible children's books-_____. Then brought-forth design-_____ edible chess-set-_____. Finally, came to exciting idea-_____ edible women's underpants-_____.] (III-38)

4   Гениа́льная иде́я! Принесёт нам три миллио́на до́лларов! Успе́х на сто проце́нтов гаранти́руется. Никако́го ри́ска. Че́рез три неде́ли мы открыва́ем фа́брику.
[Brilliant idea-_____! Will-bring us-_____ three-_____ million-_____ dollars-_____! Success-_____ on hundred-_____ percent-_____ is-guaranteed. No risk-_____. In three-_____ weeks-_____ we-_____ open factory-_____.] (III-50)

5   Э́тот душе́вный по́двиг Довла́това неповтори́м, и его́ не подде́лать бо́льше никому́, как бы кто́ ни стара́лся.
[That emotional achievement-_____ Dovlatov-_____ unrepeatable-_____, and it-_____ not fake more no-one-_____, how would who-_____ not tried.] (III-56)

6   Прави́тельство то́лько что объяви́ло о вы́пуске большо́го паке́та облига́ций на о́бщую су́мму трёх миллиа́рдов до́лларов, при́званного компенси́ровать аргенти́нцам поте́рю их ро́дственников во вре́мя так называ́емой <<гря́зной войны́>>.
[Government-_____ only that announced about issue-_____ large packet-_____ obligations-_____ for total sum-_____ three billion dollars-_____, designated-_____ compensate Argentinians-_____ loss-_____ their relatives-_____ in time-_____ so called "dirty war-_____".] (III-71)

7   Мне казáлось, что, помúмо любвú ко мне, у тебя должнó быть чýвство дóлга, но ты считáл, что ничегó не дóлжен, тогдá и я тебé ничегó не должнá.
[Me-_____ seemed, that in-addition love-_____ to me-_____, by you-_____ should-_____ be feeling-_____ obligation-_____, but you-_____ thought, that nothing-_____ not obliged-_____, then and I-_____ you-_____ nothing-_____ not obliged-_____.] (III-83)

8   Хотя публúчно Гóрький прóтив Цветáевой никогдá не выступáл, мóжно предположúть, что её сестрá в какóй-то осторóжной фóрме передалá ей нелéстное мнéние писáтеля о её твóрчестве.
[Although publicly Gorky-_____ against Tsvetaeva-_____ never not spoke-out, possible assume, that her sister-_____ in some cautious manner-_____ passed-on her-_____ unflattering opinion-_____ writer-_____ about her work-_____.] (III-111)

9   —Вы преувелúчиваете. Литерáтор дóлжен публиковáться. Разумéется, не в ущéрб своемý талáнту.
[—You-_____ exaggerate. A literary-man-_____ should-_____ publish. It-is-understood, not to detriment-_____ own talent-_____.] (III-126)

10   Начинáя с сентября япóнкам не придётся кричáть из окнá, зазывáя свойх детéй на обéд.
[Starting from September-_____ Japanese-women-_____ not come-to yell from window-_____, summoning own children-_____ to dinner-_____.] (III-139)

11   Человéк, совершúвший сáмый кровáвый террористúческий акт за всю истóрию Амéрики, был наконéц приговорён к смéртной кáзни.
[Man-_____, committed-_____ most bloody terrorist act-_____ for all history-_____ America-_____, was finally sentenced-_____ to death penalty-_____.] (III-148)

12   По его словáм, в понедéльник ýтром из Минфúна пришлó распоряжéние, соглáсно котóрому выделяемых дéнег бýдет éле-éле хватáть на зарплáты сотрýдникам.
[Along his words-_____, on Monday-_____ morning-_____ from Minfin-_____ came order-_____, agreeing which-_____ alloted money-_____ will barely suffice for wages-_____ employees-_____.] (III-167)

Dative Exercise 2, Level III

Identify the instances of the DATIVE case in the following sentences and explain why the DATIVE is used.

1   Собáка шарáхнулась от крúка и обернýла к ней удивлённую мóрду.
[Dog-_____ was-startled from scream-_____ and turned to her-_____ surprised muzzle-_____.] (III-17)

2   Растро́ганный её явле́нием, Вади́м да́же не спроси́л, отку́да ей изве́стен
    но́мер его́ телефо́на.
    [Touched-_____ her appearance-_____, Vadim-_____ even not asked, from-where
    her-_____ known-_____ number-_____ his telephone-_____.] (III-27)

3   Снача́ла нам пока́зывали каньо́н, что-то вро́де ущеля́.
    [First us-_____ showed canyon-_____, something-_____ like ravine-_____.] (III-41)

4   Но мы, сла́ва Бо́гу, защищены́ от э́того с де́тства.
    [But we-_____, glory-_____ God-_____, protected-_____ from that-_____ from
    childhood-_____.] (III-59)

5   Он переключа́ет ско́рость. Я бою́сь скоросте́й, но сейча́с мне хо́чется, что́бы
    он е́хал ещё быстре́е, хо́чется вре́заться во что́-нибудь, что́бы бо́льше не
    ду́мать.
    [He-_____ switches speed-_____. I-_____ fear speeds-_____, but now me-_____
    wants, so-that he-_____ went ever faster, wants run into something-_____, so-that
    more not think.] (III-73)

6   Весь дом находи́лся под терро́ром но́вого челове́ка, кото́рый хоте́л
    переина́чить су́тки по со́бственному усмотре́нию.
    [Whole house-_____ was under terror-_____ new person-_____, who-_____ wanted
    alter day-_____ along own discretion-_____.] (III-87)

7   Сле́дствию ну́жно бы́ло доказа́ть, что она́ завладе́ла чужи́м иму́ществом.
    [Investigative-team-_____ needed was prove, that she-_____ took-possession oth-
    ers' property-_____.] (III-119)

8   "Вы на са́мом де́ле экономи́ст.... Ну чего́ ты го́лову моро́чишь лю́дям здесь?"
    ["You-_____ in very matter-_____ economist-_____.... Well what-_____ you-_____
    head-_____ fool people-_____ here?"] (III-127)

9   Япо́нская компа́ния пейджинго́вой свя́зи выпуска́ет в прода́жу недороги́е
    пе́йджеры, специа́льно предназна́ченные для переда́чи коди́рованных
    сообще́ний де́тям.
    [Japanese company-_____ paging network-_____ puts-out to sale-_____ inexpen-
    sive pagers-_____ especially intended-_____ for transmission-_____ coded mes-
    sages-_____ children-_____.] (III-140)

10 Возмущённым роди́телям дире́ктор обеща́л вско́ре найти́ учителе́й, но в
    середи́не го́да призна́лся в своём бесси́лии и предложи́л призва́ть на по́мощь
    ча́стную фи́рму.
    [Upset parents-_____ director-_____ promised soon find teachers-_____, but in
    middle-_____ year-_____ acknowledged in own powerlessness-_____ and proposed
    summon to help-_____ private firm-_____.] (III-155)

11   А я так вот подхожу́ одна́жды к мясни́ку, говорю́, мне килогра́мма три хоро́шего мя́са бы. И подмигну́л ему́.

[And I-_____ there approach once towards butcher-_____, say, me-_____ kilogram-_____ three-_____ good meat-_____ should. And winked him-_____.] (III-165)

12   Соглаше́ние предусма́тривает созда́ние на ба́зе "Киноце́нтра" совме́стного предприя́тия, в кото́ром ка́ждой из заинтересо́ванных сторо́н бу́дет принадлежа́ть по пятьдеся́т проце́нтов а́кций.

[Agreement-_____ envisions creation-_____ on base-_____ "Cineplex"-_____ combined enterprise-_____, in which-_____ each-_____ from interested sides-_____ will belong around fifty-_____ percent-_____ shares-_____.] (III-168)

Dative Exercise 3, Level III

Identify the instances of the DATIVE *case in the following sentences and explain why the* DATIVE *is used.*

1   Он был не то́лько у́мный, но и образо́ванный и постоя́нно обнару́живал свои́ зна́ния, одна́ко не нра́вился девчо́нкам, потому́ что его́ лицо́ бы́ло покры́то ю́ношескими вулкани́ческими прыща́ми.

[He-_____ was not only smart-_____, but and educated-_____ and constantly displayed own knowledge-_____, however not pleased girls-_____, because his face-_____ was covered-_____ youthful volcanic pimples-_____.] (III-18)

2   Сего́дня равнопра́вие психи́чески больны́х, их пра́во на "со́бственное мне́ние" сво́дится к ра́вному для всех пра́ву быть обма́нутым.

[Today equal-rights-_____ mentally ill-_____, their right-_____ to "own opinion"-_____ amounts to equal-_____ for everyone-_____ right-_____ be deceived-_____.] (III-28)

3   Сейча́с газе́та мне опроти́вела, но тогда́ я был по́лон энтузиа́зма.

[Now newspaper-_____ me-_____ become-repulsive, but then I-_____ was full-_____ enthusiasm-_____.] (III-44)

4   Подойдём к ситуа́ции стро́го с то́чки зре́ния междунаро́дного пра́ва, оста́вив на вре́мя в стороне́ специфи́ческий хара́ктер взаимоотноше́ний Москвы́ с белору́сским президе́нтом.

[Approach to situation-_____ strictly from point-_____ view-_____ international law-_____, having-left for time-_____ in side-_____ specific character-_____ mutual-relations-_____ Moscow-_____ with Belorussian president-_____.] (III-63)

5   Но когда́ я пове́дал неве́сте о свое́й пробле́ме, она́ доста́ла из свое́й миниатю́рной су́мочки како́й-то прибо́р, приложи́ла к мое́й голове́ и боль исче́зла.

[But when I-_____ told fiancee-_____ about own problem-_____, she-_____ took from own miniature purse-_____ some-kind gadget-_____, placed to my head-_____ and pain-_____ disappeared.] (III-75)

6   Во́ры залеза́ют в кварти́ры ве́рхних этаже́й с кры́ши, по верёвке, привя́занной к анте́нне.
[Thieves-NOM climb in apartments-ACC upper floors-GEN from roof-GEN, along rope-DAT, tied-DAT to antenna-DAT.] (III-178)

7   Отде́лом спо́рта заве́довал доброду́шный, бессло́весный челове́к. Он неизме́нно пребыва́л в глубо́ком самозабве́нии. По темпера́менту был ра́вен мёртвой соба́ке.
[Department-_____ sport-_____ managed kind-hearted, silent man-_____. He-_____ invariably remained in deep selflessness-_____. Along temperament-_____ was equal-to dead dog-_____.] (III-121)

8   Согла́сен, Солжени́цын — э́то гора́, бы́ло бы смешно́ попыта́ться её переде́лать по на́шим ме́ркам. Де́ло тепе́рь в нас с ва́ми. Нам осмы́сливать, нам реша́ть, нам выбира́ть, куда́ идти́ да́льше.
[Agree-_____, Solzhenitsyn-_____ — this-_____ mountain-_____, was would laughable attempt it-_____ remake along our measures-_____. Matter-_____ now to us-_____ with you-_____. Us-_____ interpret, us-_____ decide, us-_____ choose, where go further.] (III-128)

9   По ро́ду свое́й рабо́ты я каждодне́вно ста́лкиваюсь с людьми́, пострада́вшими от уку́сов живо́тных.
[Along sort-_____ own work-_____ I-_____ daily bump-into with people-_____, having-suffered-_____ from bites-_____ animals-_____.] (III-142)

10   Фонд Раджи́ва Га́нди, осно́ванный е́ю, помога́ет де́тям, же́нщинам и бе́дным и стал са́мой влия́тельной неправи́тельственной организа́цией в И́ндии.
[Fund-_____ Rajiva Gandi-_____, founded-_____ her-_____, helps children-_____, women-_____ and poor-_____ and became most influential non-governmental organization-_____ in India-_____.] (III-146)

11   Лет пятна́дцать наза́д, идя́ по сне́жной лесно́й целине́ на лы́жах, мо́жно бы́ло наткну́ться и на за́ячьи, и да́же на ли́сьи следы́.
[Years-_____ fifteen-_____ ago, going along snowy forested virgin-lands-_____ on skis-_____, may was stumble-upon and on rabbit-_____, and even on fox tracks-_____.] (III-159)

12   Э́тот идио́т режиссёр заста́вил меня́ сле́довать заду́манному пла́ну.
[This idiot-_____ director-_____ forced me-_____ follow proposed plan-_____.] (III-170)

Genitive Exercise 1, Level III

Identify the instances of the GENITIVE *case in the following sentences and explain why the* GENITIVE *is used.*

1   Брази́лия явля́ется крупне́йшим в ми́ре производи́телем и продавцо́м ко́фе, выра́щивая о́коло тридцати́ проце́нтов всего́ мирово́го урожа́я арома́тных бобо́в.
[Brazil-_____ is biggest-_____ in world-_____ producer-_____ and seller-_____ coffee-_____, growing around thirty percent-_____ entire world harvest-_____ aromatic beans-_____.] (III-2)

2   У неё лицо́ соверше́нно ма́ленькой де́вочки, и э́то де́тское ли́чико нале́плено на ме́лкую, как ты́ковка, голо́вку.
[By her-_____ face-_____ completely small girl-_____, and that child's face-_____ stuck-_____ on small-_____, like little-pumpkin-_____, little-head-_____.] (III-23)

3   Ра́ньше он приходи́л к нам с жа́лобами на сосе́дей, отравля́ющих из-за сте́нки пи́щу и обжига́ющих его́ че́рез потоло́к неви́димыми луча́ми.
[Earlier he-_____ came to us-_____ with complaints-_____ on neighbors-_____, poisoning-_____ from-beyond wall-_____ food-_____ and burning-_____ him-_____ through ceiling-_____ invisible rays-_____.] (III-26)

4   Он не учени́к и не после́дователь не́коего кру́пного ма́стера, не приве́рженец како́й-либо знамени́той театра́льной шко́лы.
[He-_____ not disciple-_____ and not follower-_____ some prominent master-_____, not adherent-_____ any famous theatrical school-_____.] (III-29)

5   Плани́ровал изда́ние съедо́бных де́тских кни́г. Зате́м вына́шивал прое́кт съедо́бных ша́хмат. Наконе́ц, пришёл к волну́ющей иде́е съедо́бных да́мских тру́сиков.
[Planned publication-_____ edible children's books-_____. Then brought-forth design-_____ edible chess-set-_____. Finally, came to exciting idea-_____ edible women's underpants-_____.] (III-38)

6   Он носи́л га́лстук цве́та ру́хнувшей наде́жды.
[He-_____ wore tie-_____ color-_____ dashed hope-_____.] (III-49)

7   Подойдём к ситуа́ции стро́го с то́чки зре́ния междунаро́дного пра́ва, оста́вив на вре́мя в стороне́ специфи́ческий хара́ктер взаимоотноше́ний Москвы́ с белору́сским президе́нтом.
[Approach to situation-_____ strictly from point-_____ view-_____ international law-_____, having-left for time-_____ in side-_____ specific character-_____ mutual-relations-_____ Moscow-_____ with Belorussian president-_____.] (III-63)

8   В англи́йском го́роде Во́берн организа́торы сбо́ра средств в фонд подде́ржки кампа́нии по сохране́нию ди́кой приро́ды в стра́нах А́зии вы́вели на у́лицы трёх слоно́в из ме́стного зоопа́рка.
    [In English city-_____ Woburn-_____ organizers-_____ collection-_____ funds-_____ in fund-_____ support-_____ campaign-_____ along protection-_____ wild nature-_____ in countries-_____ Asia-_____ led-out on streets-_____ three elephants-_____ from local zoo-_____.] (III-78)

9   Реше́ние о приня́тии э́того госуда́рства, населе́ние кото́рого насчи́тывает шестна́дцать ты́сяч челове́к, в ООН Генера́льная Ассамбле́я приняла́ без голосова́ния, никто́ не возража́л.
    [Resolution-_____ about acceptance-_____ this state-_____, population-_____ which-_____ counts sixteen-_____ thousands-_____ people-_____, in UN-_____ General Assembly-_____ accepted without voting-_____, no-one-_____ not objected.] (III-90)

10 Хотя́ публи́чно Го́рький про́тив Цвета́евой никогда́ не выступа́л, мо́жно предположи́ть, что её сестра́ в како́й-то осторо́жной фо́рме передала́ ей неле́стное мне́ние писа́теля о её тво́рчестве.
    [Although publicly Gorky-_____ against Tsvetaeva-_____ never not spoke-out, possible assume, that her sister-_____ in some cautious manner-_____ passed-on her-_____ unflattering opinion-_____ writer-_____ about her work-_____.] (III-111)

11 Ко́стя сбил одея́ло, Гу́лька съе́хала с поду́шки, вы́сунула но́жку из крова́ти.
    [Kostya-_____ dislodged blanket-_____, Gulka-_____ came-down from pillow-_____, stuck-out little-leg-_____ from bed-_____.] (III-135)

12 У меня́ бы́ло два-три пла́тья, а одна́жды не́ было чуло́к, что́бы пойти́ в го́сти на Но́вый год, и тогда́ я шов нарисова́ла черни́лами на го́лой ноге́.
    [By me-_____ was two-three-_____ dresses-_____, and once not was hose-_____, in-order-to go to guests-_____ to New Year-_____, and then I-_____ seam-_____ drew ink-_____ on bare leg-_____.] (III-180)

Genitive Exercise 2, Level III

Identify the instances of the GENITIVE case in the following sentences and explain why the GENITIVE is used.

1   Предприя́тие вы́пустит шестна́дцать ты́сяч маши́н, оди́ннадцать ты́сяч из кото́рых реализу́ются за грани́цей.
    [Enterprise-_____ will-produce sixteen-_____ thousand-_____ cars-_____, eleven-_____ thousand-_____ from which-_____ will-be-sold beyond border-_____.] (III-3)

2   Мно́го говори́тся о том, что журнали́стика для литера́тора — заня́тие па́губное.

[A-lot-_____ is-said about that-_____, that journalism-_____ for writer-_____ — profession pernicious-_____.] (III-39)

3   Гениа́льная иде́я! Принесёт нам три миллио́на до́лларов! Успе́х на сто проце́нтов гаранти́руется. Никако́го ри́ска. Че́рез три неде́ли мы открыва́ем фа́брику.

[Brilliant idea-_____! Will-bring us-_____ three-_____ million-_____ dollars-_____! Success-_____ on hundred-_____ percent-_____ is-guaranteed. No risk-_____. In three-_____ weeks-_____ we-_____ open factory-_____.] (III-50)

4   Спецслу́жбы зарубе́жного госуда́рства аресто́вывают и броса́ют в тюрьму́ росси́йских гра́ждан, не соверши́вших никако́го преступле́ния.

[Special-services-_____ foreign government-_____ arrest and throw in jail-_____ Russian citizens-_____ not having-committed-_____ no crime-_____.] (III-64)

5   И о́чень любопы́тно второ́е соглаше́ние, кото́рое каса́ется тако́й гру́бой земно́й мате́рии, как тамо́жня.

[And very interesting-_____ second agreement-_____, which-_____ touches such coarse earthly material-_____, like customs-_____.] (III-91)

6   Раздраже́ние Го́рького, кото́рое чу́вствуется во всём то́не э́того письма́, несомне́нно отрази́лось и на его́ характери́стике тво́рчества Мари́ны Цвета́евой.

[Irritation-_____ Gorky-_____, which-_____ is-felt in all tone-_____ this letter-_____, certainly was-reflected also on his description-_____ work-_____ Marina Tsvetaeva-_____.] (III-112)

7   У фи́рмы бо́лее двухсо́т совме́стных предприя́тий по всему́ ми́ру, где успе́шно тру́дятся деся́тки ты́сяч са́мых высококвалифици́рованных специали́стов ра́зных национа́льностей.

[By firm-_____ more two-hundred joint businesses-_____ along all world-_____, where successfully work tens-_____ thousands-_____ most highly-qualifed specialists-_____ various nationalities-_____.] (III-136)

8   Руководи́тели фо́нда пре́жде неоднокра́тно утвержда́ли, что они́ подде́рживают не́кие свя́зи с диссиде́нтскими элеме́нтами внутри́ куби́нских вооружённых сил, кото́рые я́кобы уже́ созре́ли для переворо́та.

[Leaders-_____ fund-_____ formerly repeatedly insisted, that they-_____ support certain connections-_____ with dissident elements-_____ within Cuban armed forces-_____, which-_____ supposedly already matured for revolution-_____.] (III-144)

9   Фи́рмы, наруша́ющие э́то распоряже́ние, бу́дут лиша́ться лице́нзии на свою́
     де́ятельность.
     [Firms-_____, violating-_____ this order-_____, will be-deprived license-_____ for
     own operation-_____.] (III-153)

10   Он по́льзуется всео́бщим внима́нием и призна́нием по сию́ по́ру, когда́ не
     оста́лось в его́ жи́зни уже́ ни одно́й официа́льной подпо́рки, когда́ почти́
     забы́то, что он был председа́телем правле́ния Сою́за компози́торов, когда́
     не упомина́ют о его́ зва́ниях и награ́дах.
     [He-_____ enjoys universal attention-_____ and acknowledgment-_____ along this
     time-_____, when not remained in his life-_____ already not one official support-
     _____, when almost forgotten-_____, that he-_____ was representative-_____ board-
     _____ Union-_____ composers-_____, when not remembers about his titles-_____
     and awards-_____.] (III-156)

11   Ко́стик, две неде́ли до того́ пролежа́вший с радикули́том, в три метро́вых
     шага́ перема́хивает че́рез газо́н, а на асфа́льте, сцепи́в зу́бы от презре́ния,
     стои́т Людми́ла.
     [Kostik-_____, two-_____ weeks-_____ to that-_____ laid-up-_____ with radicu-
     litis-_____, in three-_____ meter steps-_____ leaps through lawn-_____, and on
     asphalt-_____, having-clinched teeth-_____ from disdain-_____ stands Ludmila-
     _____.] (III-172)

12   Тепе́рь я понима́ю, что в гражда́нской войне́ не быва́ет пра́вых и винова́тых,
     а есть лю́ди, по-ра́зному ви́дящие бу́дущее свое́й страны́.
     [Now I-_____ understand, that in civil war-_____ not are right-_____ and guilty-
     _____, but there-is people-_____, differently seeing-_____ future-_____ own coun-
     try-_____.] (III-181)

Genitive Exercise 3, Level III

*Identify the instances of the GENITIVE case in the following sentences and explain why
the GENITIVE is used.*

Genitive
Exercise 3
Level III

1   В Росси́и сейча́с из-за спа́да произво́дства сокраща́ется потребле́ние
     электроэне́ргии, так что изли́шки мы с удово́льствием продади́м на За́пад.
     [In Russia-_____ now from-beyond fall-_____ production-_____ declines use-_____
     electricity-_____, so that surplus-_____ we-_____ with pleasure-_____ will-sell to
     West-_____.] (III-4)

2   Да ведь э́то же и есть те́ма на́шего симпо́зиума.
     [Yes after-all that-_____ and is theme-___ our symposium-_____.] (III-40)

3   Я — ваш подпи́счик с са́мого дня рожде́ния: "Литгазе́ту" выпи́сывали ещё
     мои́ роди́тели. Мне о́чень импони́рует ва́ша ру́брика "Что сейча́с
     поде́лывает..."
     [I-_____ — your subscriber-_____ from very day-_____ birth-_____: "Litgazeta-
     _____" subscribed still my parents-_____. Me-_____ very impresses your column-
     _____ "What-_____ now does..."] (III-52)

4   Прави́тельство то́лько что объяви́ло о вы́пуске большо́го паке́та облига́ций
     на о́бщую су́мму трёх миллиа́рдов до́лларов, при́званного компенси́ровать
     аргенти́нцам поте́рю их ро́дственников во вре́мя так называ́емой <<гря́зной
     войны́>>.
     [Government-_____ only that announced about issue-_____ large packet-_____ ob-
     ligations-_____ for total sum-_____ three billion dollars-_____, designated-_____
     compensate Argentinians-_____ loss-_____ their relatives-_____ in time-_____ so
     called "dirty war-_____".] (III-71)

5   Не́когда процвета́вший жанр пеки́нской о́перы не выде́рживает зако́нов
     ры́нка.
     [Once having-blossomed genre-_____ Peking opera-_____ not withstand laws-_____
     market-_____.] (III-96)

6   Стоя́л в паску́дной о́череди, толка́лся, ждал чего́-то. И вдруг пью вино́ с
     очарова́тельной же́нщиной.
     [Stood in filthy line-_____, pushed, waited something-_____. And immediately
     drink wine-_____ with charming woman-_____.] (III-107)

7   Я не то́лько не сторо́нник, но и акти́вный проти́вник разли́чных тео́рий
     "мирово́го за́говора."
     [I-_____ not only not supporter-_____, but and active opponent-_____ various theo-
     ries-_____ "worldwide conspiracy-_____".] (III-114)

8   Начина́я с сентября́ япо́нкам не придётся крича́ть из окна, зазыва́я свои́х
     дете́й на обе́д.
     [Starting from September-_____ Japanese-women-_____ not come-to yell from win-
     dow-_____, summoning own children-_____ to dinner-_____.] (III-139)

9   Гла́вное же в том, что игра́ сбо́рной Росси́и на э́тот раз по-настоя́щему
     понра́вилась зри́телям и специали́стам, она вы́звала неподде́льное уваже́ние
     сопе́рников.
     [Main very in that-_____, that game-_____ combined Russia-_____ on this occa-
     sion-_____ along-real-_____ liked viewers-_____ and specialists-_____, it-_____
     call-forth genuine respect-_____ rivals-_____.] (III-157)

10   Боковы́м зре́нием она́ отме́тила, что на друго́й доро́жке оста́лись стоя́ть о́чень то́лстая тётенька, килогра́ммов на сто, и высо́кий ма́льчик.
[Side vision-_____ she-_____ noticed, that on other road-_____ stopped stand very fat lady-_____, kilograms-_____ to 100-_____, and tall boy-_____.] (III-171)

11   Она́ смущённо разде́лась, стыдя́сь своего́ бе́лого, ры́хлого те́ла...
[She-_____ embarrassed got-undressed, being-ashamed own white, pudgy body-_____...] (III-174)

12   С по́мощью ме́стных стару́шек, вы́сыпавших по́сле слу́жбы из це́ркви, отыска́ли под сне́гом его́ моги́лу.
[With help-_____ local old-ladies-_____, who-had-poured-_____ after service-_____ from church-_____ found under snow-_____ his grave-_____.] (III-182)

Locative Exercise 1, Level III

Locative
Exercise 1
Level III

Identify the instances of the LOCATIVE *case in the following sentences and explain why the* LOCATIVE *is used.*

1   В созда́вшихся усло́виях режи́м стреми́тся разли́чными путя́ми внести́ раско́л в оппозицио́нные ряды́.
[In created conditions-_____ regime-_____ tries different ways-_____ introduce division-_____ in opposition ranks-_____.] (III-8)

2   У меня́ сложи́лось впечатле́ние, что о токи́йской деклара́ции 1993 го́да, где бы́ло дано́ обеща́ние реши́ть территориа́льную пробле́му, в Росси́и как-то не вспомина́ют.
[By me-_____ formed impression-_____, that about Tokyo declaration-_____ 1993 year-_____, where was given-_____ promise-_____ solve territorial problem-_____, in Russia-_____ somehow not remember.] (III-20)

3   В кулуа́рах писа́теля окружи́ла толпа́ единомы́шленников и почита́телей.
[In entrance-hall-_____ writer-_____ swarmed crowd-_____ like-minded-people-_____ and admirers-_____.] (III-45)

4   На её ме́сте я поста́вила бы на сто́лик буты́лку, положи́ла бу́лочку и со всех ног бро́силась на "Мосфи́льм" снима́ться в гла́вной ро́ли.
[On her place-_____ I-_____ stood would on table-_____ bottle-_____, laid roll-_____ and from all legs-_____ throw-self at "Mosfilm-_____" be-filmed in starring role-_____.] (III-60)

5   В англи́йском го́роде Во́берн организа́торы сбо́ра средств в фонд подде́ржки
      кампа́нии по сохране́нию ди́кой приро́ды в стра́нах А́зии вы́вели на у́лицы
      трёх слоно́в из ме́стного зоопа́рка.
      [In English city-_____ Woburn-_____ organizers-_____ collection-_____ funds-
      _____ in fund-_____ support-_____ campaign-_____ along protection-_____ wild
      nature-_____ in countries-_____ Asia-_____ led-out on streets-_____ three elephants-
      _____ from local zoo-_____.] (III-78)

6   Де́вочка смотре́ла в окно́, и в её све́тлых глаза́х отража́лись дере́вья, дома́,
      не́бо. Глаза́ бы́ли пёстрые и ра́зные, в зави́симости от того́, что бы́ло за
      окно́м.
      [Girl-_____ looked in window-_____, and in her bright eyes-_____ reflected trees-
      _____, houses-_____, sky-_____. Eyes-_____ were mottled-_____ and varied-
      _____, in dependence-_____ from that-_____, what-_____ was beyond window-
      _____.] (III-105)

7   Когда́ в тридца́тые го́ды возни́кла нужда́ в духоподъёмной, спла́чивающей
      наро́д геро́ике, власть испо́льзовала для э́того и́менно Се́вер.
      [When in thirty years-_____ arose need-_____ in spiritually-uplifting-_____, gal-
      vanizing-_____ nation-_____ heroics-_____, regime-_____ used for this-_____ pre-
      cisely North-_____.] (III-116)

8   Спортсме́ны, года́ми живу́щие в экстрема́льном режи́ме, вольны́ выбира́ть
      себе́ страну́ для жи́тельства, гаранти́рующую им те усло́вия, в кото́рых им
      хо́чется жить.
      [Athletes-_____, years-_____ living-_____ in extreme regime-_____, free-_____
      choose self-_____ country-_____ for residency-_____, guaranteeing-_____ them-
      _____ these conditions-_____, in which-_____ they-_____ want live.] (III-143)

9   Он по́льзуется всео́бщим внима́нием и призна́нием по сию́ по́ру, когда́ не
      оста́лось в его́ жи́зни уже́ ни одно́й официа́льной подпо́рки, когда́ почти́
      забы́то, что он был председа́телем правле́ния Сою́за компози́торов, когда́
      не упомина́ют о его́ зва́ниях и награ́дах.
      [He-_____ enjoys universal attention-_____ and acknowledgment-_____ along this
      time-_____, when not remained in his life-_____ already not one official support-
      _____, when almost forgotten-_____, that he-_____ was representative-_____ board-
      _____ Union-_____ composers-_____, when not remembers about his titles-_____
      and awards-_____.] (III-156)

10   Свя́занные сза́ди посине́вшие ру́ки при э́том задира́лись кве́рху; каза́лось,
      он мо́лится каки́м-то необы́чным спо́собом.
      [Bound-_____ from-behind turned-blue hands-_____ in this-_____ broke upwards;
      seemed, he-_____ prays some unusual means-_____.] (III-163)

11   В телефо́нном разгово́ре в четве́рг они́ бы́ли еди́ны в том, что госуда́рствам Содру́жества Незави́симых Госуда́рств на́до реши́ть ряд вопро́сов, свя́занных с укрепле́нием ю́жных рубеже́й Содру́жества.
[In telephone conversation-_____ on Thursday-_____ they-_____ were one-_____ in that-_____, that states-_____ Commonwealth-_____ Independent States-_____ necessary decide row-_____ questions-_____, connected-_____ with strengthening-_____ southern borders-_____ Commonwealth-_____.] (III-166)

12   Геройню Щербако́вой вы легко́ мо́жете встре́тить в о́череди за дешёвыми ту́флями на распрода́же, в авто́бусе в час пик, в магази́не (то́лько не в блестя́щем суперма́ркете).
[Heroine-_____ Shcherbakova-_____ you-_____ easily may meet in line-_____ behind cheap shoes-_____ on sale-_____, in bus-_____ to time peak-_____, in store-_____ (only not in sparkling supermarket-_____.] (III-185)

Locative Exercise 2, Level III

Identify the instances of the LOCATIVE *case in the following sentences and explain why the* LOCATIVE *is used.*

Locative
Exercise 2
Level III

1   Психи́ческими неду́гами во всём их спе́ктре си́льно пью́щие поражены́ в два ра́за ча́ще, чем популя́ция в це́лом.
[Psychiatric illnesses-_____ in all their spectrum-_____ strongly drinking-_____ afflicted-_____ in two times-_____ more-frequently, than population-_____ in whole-_____.] (III-10)

2   На неда́вней конфере́нции Организа́ции азиатскотихоокеа́нского экономи́ческого сотру́дничества, уча́стники кото́рой производя́т полови́ну мирово́го валово́го проду́кта, Росси́я не уча́ствовала.
[At recent conference-_____ Organization-_____ Asian-pacific economic collaboration-_____, participants-_____ which-_____ produce half-_____ world gross product-_____, Russia-_____ not participate.] (III-21)

3   Тогда́ почему́ же я ощуща́ю себя́ на гра́ни физи́ческой катастро́фы? Отку́да у меня́ чу́вство безнадёжной жи́зненной неприго́дности? В чём причи́на мое́й тоски́?
[Then why I-_____ feel self-_____ on edge-_____ physical catastrophe-_____? From-where by me-_____ feeling-_____ hopeless life uselessness-_____? In what-_____ cause-_____ my melancholy-_____?] (III-48)

4   Во мне шла борьба́ тёмного со све́тлым, подозри́тельности с ве́рой в челове́чество.
[In me-_____ went battle-_____ dark-_____ with light-_____, suspicion-_____ with faith-_____ in humanity-_____.] (III-61)

5   Прави́тельство то́лько что объяви́ло о вы́пуске большо́го пакета облига́ций на о́бщую су́мму трёх миллиа́рдов до́лларов, при́званного компенси́ровать аргенти́нцам поте́рю их ро́дственников во вре́мя так называ́емой <<гря́зной войны́>>.
[Government-_____ only that announced about issue-_____ large packet-_____ obligations-_____ for total sum-_____ three billion dollars-_____, designated-_____ compensate Argentinians-_____ loss-_____ their relatives-_____ in time-_____ so called "dirty war-_____".] (III-71)

6   Де́ло не в том, разби́лся ты и́ли нет, про́сто я износи́ла на́ши отноше́ния. Как ту́фли. Подо́шва отлете́ла.
[Affair-_____ not in that-_____, got-hurt you-_____ or not, simply I-_____ wore-out our relationship-_____. Like shoes-_____. Sole-_____ came-off.] (III-84)

7   И тут на её горизо́нте возни́к знамени́тый эстра́дный певе́ц. Сейча́с его́ и́мя забы́то, но в шестидеся́тые го́ды он был популя́рнее Сина́тры.
[And here on her horizon-_____ appeared famous stage singer-_____. Now his name-_____ forgotten-_____, but in sixty years-_____ he-_____ was more-popular Sinatra-_____.] (III-106)

8   У́мер он во Влади́мире, хорони́ли мы его́ на мое́й ро́дине в Росла́вле, где похоро́нена моя́ родня́.
[Died he-_____ in Vladimir-_____, buried we-_____ him-_____ on my native-soil-_____ in Roslavl-_____, where buried-_____ my kin-_____.] (III-120)

9   А е́сли жена́ сжига́ет себя́ на погреба́льном костре́ му́жа, она́ удоста́ивается почти́ религио́зного поклоне́ния.
[But if wife-_____ burns self-_____ on funeral pyre-_____ husband-_____, she-_____ receives almost religious worship-_____.] (III-145)

10 Гла́вное же в том, что игра́ сбо́рной Росси́и на э́тот раз по-настоя́щему понра́вилась зри́телям и специали́стам, она вы́звала неподде́льное уваже́ние сопе́рников.
[Main very in that-_____, that game-_____ combined Russia-_____ on this occasion-_____ along-real-_____ liked viewers-_____ and specialists-_____, it-_____ call-forth genuine respect-_____ rivals-_____.] (III-157)

11 Соглаше́ние предусма́тривает созда́ние на ба́зе "Киноце́нтра" совме́стного предприя́тия, в кото́ром ка́ждой из заинтересо́ванных сторо́н бу́дет принадлежа́ть по пятьдеся́т проце́нтов а́кций.
[Agreement-_____ envisions creation-_____ on base-_____ "Cineplex"-_____ combined enterprise-_____, in which-_____ each-_____ from interested sides-_____ will belong around fifty-_____ percent-_____ shares-_____.] (III-168)

12   Потóм колúчество жéнщин, любящих Мúтю, стáло увелúчиваться в геометрúческой прогрéссии.
     [Then collection-_____ women-_____, loving-_____ Mitya-_____, began expand in geometric progression-_____.] (III-186)

Locative Exercise 3, Level III

Identify the instances of the LOCATIVE case in the following sentences and explain why the LOCATIVE is used.

1   Политúческая полúция располагáет богатéйшим архúвом, в котóром, как утверждáют, содéржатся досьé на полмиллиóна францýзов.
    [Political police-_____ have-at-disposal most-rich archive-_____, in which-_____, as claim, are-kept files-_____ on half-million-_____ French-_____.] (III-12)

2   Гóроду это бы́ло лéстно, а биóлогам — полéзно собрáться всем вмéсте и доложúть о свойх делáх, а заоднó посмотрéть Фрáнцию.
    [City-_____ this-_____ was flattering, but biologists-_____ — useful gather all-_____ together and report about own affairs-_____, but at-same-time see France-_____.] (III-22)

3   В егó движéниях — изя́щество юного кня́зя.
    [In his movements-_____ — elegance-_____ young prince-_____.] (III-51)

4   Минúстра внýтренних дел отпрáвили в отстáвку ещё в ию́не за содéйствие криминáльной эконóмике.
    [Minister-_____ internal affairs-_____ sent in dismissal-_____ already in June-_____ for collaboration-_____ criminal economy-_____.] (III-70)

5   В странé нахóдятся деся́тки ты́сяч бéженцев из Либéрии, испы́тывающих крáйнюю нуждý в продовóльствии и предмéтах пéрвой необходúмости.
    [In country-_____ are tens-_____ thousands-_____ refugees-_____ from Liberia-_____, experiencing-_____ extreme need-_____ in food-_____ and items-_____ first aid-_____.] (III-77)

6   Меня́ в четы́рнадцать лет понеслó в комсомóл, в котóром я не нашлá никакóй революциóнной ромáнтики.
    [Me-_____ in fourteen-_____ years-_____ brought to communist-youth-league-_____, in which-_____ I-_____ not found any revolutionary romance-_____.] (III-88)

7   Анастасия приехала в Сорренто ещё в начале августа, но Марина, не получая от неё известий, двадцать четвёртого августа обратилась с запросом к Горькому.
[Anastasia-_____ arrived in Sorrento-_____ already in beginning-_____ August-_____, but Marina-_____, not receiving from her-_____ news-_____, twenty fourth-_____ August-_____ turned with inquiry-_____ to Gorky-_____.] (III-110)

8   Религиозные семинары проходили в церковной библиотеке. Там собирались православные, иудаисты, мусульмане, католики. Каждой из групп было выделено отдельное помещение.
[Religious seminars-_____ went-through in church library-_____. There gathered Orthodox-_____, Jews-_____, Muslims-_____, Catholics-_____. Each-_____ from groups-_____ were assigned separate accomodation-_____.] (III-123)

9   В опубликованном у вас интервью с министром сельского хозяйства и продовольствия сказано, что Россия наконец-то будет не покупать зерно, а, наоборот, может быть, продавать.
[In published-_____ at you-_____ interview-_____ with minister-_____ village economy-_____ and foods-_____ said-_____, that Russia-_____ finally will not buy grain-_____, but, opposite, may be, sell.] (III-147)

10   Возмущённым родителям директор обещал вскоре найти учителей, но в середине года признался в своём бессилии и предложил призвать на помощь частную фирму.
[Upset parents-_____ director-_____ promised soon find teachers-_____, but in middle-_____ year-_____ acknowledged in own powerlessness-_____ and proposed summon to help-_____ private firm-_____.] (III-155)

11   Лет пятнадцать назад, идя по снежной лесной целине на лыжах, можно было наткнуться и на заячьи, и даже на лисьи следы.
[Years-_____ fifteen-_____ ago, going along snowy forested virgin-lands-_____ on skis-_____, may was stumble-upon and on rabbit-_____, and even on fox tracks-_____.] (III-159)

12   А два дня назад в Ленинградском военном округе был задержан офицер, у которого были обнаружены пистолет с двумя обоймами, один килограмм тротила в шашках по триста граммов, около 50 патронов калибра 7,62 и 5,6, пять сигнальных ракет и более шести тысяч долларов.
[But two-_____ day-_____ ago in Leningrad military district-_____ was detained-_____ officer-_____, at which-_____ were discovered-_____ pistol-_____ with two clips-_____, one kilogram-_____ TNT-_____ in charges-_____ along three-hundred-_____ grams-_____, around 50 cartridges-_____ caliber-_____ 7.62 and 5.6, five-_____ signal rockets-_____ and more six thousands-_____ dollars-_____.] (III-169)

Mixed Case Exercise 1, Level III

Identify the case uses in the sentences below and explain why those cases are used and how they interact with each other. Provide your own English translation of the sentence and compare it to the translation in the key.

1   Брази́лия явля́ется крупне́йшим в ми́ре производи́телем и продавцо́м ко́фе, выра́щивая о́коло тридцати́ проце́нтов всего́ мирово́го урожа́я арома́тных бобо́в.
[Brazil-_____ is biggest-_____ in world-_____ producer-_____ and seller-_____ coffee-_____, growing around thirty percent-_____ entire world harvest-_____ aromatic beans-_____.] (III-2)

2   Он не учени́к и не после́дователь не́коего кру́пного ма́стера, не приве́рженец како́й-либо знамени́той театра́льной шко́лы.
[He-_____ not disciple-_____ and not follower-_____ some prominent master-_____, not adherent-_____ any famous theatrical school-_____.] (III-29)

3   Я — ваш подпи́счик с са́мого дня рожде́ния: "Литгазе́ту" выпи́сывали ещё мои́ роди́тели. Мне о́чень импони́рует ва́ша ру́брика "Что сейча́с поде́лывает..."
[I-_____ — your subscriber-_____ from very day-_____ birth-_____: "Litgazeta-_____" subscribed still my parents-_____. Me-_____ very impresses your column-_____ "What-_____ now does..."] (III-52)

4   Вдру́г из чёрно-бе́лых пя́тен различа́ю среди́ засне́женных дере́вьев спи́ну ма́льчика.
[Suddenly from black-white spots-_____ make-out among snow-covered trees-_____ back-_____ boy-_____.] (III-72)

5   Значи́тельное вре́мя рабо́ты конфере́нции бы́ло посвящено́ презре́нной просту́де.
[Considerable time-_____ work-_____ conference-_____ was dedicated-_____ contemptible cold-_____.] (III-93)

6   Хотя́ публи́чно Го́рький про́тив Цвета́евой никогда́ не выступа́л, мо́жно предположи́ть, что её сестра́ в како́й-то осторо́жной фо́рме передала́ ей неле́стное мне́ние писа́теля о её тво́рчестве.
[Although publicly Gorky-_____ against Tsvetaeva-_____ never not spoke-out, possible assume, that her sister-_____ in some cautious manner-_____ passed-on her-_____ unflattering opinion-_____ writer-_____ about her work-_____.] (III-111)

7   Чита́я гениа́льные стихи́, не ду́май, каки́е оборо́ты бо́льше и́ли ме́ньше удали́сь а́втору.
[Reading brilliant poetry-_____, not think, which phrases-_____ more or less succeeded author-_____.] (III-125)

8   Он пóльзуется всеóбщим внимáнием и признáнием по сию́ пóру, когдá не
осталось в его жизни уже ни одной официáльной подпóрки, когдá почти
забыто, что он был председáтелем правлéния Союза композиторов, когдá
не упоминáют о его звáниях и нагрáдах.
[He-_____ enjoys universal attention-_____ and acknowledgment-_____ along this
time-_____, when not remained in his life-_____ already not one official support-
_____, when almost forgotten-_____, that he-_____ was representative-_____ board-
_____ Union-_____ composers-_____, when not remind about his titles-_____ and
awards-_____.] (III-156)

9   А два дня назáд в Ленингрáдском воéнном óкруге был задéржан офицéр, у
котóрого были обнарýжены пистолéт с двумя обóймами, один килогрáмм
тротила в шáшках по триста грáммов, óколо 50 патрóнов калибра 7,62 и
5,6, пять сигнáльных ракéт и бóлее шести тысяч дóлларов.
[But two-_____ day-_____ ago in Leningrad military district-_____ was detained-
_____ officer-_____, at which-_____ were discovered pistol-_____ with two clips-
_____, one kilogram-_____ TNT-_____ in charges-_____ along three-hundred-_____
grams-_____, around 50 cartridges-_____ caliber-_____ 7.62 and 5.6, five-_____
signal rockets-_____ and more six thousand-_____ dollars-_____.] (III-169)

10   Еврéи и армя́не, перенéсшие стрáшные гонéния и геноцид, хоть на йóту
утрáтили своё национáльное своеобрáзие?
[Jews-_____ and Armenians-_____, having-borne-_____ terrible persecutions-_____
and genocide-_____, even to iota-_____ lost own national originality-_____?] (III-
183)

Mixed Case Exercise 2, Level III

*Identify the case uses in the sentences below and explain why those cases are used
and how they interact with each other. Provide your own English translation of the
sentence and compare it to the translation in the key.*

1   Постановлéние о подписáнии соглашéния мéжду правительством Рýсской
Федерáции и правительством Респýблики Кипр о безвизовом режиме въéзда
и выезда подписано премьéр-министром.
[Resolution-_____ about signing-_____ agreement-_____ between government-
_____ Russian Federation-_____ and government-_____ Republic-_____ Cyprus-
_____ about visa-less procedure-_____ entering-_____ and leaving-_____ signed-
_____ prime-minister-_____.] (III-6)

2   Археóлог по крóхам восстанáвливает истóрию хазáр как раз для тогó, чтóбы
поня́ть, каким óбразом нарóды исчезáют, а на мéсто их истóрии прихóдят
апóкрифы, котóрые в силу рáзных причин принято да и удóбно считáть
истиной.

[Archeologist-_____ along fragments-_____ reconstruct history-_____ Khazars-_____ as time for that-_____ so-that understand, what means-_____ nations-_____ disappear, and on place-_____ their history-_____ come apocryphas-_____, which-_____ in strength-_____ various reasons-_____ not usual and and convenient consider truth-_____.] (III-30)

3   Влади́мир Жирино́вский, говоря́ в Ду́ме о неиспо́льзуемых прави́тельством возмо́жностях пополне́ния бюдже́та, гне́вно обвини́л после́днее в том, что оно́ не собира́ет нало́г с проститу́ток.
[Vladimir Zhirinovsky-_____, speaking in Duma-_____ about unutilized-_____ government-_____ opportunities-_____ supplement-_____ budget-_____, angrily accused latter-_____ in that-_____, that it-_____ not collect tax-_____ from prostitutes-_____.] (III-54)

4   Он переключа́ет ско́рость. Я бою́сь скоросте́й, но сейча́с мне хо́чется, чтобы он е́хал ещё быстре́е, хо́чется вре́заться во что́-нибудь, чтобы бо́льше не ду́мать.
[He-_____ switches speed-_____. I-_____ fear speeds-_____, but now me-_____ wants, so-that he-_____ went ever faster, wants run into something-_____, so-that more not think.] (III-73)

5   Активизи́руя диафра́гмы, смех углубля́ет дыха́ние, обогаща́ет кислоро́дом кровь и вентили́рует лёгкие.
[Activating diaphragms-_____, laughter-_____ deepens breathing-_____, enriches oxygen-_____ blood-_____ and ventilates lungs-_____.] (III-94)

6   Раздраже́ние Го́рького, кото́рое чу́вствуется во всём то́не э́того письма́, несомне́нно отрази́лось и на его́ характери́стике тво́рчества Мари́ны Цвета́евой.
[Irritation-_____ Gorky-_____, which-_____ is-felt in all tone-_____ this letter-_____, certainly was-reflected also on his description-_____ work-_____ Marina Tsvetaeva-_____.] (III-112)

7   —Вы преувели́чиваете. Литера́тор до́лжен публикова́ться. Разуме́ется, не в уще́рб своему́ тала́нту.
[—You-_____ exaggerate. A literary-man-_____ should-_____ publish. It-is-understood, not to detriment-_____ own talent-_____.] (III-126)

8   Гла́вное же в том, что игра́ сбо́рной Росси́и на э́тот раз по-настоя́щему понра́вилась зри́телям и специали́стам, она вы́звала неподде́льное уваже́ние сопе́рников.
[Main very in that-_____, that game-_____ combined Russia-_____ on this occasion-_____ along-real-_____ liked viewers-_____ and specialists-_____, it-_____ call-forth genuine respect-_____ rivals-_____.] (III-157)

9   Э́тот идио́т режиссёр заста́вил меня́ сле́довать заду́манному пла́ну.
[This idiot-_____ director-_____ forced me-_____ follow proposed plan-_____.]
(III-170)

10   Э́ту кни́гу почти́ все же́нщины, ю́ные и не о́чень, чита́ли и́менно так —
захлёбываясь от восто́рга.
[This book-_____ almost all women-_____, young-_____ and not very, read just so
— choking from delight-_____.] (III-184)

Mixed Case Exercise 3, Level III

*Identify the case uses in the sentences below and explain why those cases are used
and how they interact with each other. Provide your own English translation of the
sentence and compare it to the translation in the key.*

1   Прое́кт соглаше́ния предусма́тривает, что гра́ждане обо́их госуда́рств,
име́ющие де́йствующие заграндокуме́нты, мо́гут въезжа́ть на террито́рию
друго́го госуда́рства без виз на срок до девяно́ста дней.
[Draft-_____ agreement-_____ stipulates, that citizens-_____ both states-_____,
having-_____ valid international-documents-_____ can enter territory-_____ other
state-_____ without visas-_____ for period-_____ to ninety days-_____.] (III-7)

2   Вообще́ лицо́ есть, но черты́ не свя́заны одно́й те́мой и как бы взя́ты с
не́скольких лиц.
[In-general face-_____ is, but features-_____ not connected-_____ one theme-_____
and as it taken-_____ from several faces-_____.] (III-31)

3   Она́ была́ тогда́ гора́здо знамени́тее Серге́я, кото́рый глу́хо пребыва́л в
а́рмии, ниче́м никого́ особенно не занима́я; пью́щие ге́нии, вылета́ющие из
институ́тов, бы́ли тогда́ в на́ших круга́х скоре́е но́рмой, чем собы́тием.
[She-_____ was then much more-famous Sergei-_____, who-_____ quietly spent
time in army-_____ nothing-_____ no-one-_____ particularly not interesting; drink-
ing geniuses-_____, flying-out-_____ from institutes-_____, were then in our circles-
_____ rather norm-_____, what-_____ event-_____.] (III-55)

4   Предста́вьте, что вы договори́лись зае́хать ве́чером за свое́й возлю́бленной
и отпра́виться с ней в шика́рный рестора́н, а накану́не вас одоле́ли головны́е
бо́ли.
[Imagine, that you-_____ agreed go evening-_____ for your beloved-_____ and go
with her-_____ to fancy restaurant-_____, but night-before you-_____ overcame
head aches-_____.] (III-74)

5   Двойно́й станда́рт в поли́тике облада́ет сво́йством бумера́нга.
[Double standard-_____ in politics-_____ has property-_____ boomerang-_____.]
(III-95)

6   Коро́че говоря́, речь идёт о норма́льном проце́ссе борьбы́ мировы́х сил за
влия́ние и за выжива́ние.
[Shorter speaking, speech-_____ goes about normal process-_____ struggle-_____
world's powers-_____ for influence-_____ and for survival-_____.] (III-115)

7   "Вы на са́мом де́ле экономи́ст.... Ну чего ты го́лову моро́чишь лю́дям здесь?"
["You-_____ in very matter-_____ economist-_____.... Well what-_____ you-_____
head-_____ fool people-_____ here?"] (III-127)

8   Э́то гене́тик Ри́чард Сид, заяви́вший, что уже́ че́рез три ме́сяца начнёт
клони́ровать челове́ка.
[This-_____ geneticist Richard Seed-_____, announced-_____, that already through
three-_____ month-_____ begins clone man-_____.] (III-158)

9   Боковы́м зре́нием она́ отме́тила, что на друго́й доро́жке оста́лись стоя́ть
о́чень то́лстая тётенька, килогра́ммов на сто, и высо́кий ма́льчик.
[Side vision-_____ she-_____ noticed, that on other road-_____ stopped stand very
fat lady-_____, kilograms-_____ to 100-_____, and tall boy-_____.] (III-171)

10   Герои́ню Щербако́вой вы легко́ мо́жете встре́тить в о́череди за дешёвыми
ту́флями на распрода́же, в авто́бусе в час пик, в магази́не (то́лько не в
блестя́щем суперма́ркете).
[Heroine-_____ Shcherbakova-_____ you-_____ easily may meet in line-_____
behind cheap shoes-_____ on sale-_____, in bus-_____ to time peak-_____, in store-
_____ (only not in sparkling supermarket-_____.] (III-185)

Mixed Case Exercise 4, Level III
*Identify the case uses in the sentences below and explain why those cases are used
and how they interact with each other. Provide your own English translation of the
sentence and compare it to the translation in the key.*

1   Постановле́нием No. 315 глава́ областно́й администра́ции учреди́л
ежеме́сячные стипе́ндии студе́нтам ву́зов, око́нчившим шко́лу с золото́й
меда́лью.
[Decree-_____ No. 315 head-_____ regional administration-_____ established
monthly stipends-_____ students-_____ institutions-of-higher-education-_____,
graduated-_____ school-_____ with gold medal-_____.] (III-11)

2   Два́дцать лет наза́д она́ то́же была́ влюблена́ в одного́ арти́ста до поте́ри
пу́льса, и весь их класс сходи́л с ума́.
[Twenty-_____ years-_____ ago she-_____ also was in-love-_____ in one artist-
_____ to loss-_____ pulse-_____, and all their class-_____ was-going from mind-
_____.] (III-33)

3   Э́тот душе́вный по́двиг Довла́това неповтори́м, и его́ не подде́лать бо́льше
никому́, как бы кто́ ни стара́лся.
[That emotional achievement-_____ Dovlatov-_____ unrepeatable-_____, and it-
_____ not fake more no-one-_____, how would who-_____ not tried.] (III-56)

4   Но когда́ я пове́дал неве́сте о свое́й пробле́ме, она́ доста́ла из свое́й
миниатю́рной су́мочки како́й-то прибо́р, приложи́ла к мое́й голове́ и боль
исче́зла.
[But when I-_____ told fiancee-_____ about own problem-_____, she-_____ took
from own miniature purse-_____ some-kind gadget-_____, placed to my head-_____
and pain-_____ disappeared.] (III-75)

5   Предлага́ется посмея́ться над приключе́ниями трёх бра́тьев-близнецо́в,
за́нятых по́исками укра́денного алма́за уника́льной величины́ и це́нности.
[Suggests laugh over adventures-_____ three brothers-triplets-_____, occupied-
_____ searches-_____ stolen diamond-_____ unique size-_____ and value-_____.]
(III-98)

6   Когда́ в тридца́тые го́ды возни́кла нужда́ в духоподъёмной, спла́чивающей
наро́д геро́ике, власть испо́льзовала для э́того и́менно Се́вер.
[When in thirty years-_____ arose need-_____ in spiritually-uplifting-_____, gal-
vanizing-_____ nation-_____ heroics-_____, regime-_____ used for this-_____ precisely North-_____.] (III-116)

7   Согла́сен, Солжени́цын — э́то гора́, бы́ло бы смешно́ попыта́ться её
переде́лать по на́шим ме́ркам. Де́ло тепе́рь в нас с ва́ми. Нам осмы́сливать,
нам реша́ть, нам выбира́ть, куда́ идти́ да́льше.
[Agree-_____, Solzhenitsyn-_____ — this-_____ mountain-_____ ,was would laughable attempt it-_____ remake along our measures-_____. Matter-_____ now to us-
_____ with you-_____. Us-_____ interpret, us-_____ decide, us-_____ choose,
where go further.] (III-128)

8   Форма́льный по́вод для закры́тия ми́ссии тако́в: конгре́сс США ушёл на
кани́кулы, так и не продли́в де́йствие зако́на, разреша́ющего Соединённым
Шта́там име́ть дипломати́ческие конта́кты с ООН.
[Formal cause-_____ for closing-_____ mission-_____ such-_____: Congress-_____
USA-_____ left for vacation-_____, so even not extended action-_____ law-_____,
allowing-_____ United States-_____ have diplomatic contacts-_____ with UN-
_____.] (III-150)

9   Лет пятна́дцать наза́д, идя́ по сне́жной лесно́й целине́ на лы́жах, мо́жно
бы́ло наткну́ться и на за́ячьи, и да́же на ли́сьи следы́.
[Years-_____ fifteen-_____ ago, going along snowy forest virgin-soil-_____ on skis-
_____, may was stumble-upon and on rabbit-_____, and even on fox tracks-_____.]
(III-159)

10   Ко́стик, две неде́ли до того́ пролежа́вший с радикули́том, в три метро́вых шага́ перема́хивает че́рез газо́н, а на асфа́льте, сцепи́в зу́бы от презре́ния, стои́т Людми́ла.
[Kostik-_____, two-_____ weeks-_____ to that-_____ laid-up-_____ with radiculitis-_____, in three-_____ meter steps-_____ leaps through lawn-_____, and on asphalt-_____, having-clinched teeth-_____ from disdain-_____ stands Ludmila-_____.] (III-172)

Mixed Case Exercise 5, Level III

Mixed Case
Exercise 5
Level III

Identify the case uses in the sentences below and explain why those cases are used and how they interact with each other. Provide your own English translation of the sentence and compare it to the translation in the key.

1   Полити́ческая поли́ция располага́ет богате́йшим архи́вом, в кото́ром, как утвержда́ют, соде́ржатся досье́ на полмиллио́на францу́зов.
[Political police-_____ have-at-disposal most-rich archive-_____, in which-_____, as claim, are-kept files-_____ on half-million-_____ French-_____.] (III-12)

2   О́пытный престу́пник снача́ла подгото́вит себе́ кана́л бы́строго сбы́та, найдёт переку́пщиков, кото́рые суме́ют спла́вить карти́ны и украше́ния.
[Experienced criminal-_____ first prepare self-_____ channel-_____ quick sale-_____, finds second-hand-dealers-_____, who-_____ know-how get-rid pictures-_____ and decorations-_____.] (III-36)

3   Каки́е порази́тельные исто́рии мо́жно услы́шать в электри́чке от обо́рванного случа́йного сосе́да!
[What shocking stories-_____ possible hear in commuter-train-_____ from ragged random neighbor-_____!] (III-57)

4   Бы́вший чемпио́н ми́ра по бо́ксу Муха́ммед Али́, прибы́вший в африка́нскую Респу́блику Кот-д'Ивуа́р с ми́ссией до́брой во́ли — для оказа́ния по́мощи сиро́там-бе́женцам из Либе́рии, был с почётом встре́чен организа́торами его визи́та.
[Former champion-_____ world-_____ along boxing-_____ Muhammed Ali-_____, having-arrived-_____ in African Republic-_____ Cote-d'Ivoire-_____ with mission-_____ good will-_____ — for rendering-_____ assistance-_____ orphans-refugees-_____ from Liberia-_____, was with honor-_____ met-_____ organizers-_____ his visit-_____.] (III-76)

5   Вме́сте с гла́вным геро́ем мо́жно посочу́вствовать совреме́нной исто́рии не о́чень счастли́вой семе́йной па́ры, расска́занной в фи́льме <<Му́зыка для декабря́>>.
[Together with main hero-_____ possible sympathize modern story-_____ not very happy family pair-_____, told-_____ in film-_____ "Music-_____ for December-_____."] (III-99)

6   Вы бы́ли её адвока́том с того́ моме́нта, как на неё завели́ уголо́вное де́ло, и
практи́чески до оконча́ния сле́дствия.
[You-_____ were her attorney-_____ from that moment-_____, how on her-_____
brought criminal case-_____, and practically to end-_____ investigation-_____.]
(III-117)

7   Мо́жет, возьмёт тебя́ на рабо́ту литсотру́дником и́ли хотя́ бы корре́ктором.
[May, will-take you-_____ to work-_____ literary-assistant-_____ or although would
proof-reader-_____.] (III-129)

8   А е́сли жена́ сжига́ет себя́ на погреба́льном костре́ му́жа, она́ удоста́ивается
почти́ религио́зного поклоне́ния.
[But if wife-_____ burns self-_____ on funeral pyre-_____ husband-_____, she-
_____ receives almost religious worship-_____.] (III-145)

9   У меня́ есть твёрдое убежде́ние: пролива́я кровь, сча́стья для други́х не
добьёшься, а себе́ жизнь испо́ртишь.
[At me-_____ firm conviction-_____: pouring-out blood-_____, happiness-_____
for others-_____ not secure, but self-_____ life-_____ ruin.] (III-160)

10   Запо́мнить бы мне э́ти их ли́ца.
[Memorize would me-_____ these their faces-_____.] (III-173)

Mixed Case
Exercise 6
Level III

Mixed Case Exercise 6, Level III

*Identify the case uses in the sentences below and explain why those cases are used
and how they interact with each other. Provide your own English translation of the
sentence and compare it to the translation in the key.*

1   Эсто́нские роя́листы восхищены́ англи́йской мона́рхией и, в ча́стности,
при́нцем Эдва́рдом, явля́ющимся, с их то́чки зре́ния, превосхо́дным и
соверше́нным во всех отноше́ниях при́нцем.
[Estonian royalists-_____ delighted-_____ English monarchy-_____ and, in par-
ticular-_____, prince Edward-_____, being-_____, from their point-_____ view-
_____, superb-_____ and perfect-_____ in all relations-_____ prince-_____.] (III-
13)

2   Мно́го говори́тся о том, что журнали́стика для литера́тора — заня́тие
па́губное.
[A-lot-_____ is-said about that-_____, that journalism-_____ for writer-_____ —
profession pernicious-_____.] (III-39)

3   Но мы, сла́ва Бо́гу, защищены́ от э́того с де́тства.
[But we-_____, glory-_____ God-_____, protected-_____ from that-_____ from
childhood-_____.] (III-59)

4   В стране́ нахо́дятся деся́тки ты́сяч бе́женцев из Либе́рии, испы́тывающих
крайню́ю нужду́ в продово́льствии и предме́тах пе́рвой необходи́мости.
[In country-_____ are tens-_____ thousands-_____ refugees-_____ from Liberia-
_____, experiencing-_____ extreme need-_____ in food-_____ and items-_____
first aid-_____.] (III-77)

5   Невдалеке́ от меня́ сиде́л оди́н из танки́стов, ростовча́нин, ро́слый хму́рый
ста́рший лейтена́нт.
[Not-far from me-_____ sat one-_____ from tank-crew-members-_____, Rostovian-
_____, tall gloomy older lieutenant-_____.] (III-100)

6   Моше́нничество — э́то ли́бо завладе́ние ли́чным иму́ществом гра́ждан, ли́бо
приобрете́ние пра́ва на завладе́ние иму́ществом путём обма́на и́ли
злоупотребле́ния дове́рием.
[Swindling-_____ — that-_____ either taking-possession-_____ personal property-
_____ citizens-_____, or acqusition-_____ right-_____ on taking-possession-_____
property-_____ way-_____ deceit-_____ or abuse-_____ trust-_____.] (III-118)

7   Хозя́йка ланчоне́та ми́ссис Бо́но с гро́хотом поднима́ет желе́зную решётку.
[Owner-_____ luncheonette-_____ Mrs. Bono-_____ with crash-_____ lifts iron
grill-_____.] (III-130)

8   Фонд Раджи́ва Га́нди, оспо́ванный е́ю, помога́ет де́тям, же́нщинам и бе́дным
и стал са́мой влия́тельной неправи́тельственной организа́цией в И́ндии.
[Fund-_____ Rajiva Gandi-_____, founded-_____ her-_____, helps children-_____,
women-_____ and poor-_____ and became most influential non-governmental or-
ganization-_____ in India-_____.] (III-146)

9   Под землёй че́рез не́сколько сантиме́тров лёд, ве́чная мерзлота́, све́рху снег.
[Under ground-_____ through several-_____ centimeters-_____ ice-_____, eternal
frost-_____, on-top snow-_____.] (III-161)

10 Он уда́рился гру́дью о водопрово́дную трубу́, кото́рая проходи́ла по газо́ну.
[He-_____ hit chest-_____ against water pipe-_____, which-_____ ran along lawn-
_____.] (III-175)

Mixed Case Exercise 7, Level III

*Put the following words and phrases into the necessary case. Provide your own
English translation of the sentence and compare it to the translation in the key.*

1   Пе́рвые 169 специа́льпо отобранные военнослу́жащие и доброво́льцы уже́
на́чали специа́льная четырёхнеде́льная подгото́вка, чтобы в слу́чай
необходи́мость бы́ть гото́вые отпра́виться в любо́й райо́н плане́та под фла́г
ООН. (III-14)

2　Снача́ла <u>мы</u> пока́зывали <u>каньо́н</u>, <u>что́-то</u> вро́де <u>уще́лье</u>. (III-41)

3　<u>Росси́йская власть</u> демонстри́рует <u>по́лное бесси́лие</u>, <u>неспосо́бность</u> защити́ть <u>свои́ гра́ждане</u> и <u>гото́вность</u> сле́по идти́ на <u>по́вод</u> Алекса́ндр Лукаше́нко, принима́я <u>его́ аргумента́ция</u> и <u>его́ пра́вила игра́</u>. (III-62)

4　В <u>англи́йский го́род</u> Во́берн <u>организа́торы</u> <u>сбор</u> <u>сре́дства</u> в <u>фонд</u> <u>подде́ржка</u> <u>кампа́ния</u> по <u>сохране́ние ди́кая приро́да</u> в <u>стра́ны</u> <u>А́зия</u> вы́вели на <u>у́лицы</u> <u>три слоны́</u> из <u>ме́стный зоопа́рк</u>. (III-78)

5　Тут спра́ва из <u>сара́й</u> вы́бежал <u>молодо́й челове́к</u> и, перепры́гнув через <u>коры́то</u>, на <u>кото́рое</u> среди́ <u>помо́и</u> лежа́ла <u>свинья́</u>, с <u>крик</u> побежа́л к <u>воро́ты</u>. (III-101)

6　<u>Сле́дствие</u> ну́жно бы́ло доказа́ть, что <u>она́</u> завладе́ла <u>чужо́е иму́щество</u>. (III-119)

7　<u>Я</u> перепи́сываю в <u>дневни́к</u> <u>результа́ты вчера́шний о́пыт</u>, укла́дываю в <u>коро́бка</u> <u>бро́шенные вчера́ образцы́</u>, рву и выки́дываю <u>черновики́</u> с <u>расчёты</u>. (III-132)

8　В <u>опублико́ванное</u> у <u>вы</u> <u>интервью́</u> с <u>мини́стр</u> <u>се́льское хозя́йство</u> и <u>продово́льствие</u> ска́зано, что <u>Росси́я</u> наконе́ц-то бу́дет не покупа́ть <u>зерно́</u>, а, наоборо́т, мо́жет быть, продава́ть. (III-147)

9　<u>Он</u> до́лго пил из <u>ведро́</u>, пролива́я пря́мо на <u>гимнастёрка</u>, на <u>грудь</u>, пото́м сле́по шагну́л в <u>сторона́</u> и, не выбира́я где, свали́лся в <u>кусты́</u> спать. (III-162)

10　Пото́м <u>ка́ждый раз</u>, где бы <u>они́</u> ни́ были, <u>он</u> <u>она́</u> <u>глаз</u> заце́пит и де́ржит, как <u>ко́шка цыпля́</u>. (III-176)

Mixed Case Exercise 8, Level III

Put the following words and phrases into the necessary case. Provide your own English translation of the sentence and compare it to the translation in the key.

1　<u>Он</u> всегда́ приноси́л с <u>себя́</u> <u>буты́лка вино́</u>, выпива́л <u>она́ оди́н</u>, <u>вдова́ то вре́мя</u> укла́дывала <u>ребёнок</u> спать, нареза́ла <u>како́й-то просто́й сала́т</u>, что бы́ло под <u>рука́</u>, то ли вари́ла <u>яйцо́</u> вкруту́ю, коро́че, хлопота́ла, но не о́чень. (III-16)

2　Кро́ме <u>официа́льные уча́стники</u> <u>до́лжен</u> съе́хаться <u>так называ́емые го́сти</u>. (III-43)

3　Неуже́ли <u>росси́йская власть</u> по́лностью утра́тила <u>уваже́ние</u> не то́лько к <u>свои́ гра́ждане</u>, но и к <u>сама́ себя́</u>? (III-65)

4   Óчень мóжет стáться, что <u>жизнь задýман</u>, как <u>дорóга</u> к <u>вершúна</u>. Дойдý ли <u>я</u> до <u>своя вершúна</u> úли устáну и вернýсь, чтóбы лечь на <u>дивáн</u>? (III-82)

5   <u>Взяв я</u> в <u>своя грýппа</u> и поручúв <u>я</u>, <u>полгóда</u> назáд, <u>испытáния нóвый материáл</u>, <u>дирéктор</u>, конéчно, рисковáл. (III-102)

6   <u>Отдéл спорт</u> завéдовал <u>добродýшный, бессловéсный человéк</u>. Он неизмéнно пребывáл в <u>глубóкое самозабвéние</u>. По <u>темперáмент</u> был <u>рáвен мёртвая собáка</u>. (III-121)

7   <u>Я</u> мóлча вытáскиваю <u>рукá</u> из-под <u>одеяло</u> и протягиваю к <u>он</u>. (III-133)

8   <u>Человéк</u>, <u>совершúвший сáмый кровáвый террористúческий акт</u> за <u>вся истóрия Амéрика</u>, был наконéц <u>приговорён</u> к <u>смéртная казнь</u>. (III-148)

9   <u>Свя́занные сзáди посинéвшие рýки</u> при <u>э́то</u> задирáлись квéрху; казáлось, <u>он</u> мóлится <u>какóй-то необы́чный спóсоб</u>. (III-163)

10   Со <u>врéмя</u> станóвится очевúдно, что с <u>сáмое начáло</u> былá <u>сдéлан ошúбка</u>: вмéсто <u>дешёвый электромеханúческий замóк</u>, лýчше установúть в <u>дверь электромагнúтный замóк</u>! (III-177)

Mixed Case Exercise 9, Level III

Put the following words and phrases into the necessary case. Provide your own English translation of the sentence and compare it to the translation in the key.

1   У <u>я</u> сложúлось <u>впечатлéние</u>, что о <u>токúйская декларáция 1993 год</u>, где бы́ло <u>дан обещáние</u> решúть <u>территориáльная проблéма</u>, в <u>Россúя</u> как-то не вспоминáют. (III-20)

2   Сейчáс <u>газéта я</u> опротúвела, но тогдá <u>я</u> был <u>пóлон энтузиáзм</u>. (III-44)

3   <u>Президéнт центр хирургúя</u> нáзвал <u>чýдо то</u>, что <u>семидесятишестилéтний человéк</u>, <u>перенёсший сорокоминýтная клинúческая смерть</u>, живёт ужé <u>две недéля</u>. (III-67)

4   <u>Я</u> казáлось, что, помúмо <u>любóвь</u> ко <u>я</u>, у <u>ты дóлжен</u> быть <u>чýвство долг</u>, но <u>ты</u> считáл, что <u>ничтó</u> не <u>дóлжен</u>, тогдá и <u>я ты ничтó</u> не <u>дóлжен</u>. (III-83)

5   <u>Кýхня</u> превратúлась в <u>электрúческое пóле</u> с <u>разнозаряжённые частúцы</u>, <u>котóрые</u> стáлкиваются. (III-104)

6   <u>Религиóзные семинáры</u> проходúли в <u>церкóвная библиотéка</u>. Там собирáлись <u>правослáвные, иудаúсты, мусульмáне, катóлики</u>. <u>Кáждая</u> из <u>грýппа</u> бы́ло <u>вы́делен отдéльное помещéние</u>. (III-123)

7   Жа́лость и <u>тёплая вода́</u> де́лают <u>своё де́ло</u> — из-под <u>душ</u> <u>я</u> выхожу́ <u>подобре́вшая и освежённая</u>. (III-134)

8   <u>Ли́ца</u> <u>все сиде́вшие</u> в <u>зал</u> окамене́ли. (III-149)

9   <u>Она́</u> утыка́ется <u>голова́</u>, <u>рот</u> <u>он</u> в <u>грудь</u>; хо́чется <u>слова́</u> <u>утеше́ние</u>... (III-164)

10   <u>Во́ры</u> залеза́ют в <u>кварти́ры</u> <u>ве́рхние этажи́</u> с <u>кры́ша</u>, по <u>верёвка</u>, <u>привя́занная</u> к <u>анте́нна</u>. (III-178)

Mixed Case Exercise 10 Level III

Mixed Case Exercise 10, Level III
Put the following words and phrases into the necessary case. Provide your own English translation of the sentence and compare it to the translation in the key.

1   На <u>неда́вная конфере́нция</u> <u>Организа́ция</u> <u>азиатскотихоокеа́нское экономи́ческое сотру́дничество</u>, <u>участники</u> <u>кото́рая</u> произво́дят <u>полови́на мирово́й валово́й проду́кт</u>, <u>Росси́я</u> не уча́ствовала. (III-21)

2   В <u>кулуа́ры</u> <u>писа́тель</u> окружи́ла <u>толпа́</u> <u>единомы́шленники</u> и <u>почита́тели</u>. (III-45)

3   <u>Реанимато́логи</u> беспреры́вно де́лали <u>прямо́й масса́ж</u> <u>се́рдце</u>, и все со́рок <u>мину́т</u> <u>клини́ческая смерть</u> <u>кровь</u> поступа́ла в <u>головно́й мозг</u>. (III-68)

4   <u>Я</u> по́днял <u>рука́</u> и потяну́л на <u>себя́</u> <u>чемода́н</u>.   Све́рху лежа́ли <u>раке́ты</u> для <u>бадминто́н</u>. <u>Они́</u> пое́хали и упа́ли на́ <u>пол</u>. (III-86)

5   <u>Де́вочка</u> смотре́ла в <u>окно́</u>, и в <u>её све́тлые глаза́</u> отража́лись <u>дере́вья</u>, <u>дома́</u>, <u>не́бо</u>. <u>Глаза́</u> бы́ли <u>пёстрые</u> и <u>ра́зные</u>, в <u>зави́симость</u> от <u>то</u>, что бы́ло за <u>окно́</u>. (III-105)

6   <u>Поэ́т</u> возврати́лся к <u>стол</u>. У <u>он</u> бы́ло <u>ра́достное</u>, соверше́нно <u>измени́вшееся</u> от <u>это</u> <u>лицо́</u>. <u>Он</u> поклони́лся <u>актри́са</u>. (III-124)

7   У <u>фи́рма</u> бо́лее <u>двести</u> <u>совме́стные предприя́тия</u> по <u>весь мир</u>, где успе́шно тру́дятся <u>деся́тки</u> <u>ты́сячи</u> <u>са́мые высококвалифици́рованные специали́сты</u> <u>ра́зные национа́льности</u>. (III-136)

8   Вско́ре по́сле <u>оглаше́ние</u> <u>реше́ние</u> <u>суд</u>, во вре́мя <u>чте́ние</u> <u>кото́рое</u> <u>террори́ст</u> был абсолю́тно <u>споко́ен</u>, <u>он</u> перевели́ в <u>тюрьма́</u> с макси́мально <u>уси́ленный режи́м безопа́сность</u> в <u>штат Колора́до</u>. (III-151)

9   А <u>я</u> так вот подхожу́ одна́жды к <u>мясни́к</u>, говорю́, я <u>килогра́мм</u> три <u>хоро́шее мя́со</u> бы. И подмигну́л <u>он</u>. (III-165)

10   Соверши́в кра́жа, во́ры покида́ют подъе́зд уже́ неузнава́емые: они́
      "переки́дываются" оде́жда на бег, в лифт. (III-179)

Mixed Case Exercise 11, Level III
Put the following words and phrases into the necessary case. Provide your own
English translation of the sentence and compare it to the translation in the key.

1   У она́ лицо́ соверше́нно ма́ленькая де́вочка, и э́то де́тское ли́чико нале́плен
     на ме́лкая, как ты́ковка, голо́вка. (III-23)

2   Дека́брьское у́тро про́шлый год я отосла́л це́лая па́чка расска́зы в журна́л
     "Но́вый мир". Открове́нно говоря́, я не пита́л иллю́зии. (III-46)

3   Де́ти ся́дут за па́рты, как обы́чно, в пе́рвый день о́сень, а слу́хи появи́лись в
     связь с предстоя́щие торжества́ в честь юбиле́й го́род. (III-69)

4   По-мо́ему, он не понима́л, что э́то ко́нчится, хотя́ и сказа́л, что обя́зан лечь
     поперёк дверь и я не пусти́ть, но понима́ет, что тогда́ я вы́прыгну в окно́.
     (III-89)

5   И тут на её горизо́нт возни́к знамени́тый эстра́дный певе́ц. Сейча́с его́ и́мя
     забы́т, но в шестидеся́тые го́ды он был популя́рнее Сина́тра. (III-106)

6   Стоя́л в паску́дная о́чередь, толка́лся, ждал что́-то. И вдруг пью вино́ с
     очарова́тельная же́нщина. (III-107)

7   В ию́ль в ход визи́т в Москва́ мини́стр иностра́нные дела́ Великобрита́ния
     заверши́л обсужде́ние прое́кт двухсторо́ннее соглаше́ние по сотру́дничество
     в борьба́ с организо́ванная престу́пность. (III-138)

8   По род своя́ рабо́та я каждодне́вно ста́лкиваюсь с лю́ди, пострада́вшие от
     уку́сы живо́тные. (III-142)

9   Накану́не швейца́рская встре́ча противоре́чие ме́жду общи́ны на Ки́пр
     неожи́данно обостри́лись: шесто́е а́вгуст никто́, кро́ме Анкара́, не
     при́знанная <<Туре́цкая респу́блика Се́верный Кипр>> и материко́вая
     Ту́рция подписа́ли соглаше́ние об организа́ция так называ́емый
     <<интеграцио́нный сове́т>>. (III-152)

10   У я бы́ло два-три пла́тье, а одна́жды не́ было чулки́, чтобы пойти́ в го́сти на
     Но́вый год, и тогда́ я шов нарисова́ла черни́ла на го́лая нога́. (III-180)

Mixed Case Exercise 12, Level III
Put the following words and phrases into the necessary case. Provide your own English translation of the sentence and compare it to the translation in the key.

1   <u>Растро́ганный</u> <u>её</u> <u>явле́ние</u>, <u>Вади́м</u> да́же не спроси́л, отку́да <u>она́</u> изве́стен <u>но́мер</u> <u>его́ телефо́н</u>. (III-27)

2   Тогда́ почему́ же <u>я</u> ощуща́ю <u>себя́</u> на <u>грань</u> <u>физи́ческая катастро́фа</u>? Отку́да у <u>я</u> <u>чу́вство</u> <u>безнадёжная жи́зненная неприго́дность</u>? В <u>что</u> <u>причи́на моя́ тоска́</u>? (III-48)

3   <u>Мини́стр</u> <u>вну́тренние дела́</u> отпра́вили в <u>отста́вка</u> ещё в <u>ию́нь</u> за <u>соде́йствие криминáльная экономи́ка</u>. (III-70)

4   <u>Реше́ние</u> о <u>приня́тие</u> <u>э́то госуда́рство</u>, <u>населе́ние</u> <u>кото́рое</u> насчи́тывает <u>шестна́дцать ты́сяча челове́к</u>, в <u>ООН</u> <u>Генера́льная Ассамбле́я</u> приняла́ без <u>голосова́ние</u>, <u>никто́</u> не возража́л. (III-90)

5   По́мню <u>огро́мный, краси́вый, мра́чный Довла́тов</u>, <u>выходя́щий</u> с <u>то́лстая па́пка</u> в <u>ру́ки</u> из <u>журна́л</u> <u>“Нева́”</u>. (III-108)

6   <u>Япо́нская компа́ния</u> <u>пейджинговая связь</u> выпуска́ет в <u>прода́жа</u> <u>недороги́е</u> пейджеры, специа́льно <u>предназна́ченные</u> для <u>переда́ча</u> <u>коди́рованные сообще́ния</u> <u>де́ти</u>. (III-140)

7   <u>Спортсме́ны</u>, <u>го́ды</u> <u>живу́щие</u> в <u>экстрема́льный режи́м</u>, <u>во́лен</u> выбира́ть <u>себя́</u> <u>страна́</u> для <u>жи́тельство</u>, <u>гаранти́рующая</u> <u>они́</u> те усло́вия, в <u>кото́рые</u> <u>они́</u> хо́чется жить. (III-143)

8   <u>Фи́рмы</u>, <u>наруша́ющие</u> <u>э́то распоряже́ние</u>, бу́дут лиша́ться <u>лице́нзия</u> на <u>своя́ де́ятельность</u>. (III-153)

9   В <u>телефо́нный разгово́р</u> в <u>четве́рг</u> <u>они́</u> бы́ли <u>еди́н</u> в <u>то</u>, что <u>госуда́рство Содру́жество Незави́симые Госуда́рства</u> на́до реши́ть <u>ряд</u> <u>вопро́сы</u>, <u>свя́занные</u> с <u>укрепле́ние</u> <u>ю́жные рубежи́ Содру́жество</u>. (III-166)

10   Тепе́рь <u>я</u> понима́ю, что в <u>гражда́нская война́</u> не быва́ет <u>пра́вые и винова́тые</u>, а есть <u>лю́ди</u>, по-ра́зному <u>ви́дящие</u> <u>бу́дущее своя́ страна́</u>. (III-181)

Mixed Case Exercise 13, Level III
Put the following words and phrases into the necessary case. Provide your own English translation of the sentence and compare it to the translation in the key.

1   Сего́дня <u>равнопра́вие</u> <u>психи́чески больны́е</u>, <u>их пра́во</u> на <u>“со́бственное мне́ние”</u> сво́дится к <u>ра́вное</u> для <u>все пра́во</u> быть <u>обма́нутый</u>. (III-28)

2 В <u>его движе́ния</u> — <u>изя́щество</u> <u>ю́ный князь</u>. (III-51)

3 <u>Прави́тельство</u> то́лько что объяви́ло о <u>вы́пуск большо́й паке́т облига́ции</u> на <u>о́бщая су́мма</u> <u>три миллиа́рда до́лларов</u>, <u>при́званный</u> компенси́ровать <u>аргенти́нцы поте́ря их ро́дственники</u> во вре́мя <u>так называ́емая <<гря́зная война́>></u>. (III-71)

4 Одна́ко далеко́ не <u>все фи́льмы</u>, <u>предста́вленные</u> на <u>пари́жский фестива́ль</u>, <u>окра́шен траги́ческий и́ли драмати́ческий па́фос</u>. (III-92)

5 <u>Анастаси́я</u> прие́хала в <u>Сорре́нто</u> ещё в <u>нача́ло а́вгуст</u>, но <u>Мари́на</u>, не получа́я от <u>она́ изве́стии</u>, <u>два́дцать четвёртое а́вгуст</u> обрати́лась с <u>запро́с</u> к <u>Го́рький</u>. (III-110)

6 Есть, по-мо́ему, <u>уда́чное реше́ние пробле́ма захороне́ние те́ло Ле́нин</u>, кото́рая сего́дня столь боле́зненно воспринима́ется <u>разли́чные круги́ росси́йское о́бщество</u>. (III-141)

7 <u>Руководи́тели фонд</u> пре́жде неоднокра́тно утвержда́ли, что <u>они́</u> подде́рживают <u>некие свя́зи</u> с <u>диссиде́нтские элеме́нты</u> внутри́ <u>куби́нские вооружённые си́лы</u>, <u>кото́рые</u> я́кобы уже́ созре́ли для <u>переворо́т</u>. (III-144)

8 <u>Возмущённые роди́тели дире́ктор</u> обеща́л вско́ре найти́ <u>учителя́</u>, но в <u>середи́на год</u> призна́лся в <u>своё бесси́лие</u> и предложи́л призва́ть на <u>по́мощь ча́стная фи́рма</u>. (III-155)

9 По <u>его́ слова́</u>, в <u>понеде́льник у́тро</u> из <u>Минфи́н</u> пришло́ <u>распоряже́ние</u>, согла́сно <u>кото́рое выделя́емые де́ньги</u> бу́дет е́ле-е́ле хвата́ть на <u>зарпла́ты сотру́дники</u>. (III-167)

10 С <u>по́мощь ме́стные стару́шки</u>, <u>вы́сыпавшие</u> по́сле <u>слу́жба</u> из <u>це́рковь</u>, отыска́ли под <u>снег его́ моги́ла</u>. (III-182)

Multi-Case Preposition Exercise 1, Level III
Choose the correct preposition and case from the choices below.

1 Предприя́тие вы́пустит шестна́дцать ты́сяч маши́н, оди́ннадцать ты́сяч из кото́рых реализу́ются <u>за грани́ца/за грани́цу/за грани́цей</u>.
The enterprise will produce sixteen thousand cars, eleven thousand of which will be sold abroad. (III-3)

2   Áня всерьёз купи́ла биле́т <u>на пра́здник/на пра́зднике</u> Но́вого го́да, не
подозрева́я <u>о то/о том</u>, что <u>на э́тот пра́здник/на э́том пра́зднике</u> должны́
быть таки́е же одино́чки, как она́ сама́, те, кого́ не при́няли, отве́ргли
студе́нческие вечери́нки.
Anya bought the ticket for the New Year's party in all seriousness, not suspecting
that at this party would be the same kind of lonely women like herself, those who
weren't accepted, and who were spurned at the student parties. (III-15)

3   Два́дцать лет наза́д она́ то́же была́ влюблена́ <u>в одного́/в одно́м</u> арти́ста до
поте́ри пу́льса, и весь их класс сходи́л <u>с ум/с ума́/с умо́м</u>.
Twenty years ago she also was in love with an artist, to the point of losing her pulse,
and their whole class was going crazy. (III-33)

4   <u>На её ме́сто/На её ме́сте</u> я поста́вила бы <u>на сто́лик/на сто́лике</u> буты́лку,
положи́ла бу́лочку и <u>со все́ ноги/со всех ног/со все́ми нога́ми</u> бро́силась <u>на
"Мосфи́льм"/на "Мосфи́льме"</u> снима́ться <u>в гла́вную ро́ль/в гла́вной ро́ли</u>.
In her place, I would put the bottle on the table, lay down the roll, and would run at
full speed to "Mosfilm" to be filmed in a starring role. (III-60)

5   Мы стои́м <u>с неё/с ней</u> <u>по ра́зные концы́/по ра́зным конца́м</u> го́рода, как два
бара́на <u>на мо́стик/на мо́стике</u> горба́том, ка́ждый <u>со свою́ пра́вду/со свое́й
пра́вды/со свое́й пра́вдой</u>.
She and I are on different ends of the city, like two rams on a hump-backed bridge
— each with his own truth. (III-79)

6   Тут спра́ва из сара́я вы́бежал молодо́й челове́к и, перепры́гнув через коры́то,
<u>на кото́рое/на кото́ром</u> среди́ помо́ев лежа́ла свинья́, <u>с крик/с кри́ка/с кри́ком</u>
побежа́л к воро́там.
Just to the right a young man ran out of the barn, jumped over the trough in which a
pig lay in the slop, and ran up twards the gate with a shout. (III-101)

7   Раздраже́ние Го́рького, кото́рое чу́вствуется <u>во весь тон/во всём то́не</u> э́того
письма́, несомне́нно отрази́лось и <u>на его́ характери́стику/на его́
характери́стике</u> тво́рчества Мари́ны Цвета́евой.
Gorky's irritation, which is felt all through the tone of this letter, was certainly reflected in his description of Marina Tsvetaeva's work. (III-112)

8   У́мер он <u>во Влади́мир/во Влади́мире</u>, хорони́ли мы его́ <u>на мою́ ро́дину/на
мое́й ро́дине</u> в <u>Росла́вль/в Росла́вле</u>, где похоро́нена моя́ родня́.
He died in Vladimir, and we buried him in my native soil in Roslavl where my kin
are buried. (III-120)

9   В июль/В июле в ход/в ходе визита в Москву/в Москве министр иностранных дел Великобритании завершил обсуждение проекта двухстороннего соглашения по сотрудничество/по сотрудничеству в борьбу/в борьбе с организованную преступность/с организованной преступности/с организованной преступностью.
In the course of his July visit to Moscow, the foreign affairs minister of Great Britain completed the discussion of a project of bilateral agreement for cooperation in the struggle against organized crime. (III-138)

10   Вскоре после оглашения решения суда, во время/во времени чтения которого террорист был абсолютно спокоен, его перевели в тюрьму/в тюрьме с максимально усиленный режим/с максимально усиленного режима/с максимально усиленным режимом безопасности в штат/в штате Колорадо.
Soon after the announcement of the court's decision, during the reading of which the terrorist was absolutely calm, they took him to a maximum security prison in the state of Colorado. (III-151)

11   Со время/Со времени/Со временем становится очевидно, что с самое начало/с самого начала/с самым началом была сделана ошибка: вместо дешёвого электромеханического замка, лучше установить в дверь/в двери электромагнитный замок!
With time it becomes obvious, that a mistake was made from the very beginning: instead of a cheap electromechanical lock, it is better to install an electromagnetic lock in the door! (III-177)

Multi-Case Preposition Exercise 2, Level III
Choose the correct preposition and case from the choices below.

Multi-Case
Preposition
Exercise 2
Level III

1   В создавшиеся условия/В создавшихся условиях режим стремится различными путями внести раскол в оппозиционные ряды/в оппозиционных рядах.
Given the present conditions, the regime is trying various means to introduce division among the ranks of the opposition. (III-8)

2   Городу это было лестно, а биологам — полезно собраться всем вместе и доложить о свой дела/о своих делах, а заодно посмотреть Францию.
It was flattering for the city, and for the biologists, and useful to gather together to give reports on their affairs, and at the same time to visit France. (III-22)

3   При взгляде на эту комнату/на этой комнате с лежащий/с лежащего/с лежащим посредине на пол/на полу трупом старой женщины почему-то возникала ассоциация с Достоевского/с Достоевским.
At the sight of that room with the corpse of an old woman lying in the middle of the room, an association with Dostoevsky somehow sprung up. (III-34)

4   Подойдём к ситуа́ции стро́го <u>с то́чку</u>/<u>с то́чки</u>/<u>с то́чкой</u> зре́ния междунаро́дного пра́ва, оста́вив <u>на вре́мя</u>/<u>на вре́мени</u> <u>в сто́рону</u>/<u>в стороне́</u> специфи́ческий хара́ктер взаимоотноше́ний Москвы́ <u>с белору́сского президе́нта</u>/<u>с белору́сским президе́нтом</u>.
Let's approach the situation strictly from the point of view of international law, leaving aside for the time being the specific character of the mutual relations between Moscow and the Belorussian president. (III-63)

5   Весь дом находи́лся <u>под терро́р</u>/<u>под терро́ром</u> но́вого челове́ка, кото́рый хоте́л переина́чить су́тки <u>по со́бственное усмотре́ние</u>/<u>по со́бственному усмотре́нию</u>.
The whole house was being terrorized by the new person, who wanted to alter the daily rhythm according to his own discretion. (III-87)

6   Спуска́юсь вниз, толка́ю дверь <u>на пружи́ну</u>/<u>на пружи́не</u>, навстре́чу мне вырыва́ется волна́ шу́ма, но я преодолева́ю её и прохожу́ <u>за стекля́нная перегоро́дка</u>/<u>за стекля́нную перегоро́дку</u>/<u>за стекля́нной перегоро́дкой</u>.
I go downstairs, push the swinging door, and a wave of noise rushes out toward me, but I overcome it and walk over behind the glass barrier. (III-103)

7   Коро́че говоря́, речь идёт <u>о норма́льный проце́сс</u>/<u>о норма́льном проце́ссе</u> борьбы́ мировы́х сил <u>за влия́ние</u>/<u>за влия́нием</u> и <u>за выжива́ние</u>/<u>за выжива́нием</u>.
To put it briefly, the subject is the normal way in which the world's powers struggle for influence and survival. (III-115)

8   <u>Под э́тот аккомпанеме́нт</u>/<u>Под э́тим аккомпанеме́нтом</u> я потихо́ньку перета́скиваю все свёртки к нам <u>в лаборато́рию</u>/<u>в лаборато́рии</u>.
To this accompaniment I noiselessly drag all of the bundles to our laboratory. (III-131)

9   Начина́я <u>с сентя́брь</u>/<u>с сентября́</u>/<u>с сентябрём</u> япо́нкам не придётся крича́ть из окна́, зазыва́я свои́х дете́й <u>на обе́д</u>/<u>на обе́де</u>.
Starting in September, the Japanese women won't have to cry out from the window when summoning their children to dinner. (III-139)

10   Жизнь же <u>в Арме́нию</u>/<u>в Арме́нии</u>, и <u>в ча́стность</u>/<u>в ча́стности</u> <u>в Ерева́н</u>/<u>в Ерева́не</u>, переста́в быть невыноси́мой, перешла́ <u>в катего́рию</u>/<u>в катего́рии</u> терпи́мой и уже́ подбира́ется к отме́тке <<бли́зко к челове́ческой>>.
Life in Armenia, and in part in Yerevan, having stopped being unbearable, has moved into the category of bearable and already is approaching the mark "close to human". (III-154)

Multi-Case Preposition Exercise 3, Level III
Choose the correct preposition and case from the choices below.

1   Психи́ческими неду́гами <u>во весь их спе́ктр/во всём их спе́ктре</u> си́льно пью́щие поражены́ <u>в два ра́за/в двух ра́зах</u> ча́ще, чем популя́ция <u>в це́лое/в це́лом</u>.
    Heavy drinkers are afflicted with the whole range of psychiatric illnesses twice as frequently as the population as a whole. (III-10)

2   Ра́ньше он приходи́л к нам <u>с жа́лобы/с жа́лоб/с жа́лобами</u> <u>на сосе́дей/на сосе́дях</u>, отравля́ющих из-за сте́нки пи́щу и обжига́ющих его́ че́рез потоло́к неви́димыми луча́ми.
    He used to come to us with complaints about his neighbors, who poisoned his food through the wall and burned him through the ceiling with invisible rays. (III-26)

3   Слон был похо́ж <u>на грома́дную копну́/на грома́дной копне́</u> се́на.
    The elephant looked like an enormous hay-stack. (III-47)

4   Де́ти ся́дут <u>за па́рты/за па́ртами</u>, как обы́чно, <u>в пе́рвый день/в пе́рвом дне</u> о́сени, а слу́хи появи́лись <u>в связь/в связи́</u> <u>с предстоя́щие торжества́/с предстоя́щих торже́ств/с предстоя́щими торжества́ми</u> <u>в честь/в чести́</u> юбиле́я го́рода.
    Children start school on the first day of fall, as usual, but the rumors got started in connection with the upcoming festivities for the city's anniversary. (III-69)

5   Меня́ <u>в четы́рнадцать лет/в четы́рнадцати года́х</u> понесло́ <u>в комсомо́л/в комсомо́ле</u>, <u>в кото́рый/в кото́ром</u> я не нашла́ никако́й революцио́нной рома́нтики.
    At age fourteen I was brought to the communist youth league, where I didn't find any revolutionary romance. (III-88)

6   По́мню огро́много, краси́вого, мра́чного Довла́това, выходя́щего <u>с то́лстую па́пку/с то́лстой па́пки/с то́лстой па́пкой</u> <u>в ру́ки/в рука́х</u> из журна́ла "Нева́."
    I remember a huge, handsome, gloomy Dovlatov, emerging with a thick file in his hands from the journal "Neva." (III-108)

7   Вы бы́ли её адвока́том <u>с тот моме́нт/с того́ моме́нта/с тем моме́нтом</u>, как <u>на неё/на ней</u> завели́ уголо́вное де́ло, и практи́чески до оконча́ния сле́дствия.
    You were her attorney from the moment a criminal case was brought against her and nearly until the end of the investigation. (III-117)

8   Сейча́с он живёт вме́сте <u>с жену́ и сынове́й/с жены́ и сынове́й/с жено́й и сыновья́ми</u> в Мона́ко, одна́ко склоня́ется к тому́, что́бы перебра́ться <u>в Шве́цию/в Шве́ции</u>.
    Now he lives together with his wife and sons in Monaco, however he is leaning towards moving to Sweden. (III-137)

9   Лица всех сидевших <u>в зал</u>/<u>в зале</u> окаменели.

The faces of all those sitting in the hall turned to stone. (III-149)

10   Соглашение предусматривает создание <u>на базу</u>/<u>на базе</u> "Киноцентра" совместного предприятия, <u>в которое</u>/<u>в котором</u> каждой из заинтересованных сторон будет принадлежать <u>по пятьдесят процентов акций</u>/<u>по пятидесяти процентам акциям</u>.

The agreement envisions the creation of a combined enterprise on the scale of a Cineplex, in which each of the interested sides will have around fifty percent of the shares. (III-168)

English Index

[All numbers refer to page numbers in the text. Page numbers followed by T refer to items appearing in tables.]

H

I

Russian Index

успе́х(и) в 'success in' +LOC, 142T
устра́иваться/устро́иться 'get a job (as)' +INST, 38T
уступа́ть/уступи́ть 'yield to' +DAT, 103T
усту́пка 'concession, compromise' +DAT, 103T
у́тром 'in the morning', 22
уча́ствовать в 'participate in' +LOC, 142T
уча́ствующий в 'participant in' +LOC, 142T
уча́стие в 'participation in' +LOC, 142T
уча́щийся 'student' +DAT, 103T
учи́ться/научи́ться 'study' +DAT, 103T
ущéрб 'detriment' +DAT, 94T

Х

хвали́ться/похвали́ться 'boast of' +INST, 33T
хвата́ть 'suffice, be enough' +DAT/+GEN, 95T, 131T
хло́пать/хло́пнуть две́рью 'slam a door', 26T
ходи́ть на (лы́жах/паруса́х) 'go (skiing/sailing, etc.)'
        +LOC, 147T
ходьба́ на (лы́жах/паруса́х) 'going (skiing/sailing, etc.)'
        +LOC, 147T
хоте́ть/захоте́ть 'want' +GEN or +ACC, 124T
хоте́ться/захоте́ться 'feel like, want to' +DAT, 100T;
        +GEN, 124T

Ч

чем X, тем Y 'the more X...the more Y', 29
чéрез 'across, after; in, at the end of; through, every other'
        +ACC, 54T, 75, 77, 78-80, 79T
    'across, after; in, at the end of' +ACC in domain of
        space, 54T, 78
    'after, in' +ACC in time running forward expressions,
        79-80, 79T
    'every other' +ACC in domain of space, 78
    'through' +ACC with various activities, 54T, 75, 77
чéрез посре́дство 'by means of' +GEN, 129T
чéрез стро́чку 'skip lines, double-spaced', 78
числи́ться 'be listed (as)' +INST, 38T
чи́слиться в 'be counted among' +LOC, 142T
чита́ть/прочита́ть (вслух) 'read (out loud) to' +DAT, 88T
что за Y-NOM 'what kind of Y is that?', 14
что тако́е Y-NOM 'what is Y', 14
чу́вствовать/почу́вствовать себя́ 'feel (like)' +INST, 38T
чужда́ться 'shun, stand aloof' +GEN, 118T
чу́ждый 'alien' +DAT, 94T

Ш

ша́гом 'at a walk', 28

Э

эконо́мить/сэконо́мить на 'economize on, save on'
        +LOC, 147T
эконо́мия на 'economizing on' +LOC, 147T

Я

явля́ться 'be' +INST, 38T